GOD'S TRAITORS

Jessie Childs won the Elizabeth Longford Prize for Historical Biography with her first book *Henry VIII's Last Victim: The Life and Times of Henry Howard, Earl of Surrey*. She has written and reviewed for several newspapers and magazines, including the *Daily Telegraph*, *Sunday Telegraph* and *Literary Review*. She took a First in History from the University of Oxford and lives in London with her husband and two daughters. *God's Traitors* is her second book, and was longlisted for The Samuel Johnson Prize for Non-Fiction, and shortlisted for the Longman-*History Today* Book of the Year award.

www.jessiechilds.com
@childs_jessie

JESSIE CHILDS

God's Traitors

Terror and Faith in
Elizabethan England

VINTAGE BOOKS
London

Published by Vintage 2015

2 4 6 8 10 9 7 5 3 1

Copyright © Jessie Childs 2014

Jessie Childs has asserted her right under the Copyright, Designs
and Patents Act 1988 to be identified as the author of this work

First published in Great Britain in 2014 by
The Bodley Head

Vintage
20 Vauxhall Bridge Road,
London SW1V 2SA
www.vintage-books.co.uk

A Penguin Random House Company

Penguin
Random House
UK

global.penguinrandomhouse.com

A CIP catalogue record for this book
is available from the British Library

ISBN 9781784700058

Penguin Random House is committed to a sustainable future for our
business, our readers and our planet. This book is made from Forest
Stewardship Council® certified paper.

Typeset in Sabon by Palimpsest Book Production Limited,
Falkirk, Stirlingshire
Printed and bound in Great Britain by
CPI Group (UK) Ltd, Croydon CR0 4YY

To my mother and sister

No man is an island, entire of itself; every man is a piece of the continent, a part of the main; if a clod be washed away by the sea, Europe is the less, as well as if a promontory were, as well as if a manor of thy friends, or of thine own were; Any man's death diminishes me, because I am involved in Mankind; And therefore never send to know for whom the bell tolls; It tolls for thee.

John Donne, *Devotions upon Emergent Occasions* (1624)
17 Meditation, sig. T4

Contents

Author's Note

Two calendars were in use in this period: the Gregorian (or New Style) and the Julian (or Old Style). In 1582, Spain, Italy and France adopted the former, which put them ten days ahead of Protestant England, which kept the latter until 1752. Unless otherwise stated, I give Old Style dates, but take the year to begin on 1 January, instead of Lady Day (25 March), which was also retained in England until the eighteenth century.

In this pre-decimal period, a shilling was twelve pence and a pound was twenty shillings. The mark was worth two-thirds of a pound and there were six Dutch florins to one pound sterling.

The letters 'S.J.' after a name denote a member of the Society of Jesus.

Spelling and punctuation have, for the most part, been modernised.

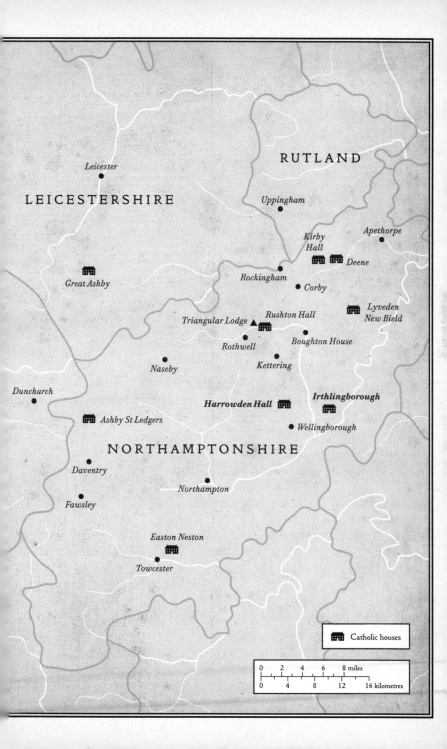

LEICESTERSHIRE

Leicester

RUTLAND

Uppingham

Kirby Hall

Apethorpe

Deene

Great Ashby

Rockingham

Corby

Lyveden New Bield

Triangular Lodge

Rushton Hall

Rothwell

Boughton House

Naseby

Kettering

Dunchurch

Harrowden Hall

Irthlingborough

Ashby St Ledgers

Wellingborough

NORTHAMPTONSHIRE

Daventry

Northampton

Fawsley

Easton Neston

Towcester

Catholic houses

| 0 | 2 | 4 | 6 | 8 miles |
| 0 | 4 | 8 | 12 | 16 kilometres |

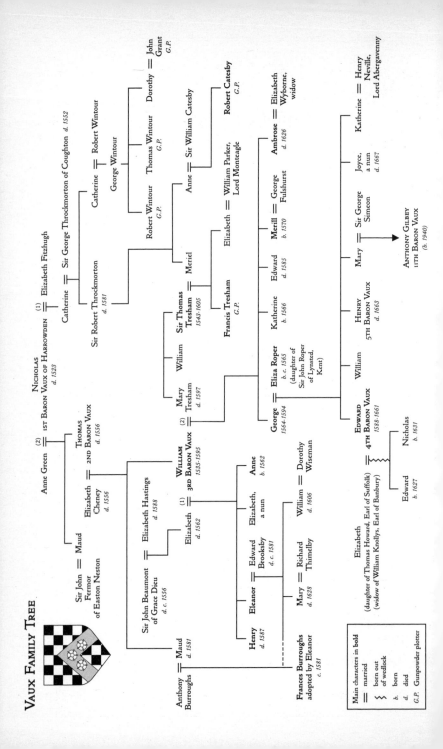

Vaux Family Tree

Nicholas, 1st Baron Vaux of Harrowden (d. 1523)
(1) = Elizabeth Fitzhugh
(2) = Anne Green

Sir George Throckmorton of Coughton (d. 1552) = Catherine

Catherine = Robert Wintour

George Wintour

Catherine = Sir George Throckmorton of Coughton

Thomas Wintour G.P.

Dorothy = John Grant G.P.

Robert Wintour G.P.

Anne = Sir William Catesby

Robert Catesby G.P.

Sir Robert Throckmorton (d. 1581)

Robert Wintour G.P.

Elizabeth = William Parker, Lord Monteagle

Ambrose (d. 1626) = Elizabeth Wyborne, widow

Sir John Fermor of Easton Neston = Maud

Thomas, 2nd Baron Vaux (d. 1556) = Elizabeth Cheney (d. 1556)

William, 3rd Baron Vaux 1535-1595

Meriel

Mary Tresham (d. 1597) = William Tresham

Sir Thomas Tresham 1543-1605

Francis Tresham G.P.

Edward (b. 1585)

Katherine (b. 1566)

Merill (b. 1570) = George Fulshurst

Joyce, a nun (d. 1667)

Katherine = Henry Neville, Lord Abergavenny

Sir John Beaumont of Grace Dieu (d. c. 1556)

William Vaux 1535-1595

Elizabeth Hastings (d. 1588)

(1) = Elizabeth Hastings (d. 1588)

George 1564-1594 = Eliza Roper (b. c. 1565) (daughter of Sir John Roper of Lynsted, Kent)

William

Henry 5th Baron Vaux (d. 1663)

Mary = Sir George Simeon

Anthony Gilbey 11th Baron Vaux (b. 1940)

Anthony Burroughs = Maud (d. 1581)

Elizabeth (d. 1562) = Edward Brooksby (d. c. 1581)

Elizabeth, a nun

Anne (b. 1562)

(1) = Elizabeth Hastings

Mary (d. 1628) = Richard Thimelby

William (d. 1606) = Dorothy Wiseman

Edward 4th Baron Vaux 1588-1661

Elizabeth (daughter of Thomas Howard, Earl of Suffolk) (widow of William Knollys, Earl of Banbury)

Edward (b. 1627)

Nicholas (b. 1631)

Henry (d. 1587)

Eleanor

Frances Burroughs adopted by Eleanor c. 1581

Main characters in bold
= married
⌇ born out of wedlock
b. born
d. died
G.P. Gunpowder plotter

Principal Characters

Members of the Vaux Family

William, 3rd Baron Vaux of Harrowden – the gentle patriarch. Father of:

Henry Vaux – precocious child poet and Catholic underground operative, heir to the barony but 'resolutely settled not to wife'

Eleanor Brooksby – 'the widow'

Anne Vaux (alias Mistress Perkins) – 'the virgin'

Frances Burroughs – sprightly niece of Lord Vaux, adopted by Eleanor Brooksby upon the death of her mother

Mary, Lady Vaux (née Tresham) – William's second wife. Mother of:

Ambrose Vaux – the black sheep

Merill Vaux – youngest daughter of Lord Vaux, elopes with her uncle's servant

George Vaux – forfeits his right to the Vaux inheritance when he engages in a 'brainless match' with:

Eliza Vaux (née Roper) – daughter of John Roper of Lynsted, Kent; possessor of 'irresistible feminish passions'. Children include:

Edward and *Henry* – the 4th and 5th Barons Vaux of Harrowden

Kinsmen and Friends

Anthony Babington – Vaux associate, conspires to assassinate Queen Elizabeth in 1586

Robert Catesby – Vaux cousin and leader of the 1605 Gunpowder Plot

Sir Everard Digby – glamorous Catholic convert, late recruit to the Gunpowder Plot

Sir Thomas Tresham of Rushton Hall – brother-in-law of Lord Vaux, recusant spokesman, father of a gunpowder plotter, architect, theologian, serial litigant

Priests

William Allen – founder of the Douai/Rheims seminary and unofficial leader of the English Catholics in exile, supports the invasion of England by the powers of Catholic Europe

Claudio Aquaviva, S.J. – Jesuit Superior General, based in Rome

Edmund Campion, S.J. – former schoolmaster at Harrowden Hall, launches the Jesuit mission in England with Robert Persons

Henry Garnet, S.J. – Jesuit Superior in England between 1586 and 1606; harboured by Anne Vaux and Eleanor Brooksby

John Gerard, S.J. – 'Long John with the little beard', swashbuckling missionary harboured by Eliza Vaux

Edward Oldcorne, S.J. – chaplain at Hindlip, Worcestershire

Robert Persons, S.J. – first Jesuit missionary, later an exile agitating for a Catholic invasion of England

Robert Southwell, S.J. – poet and polemicist, runs the London end of the mission, harboured by the Vauxes

Oswald Tesimond, S.J. – confessor to several gunpowder plotters including the ringleader, Robert Catesby

Heads of State and Foreign Dignitaries

Elizabeth I – Queen of England and Ireland, 'Defender of the Faith', daughter of Henry VIII

Guise, Henri, Duke of – cousin of Mary Queen of Scots, founder of the French Catholic League, keen to dethrone Elizabeth I, assassinated in 1588

James VI and I – King of Scotland and (from March 1603) King of England and Ireland, Protestant son of:

Mary Queen of Scots – great-niece of Henry VIII, Catholic pretender to Elizabeth's throne

Bernardino de Mendoza – Spanish ambassador in London, 1578–84

Philip II – King of Spain, widower of 'Bloody' Mary Tudor, imperialist for whom 'the world is not enough', sends the Great Armada against England in 1588

Pope Pius V (1566–72) – excommunicates Queen Elizabeth in February 1570; 'Impious Pius' according to English Protestants

Pope Gregory XIII (1572–85) – founder of the Gregorian calendar, supporter of various plots against Queen Elizabeth, sends the Jesuits to England in 1580

Pope Sixtus V (1585–90) – endorses the 1588 Armada

Government Officials

Sir William Cecil, Lord Burghley – Lord Treasurer, Elizabeth's chief minister and 'spirit'. Father of:

Sir Robert Cecil, 1st Earl of Salisbury – Secretary of State to Elizabeth and James

Sir Edward Coke – Attorney General, leads the prosecution in the Gunpowder Plot trials

Sir Walter Mildmay – Chancellor of the Exchequer, Vaux neighbour, no friend to the 'stiff-necked Papist'

Sir Francis Walsingham – Elizabeth's Secretary and spymaster

Richard Topcliffe – priest-catcher, torturer, lecher

Richard Young – chief London justice, in charge of the raid on the Vaux house in Hackney in November 1586

Others

Maliverey Catilyn – government spy known as 'II'

Richard Fulwood – smuggler

John Lillie – lay assistant to the missionary priests

Nicholas Owen – 'Little John', builder of priest-holes

Thomas Phelippes – Walsingham's decipherer and forger

Sara Williams – Lady Vaux's teenaged maid, exorcised by the priests
   at Hackney in 1586, later Sara Cheney

Introduction

Four months after the discovery of the Gunpowder Plot, Anne Vaux awoke in a prison cell. She had been on the run, changing her lodging every two to three days. Her confessor had hoped that she would have 'kept herself out of their fingers', but the authorities had tracked her down and taken her to the Tower of London. She was placed in solitary confinement and interrogated.

There were three chief lines of enquiry, all concerning Anne's fraternisation with known, or suspected, conspirators.[1] The first focused on White Webbs, a house she kept in Enfield Chase. It had been used by her cousin, the plot's ringleader, 'Robin' Catesby, as a rendezvous. One official called it 'a nest for such bad birds'.

Who had been paying for the house's upkeep? Anne's interrogators demanded.

Who had visited?

When?

What had they talked about?

Where else had she stayed and with whom?

Anne was pressed about the pilgrimage she had recently undertaken with several of the conspirators and their families to St Winifred's Well in Wales.

When did she go?

With whom?

What had been the purpose of the trip and where had they lodged?

Had she seen or heard anything to make her suspicious?

And what had some of the wives meant when they had asked her where she would bestow herself 'till the brunt were past, that is till the beginning of the Parliament'?

Finally, Anne was asked about Garnet: Father Henry Garnet *alias*

Measy, *alias* Walley, *alias* Darcy, *alias* Farmer, *alias* Roberts, *alias* Philips: the superior of the Society of Jesus in England.

What advice had she heard him give the traitors?

Why, after he had been proclaimed a 'practiser' in the plot on 15 January 1606, had she helped him evade arrest?

Why, after his capture twelve days later, had she followed him to London and sent him secret letters etched in orange juice?

And what was the nature of their relationship? Was she his sister? Benefactor? Confederate? . . . Lover?

Anne's nerve had been tested many times. She had faced down spies in her household, slurs against her name and raids on her home. She was well lessoned in the art of equivocation and had heard enough prison tales to have some expectation of her treatment. But nothing could prepare her for the indignity of incarceration, nor the odium concentrated upon those Catholics suspected of involvement in the plot to annihilate King James I, his family and the political and spiritual elite of the realm.

It was reported that 'to more weighty questions she responded very sensibly'. She revealed the names of some of her house guests, though was hazy on 'needless' details, and she admitted that her suspicions had been raised on the pilgrimage, when she had feared that 'these wild heads had something in hand'. But when her interrogators accused her of impropriety with her priest, Anne's manner shifted. She 'laughed loudly two or three times', then rounded on them:

'You come to me with this child's play and impertinence, a sign that you have nothing of importance with which to charge me.'

Of course, she sneered, she had known about the powder treason. She was, after all, a woman, and women make it their business to know everything. And of course Garnet had been involved: since he was the greatest traitor in the world, he wouldn't have missed it. Then she thanked her guards for giving her board and lodging, as no one else in London was prepared to put her up.

'She is really quite funny and very lively,' wrote an admirer. 'She pays no attention whatsoever to them, and so she has them amazed and they are saying, "We absolutely do not know what to do with that woman!"'

★

That woman was one of several ardent, extraordinary, brave and, at times, utterly exasperating members of the Vaux* family. In many ways they were perfectly typical of the lower ranks of the Elizabethan aristocracy. They owned grand houses and estates. They patronised local people and places. They married folk similar to themselves. William, third Baron Vaux, was a gentle soul, seldom happier than with his hounds and hawks. He was a proud father, an affable host, a bit deaf and not good with money. His eldest daughter, Eleanor, was a 'very learned and in every way accomplished lady'; his youngest, Merill, ran off with her uncle's servant. One grandson inherited the barony and married the daughter of an earl; another murdered a merchant in Madrid.

There were squabbles within this family and disputes without it. There were heady romances, clandestine marriages and some very embarrassing lawsuits. There was even the proverbial black sheep: ever-indebted Ambrose, 'an untoward and giddy headed young man', who took to brawling at Shakespeare's Globe.[2] The private lives of other Elizabethan families were probably just as entertaining, if not so well documented. The Vauxes were not, in other words, unique. But there was something that made them remarkable, that defined them and in turn helps them define the age in which they lived, for it was the ill fortune of the Vaux family, at a time of Protestant triumphalism, to be Roman Catholic.

Specifically, the Vauxes were 'recusants'. They refused to go to church every Sunday (the word stems from the Latin *recusare*: to refuse). Not for them the awkward compromises, the crossed fingers and blocked ears at official service, the hasty confession and secret Mass at home afterwards. Once the men in Rome decreed that it was not good enough to be a 'church papist', as those who chose outward conformity were derisively termed, the Vauxes stayed at home. They needed the sacraments. They needed to confess their sins and consume what they believed to be the real presence of Christ at the Sacrifice of the Altar, but this required an agent of sacramental grace. Here was another problem, since Catholic priests were effectively outlawed. So for upholding their faith, the Vauxes committed the passive crime of not going to church and the more active one of harbouring priests. Other laws passed during the reign of 'Good Queen Bess' banned the

* The name is pronounced 'Vorx'.

receipt of images, crucifixes, rosaries and other 'popish trash' that was so ingrained in the Catholic way of life.

The penalties for disobedience – for what was widely perceived as a challenge to monarchical authority and a deliberate fracturing of society – were fines, controls on movement, the loss of public office, property, liberty and, in some cases, loss of life. Few Elizabethans would have disputed that obedience was a Christian duty, but after the Pope excommunicated Queen Elizabeth in 1570, it became increasingly difficult for English Catholics to maintain a dual allegiance to their God and their Queen.

The international situation hardly helped. The Protestant Reformation may have taken root in England, but in other parts of Europe the Counter-Reformation was rampant. Protestants were massacred in France and the Low Countries, Armadas were launched from Inquisition Spain, rebellion was fomented in Ireland and, from across the Scottish border, a rival queen with Tudor blood pitched up and became the willing instrument of Elizabeth's enemies. Militant religious orders were sent on missions to save souls, both in the New World and in the Old. The Queen and her Council felt under siege from Catholic Europe. This was the age of assassination; with every attempt on Elizabeth's life, fears for national security grew and increasingly draconian laws were passed to protect it.

Distrust and hatred from both sides fed each other. 'Only the question is,' wrote the Queen's godson Sir John Harington, '(which in my conscience I cannot certainly decide): which was first? I mean, whether their sinister practises drew on these rigorous laws, or whether the rigour of these laws moved them to these unnatural practises. But thus, in the end, acts of religion became to be treasons.'[3]

For many Catholics the Elizabethan 'Golden Age' is an alien concept. Almost two hundred of their co-religionists were executed.[4] Others perished in prison. Torture, though formally unlawful, was used more than at any other time in England's history. One Catholic woman, destined for the gallows for organising the escape of a priest, protested that 'the Queen herself, if she had the bowels of a woman, would have done as much if she had known the ill-treatment he underwent'.[5] But it was the heart and stomach of a king that were required for England's defence. It was the Queen's sworn Christian duty to protect the Church and extirpate heresy. Toleration was unthinkable.

This book attempts to go some way towards explaining how 'acts of religion became to be treasons' and why 'unnatural practises' were motivated by faith. It follows the Vauxes of Harrowden Hall into the heart of the underground movement and explores the conflicts of loyalty that they, as Catholics and Englishmen, faced in a violent, volatile world. It is a story of stately homes and Thames-side taverns, spy rings and torture chambers, priest hunts, exorcisms and a swashbuckling escape from the Tower of London: sensational stuff that was sensationalised at the time and has proved a rich seam for historical novelists. But it also seeks to enter the shuttered world of the Elizabethan recusant household and look at how parents, children and servants tried to keep the faith on a daily basis. Their lives were not reflective of the common Catholic experience; there was no such thing and the Vauxes took more risks than most in their zeal to preserve and promote Catholicism in England. But I hope that for the general reader it might throw a shaft of light on a rather murky corner of England's past, one that was for a long time kept hidden.

Recusant families would conceal their papers (as well as their priests) under floorboards and in cavity walls. Centuries might pass before workmen or curious children pulled them out again. The Tresham Papers, which contain wonderful details about the Vaux family, were only exposed when builders knocked through a wall at Rushton Hall in 1828. Around seventy years later, a secret room with a swinging-beam entrance was discovered by a boy exploring a derelict wing of Harvington Hall, near Kidderminster. In 1959, electricians working in the attic at Lyford Grange found a small box containing an Agnus Dei* and papers dated 1579. One contemporary recorded his plan to bind up his documents 'with the string of secrecy & for a time to bury & entomb them in their sepulchre, till some joyful day cause their happy resurrection, that then with free egress they may pass uncontrolled'.[6] They were preserved for years by the Brudenells of Deene, and now, as long as the rules of the Bodleian Library are observed, 'may pass uncontrolled' to all readers.

It is impossible to know how many Catholics there were in Elizabethan

---

* A small wax disc made from the paschal candle, bearing the imprint of a cross and a lamb, and blessed by the Pope. The Agnus Dei ('lamb of God') was usually worn round the neck and was thought to protect its bearer from evil influences. After 1571 anyone caught bringing one into the country risked forfeiture of lands and goods.

England – more at the beginning than the end, certainly, but they did not advertise their membership. John Bossy estimated some forty thousand in 1603, less than one per cent of the population. The recusants, the 'obstinate papists', were a tiny, noisy fraction of that minority: thousands rather than tens of thousands.[7] More were dreaded. Seemingly backed by the powers of Catholic Europe, they aroused fears of a fifth column poised to strike at the heart of the commonwealth. 'Anti-popery' became an ideology, a cultural force. Not only did it shape the life and policy of Elizabeth I, but also those of her successors. It was a contributory factor in the Civil War and left some weeds in the British constitution. It needs to be looked at in the context of its time, not ours, but if we are to gain a rounded sense of our past, it is important to know about the priest-holes as well as the palaces.

Prelude: The Calm before Campion

When Henry Vaux's old tutor returned to England in the summer of 1580, he was disguised as a jewel merchant. On reaching London, he changed his outfit, acquired arms and a horse, and became a gentleman. He later toured the English countryside 'in apparel to myself very ridiculous; I often change it and my name also'.[1] The subterfuge was necessary because he was a Roman Catholic priest. He was a member of a new religious order called the Society of Jesus and he had undergone several years of intensive training to prepare for this moment. In a previous incarnation he had dazzled Queen Elizabeth at Oxford University. Now he aimed to employ his rhetorical skills in a more expansive arena. He was forty years old, his name was Edmund Campion and his mission was the restoration of the Catholic faith in England.

One of the first people to welcome him home was his former pupil Henry, now a member of an underground group helping priests evade arrest. When Campion came to Northamptonshire, Henry's father, William, third Baron Vaux of Harrowden, offered him hospitality 'sundry times' and invited influential neighbours to hear Mass.[2] The last time Campion had been at Harrowden Hall was as a tutor just over a decade earlier. It had been a short tenure, but left a lasting impression. 'From the day your father first asked me to see you and superintend your education,' Campion had written to Henry in 1570, 'I have become amazingly attached to you, for I marvelled and was almost perplexed when I saw a boy who had not yet completed his ninth year, scion of a notable family, of such pleasant demeanour and refinement.' Campion had been touched by Lord Vaux's 'fatherly pride', his 'anxious and solicitous care for you all' and 'his pleasant and easy manner'. Indeed, 'a more illustrious example of affability and integrity than your father,' Campion informed Henry, 'I do not think it is possible for you to see.'[3]

Lord Vaux faced a dilemma in 1580. Campion was no longer the darling of Oxford. Nor was he a client of Queen Elizabeth's favourite, the Earl of Leicester, as he had been in the late 1560s. Having him at Harrowden then had been a matter of good patronage. In 1580 it was a controversial and defiant act. Father Edmund Campion, S.J., was a wanted man. His mission to reconcile Elizabeth's subjects to Rome was potentially treasonous. Anyone who harboured or aided him was liable to loss of goods and life imprisonment. When Lord Vaux decided to open his gates in 1580, it wasn't just Campion he was letting in, but the wrath of the law. For a man so 'anxious and solicitous' for the care of his children, the decision could not have been easy. Vaux knew he was taking a risk in 1580, but he could never have foreseen quite how dramatically his life, and the lives of those around him, would change.

Forty-five years earlier, in 1535 when William Vaux was born, the prospect of a Catholic priest being a fugitive for his faith in England would have been greeted with derision. Priests were regarded by most Englishmen as the indispensable channels of saving grace and no matter how far some individuals fell short of the ideal, they represented an institution that was revered. The Mass remained the cornerstone of Christian worship. Denial of the Real Presence – that is, the physical body and blood of Christ in the consecrated bread and wine – was a capital offence and continued to be for the rest of Henry VIII's reign.

But change was afoot. On 6 July 1535, the month before William's birth, Thomas More had climbed the scaffold for his refusal to endorse Henry VIII as the Supreme Head of the Church of England. He had been willing to pledge allegiance to Queen Anne Boleyn, but not to renounce the spiritual primacy of the Pope. New legislation declared that England was 'governed by one Supreme Head and King', who was furnished with 'plenary, whole and entire power, pre-eminence, authority, prerogative and jurisdiction' over Church and State. No interference from 'foreign princes or potentates' would be countenanced. The ancient problem of dual allegiance had resurfaced. 'Render unto Caesar,' Christ had counselled, 'the things which be Caesar's and unto God the things which be God's' (Matthew 22:21).

It had never been an easy distinction to make in practice. Henry VIII's welding of the spheres, and assertion of supremacy over both, made it even harder.

The Vauxes had more reason than most to acknowledge England's Caesar as God's chief spokesman. They owed everything to the Tudors. The Northamptonshire family, which could trace its descent at least as far as the thirteenth century, was staunchly Lancastrian. Attainder in 1461 under the Yorkist Edward IV had taken away their fortune – a sizeable living accrued from solid county service and canny marriages to local heiresses. The Battle of Tewkesbury a decade later claimed the life of Sir William Vaux (1437–71) and left his widow, Katharine, destitute with 'none earthly thing for her and her children to live upon'.[4] When her mistress, Margaret of Anjou (Shakespeare's 'she-wolf of France'), went into exile, Katharine was one of the few ladies by her side. Steadfast loyalty to unpopular causes would prove to be a family trait.

Vaux constancy was vindicated at Bosworth Field. Henry VII's first Parliament restored the family lands to Katharine's son Nicholas and reversed the attainder. A knighthood quickly followed, reward for Nicholas's military service against the early pretenders who challenged Tudor rule. His sister Jane, Lady Guildford, became governess to Henry VII's daughters – Princess Mary called her 'my mother Guildford'* – and in 1502 Nicholas was appointed Lieutenant of Guînes, a military and diplomatic post that he held till his death.

Towards the end of Henry VII's reign, Nicholas married Anne Green, a wealthy heiress, who brought him lands in Northamptonshire and six other counties stretching from Yorkshire to Kent. He consolidated his holdings on the accession of Henry VIII, when he was granted a slew of offices and manors.[5] Thenceforth, Vaux prosperity seemed assured. Nicholas served three times as sheriff of Northamptonshire and established the family seat at Harrowden Hall, near Wellingborough. Henry VIII visited 'Sir Nicholas Vaux place' once,

---

*Lady Guildford was attendant on the young Catherine of Aragon on the night of her wedding to Prince Arthur (Henry VIII's older brother). According to her later testimony, made during Henry VIII's annulment proceedings, Lady Guildford had seen the young couple 'lying in bed together alone and sole, and in mind and intent, as she believeth, to have carnal cognition together as man and wife'. (PRO SP 1/65, f. 19r)

on 27 July 1511, a Sunday, when he heard Mass and made his usual offering of six shillings and eightpence.[6]

At court Nicholas had a fondness for ceremonial and a sartorial flair that was appreciated by the chroniclers. In 1520 he helped organise the Anglo-French conference known as the Field of Cloth of Gold, at which Henry VIII attempted to outdo Francis I in a series of costly spectacles. A fleeting cloud of suspicion passed over Nicholas the following year at the fall of the Duke of Buckingham – it was later discovered that he had employed a chaplain of the executed peer[7] (harbouring suspect priests was another family trait) – but he retained the King's favour. In April 1523, Sir Nicholas Vaux was elevated to the peerage as the first Baron Vaux of Harrowden. His creation was by writ of summons. The following month, he died.

Nicholas had been a devout Catholic at a time when the term was synonymous with being a devout Christian. It was his son Thomas, second Lord Vaux, and later his grandson William, the third Baron, who had to navigate the treacherous waters stirred up by the Break with Rome and Henry VIII's peculiarly avaricious brand of Reformation.

Thomas was fourteen and newly married when his father died in 1523. Four years later, he attended Cardinal Wolsey on embassy in France and in January 1531, having reached his majority, the second Lord Vaux took his seat in the House of Lords.[8] In 1532 he accompanied Henry VIII and Anne Boleyn when they crossed the Channel to secure French support for Henry's campaign to annul his marriage to Catherine of Aragon. The following year, on 30 May 1533, Thomas was created a Knight of the Bath in anticipation of Anne's coronation the following day.

A gap in the Lords Journal makes it impossible to monitor Vaux's attendance before 1534, but he was seated in the Upper House many times in February and March that year and was present during several readings of the bill concerning the 'usurped authority' of the Pope. He also attended the formal closing of the session on 30 March 1534, when, in the King's presence, the Lord Chancellor gave the royal assent to the legislation and announced that all members would have to take an oath of allegiance 'alonely to the King's Majesty and to the heirs of his body'.[9]

There was no sign of Lord Vaux when Parliament reassembled in November. His seat was cold at the next session and the next. Indeed, only once, in order to ensure his wife's jointure in 1536, would he return during Henry VIII's reign. He presented himself for one day at the first session of Edward VI's Parliament in 1547, but ignored all subsequent summons.[10] It was only on the accession of Mary I that Thomas's record improved. It is tempting to infer that faith was a determining factor. He clearly supported Mary more than her father or brother and inclined her way, the Roman Catholic way. But one must beware of reading the Vaux story backwards; that is to say, of tracing the family's subsequent recusancy and uncompromising attitude to faith earlier than the record allows. If Lord Vaux was not the pliable peer for which the government had probably hoped when he was dubbed a Knight of the Bath before Anne's coronation, nor was he an engagé. Other Catholics tried to resist reform, either from within or in open opposition. Lord Vaux chose to withdraw from the fray. Apart from seven months in 1536 when he served as Governor of Jersey and two occasions – in 1551 and 1554 – when he sat on county commissions, he seems to have avoided public office.

It is evident from his business dealings that Vaux shied away from confrontation. His wife, the redoubtable Elizabeth (née Cheney), negotiated property transactions on his behalf. On one occasion, she 'dashed the matter' of an unfavourable sale of land to Thomas Cromwell. 'The man is of such constancy,' Cromwell's agent reported of Lord Vaux, 'that he would be turned in a minute of an hour from the most earnest matter that ever he was resolved in.' No doubt aware of this flaw in his character, Vaux had sent Elizabeth as his proxy 'and he said he would make me no further answer therein till my Lady his wife had spoken with you'.[11] Perhaps he knew that in politics, as in business, he didn't have the stomach for resistance.

The second Lord Vaux should be remembered for his poetry. If he was not quite as pioneering or polished a poet as his contemporaries Wyatt and Surrey, he nevertheless stood high on the second rank in the generation before Shakespeare. His verse was included a year after his death in *Tottel's Miscellany*, the most popular anthology of the day, and his work will forever live on in *Hamlet*, for it is Vaux's lyrics that Shakespeare adapted for the song of the gravedigger.*[12]

Thomas, second Lord Vaux of Harrowden, died in October 1556 at the age of forty-seven. Elizabeth followed her husband to the grave

---

* *Hamlet*, Act 5, Scene 1. Two centuries later Goethe would use two stanzas of Vaux's poem in *Faust* (Part II, v. 6).

the following month. It is possible that they both succumbed to the plague that ravaged England that year. Perhaps it is not too fanciful to read an apologia of sorts in the following lines:

> Companion none is like unto the mind alone,
> For many have been harmed by speech, through thinking few
>   or none:
> Fear oftentimes restraineth words, but makes not thoughts to
>   cease,
> And he speaks best that hath the skill when for to hold his
>   peace.[13]

*

We return now to Thomas's son William, third Baron Vaux of Harrowden, the man 'by whom,' Edmund Campion wrote, 'I am dearly loved, and whom I particularly revere'. He would hold the dubious honour of being the only peer convicted of recusancy under Queen Elizabeth, but before his loyalty was tested, he had muddled along fairly well.[14]

He was born in 1535 and brought up at Harrowden Hall within a household of almost fifty people that included grooms, laundresses, the cook, the baker, an embroiderer, the chaplain and the steward. An account book survives for the year of his birth revealing payments for a birdcage, soap, swaddling and, on 14 August, five shillings 'to buy ale for the nurse'.[15] William grew up as monumental religious changes enveloped the country. He was too young to notice the dissolution of the smaller monasteries in 1536, but when the larger ones were targeted in 1539, he was four, old enough to wonder at the assault on the big, beautiful landmarks of his infancy.

Followers of the New Learning, as it was known, were convinced that salvation could only be attained by faith in Christ. For centuries Christians had believed that good works – prayers, charitable deeds, fasting and so on – could be stockpiled against the day of judgement. The more good works done in this life, the less time one would have to suffer the pains of purgatory before moving on to heaven. If 'indulgences' were obtained (either through some devotional exercise such as pilgrimage or by purchase from the papacy), and if the departed soul was prayed for on earth, then further remission was granted.

The reformers argued that this was superstitious nonsense. Purgatory was not mentioned in the Bible; therefore it did not exist. The primacy of the Pope was grounded on tradition, not Scripture; therefore he had no more authority over Christian souls than any other bishop. Indeed in perverting doctrine and deceiving the people, he was Antichrist. And the Mass – the sacrament around which most Christians shaped their lives – was a mummery. The more radical reformers argued that when Christ had broken the bread at the Last Supper and said 'take, eat, this is my body', he had not meant it literally. They believed that communion was valid as a commemoration of the Passion, but any notion that a priest could re-enact Christ's sacrifice on an altar, mutter some Latin and thereby transform the bread and wine into Christ's 'real presence' was idolatry of the worst kind. To reformers, the Roman Catholic priest was a charlatan who used stage tricks and sorcery to gull his congregation.*

This was, of course, vile heresy to Catholics. They revered the Mass, 'that Sacrament of Sacraments', as the renewal of Christ's redemption and the manifestation of the divine.[16] Catholics examined their consciences and confessed their sins before communion so they could receive in a state of grace. During the ceremony their senses were heightened by music, incense, candles, relics, a great crucifix, painted images and other 'godly ornaments' in order to repel the devil, bring themselves closer to God and evoke the reverence appropriate for worship. They believed that 'the very Passion of our Saviour is there lively represented'. The priest originally wore an alb, for example, because Herod had sent Christ back to Pilate in a white coat, 'reputing him as a fool'. The girdle 'betokeneth the scourge wherewith Christ was whipped'.[17] Vestments were so important to Catholics – and were later made and preserved by recusants despite the high risk of discovery – partly because each article worn by the celebrant memorialised an aspect of the Passion. And thus, at the moment when the priest, representing Christ, recited his words, the substances of bread and wine were transformed – 'transubstantiated' – into the body and blood of Christ. When, at least every Easter, communicants received the consecrated bread themselves, they believed they were consuming Christ.

---

*The seventeenth-century term *hocus-pocus* may be a corruption or parody of the words of consecration: *'hoc est (enim) corpus (meum)'*.

And by feeding on Him, they were nourishing their souls and participating in a common union. They renewed their faith and, in turn,
received the pledge that they would share in life everlasting.

The Mass was one of the chief bones of contention between
Catholics and Protestants and amongst the reformers themselves.
For the increasingly beleaguered Catholic community, it would be
a symbol of continuity and collective suffering: 'We many be one
bread and one body.'[18] The Mass was the source of Christian fellow-
ship, a symbol of the visible Church at a time when individual
Catholics would increasingly have to become invisible. It later
reminded those in prison, or on the run, or leading a double life of
outward conformity, that they were not alone. It would be the life-
blood of the recusant community and people would be prepared to
pay the ultimate price to preserve it.

A Reformation of ideas and faith may have been sweeping through
Europe and across the Channel, but at Harrowden Hall life carried
on much as usual. Under the instruction of the family chaplain, young
William read his catechism and his primer.[19] He recited the paternoster
and the Ave Maria. He read the lives of the saints and chose his
favourites. He joined the household in observing the fasts and celebrating the feasts. He prayed for his family and for the souls of his
dead ancestors. And he was taught what to do at his First Communion:
with his heart 'inflamed in fervent love and charity', his hands at his
breast, his head 'conveniently lifted up', his mouth 'reasonably open
& not gaping', and his tongue 'not too much put forth', he had to
receive the consecrated wafer and swallow it without chewing and
without letting it touch the roof of his mouth. For a quarter of an
hour after receiving, he was not allowed to spit, or if it was absolutely
necessary, 'at the least it is decent to spit where it may not be trodden
on'. Likewise, he had to refrain from eating meat for a while, 'lest
thou mix corruptible food with that divine and heavenly food which
thou so lately receivest'.[20]

Children could only receive their First Communion when they were
deemed old enough to understand transubstantiation. This was usually
around the age of twelve.[21] Just as William reached this important
milestone everything that he had been taught was overturned. What
had been radical heresy under Henry VIII became orthodoxy in the

reign of his son and what had been considered traditional worship was denounced as idolatry. William was twelve years old at the change of monarch in 1547 and eighteen when Edward VI died in 1553. As the boy became a man, England was transformed into a Protestant country.

One of the early casualties of Edward VI's reform programme was the Vaux chantry. William's grandfather Nicholas, the first baron, had left instructions in his will for its foundation at Harrowden. He endowed a priest 'and his successors . . . to sing for the soul of me and the souls of my grandfather, my father, my mother, my wives, my children and other my ancestors' souls, and all Christian souls'.[22] In November 1547, Edward VI's first Parliament abolished the chantries with the reformed logic that as there was no such thing as purgatory, prayers were wasted on the dead. At a stroke, Lord Vaux's foundation was rendered obsolete.

Edward VI was hailed by reformers as the new Josiah, the boy-king who would destroy the temple of false worship. He did not disappoint. Whitewash and the axe were the preferred agents for purging the church of idolatry. Before Edward's reforms, the parish church was an assault on the senses – gleaming chapel plate, painted walls and ceilings, stained glass, elaborate statuary, reliquaries and shrines lit by wax tapers and tallow candles. Dominating the interior was a great rood, or crucified Christ, often flanked by images of the Virgin and St John. The church was a stage, especially during the holy days: there were Candlemas candles, Ash Wednesday ashes, Palm Sunday palms and 'creeping to the cross' on Good Friday, when the clergy and heads of houses crawled barefoot towards a veiled crucifix. There was 'singing, ringing and organs piping'.[23]

After the Edwardian 'purification', the church was a pared-down affair. All vestiges of popery were ripped out, smashed up or daubed over. It was not entirely colourless: bright coats of arms replaced the religious murals, scriptural quotations were inscribed in striking black lettering that was decorative as well as edifying. But the overall effect must have been stark. The roods were pulled down and the side altars demolished along with anything else that diverted attention from the pulpit and lectern. Nothing was screened or hidden. The new church was a monument to the plain and lively word of God. The Bible was freely available and if there were no more palms or ashes or holy day processions, there was an increased stress on the participation of the congregation in everyday worship. The sounds were plainer: bell ringing was minimised and metrical psalms replaced elaborate polyphony.*[24]

Perhaps the most revolutionary aspect of the Edwardian Reformation was the assault on the Mass, for reformers the most ingrained and pernicious form of adoration. As Bishop John Hooper put it, 'as long as the altars remain, both the ignorant people and the evil-persuaded priests will dream always of sacrifice.' The 1552 Prayer Book insisted that the 'Lord's Supper' was a commemorative rite only. Stone altars were replaced with wooden tables and positioned lengthwise down the nave or chancel. Communion was to be 'in both kinds' (bread and wine) when previously parishioners had only received the bread. The service was to be in English, not Latin, and the priest had to substitute his richly embroidered vestments for a simple white surplice. Indeed, the priest was no longer a priest, no longer the pure – and celibate – demi-God that William Vaux had been brought up to revere, but a simple minister who could marry and have children.

For many of Edward VI's subjects, 'the stripping of the altars' was welcome. Indeed, in some areas iconoclasm anticipated policy: at least eighteen London parishes demolished their altars before it became an official requirement.[25] Compliance was the norm. Edward may have been a minor, but he was a divine-right king to whom every Christian subject owed obedience. Resistance imperilled body and soul, as several thousand Cornish and Devonshire rebels learned at the cost of their lives when their demands over the summer of 1549 for (among other things) a reversion to the old Latin prayer book were ruthlessly suppressed.

---

*In terms of aesthetics, it is easy to lament what was lost, but modern sensibilities should be resisted. Edward VI's iconoclasts were not artistically motivated. Their God was a jealous God who had forbidden graven images. Similarly, it was to destroy the idols of false gods that the Catholic conquistadors demolished the monuments of native religion in the New World.

Keith Thomas makes an interesting point: 'Nowadays, when we gaze happily and indiscriminately at altarpieces of the virgin Mary and Greek statues of Apollo and Hindu sculpture and Japanese Buddhas and masks from Benin, are we showing the catholicity of our taste or simply our indifference to religious values? For it would still be almost impossible for us to appreciate an artefact, however exquisite, if we found its symbolic overtones too repugnant. What would we do if we were given, say, a beautifully carved and bejewelled swastika? . . . Perhaps the gulf separating us from the Tudor and Stuart iconoclasts is narrower than we think.' (Thomas, 'Art and Iconoclasm', p. 40)

Parishioners were nothing if not resourceful. When, in 1551, the government sent commissioners into the shires to seize superfluous church property, much was sold off or adapted to secular use. At the Northamptonshire parish of Moulton, a chalice was sold 'by the common assent of the parish' and the proceeds were 'employed towards the furnishing of one soldier for all things belonging unto him'. Another memorandum revealed that two Moulton men had bought one of the church bells and, 'by the consent of the whole parish', converted it into the 'clock-bell'. It was to be rung 'when any casualty shall chance and for the gathering together of the inhabitants of the said town . . . and not given to the said church'.[26]

One gets a sense here of the spirit of the English parish – pragmatic, resilient, protective of its community and its materials, adaptable and perhaps also a little bloody-minded. Many of the objects that the commissioners hoped to confiscate were bequests from parishioners' ancestors. If their local church could no longer have them, they made sure that the government could not take them. The people of Moulton naturally obeyed the law, but in as much as it was possible, they strived to do so on their own terms. Parochialism usually trumped patriotism. It was this attitude that enabled the people of Moulton to carry on and to thrive during the early phases of the English Reformation. Perhaps, too, it was the kind of mindset that lay behind the 'stolid conformity' of the vast majority of subsequent generations of English men and women.[27]

Before the Reformation could take firm root in England, there was the reign of Mary I. She was so resolutely Catholic that it was inevitable that her reign would be assessed for a long time afterwards on confessional lines. For Protestant polemicists, she was the ugly sister of the Tudor dynasty, a throwback to a time when England was shrouded in darkness and superstition. Mary may have been Great Harry's child, but reformers loathed her as the daughter of Aragon, the bride of Spain and the creature of Rome. At the end of her reign, she surrendered Calais to the French, further evidence, if any were needed, that she was no patriot.

For Catholics like the Vauxes, however, Mary was the answer to their prayers, a genuine Defender of the Faith, who would guide them back to the truth. The Queen tried valiantly and imaginatively to revitalise Catholicism in her land. The papal supremacy was restored with the sensible proviso that redistributed monastic wealth could remain in lay hands. The Mass and traditional ceremonies returned, and the parish church was reinvested with altars, vestments, roods, bells and images. Protestant Bibles were removed from the churches, but a new, acceptably Catholic translation was conceived. Mary's cousin and Archbishop of Canterbury, Cardinal Reginald Pole, led a concerted drive to re-educate the clergy and raise their moral standards. He planned a 'seed-bed' (*seminarium*) for the training of priests in every diocese. Preaching was encouraged and new catechisms and collections of homilies were printed and distributed. Recruitment to the clergy began to rise for the first time in a decade.[28]

It is remarkable how much was achieved in the five years from 1553 to 1558 that Mary ruled England, especially in light of the harvest failures and epidemics that blighted her reign. But it would have taken decades fully to undo the work of her father and brother. Mary's early demise and the subsequent longevity of her Protestant sister's reign ensured that any changes were short-lived. It also meant that Mary would be associated less with renewal than repression.* She was the queen who put the torch to the human bonfires. More than 280 men and women were roasted alive for refusing to accept her version of Christianity. Toleration was not a word that had any currency with sixteenth-century rulers. Within their kingdom, there was one truth faith – their own. All else was error and it was the duty of the godly magistrate to provide correction. Nevertheless, the scale and intensity of the Marian burnings between February 1555 and November 1558 were unprecedented and shocked even those who were familiar with the Spanish Inquisition. The sight of 'fat, water and blood' dripping from roasting bodies, or lips moving in prayer till 'shrunk to the gums', lived long in the memory.[29]

The burnings were horrific and contemporaries thought so at the time, but they were also deemed by many to be an appropriate punishment for heresy. If, as Christians fervently believed, unrepentant heretics would burn in the flames of hell for eternity, then death by fire was a fitting appetiser to the torment to which they had condemned

---

* As with much of *1066 and All That* (1930), Sellar and Yeatman's gentle parody of posterity's verdict is astute: 'Broody Mary's reign was . . . a Bad Thing, since England is bound to be C of E, so all the executions were wasted.'

themselves. The Protestant preacher John Rogers argued as much under Edward VI when he supported the burning of Joan Butcher in 1550. Her sentence, he urged, was 'sufficiently mild' for an Ana-baptist.[30] It is doubtful that he found it so mild when, on 4 February 1555, he was himself tied to the stake at Smithfield, but he refused to recant:

> He was the first protomartyr of all that blessed company that suffered in Queen Mary's time, that gave the first adventure upon the fire. His wife and children, being eleven in number, ten able to go, and one sucking on her breast, met him by the way as he went towards Smithfield. This sorrowful sight of his own flesh and blood could nothing move him, but that he constantly and cheerfully took his death with wonderful patience in the defence and quarrel of Christ's Gospel.[31]

The words come from John Foxe's *Actes and Monuments*, a work first published in English in 1563 and popularly known as the 'Book of Martyrs'. Celebrating Mary's Protestant victims as the true heirs of the Apostles, the emotive text and accompanying woodcuts cata-logued each stake-side speech and every detail of death. It sought to destroy the religious credibility of Roman Catholicism, but even more damaging to English Catholics in the long run was the undermining of their patriotic credentials. Ministers were urged to place the 'Book of Martyrs' alongside the Bible in their churches. Sir Francis Drake sailed with a copy and read extracts to his crew. Protestantism – an import from the free towns of Germany and Switzerland – increas-ingly came to be seen as the 'true religion' of England. Catholicism, by contrast, was regarded as an alien faith characterised by obscur-antism, persecution and tyranny. People began to question if it was even possible for an English Catholic to be a true patriot.

There was one recorded burning in Northamptonshire: John Kurde, a shoemaker from Syresham, perished 'in the stonepits' just outside the north gate of Northampton on 20 September 1557.[32] It is not known if William, who had become the third Lord Vaux upon the death of his father the previous year, attended. William had recently married Eliza-beth Beaumont, the daughter of the lawyer Sir John Beaumont of Grace

Dieu in Leicestershire.* She brought to her marriage four hundred pounds and a 'holiness of life'. According to Edmund Campion, she was noted for her 'natural ability' and 'admirable shrewdness', qualities that may have reminded William Vaux of his recently deceased mother.[33]

Elizabeth bore William four children in four years – Henry, Eleanor, Elizabeth and Anne. The birth of the last may have claimed her life. The register for the Northamptonshire parish of Irthlingborough, where the Vauxes had a manor house, reveals that on 12 August 1562, twenty-four days after Anne's baptism, 'Elizabeth, wife of the Lord Vaux', was buried.[34] That same month, William turned twenty-seven.

He seems to have coped with Elizabeth's death in the conventional way: after a period of mourning, he went in search of a second wife. He did not have to look far. Mary Tresham was a Northamptonshire gentlewoman of good Catholic stock. Her grandfather, Sir Thomas Tresham of Rushton Hall, had given the order for John Kurde's burning in Northampton's stonepits. Her brother Thomas would become a prominent recusant in the latter half of Elizabeth's reign. There was a long history of friendship between the two families, who were already kin due to an inter-marriage in the fifteenth century. Vauxes and Treshams had witnessed each other's wills, exchanged land, worked together on the county bench and been brothers in arms during the Wars of the Roses.

Marriage to the third Lord Vaux must have been an attractive proposition for Mary Tresham. Here was a young, good-looking baron with a rich estate and one great mansion, Harrowden Hall. With a male heir and three daughters, he had a good record in procreation. He was convivial and enjoyed music and theatre. Lord Vaux's players toured the country and his 'bearward' was recorded baiting his animals in Bristol, Ipswich and once at Chesterton near Cambridge, where he got into trouble for diverting 'a great multitude of young scholars' from the afternoon sermon.[35]

William's piety did not prevent him from revelling in the noble pursuits of the country. He was particularly fond of his hawks. He liked to spend money – 'thrift,' his brother-in-law wrote, 'is with him

---

* Sir John Beaumont, a bencher of the Inner Temple, had attained the office of Master of the Rolls in the reign of Edward VI, but lost it, along with his estate, under charges of corruption and fraud.

against the stream.'[36] If, like his father, William had no head for business, it seemed to matter little with such a vast estate and sufficient funds to employ those who did. And if, also like his father, he was easily led, then Mary Tresham, who was every bit as shrewd as William's mother and first wife had been, would just have to keep his inconstancy in check. Marriage was a solemn undertaking for any bride, but seldom would the vows be more straitly tested than those taken by Mary Tresham.

William and Mary had five children. The first was George, whose baptism was recorded in the Harrowden parish register on 27 September 1564.[37] He was followed by Katherine, Edward, Merill and Ambrose. Although the children were privately raised as Catholics, the official registration of some of their baptisms shows that Lord Vaux was using the services of his parish church from time to time.

He strived to avoid the politics of religion. He had been one of the noblemen appointed to escort Queen Elizabeth from Hatfield to London upon her accession in 1558, but he stayed away from Parliament, despite having taken his seat in Mary's reign, and gave his proxy to a Protestant.[38] This meant that he missed the crucial events of 1559 when England once again broke with Rome and the Elizabethan religious 'settlement' was hammered out. He did not witness the uproar in the House of Lords over the bill for the Queen's supremacy, nor the refusal of all but one of the bishops to take the compromise oath acknowledging Queen Elizabeth as 'the only Supreme Governor' of Church and State. Indeed, when Viscount Montague made an impassioned speech against the bill, it was Lord Vaux's proxy, the Earl of Bedford, who sought to discredit him by asking if Montague had been offered whores by the Roman cardinals when he had delivered Mary I's submission to the Pope.[39]

Lord Vaux's surrendered vote went towards the imposition of what was, in essence, a variant of Edward VI's Church, watered down and frozen in time.[40] The Mass, for example, was abolished – there was to be no Latin canon, no sacrificial altar, no elevation of the host, no clerical exclusivity – but the new communion service was circumlocutory enough to hint at the possibility of Christ's 'real presence' for those wishing to find it. Any attempt to shunt the Church either back or forth risked prosecution. Criticism of the prayer book or the maintenance of any other form of liturgy incurred a fine of 100 marks for the first offence and 400 marks for the second. Forfeiture of goods and life imprisonment awaited anyone who dared offend a third time. Subjects were required to attend their parish church every Sunday and holy day upon pain of a twelve-pence fine. The royal supremacy had to be declared, on oath, by all those holding office under Church or Crown. Defence of the spiritual primacy of the Pope incurred forfeiture of goods and, if possessions were worth less than twenty pounds, prison for a year. Serial offenders ran the risk of a traitor's death.

Subjects who failed these tests of allegiance came to be known as recusants. At this stage, Lord Vaux was not of their number. Noble privilege exempted him from the oath of supremacy and allowed him to worship in his private chapel. The official prayer book had to be used, of course, but as long as Vaux remained quiescent and discreet – and his father had taught him well – his inner sanctum was not violated. He probably hoped that the Queen, like her siblings, would not live long enough for the 'alteration of religion' to take hold. He had, after all, seen it all before.

For the first decade of Elizabeth's reign the letter of the law was not rigorously enforced. Those who raised their heads above the parapet were usually shot down, but the majority of Catholics avoided confrontation and were not subjected to unnecessary scrutiny. Queen Elizabeth, in common with most of her leading ministers, had conformed during Mary's reign, and she seemed genuine in her reluctance to intrude on private thoughts.*

The Queen was also acutely aware of her vulnerability on the international stage. According to the leaders of Catholic Europe, she was not the rightful ruler of England, but the bastard child of an invalid union that had subsequently been recognised as such by her own father. (Although Henry VIII named Elizabeth in the 1544 Act of Succession, and in his last will, he never formally repealed the Act of

---

*The famous, but often misquoted, assertion that Queen Elizabeth did not like 'to make windows into men's hearts and secret thoughts' was made by Francis Bacon towards the end of the reign. As Diarmaid MacCulloch points out, 'the heart is not the seat of salvation as is the soul. It would not be inconsistent with protestantism for the Queen to care less about feelings or opinions than about salvation.' (J. Spedding, *The Letters and the Life of Francis Bacon*, I, 1861, p. 178; MacCulloch, 'Latitude', p. 49)

1536 that had declared her illegitimate.) The 1559 treaty of Cateau-Cambrésis ensured that France and Spain were no longer at logger-heads, thus opening up the terrifying prospect, to Elizabethan eyes, of a Catholic world order.

In the event, both countries would have their own domestic trials. France would be destabilised by four decades of religious civil war and Philip II, upon returning to Spain in the autumn of 1559, initially poured his energies into the Inquisition and his battle against growing Protestant activism in the Low Countries. Yet he was always very interested in English affairs, not just because he was the self-styled champion of Catholic Europe and because Dutch Protestant exiles found a safe haven across the North Sea, but also because he had been married to Mary I for four years and enjoyed the 'crown matrimonial' of England. 'God has already granted that by my intervention and my hand that kingdom has previously been restored to the Catholic Church once,' Philip later declared in an ominous statement of chutzpah and intent. He did not mourn Mary much or his departure from the country that had received him with such ill grace, but he had relished his role as joint Defender of the Faith and even contem-plated reclaiming the title long after Mary's death.[41] Elizabeth I was wise indeed to avoid making waves at the start of her reign.

She was, nevertheless, determined to kill off Catholicism in her kingdom. She was happy to procure a slow death by gradually starving the community of its sacraments. Once the old generation of Marian 'mass-mongers' had died out, and once the schoolmasters, who after 1563 were required to take the oath of supremacy, had worked on the next generation, the demand for the Catholic sacraments would dwindle. That was the theory. It did not take into account the resilience and resourcefulness of the Catholic community. Nor the efforts of an Oxford academic in exile called William Allen, who circumvented the ban on domestic ordination by setting up a seminary in Douai, Flanders. Within six years of its foundation in 1568, Allen was sending newly trained priests across the Channel for the sustenance of hungry Catholic souls.

Another event in 1568 caused even graver consternation. Mary Queen of Scots, the young Catholic widow of Francis II of France, and the great-niece of Henry VIII, sailed into England seeking refuge from the Scottish Protestants who had forced her abdication. Elizabeth I was in a bind. Until she married and had children, her cousin Mary was the heir presumptive to the English throne. By quartering her arms with those of England, Mary had signalled her desire to be enthroned at Westminster. Whether she hoped to achieve this by deposition or succession was unclear, but many of her supporters, including militant leaders in Spain, Rome and France, seemed to favour the former.

Elizabeth's Secretary, William Cecil (Lord Burghley from February 1571), was convinced that Mary posed a mortal threat to his Queen. Five years earlier, he had even tried to introduce a bill that would have given the Privy Council, in the event of Elizabeth's death, temporary control of government, allowing time for Parliament to elect a suit-able (Protestant) successor. It was a radical proposal and ahead of its time. The Glorious Revolution of 1688–9 would later justify Cecil's vision, but in 1563 Queen Elizabeth was far too wedded to the concept of inviolable hereditary monarchy to legislate for such a provision.[42] The bill was dropped, but Cecil never gave up and nor did Mary or her supporters. 'There is less danger in fearing too much than too little,' Francis Walsingham wrote to Cecil towards the end of 1568.[43]

Despite noble privilege and official reluctance to intrude upon private worship at Harrowden, Lord Vaux was doubtless observed with a weather eye. He was known on the Continent as a friend of Rome: a document in the Vatican archives from December 1567 lists him as one of thirty-one English Catholic peers.[44] Two years earlier he had granted the advowson of a church living to a 'clarke' who subsequently 'changed his habit' and ministered as a priest to the Catholic commu-nity. From 1571, the priest was receiving ten pounds a year from Lord Vaux. The following year, he was imprisoned by the Bishop of London. One of Burghley's spies, who suspected the priest of associating with confederates of the Scottish Queen, reported from London that he had been living 'very gentlemanlike in this town, resorting familiarly to the French ambassador & is favoured of a great number of papists'.[45] Lord Vaux may have been adopting a conformist pose, but it must be wondered how many other priests were receiving his aid behind the scenes.

The letter that Edmund Campion wrote to Lord Vaux's first son, Henry, is suggestive: 'During the period of several months when I was a guest at your father's house,' he wrote, in reference to his sojourn at Harrowden Hall around 1568, 'his daily speech and intimate conversation brought home to me the great work he was doing for all men of learning.' Campion concluded by sending his infinite good wishes to Henry 'and your family, by whom I am so sumptuously maintained and so honourably encouraged'.

Within a month of writing this letter, which he addressed from Oxford on 28 July 1570, Campion had left England for Ireland, where he wrote *Two Bokes of the Histories of Ireland*, dedicated to the Chancellor of Oxford University, and Queen Elizabeth's favourite, the Earl of Leicester. The following summer, he travelled to Allen's seminary in Douai, where he studied scholastic theology for nearly two years before moving to Rome and joining a religious order, the Society of Jesus. He was ordained in Prague in 1578 and celebrated his first Mass on 8 September. Two years later he returned to England 'to cry alarm spiritual against foul vice and proud ignorance wherewith many my dear countrymen are abused'.[46]

It would be putting the cart before the horse to anticipate all this in the summer of 1570 when Campion gratefully acknowledged Lord Vaux's continued support. However, he did write his letter at a crossroads. In the late 1560s, the Oxford scholar had composed a long Latin poem on the tribulations of the early Church that juxtaposed the permanence of the Roman Church with the transitoriness of the Empire. 'The strong pillar of faith stood firm,' Campion wrote, 'and the sure barque of Peter, never to sink, sailed bravely forward despite the tyrant.' He wrote in the classical hexameters of Virgil and dedicated his work to 'one of the most heroic men alive': Viscount Montague, a prominent Catholic nobleman, who had spoken against the oath of supremacy in Parliament, but retained the favour of the Queen.[47]

Towards the end of 1568, Campion had sacrificed his exhibition with the Grocers' Company because he had not fulfilled their request to 'utter his mind in favouring the religion now authorised' in a public sermon. On 19 March 1569, after five years studying theology at Oxford, he had supplicated for the degree of Bachelor of Theology, something that he was unlikely to have done had he been unable to defend the established Church (the degree required public disputation). It seems that around this time Campion also 'suffered himself to be ordained' into the Anglican Church. Yet he did not take his degree in the summer, possibly, as his fellow missioner Robert Persons maintained, because of 'a remorse of conscience and detestation of mind' against his ordination, which prompted him to forsake the established Church and, for a time, his country. According to one scholar, Campion was 'an avowed Catholic' when he arrived in Ireland on 25 August 1570.[48]

The chronology is important because it helps to assess Campion's frame of mind when he wrote his letter to Henry Vaux from Oxford on 28 July 1570. We cannot know what 'intimate conversation' Campion and Henry's father had shared in 1568, nor the exact nature of 'the great work' Lord Vaux had been doing for 'all men of learning'. But if, as now seems likely, Campion was a recent convert to Catholicism when he wrote his letter, then his gratitude to Lord Vaux for his sumptuous maintenance and honourable encouragement well over a year after he had left his employ is intriguing. The two men had not seen each other for a while – 'I have been separated from him longer than I anticipated (not my by own wish, but by reason of my way of life),' Campion wrote, possibly in reference to his acceptance of the Anglican diaconate, which may have temporarily alienated Lord Vaux.[49] But they had recently been in touch as Campion had written the letter at Vaux's request – 'your Father (by whom I am dearly loved, and whom I particularly revere) has easily persuaded me that my voice and advice should come to you.'

Whatever Campion's subsequent vocation and whenever he resolved upon it, his job at Harrowden Hall had been to tutor Henry Vaux. He was hugely impressed with the boy, who at nine had already mastered Latin and was composing poetry. This was astonishing to Campion because:

> among men of your rank we very seldom come across any who have even a slight acquaintance with literature. Many are overburdened with leisure; they concern themselves with trifles, waste the possessions of others and squander their own; they ruin the prime of life with women and pleasure. All the more rightly, then, do I congratulate you on your intellectual outlook.

Campion also had high praise for Henry's sister, 'your rival in study and work'. This was probably the eldest Vaux girl, Eleanor, who was about eight in 1568. If Henry continued to fly 'the flag of promise' and encourage his sibling, then Campion predicted great things:

You and your sister will be a matchless pair; you will reach the delights you so eagerly seek for, you will shine with marvellous lustre, you will be filled with the desire to do your duty and act generously, and you will be surrounded by fame and affection in the sight of all men.

It might seem a curious letter to write to a young boy, but such compositions, offering students praise and advice in elegant Latin, were fairly commonplace in sixteenth-century England. We cannot now know if the lessons at Harrowden Hall strayed towards issues of faith. Campion's language is suggestive, but circumspect. Any direct references to religion are neutral: 'Love God and serve Him.' Henry and Eleanor would both commit their lives to the Catholic cause and, if not exactly regarded with affection 'in the sight of all men', to many Catholics at least, Campion's words were prophetic.

The turn of the decade was not a good time to be a Catholic peer. National security was under threat. A series of diplomatic skirmishes damaged the uneasy relationship between England and the Catholic monarchy in France, while the English seizure of a treasure fleet destined for the Spanish Netherlands in November 1568 brought latent hostility between Elizabeth I and Philip II of Spain into the open. Early in 1569 Secretary Cecil wrote a memorandum outlining his fears of an international Catholic conspiracy against Elizabeth. Everywhere he looked – Rome, France, Spain, the Low Countries, Ireland, Scotland, even at home, where Mary Stuart now resided – he saw 'perils . . . many, great and imminent'.[50]

In November 1569, there was a rising in the north of England. The causes were as much political as religious, but the Earls of Northumberland and Westmorland had rallied their tenants under a Catholic banner and heard Mass in Durham Cathedral. The plan, in as much as there was one, was to free Mary Stuart from house arrest in Tutbury Castle, Staffordshire, and 'thereby to have some reformation in religion'.[51] The Duke of Norfolk, already in prison for conspiring to marry Mary, was implicated. Spanish aid was sought, but not forthcoming, and the rising was crushed with ruthless efficiency. Retribution was swift and terrible. Hundreds of rebels were executed under martial law; 450 dead is the conservative estimate, though a convincing argument has been made for the figure to be doubled.[52]

The rising had occurred miles from Northamptonshire and Lord Vaux, serving on the county commission for musters, had had nothing to do with it. He felt the heat nonetheless. On 18 November 1569, he subscribed to a statement of loyalty tendered to past and present justices of the peace. He promised to worship 'devoutly' according to the official prayer book, at church 'or upon reasonable impediment' in his chapel, and to oppose anything said or done in contempt of the established religion. A couple of months later, the baptism of his youngest daughter, Merill, was registered at Irthlingborough parish church.[53]

Such tokens of conformity were no longer deemed sufficient proof of loyalty. The northern rising had exposed the Catholic Church militant in England and undermined the claims of all its worshippers to be good Elizabethans. Far from winning allegiance, the Queen's 'natural clemency' had apparently emboldened rebellious spirits. The shooting in Scotland of Regent Moray on 23 January 1570 confirmed Protestant fears that assassins were active in the British Isles. If there was any doubt that Elizabeth I was also a target, it was removed the following month when she was excommunicated by the Pope.

The papal bull *Regnans in Excelsis* condemned Elizabeth as a heretic, whose 'monster-like' usurpation of the English throne had brought 'miserable ruin' upon the kingdom. It deprived her of 'the right which she pretends' and absolved all Catholics from any previous oaths of allegiance. The time had come for absolute obedience to the papacy: 'there is no place left for any excuse, defence, or tergiversation.' Thenceforth, any Catholic peer or subject (the bull made the distinction) 'shall not once dare to obey her or any her directions, laws, or commandments, binding under the same curse those who do anything to the contrary'.[54] The 'curse' was the sentence of anathema. Catholics could either obey their Queen and consign their souls to damnation or they could obey the Pope and surrender their bodies to temporal punishment. They could not, in good conscience, do both. It was the choice of two betrayals and theoretically it put Lord Vaux and his co-religionists in an impossible position.

The irony of *Regnans in Excelsis* is that it did more damage to the English Catholic community than any Protestant proclamation could have done. Pope Pius V had issued it at the behest of the northern earls, but by the time it appeared in England, all that was left of the rebellion were the corpses, hanging 'for terror' in the marketplace.[55] Many Catholics resented the insensitivity of the Pope's ultimatum and, according to William Allen, 'did think hardly of that deed', wishing that 'so great a matter' had been left to the judgement of God. Even Philip II of Spain was vexed, but chiefly because he had not been consulted: 'My knowledge of English affairs is such that I believe I could give a better opinion upon them and the course that ought to have been adopted under the circumstances than anyone else,' he huffed in a letter to his ambassador in London.*[56]

The Protestant backlash was inevitable. Those who had always suspected that the true colour of English Catholicism was papal purple now felt vindicated in their attacks on the community. 'Papists' were portrayed as the enemy within, potential fifth columnists, who were biding their time in feigned conformity until the call to strike. In Lord Vaux's county, a gloating tract was 'cast in the streets of Northampton':

> And this is true, the time is come,
>   I'll tell you truer news:
> All papists which have traitorous hearts
>   and do their prince refuse,
> Must now relent, and turn forthwith,
>   and true become God knows:
> Or else prepare to give their flesh,
>   at once to feed the crows.
>
>   . . .
>
> Your wresting long of God's true word
>   can nothing you prevail:
> Have done I say, dispatch therefore,
>   pluck down your peacock's tail.
> Down on your knees you asses stout,
>   pray God and Queen for grace:
> You can no longer now prevail,

---

*Memories of the mistimed Bull took a long time fading: 'Pius's action was so generally recognized as a political blunder that it was even remembered in the 1930s when the papacy considered how to react to Adolf Hitler's regime: discreet voices in the Vatican privately recalled the bad precedent, and behind the scenes it was a factor in preventing a public papal condemnation of Nazism.' (MacCulloch, *Reformation*, p. 334)

> your practise takes no place.
> It boots you not to Pius now
>   for mercy for to seek:
> For you be traitors proud at home,
>   his Bull is not worth a leek.
> Therefore as thousand traitors are,
>   by thousands all agree:
> To turn to God, or else make haste,
>   to scale the gallow tree.[57]

The official response was more measured, though hardly less hostile. Parliament was called with the intention of flushing out all the 'traitorous hearts' and, for the first time in the reign, Lord Vaux answered the summons to attend. He sat in the Lords alongside the newly ennobled William Cecil, Baron of Burghley, on almost every day that the House was in session. New treason legislation was enacted condemning anyone who questioned the validity of the Queen's religion or her right to rule. It became high treason to 'reconcile' anyone to Rome using papal bulls or instruments, and for anyone to be thus reconciled. Abetters and harbourers of such people were liable to loss of lands and goods. The 'Act against Fugitives over the Sea' demanded the return, within six months, of anyone who had gone abroad without permission since the beginning of the reign. Those who stayed away risked forfeiture of goods, chattels and estate profits. 'An Act against the bringing in and putting in execution of Bulls and other Instruments from the See of Rome' ruled that knowingly to import, receive or handle documents stamped with the pretended powers of the papacy was treason. The real sting in the Act came in the fourth section, which also banned any Agnus Dei, cross, picture, bead 'or such like vain and superstitious things' blessed by the Pope or his priests. The importation or receipt of such 'hallowed' objects would incur the forfeiture of lands and goods.[58] It was a blatant assault on traditional piety. From thenceforth, even the simple act of owning a rosary was considered dubious.

Despite his regular attendance in the Upper Chamber, there is no recorded objection from Lord Vaux to any of the legislation that was passed. One bill did, however, compel him to break his silence. The bill 'for coming to the church, and receiving the Communion' insisted upon full ecclesiastical conformity and was the most controversial of the parliamentary session. Two clauses in particular aroused strong feeling in both Houses. The first concerned the proviso that exempted anyone of or above the rank of a gentleman who had a private chapel from having to attend his parish church. 'There should be no difference between man and man,' argued Mr Aglionby, Member for Warwick, and his colleagues in the Commons appear to have agreed that the exemption should be lifted.

Aglionby did, however, dispute the second major issue, which concerned the Lord's Supper. Hearing divine service was one thing, he argued, but no law should 'enforce consciences' to receive communion: 'The conscience of man is internal, invisible, and not in the power of the greatest monarch in the world, in no limits to be straitened, in no bonds to be contained.'[59] Thomas Norton, a protégé of Lord Burghley, countered that the exposure of 'the very secrets of the heart' was necessary in order to identify 'the good seed so sifted from the cockle'.* The time for harvest had come. Enforced communion would lead to the exposure of 'those rebellious calves whom the Bull hath begotten'.[60]

The bill was sent up to the Lords on 5 May 1571 with an escort of twenty-nine members, a sure sign of its significance. Letters from the French ambassador suggest that some peers resented the intrusion upon noble privilege.[61] This deeply affected Lord Vaux. Hitherto he had avoided scrutiny by worshipping in his private chapel. Compulsory attendance at the parish church and, worse still, enforced communion would openly expose him as a traitor to his faith or, if he refused to attend, a recusant.

He heard all three readings of the bill and, on 17 May, voted against it with three other Catholic peers (Worcester, Southampton and Windsor).[62] Vaux had finally made a stand, though whether it was for noble privilege or general freedom of conscience cannot be conclusively determined. Given his previous record, the inclination to be ungenerous and assume the former motivation is strong. However,

---

* This is an arresting image. The cockle was a purple-flowering weed that blighted the cornfields. In the Parable of the Weeds (Matthew 13:24–30), Jesus advised against uprooting the weed too soon, 'lest perhaps, gathering up the cockle, you root up the wheat also together with it. Suffer both to grow until the harvest, and in the time of the harvest, I will say to the reapers: Gather up first the cockle and bind it into bundles to burn, but the wheat gather ye into my barn.'

before voting, the Lords had made some alterations to the bill and, according to the parliamentary historian J. E. Neale, 'the odds are that the Upper House reinserted the proviso' of noble exemption.[63] If this was indeed the case – and the reaction of the Commons seems to point that way – then Lord Vaux did not vote out of self-interest, but on behalf of all his co-religionists.

Although his own efforts could not defeat the bill, Vaux found an unlikely ally in the Queen, who asserted her power of veto at the end of the session. Despite the northern rising and the papal bull, and despite the long hours put into the bill by both Houses, Elizabeth remained true to her declaration of the previous year: she was 'very loath' to substitute 'princely severity' for 'natural clemency'; she would not force 'an inquisition' upon her subjects. If, however, any of them dared to break her laws – and after the 1571 Parliament there were more to break – 'then,' she warned, 'she cannot but use them according to their deserts, and will not forbear to inquire of their demeanours and of what mind and disposition they are.'[64] This was lenience sixteenth-century style.

The sun had briefly shone on the application of Elizabeth I's veto, but there had been too many dark clouds in the 1571 Parliament for celebration. Lord Vaux had anticipated stormy weather. On 10 February 1571, two months before taking his seat in the Lords, he had signed a deed that tied up his estates in a series of trusts. Perhaps mindful that cash might not always be available, he also made provision for the dowries of Eleanor, Elizabeth and Anne, his three daughters by his first wife. The agreement bound his brother-in-law, Thomas Tresham, to pay £500 for each of the girls at the time of their marriage. In return, Lord Vaux would give Tresham £100 annually for fifteen years.

The deed also entrusted the three girls and their brother Henry to the custody of their grandmother Elizabeth Beaumont. They were to go and live with her in Leicestershire for ten years. Lord Vaux would pay £20 a year for 'the education, finding and bringing up' of Henry, and £10 a year for each of the girls. The rest of the six-page document secured the jointure of the current Lady Vaux, and the inheritance of Vaux's sons by both his marriages. It bore the seals of ten men and committed a number of neighbours and kinsfolk to the preservation of the Vaux patrimony. Two names stand out: Tresham and Catesby. These two families were closely bound to the Vauxes long before the Gunpowder Plot would make their association infamous.[65]

In the Vatican archives there is a document written in Italian and set in cipher. Undated, but belonging to March 1571, it is purportedly a letter of instruction from the Duke of Norfolk to a Florentine banker called Roberto Ridolfi. The banker was to travel 'with all possible celerity' to the Pope in Rome and thence to Philip II in Madrid. He was to advise them on 'the miserable plight in which this island is', and 'the afflictions and cruel usage to which the Queen of Scotland and myself, as also all the Catholics of these kingdoms are subjected'. Ridolfi's brief was to secure aid:

> in the just enterprise, which has the promise of assured success if they would but grant the succour that is craved for the furtherance of the Queen of Scotland's title, the re-establishment of the Catholic religion, and the suppression of those that are of the opposite side.[66]

The 'succour' was to take the form of men, money, munitions and 'a person experienced in leading an army'. As Philip II understood the plan, Elizabeth I was to be 'either killed or captured'.[67] According to the Vatican document, there were forty English noblemen who had pledged 'to expose themselves to all peril of battle'. They could muster many thousands of men and were, allegedly, at Norfolk's 'beck and call'.

This 'tree of treason and rebellion', as Lord Burghley later termed it, had many branches.[68] In addition to Norfolk's brief, Ridolfi travelled with a letter of credit from Mary Stuart. He also visited the Grand Duke of Tuscany and Philip II's governor-general in the Netherlands, the Duke of Alba. Everyone, except Alba whose objections were largely practical, embraced the proposal. Philip II, whose policy, it has been argued, was guided by a 'messianic vision', truly seemed to believe that he had God's mandate for 'the Enterprise of England'. He announced that 'this was the occasion and the opportunity for which he had waited' and no matter how flawed the strategy, God would help them 'get things right'.[69]

But Ridolfi had also been talking to the English government. Since the late 1560s he had been on Lord Burghley's radar. In September 1569 he had transferred papal funds to the Queen of Scots and the following month, just before the northern rebellion, he was arrested and imprisoned in Francis Walsingham's house in Seething Lane. Although he faced twenty-five separate charges, he was soon released. A year later, at a meeting with Walsingham about the Anglo-Spanish trade war, he offered to mediate between the two courts. Walsingham wrote to Burghley of his hope that the Florentine would behave 'both discreetly and uprightly'. In March 1571, on the eve of his departure for the Catholic courts of Europe, Ridolfi had an audience with Elizabeth I, ostensibly about trade. He received 'a very favourable passport' and, armed with 'Instructions' from the Duke of Norfolk and the Scots Queen, he went on his conspiratorial way.[70]

Clearly more than just a messenger, Ridolfi seems to have been playing a double game, but on whose behalf? Norfolk, Mary and the Catholic leaders they petitioned for aid? Or Burghley, Walsingham and Elizabeth, who granted him easy passage to the Continent? Or was he a maverick, who thrilled to the spying game and was happy to play each side off against the other as long he retained access to powerful people and a hand in their purses? We will probably never know quite who were the players and who were the pawns in the Ridolfi Plot. The eponymous conspirator would resurface in Florence as a papal senator; he clearly relished intrigue.

By the autumn of 1571, Burghley had gathered enough evidence – from intercepted letters and ciphers, spy reports and interrogations under the threat of torture – to expose many branches of the conspiracy. He did so very publicly, using the printing press to leak the details of the plot and smear one suspect in particular: Mary Queen of Scots. Now the English public and the courts of Europe could read, in a work translated from Latin into imitation Scots under Burghley's commission, the dossier of evidence that had previously been gathered against Mary 'touching the murder of her husband, and her conspiracy, adultery and pretended marriage with the Earl of Bothwell'. Although Mary had been discreet in her involvement with Ridolfi, Burghley was convinced that she had transferred her murderous inclinations on to Queen Elizabeth. 'Now judge, Englishmen,' the final words of the work exhorted,

if it be good to change queens. Oh uniting confounding! When rude
Scotland has vomited up a poison, must fine England lick it up for a
restorative? Oh vile indignity! While your Queen's enemy liveth, her
danger continueth. Desperate necessity will dare the uttermost . . .[71]

In blackening Mary's reputation, Burghley arguably benefited a
great deal from the exposure of the Ridolfi Plot, but he failed in his
ultimate aim to have the Scottish Queen destroyed. When Parliament
met in May 1572, Mary was denounced as a Jezebel, a murderess and
a 'most wicked and filthy woman', but Elizabeth refused to heed the
clamour for her execution. Nor would she formally exclude Mary
from the succession. Instead, after much temporising, she surrendered
the head of another conspiratorial cousin, Thomas Howard, fourth
Duke of Norfolk. He was executed for his part in the Ridolfi Plot on
2 June on Tower Hill, where, some twenty-five years earlier, his father,
the poet Earl of Surrey, had also placed his neck on the block.

The failure of the Ridolfi Plot did little to blur Philip II's 'messianic
vision'. Victory for his half-brother, Don John of Austria, over the
Turks at Lepanto in October 1571 and news from France the following
August of the 'St Bartholomew's Day Massacre' were welcomed in
Madrid as God's handiwork. The Spanish ambassador in France could
hardly contain his delight at the slaughter of so many Protestants:

> As I write, they are killing them all, they are stripping them naked, drag-
> ging them through the streets, plundering the houses and sparing not
> even children. Blessed be God who has converted the French princes to
> His cause. May he inspire their hearts to continue as they have begun.[72]

For the Protestants of Europe, there was nothing sanctified about
the slaughter of their brethren at the hands of the French Catholics.
It was an atrocity that few witnesses – including Francis Walsingham,
on secondment at the English embassy in Paris – would forget. Many
French Protestants sought refuge in England, each arriving with his
own harrowing tale of Catholic bloodlust.* According to the French

---

* A century later, the massacre, along with the Marian burnings, was still used to
stir up a visceral fear of Catholicism. In order to fathom 'the last time Popery reigned
amongst us,' wrote Charles Blount in 1679, the reader must imagine a town in flames,

ambassador in England, many believed 'that it was the Pope and the King of Spain who kindled the fire in France . . . and that there is something evil afoot from all three of them against England'.[73]

Philip II reportedly laughed at the news of the massacre. It was, he said, 'one of the greatest moments of satisfaction that I have had in all my life'. Not only would it reduce French interference in the Netherlands, but it also provided reassurance that in those apocalyptic times he was indeed a messiah who could discern God's purpose. When, a decade later, a medal was struck to commemorate the Spanish annexation of Portugal of 1580, it bore the legend: *Non sufficit orbis* – The world is not enough.

Despite the setback of the Ridolfi business, Philip was sure that one day God would help him dethrone England's heretic Queen. He had to be careful; in April 1572 Elizabeth I signed a treaty of mutual defence with France. As long as the French had the power to intervene across the Channel, peace – no matter how strained – was the defining characteristic of Anglo-Spanish relations. But Philip remained determined to honour his 'special obligation to God'.[74] The Enterprise of England was not abandoned.

Lord Vaux's reaction to the atrocities in France is nowhere recorded, nor is his response to the Ridolfi Plot, though he was hardly a disinterested observer. His attendance at the 1572 Parliament that was called to deal with Norfolk, Mary and the 'safety' of Elizabeth and her realm suggests that he was still engaged by the issues of the day. He may also have wanted to demonstrate his loyalty to the Queen, for the Italian letter of March 1571 (set under Norfolk's name, but more probably drawn up by Ridolfi himself) allegedly represented the views of 'the more part of the nobles of this realm'. Indeed, it had gone further, suggesting that Norfolk could muster 'twenty thousand

---

'at the same instant, fancy amongst the distracted crowd you behold troops of papists ravishing your wives and daughters, dashing your little children's brains out against the walls, plundering your houses and cutting your own throats . . . Then represent to yourselves the Tower of London playing off its cannon and battering down your houses about your ears. Also, casting your eye towards Smithfield, imagine you see your father or your mother or some of your nearest and dearest relations tied to a stake in the midst of flames, when with hands and eyes lifted up to heaven, they cry out to God for whose cause they die.' (Justin Champion, 'Popes and Guys and Anti-Catholicism', in Buchanan et al., *Gunpowder Plots*, pp. 93–6)

foot and three thousand horse' by forty English Catholics, who were 'well disposed and ready to act'. Lord Vaux's name was on the list.[75]

It is highly unlikely that Vaux was aware of what was, in all probability, the arrogation of his name. Ridolfi undermined his claim by further asserting that 'many' Protestants would afford aid, 'being concerned rather with the question of succession than with that of religion'. He even named the Earl of Leicester as a fence-sitting 'neutral'. A thorough investigation into the Ridolfi Plot implicated the Catholic peers Arundel and Lumley, but Vaux was not mentioned in the associated intelligence. The following year, however, a priest on his pension, who had been 'resorting familiarly to the French ambassador', was named by one of Burghley's spies as a person of interest in the ongoing investigation into Mary Stuart. Committed to prison by the Bishop of London, the priest, 'one Dowglas', was briefly suspected of 'familiarity' with some of the Scottish Queen's supporters and 'hath confessed somewhat of them'.[76] The spy does not elaborate and 'Dowglas' does not appear in his later reports. Burghley, it seems, did not pursue the matter, but any perceived association with Mary Stuart, even by several degrees of separation, did not augur well for Lord Vaux.

Whatever secret sympathies he may or may not have harboured, Lord Vaux was, on the face of it, a loyal and trusted citizen. Not only did he attend Parliament in 1572, but he also sat on the county commission for musters in 1569 and 1570, on a committee dealing with vagabonds in 1572, and on the commission for gaol delivery in 1579. Indeed, for much of the decade, it was county business that dominated his agenda. When Parliament met again in 1576, he nominated Lord Burghley as his proxy – an unlikely choice in terms of religion, but Burghley was a close neighbour who could be relied upon to defend local interests.[77]

Vaux could not avoid religious controversy by withdrawing from Westminster, however. Another near neighbour was the Chancellor of the Exchequer, Sir Walter Mildmay, an outspoken Protestant who liked to lambast 'the usurped tyranny of Rome' at any given opportunity.[78] There was a strong Puritan element in the county. Indeed, it was a Northamptonshire Puritan, Percival Wiburn, who would coin the phrase 'the hotter sort of Protestants' to describe those godly activists who sought further reform in Church and society and campaigned for a preaching ministry throughout the realm.[79]

There were some very substantial Catholics in the shire too. In addition to the Treshams, Lord Vaux could find allies among the Mordaunts of Drayton, the Griffins of Dingley and the Brudenells of Deene, but their influence was counterbalanced by men like Sir Edward Montagu of Boughton and Sir Richard Knightley of Fawsley – Puritan sympathisers who came to dominate the county bench. The religious polarisation of the region did not correspond with any clear-cut geographical division. Puritans and recusants lived side by side and although there were moments of friction, harmony was the norm.

Lord Vaux and Sir Edward Montagu, for example, shared many local interests and seem to have spoken with one voice when they bailed poachers and punished vagabonds in the 1570s. Indeed, the two were good friends and Montagu entertained Vaux 'many times' at Boughton House.[80] The Vauxes were also welcome at Fawsley, Sir Richard Knightley's home, where, on one occasion, Henry Vaux composed a Latin poem *ex tempore* at the encouragement of a fellow guest. The proposed theme was the Ciceronian maxim *Honos alit artes* (Honour nourishes the arts).[81] Fawsley would become a Puritan stronghold under Knightley's patronage, but at least in this instance, the religious differences of the neighbours did not prevent them from enjoying some traditional pastime with good company.

Occasionally, however, simmering religious tensions boiled over. On Friday, 13 April 1576, for instance, Henry Norwich, a Protestant, was badly beaten up by a group of Catholics that included two of his nephews and Lord Vaux's brother-in-law, Sir Thomas Tresham. According to Norwich, his assailants, 'arrayed with swords, bucklers, daggers, long-picked staves, cudgels, bastinadoes and sundry other weapons, as well invasive as defensive', had set upon him in Kettering market and would have killed him had he not escaped to a nearby house. He alleged that other attempts had been made on his life before and since. He sought redress at the Northampton quarter sessions, but was not happy with the verdict delivered by Lord Vaux and his fellow officials there. He claimed that the defendants were 'supported by some in authority' and in 1578 he appealed to the Star Chamber. The case evidence exposes the murderous divisions within the Norwich family. Henry Norwich testified that his assailants were utterly contemptuous of the law:

And such is their liberty and especially the said Simon [his nephew] that he dare openly profess popery or any superstition and to manifest the same he hath not been at any divine service nor received any sacrament sithence your Majesty's reign, unless it have been at any armitage [Hermitage] in the woods near his house where sometimes, with divers vagrant persons known to be massing priests, he heareth Mass.[82]

Henry Norwich was an informer against Catholics, all Catholics it seems, even those who happened to be his nephews. He also accused Simon of smuggling papal bulls into the country, defaming the English Bible and supporting Catholic priests both at home and abroad. Evidently his nephews felt that Uncle Henry had meddled one time too many in their affairs and at Kettering market they had meted out their own brand of rough justice. The case is a reminder not only of local resentment to the implementation of the recusancy laws, but also to the inherent violence of the age.

Henry Norwich won his case in the Star Chamber and continued to hound local Catholics. Sixteen years after the affray at Kettering, 'her Majesty's servant' would be 'assaulted and wounded' again, this time 'by the procurement' of George and Ambrose Vaux, two of Lord Vaux's sons by his second marriage. The cause was the same: 'for splena [sic] and displeasure borne by them unto him for prosecuting some of their friends for recusancy'. As before, Norwich was dissatis-fied with the reaction – or rather inaction – of the local authorities and complained to the Privy Council that his assailants were persisting in 'their riotous and disorderly proceedings'.[83] Despite the law of the land and the ferocity and ubiquity of anti-Catholic rhetoric in Eliza-bethan England, it seems that, in Northamptonshire at least, informing on one's neighbours with what was deemed unnecessary fervour was an unpopular and risky endeavour.

In 1580 Lord Vaux turned forty-five. This was around the time, according to contemporary experts, of the onset of old age. It was believed that the body would begin to dry up, strength would decline and the mind would become 'more sedate and quiet in its motions'.[84] Wisdom and discretion would replace the passion and folly of youth. This probably suited Vaux just fine.

He had lived through three changes of monarch (four if one includes the abortive reign of Lady Jane Grey). He had seen the Mass abolished, restored and abolished again. He had subscribed to a religious settlement, in which he did not believe, and promised to defend a Church whose authority he did not recognise. He had witnessed the publication of Foxe's 'Book of Martyrs' and the excoriation of his faith. He had been forced to serve God in secret and conceal aspects of worship of which he was proud. Priests, whom he revered, had been exiled, imprisoned and even put to death. He had buried his parents and his first wife. He had sired nine children and was the grandfather of two. Towards the end of the decade, his daughter Eleanor, who had married Edward Brooskby, had a boy and a girl, William and Mary. Raised from birth as Catholics, they joined an embattled minority. It has been estimated that by 1580 more than half of the population had been baptised in the Elizabethan Church.[85]

'Learn thou hereby not to faint,' Lord Vaux may have read in *The Exercise of a Christian Life* issued from a secret Catholic press in England in 1579,

> or to be discouraged when thou art persecuted, tempted and afflicted, but with faith to expect our good Lord his hour, who after a tempest sendeth fair weather, after troubles quietness.[86]

Lord Vaux knew all too well that the better part of valour was discretion. Even the hardest heart might have forgiven him for wanting to live out the rest of his days in quiet expectation of future fair weather: to enjoy his hounds and hawks, to muddle along with Puritan neighbours and to let the next generation champion the cause with the vigour of youth. Then a familiar friend turned up at his gates and Lord Vaux, ever the hospitable nobleman, welcomed him inside. In so doing, he condemned the rest of his life to imprisonment, pecuniary pain and 'inspeakable misery'.[87]

The tempest was only just beginning to stir.

PART ONE

WILLIAM AND HENRY

I

The Enterprise is Begun

And touching our Society, be it known unto you that we have
made a league – all the Jesuits in the world, whose succession
and multitude must overreach all the practices of England – cheerfully to carry the cross that you shall lay upon us and never to
despair your recovery while we have a man left to enjoy your
Tyburn, or to be racked with your torments, or to be consumed
with your prisons. The expense is reckoned, the enterprise is
begun; it is of God, it cannot be withstood. So the faith was
planted, so it must be restored.

Campion's 'Brag', 1580[1]

Lord Vaux's first son, Henry, had been eleven when he had left home
with his sisters to live with his maternal grandmother in Leicestershire.
There was nothing particularly unusual in the arrangement; children
often completed their education in the households of their relatives
and Lord Vaux could rely on his mother-in-law to bring up his children
the right way, which is to say, the Catholic way.

Elizabeth Beaumont was born a Hastings. She was distantly related
to the Puritan Earl of Huntingdon and his brother, Francis Hastings,
a fervid Protestant, who was convinced that no Catholic could be a
good Englishman. He persistently railed against the 'viperous brood'
of priests and their 'popish poison'. Their harbourers, he wrote, were
'dangerous people (for subjects I cannot call them till they obey better)',
who threatened to 'infect the heart and mind of many a simple
subject'.[2] Despite her relation's best efforts to rid the county of 'this
pernicious sect of papists', Elizabeth Beaumont, a widow and therefore
possessed of a certain amount of independence, continued to worship
the old faith in her home.

Henry Garnet, the Jesuit leader who was active in England from 1586, would praise Elizabeth's service to the mission. 'It was her pleasure,' he wrote, 'to look after the priests' rooms and to cook their food so that their presence might be kept more secret. And she showed great devotion to me without my meriting it in any way.' Priests had been resorting to her house long before the first missionaries came to England in 1574. Garnet mentions that her son Francis Beaumont had grown up hearing Mass secretly at home before disappointing them all in adulthood by attending the services of the 'new religion'.[3]

In addition to Elizabeth Vaux, Beaumont had another daughter, Jane, who was the second wife of Robert Brooksby of Shoby, one of those dangerous non-subjects whose 'obstinacy' in his faith Francis Hastings deemed so malignant.[4] Around 1577, Brooksby's son by his first marriage, Edward, married the eldest Vaux girl, Eleanor. Little is known about the middle Vaux girl, Elizabeth, who sailed away to France in 1582 to become a nun, but Eleanor and the youngest, Anne – of whom much more later – would both dedicate their lives to the English mission. The little evidence that survives suggests that the girls, whose mother had died within a month of Anne's birth, were devoted to their only living grandparent. When she lay dying in 1588, it was a priest under their care who would administer the last rites. Many years later, Anne was still in possession of some of her grandmother's greatest treasures: 'a tawny rouge mantle' and 'a gold cross full of relics'.[5]

Henry Vaux's erstwhile tutor, Edmund Campion, also approved of Elizabeth Beaumont. 'I congratulate you on your intellectual outlook,' he wrote in his letter to Henry of July 1570, 'your distinguished father, your grandmother, your relations and kinsfolk: all of them are and were your teachers.'

I congratulate you on the result of their teaching, namely, that you truly count it a thing admirable and splendid, excellent and glorious, to consider the ornaments of virtue and not fleeting imaginings to be the real fame; not to waste your talents in idleness, not to gamble away your life, not to be puffed up, not to live licentiously and for pleasure; but to serve God, to avoid vicious practices, to seek the best in culture and in art.[6]

Henry, who may have inherited his literary skills from his father's father, the second Lord Vaux, was a precocious student. Campion noted that he was composing verse at the age of nine. Three surviving poems, including a Latin meditation on the Passion of Christ, were written when he was thirteen.[7] The priest John Gerard described Henry as 'a very scholarly man, well known for his piety',[8] but this was not just the pensive piety of his grandfather, who had deemed it 'the sweetest time in all his life in thinking to be spent'. Henry's was the active, determined piety of a young man. There was no question of him sitting out Elizabeth's reign in the safe house of his grandmother. Latin meditations, even on the Passion, could only exercise him so far. But Henry and other young Catholics who resolutely adhered to the Church of Rome had to accept a life of diminished scope. If they refused to take the oath renouncing papal sovereignty, they could not graduate from university or hold office under the Crown. They could not be magistrates or members of Parliament or command the Queen's forces. Prominent public roles, in any case, made absenteeism from church more visible and harder for the authorities to disregard. Nor was overseas travel an easy option as a licence was required and tricky questions were asked.

A great many Catholics opted for occasional conformity and suffered the label 'church papist' for their sins. They participated in public worship and were discreet about their private devotions. Some heard Mass at home secretly after church. Others, like the composer William Byrd, conformed at court, but refused to attend the services of his local parish. A common ruse was the division of the responsibilities of the household: the men, who were more vulnerable to the penal laws, would go to church and avoid the fine, while the women would say their prayers and foster the young – and sometimes the priest – behind closed doors. Sir Arthur Throckmorton complained of this practice in Northamptonshire in 1599: 'Such here have a common saying that the unbelieving husband shall be saved by the believing wife.'

Ralph Sheldon of Beoley in Worcestershire came up with a novel solution. On the north side of his parish church he built himself a chapel that housed an elaborate stone altar, which still survives. He entered it through the churchyard, thus bypassing the main body of the church. Few Catholics had the resources to construct such solid defences, but they still managed to qualify their conformity with mini-protests designed to prove the impenetrability of their souls. Simon Mallory of Northamptonshire, 'a very inward man with Sir Thomas Tresham and the Lord Vaux', went to church and heard the sermon, but afterwards 'scoffeth at the preacher'. Another Northamptonshire family tight with Tresham and Vaux were the Flamsteads. William, who was in his eighties, read a book during the sermon 'in contempt of the word preached', while Roger kept his hat on during the prayers for Queen and country. They were reported by the Puritan minister of Preston, a stickler for transgressions at which his more moderate colleagues might have winked. In 1585 he informed on one of his own churchwardens for 'prating and talking' during a baptism.

Excuses for abstention from the Lord's Supper proliferated. Being out of charity with a neighbour was a frequent plea as it rendered the parishioner unfit for communion. Others, in common with William Shakespeare's father, John, were thought to forbear the church 'for fear of process for debt'. Mrs Kath Lacy of Sherburn in North York-shire took communion in 1569, but, instead of consuming the sacra-ment, trod 'the same bread under her foot'. There is the suspicion that some parishioners, like Sir Richard Shireburn, who blocked his ears with wool when he attended church throughout the 1560s and 1570s, might have rather enjoyed their little rebellions. The reports of irreverent behaviour can sometimes read like the actions of overgrown schoolchildren testing the patience of sober ministers. But their motives were serious. There was nothing light-hearted about the attempted suicide of John Finche of Manchester, who tried to drown himself after attending public worship.[9]

The Elizabethan Catholic experience was a wide and wavering spectrum, as sensitive to the dictates of conscience and the vagaries of local law enforcement as to shifts in domestic policy and pressures from abroad. It ranged from those who were, to all intents and purposes, Protestant, and were only reconciled on their deathbed, through all the subtle variegations of church papistry (or moderated recusancy), towards those professed papists who actively resisted what they regarded as a heretical regime. The Vauxes were situated at the less obedient, or from Rome's viewpoint the more obedient, end of the spectrum. The Council of Trent, a general synod responsible in the mid-sixteenth century for devising ways of countering the

Protestant advance and revivifying the Catholic Church, had ruled in August 1562 that conformity to the Elizabethan Settlement, even if only outward and occasional, was against the law of God. According to the Declaration of the Fathers of the Council of Trent:

> It is expedient for your souls' salvation rather to forsake your country, or with stout and invincible courage to abide the strokes of howsoever miserable and afflicted fortune, than any way to obey most wicked laws, to the shame and reproach of your faith and religion.[10]

There would be no hat wearing or ear blocking in church for the Vauxes.

Recusants argued that their cause was religious and their motivations spiritual. They were loyal citizens who simply sought freedom of worship. Their refusal to attend prayer-book services was purely a matter of conscience. It was a defence for which some local officials had a measure of sympathy. It was not uncommon for churchwardens to use their discretion or for communities to treat their recusants as local eccentrics. There seems to have been more mischief than malice behind John Wood's decision on Ascension Day, 1612, to lead a recusant's horse into the church porch of North Petherton, Somerset, with the words: 'If thou wilt not go to the church, thy horse shall!'[11]

On the other hand, there was an inescapable logic to the Protestant argument that any unwillingness to accept the Queen's religious settlement was a challenge to her sovereignty. Resistance to the Act of Uniformity, as to any statute, was political, even if not politically motivated. And since the papacy had not only excommunicated Elizabeth, but also deprived her of 'the right which she pretends' to rule England,[12] the maintenance of any form of Roman Catholic devotion was arguably damaging to the unity of the commonwealth. As Francis Hastings put it, papists were 'unprofitable' to the body politic, 'for they have dismembered themselves from us'.[13] A similar terminology infused Catholic writing. Those who oscillated between Protestant and Catholic forms of worship were branded 'schismatic'. A great deal of contemporary ink was spilled on a circular argument that could never be squared. Service to God and Caesar could not fruitfully be separated, not for those Protestants who upheld the absolute jurisdiction of the monarch in matters of faith, nor for the Roman

Catholics whose God, through his papal deputy, had denied the authority of the Queen.

Sometime around the turn of the decade – perhaps in 1579 when he celebrated his twentieth birthday and began to receive a fifty-pound annuity[14] – Henry Vaux ventured to London. If he felt at all 'dismembered' from society or any sense of frustrated ambition, then he soon found a sense of purpose in the sprawling metropolis. The gambling dens and brothels that Campion had feared were so popular with young men of Henry's rank offered no temptation. Instead, he fell in with a group of like-minded individuals who wanted to channel their passions and their cash more productively.

Henry already knew several from home. Those whose families were intertwined on the trellis of Midlands Catholicism included Edward and Francis Throckmorton – distant cousins, whose grandmother had been a Vaux – and William Tresham, whose brother was married to a Throckmorton and whose sister was Henry's stepmother. Edward Brooksby was married to Henry's sister Eleanor, but most were unencumbered by wife or office. They were, chiefly, twenty-something, second-generation Catholic gentlemen, who shared an ardent desire to defend their embattled faith.

Some had raised the standard at a young age. Edward Throckmorton had belonged to a Warwickshire gang of boys who had pledged to endure all manner of worldly pain for refusing to go to church. Others spent time overseas visiting foreign courts and English Catholics in exile. At Spa in the Low Countries, Francis Throckmorton conferred with the Queen's enemies 'touching the altering of the state of the realm' in England 'and how the same might be attempted by foreign invasion'.[15]

Stephen Brinkley was engaged in a more sedate, but no less hazardous, endeavour. In 1579 his translation of a devotional handbook, composed in Italian by the Spanish Jesuit Gaspar Loarte, was issued from a secret printing press. Not only was its publication a flagrant defiance of the law, but Brinkley, under the pseudonym 'James Sancer', had added insult to injury by dedicating *The Exercise of a Christian Life* to the Society of Jesus. In the eyes of the English government, the Society, founded in 1540 by a Spaniard, Ignatius Loyola, was the most militant and threatening religious order to come out of Counter-Reformation Europe. In his dedicatory epistle, Brinkley acknowledged his debt to the Jesuits for 'the means you gave me to attempt and finish this work' and offered it up 'as a testimony of a reverent zeal I bear to your whole Society'. Signing off as 'your most bounden beadsman and dutiful friend forever', Brinkley prayed that God would 'preserve, increase and strengthen you forever; and grant me and all others grace to follow your good instructions'.[16]

The 'good instructions' in the book – an aid to prayer, meditation and 'the exercises, which every good Christian ought to occupy himself in' – shed some light on the way Brinkley, Henry Vaux and their fellows tried to shape their lives. Although 'principally intended for the simple and more ignorant sort', *The Exercise* would, its author hoped, 'profit each one that with good and godly intent will vouchsafe to read it'. It prescribed methods based on the 'Spiritual Exercises' taught by Jesuit retreat masters and was recommended by the Society as a foundation text for practical Christian worship.[17] Although it may not reveal the actual lifestyle of the London Catholics, it presents the ideal to which they would have strived.

The book directed readers to 'fly such places where God is customably offended, as be dicing houses, taverns, dancing schools and such like'. They had to avoid idleness and 'all excess in eating, drinking, sleeping and clothing'. Abstinence, fasting and 'other afflictions and corporal chastisements' were recommended, but only if 'moderately applied'; any 'indiscreet mortifying of the flesh' was considered counterproductive as it could lead to infirmity. After night-time prayers and a complete examination of his conscience, the good Christian, 'making the sign of the holy cross', could lie down on his bed, but he should beware, the book warned, 'in any wise of loving too dainty and soft a bed, calling to mind that narrow and hard couch of the cross, which for thy sake our Saviour lay upon'.

Prayers and meditations were an integral part of the daily routine, designed to help the layman get to know God intimately. There were chapters on 'how to pray mentally' – the mind was to be lifted up to God in silent, concentrated prayer for 'one hour in the morning, and another in the evening (little more or less)' – on appropriate behaviour during holy days, and on the mysteries of the rosary – 'the whole rosary to be said at least once every week'. A large number of prayers were provided at the end of the book for specific moments: 'in the morning before all other business', 'before Sacramental Confession', 'before Mass', 'in time of sickness'. Chapter nine prescribed meditations for every day of the week: Monday was for the reflection of past sins, Tuesday for present sins. On Wednesday the reader should concentrate his mind on death and on Thursday the last day of judgement. The pains of Hell were to be dwelt upon on Friday ('for the meditating whereof it shall be convenient thou frame in thine imagination some horrible and hideous place, as might be an infernal pit, or dungeon without any bottom, dark and full of fire; whereinto the damned souls shall be thrown headlong down'). Saturday was to be awakened with the joys of Heaven and Sunday with thoughts and thanksgiving for 'that Sacrament of Sacraments', the Mass. There was a separate chapter on 'the utility and profit that is reaped by often receiving the holy sacrament', a requirement not easy to fulfil in a country where the Mass was prohibited.

At the end of his translation Brinkley appended the report of a discovery in July 1578 of 'a most strange and excellent monument', chanced upon by men digging for black sand in a vineyard about two miles from Rome. Further excavation had exposed a Roman catacomb, one of the underground cemeteries built between the second and fifth centuries AD, but forgotten since the Middle Ages. This one, the catacomb of St Priscilla, was the first to be rediscovered and had reportedly brought tears to the eyes of its beholders. In the vivid account printed by Brinkley, 'it seemeth an under-earth city of dead men . . . even like a labyrinth, the circuit whereof is supposed to be a mile'. At the end of one of the subterranean passages was 'an inner room, a chapel, with a little altar found, where the picture of the crucifix is to be seen', flanked by images of the saints.

Contrary to popular legend, the catacombs were not the product of persecution; they were, chiefly, a practical solution to a lack of space for Christians who wanted to bury their dead together, but did not have the money to buy land for open-air cemeteries. In the early days of the persecution however, Christians had occasionally resorted to the catacombs to hear Mass and had used the underground space to display the symbols of their faith. For Brinkley and his fellows, who identified with the early Christians and used their suffering as a reference for their own experience, there was nothing accidental about the discovery. It was, 'as God would have it', a thrilling and timely revelation:

By this most worthy monument we may easily gather how great the persecutions and miseries, as also the piety of those godly persons were in the primitive Church.

Here may every man see, to the singular confirmation of our undoubted and Catholic Religion and of the Catholic rites and observances, the religion, care and diligence which those good friends of God used in the burying of the dead. Here may we witness apparently with our own eyes how, when those holy and devout friends of God could not in the Ethnikes' and Idolators' days paint and reverence pictures in open place and public show, yet did they paint and reverence them in caves and secret corners.

By binding the tale of the catacomb's discovery with the pages of the devotional manual, Brinkley was seeking to authenticate the message of his text. The finding seemed to prove 'the reverend antiquity of our Catholic Religion' and its resilience in times of hardship. 'Catholic rites and observances' had provided strength and comfort then, just as they would help true Christians overcome the 'intolerable blindness of our days'. This sense of community in suffering bound the 'good friends of God' to the Church Universal. In revealing the catacombs at this time, God, through the agency of Stephen Brinkley and an illicit printing press, was apparently reminding the English Catholics of their common union with Christ.

Brinkley and his fellows may have been coming up with imaginative ways of reigniting the faith, but all the brotherly love in the world could not make priests out of laymen – not in Elizabethan England, where the ordination of the Catholic clergy was banned. But it was priests that were so desperately needed. One of the first directives of *The Exercise of a Christian Life* was for the confession of sins to 'the best learned and most virtuous confessor thou mayest possibly find'. And while it was comforting to be reminded of one's common union with Christ, it was no substitute for actual communion with Christ in the Mass, which, the *Exercise* again made clear, was to happen on a regular basis.

But if they could not minister the sacraments, they resolved to do the next best thing: they would help those priests who had attended the continental seminaries return home and find their wandering flocks. William Allen's foundation (transferred from Douai to Rheims in 1578) was the model for subsequent English colleges in Rome and elsewhere in Europe. Applying the decrees of the Council of Trent, which had themselves been inspired by the proposals of Archbishop Pole in the reign of Mary I, the seminary provided a thorough schooling in Counter-Reformation discipline, dogma and spirituality. As much a training ground for the mission as a school of theology, it produced a corps of professional priests, equipped for disputation in religious controversy and the practical skills necessary to minister in a hostile environment.

What it could not provide, in an age when communication was not instantaneous, was a sound knowledge of the situation on the ground. Since 1574, when the first four graduates had launched the English mission, the numbers of seminarians smuggled into England had swollen. There had been seven new arrivals in 1575, eighteen the following year and fifteen the next. By 1580, there were about a hundred new priests in England seeking the conversion of its inhabitants.[18] The government, alarmed by the means as well as the motives of these seminary men who received subsidies from Spain and Rome, had reacted with its laws and proclamations. Border patrols were stepped up and the circle of intelligence widened. In 1577 Cuthbert Mayne became the 'protomartyr' of Allen's seminary for bringing a papal bull into the country and having an Agnus Dei around his neck. He was hanged, drawn and quartered for treason in Launceston market-place.

In order to avoid his fate, incoming priests needed current information on the ports, roads, inns and people. This is where Henry Vaux and his friends came in. They offered lodging, clothes, funding and an escort through the country. Not only did they provide cover for the priests, but also, and just as crucially, they safeguarded the Catholic hosts who were risking their livelihoods. Priests did not carry papers of identification any more than householders advertised their Catholic credentials. Both had to rely on the lay companions to ensure there were no renegades in their midst.

The apparent leader of this group was a convert, George Gilbert. He had been raised a Protestant and had been attracted to the intensity of Puritanism before travels in Europe and an encounter with the Jesuit Robert Persons convinced him that his true calling lay in 'advancing the Catholic cause' at home. He returned to London in 1579 and, according to Persons, 'put in execution so much as had been counselled him, drawing diverse principal young gentlemen to the same purpose'. Each man offered 'his person, his ability, his friends and whatsoever God had lent him besides'. They were eager to make sacrifices and pledged 'to content themselves with food and clothing and the bare necessaries of their state, and to bestow all the rest for the good of the Catholic cause'.

Gilbert arranged for some of them to live under the same roof 'in the chief pursuivant's house'. A 'pursuivant' was a liveried messenger of the Queen, often charged in this period with finding Catholic priests. Their new landlord was 'of most credit' with the Bishop of London and although he and the Bishop's son-in-law were in Gilbert's pay, it was an astonishingly reckless choice of lodging. They lived there for 'divers years and had access of priests unto them & sundry Masses daily said in their house until,' Robert Persons recalled, 'the Jesuits came in when times grew to be much more exasperated'.[19]

Persons was writing from experience, for he was one of the two Jesuit priests sent by the Society to launch its first mission in England. The other was Edmund Campion, Henry Vaux's one-time tutor and his father's old friend. The Jesuit mission would indeed exasperate the times for the English Catholics, but it exasperated Elizabeth I and her government no less. The Jesuits were members of a fledgling religious order, bound by a Rule. In addition to the traditional vows of poverty, chastity and obedience, the professed fathers of the Society of Jesus took a fourth vow of special obedience to the Pope. They trained according to a carefully regimented programme of prayer, meditation and self-examination known as the Spiritual Exercises. They saw themselves, as one English member put it, as 'instruments of Christ' with a vocation to heal souls 'in this last era of a declining and gasping world'.[20] They strived to live and work every day according to their motto, *Ad maiorem Dei gloriam*: To the greater glory of God.

Their founder, Ignatius Loyola (1491–1556), was a Spaniard and former soldier whose knightly training was evident in his adoption of military terminology (the *Company* of Jesus, the Society *General*, the Spiritual *Exercises*) and in the practical spirituality he espoused for the maintenance of an effective working mission. The Jesuits were

proselytisers and educators as well as ministers. By 1580, there were
150 schools staffed by the Society across the world. That year there
were five thousand recruits and, before coming to England, they
had made inroads into India, the Congo, Ethiopia, Brazil, Mexico,
Peru, Japan and China.[21] To some degree they were victims of their
own success, feared or revered as the vanguard of the Counter-
Reformation. They were a testament to the new Tridentine drive for
efficiency and it was, in part, their reputation for meticulous planning
that made the timing and agenda of their mission to England seem
so suspicious.

The launch dovetailed with the arrival in Ireland of Nicholas
Sander, a prominent English Catholic and papal nuncio, who was
supporting a Spanish-assisted insurrection against English rule. From
the government's viewpoint, it looked very much as though Campion
and Persons were papal-Spanish agents bent on subversion, not
conversion. Pius V's bull of excommunication against Elizabeth was
still in force and although the new Pope, Gregory XIII, would send
the priests into England with a resolution that the bull should not
be implemented 'under present circumstances', this was scant comfort
for the Queen – the effective message being that she should still be
deposed, just not quite yet.[22]

The very deed of carrying the papal *Explanatio* into the country was,
in any case, an act of treason. Moreover, the Pope had ridden rough-
shod over English law by granting the mission a number of subversive
faculties, including the celebration of Mass and permission to print
books anonymously. Gregory XIII also solemnly blessed the priests' lay
helpers.[23] There were further concerns that Campion and Persons would
try to exploit the potentially advantageous situation created for court
Catholics by the negotiations for a marriage between the Queen and
the Duke of Anjou.[24] By accident or design, therefore, the first Jesuit
mission to England contained political overtones beyond the inherent
threat that any such venture already posed to the unity of the commonwealth.

The Jesuit General in Rome, Everard Mercurian, had grave reserva-
tions about sending Campion and Persons into such a hostile environment. He issued a set of instructions that he hoped would dampen
the controversy and mitigate the risks to his men. They were to operate
prudently and with circumspection, only working with faithful or

lapsed Catholics. 'They must so behave that all may see that the only gain they covet is that of souls.' They were to steer clear of Protestants and the affairs of state. They should avoid disputation unless 'necessity force them'.[25] Persons was designated superior of the mission and Campion, who had been happily ensconced in Prague, was summoned to Rome. They were joined by a number of laymen and secular priests* and left Rome on 18 April 1580, only nine days after Campion's arrival. He, too, had been less than enthusiastic about the venture, but his vow of obedience ('which by the grace of God I will in no case violate'[26]) and the prospect of possible martyrdom were strong inducements.

The missioners did not exactly assume a low profile on their journey towards England. Speeches were made at Bologna and Milan, and instead of passing quietly through Geneva, which was Calvin country, they tried to provoke the reformer Theodore Beza into a disputation. (Beza claimed to be too busy to deal with them, but they stood their ground and only agreed to leave when his wife intervened.) By the time they reached France, the mission was well telegraphed and the Channel ports were on alert. Campion wrote to the General that 'something positively like a clamour' heralded their approach. He was eager now to carry the banner to England, but was aware of the risk: 'It often happens that the first rank of a conquering army is knocked over.'[27]

For safety's sake, the party split up and resolved to enter England separately. Persons was the first to make the night voyage from Calais. Dressed in a buff leather coat trimmed with gold braid and a feather in his hat, he assumed the guise of a mercenary captain and was so convincing, Campion marvelled, 'that a man needs must have very sharp eyes to catch a glimpse of any holiness and modesty shrouded beneath such a garb'.[28] On 16 June 1580, Persons – 'such a peacock, such a swaggerer' – sailed into Dover and through customs. One port official even procured a horse for his onward journey and agreed to forward a letter to a certain 'Edmunds', a jewel merchant in St Omer, who was to make haste to London, where profitable opportunities awaited.

It was only when he reached Southwark that Persons ran into problems. It was four in the morning, there was no lookout and no

* Those priests not part of a religious order like the Jesuits or the Benedictines.

immediate way of finding George Gilbert and his friends. Recent events and proclamations had made the innkeepers twitchy and they refused to let in the strange mercenary knocking on their doors in the small hours. After a frustrating morning, Persons decided to risk a visit to the Marshalsea prison, one of the few places in south London where he was sure to find some Catholics. There he met Thomas Pounde, a layman who had been in the prison for over four years. As chance would have it, Pounde also received a visit that day from Edward Brooksby, Henry Vaux's brother-in-law and a member of Gilbert's circle. Brooksby escorted the Jesuit to their shared house in the city. Persons had made contact.

Meanwhile, Campion, *alias* 'Edmunds' the jewel dealer, was waiting in Calais for a fair wind. He set sail on the evening of 24 June, accompanied by his 'little man', the lay brother Ralph Emerson. They reached Dover before daylight the following morning and were subjected to a rigorous interrogation. Lacking the bravura of his colleague, Campion failed to convince as a jeweller. It did not help that he bore a superficial resemblance to Gabriel Allen, the seminary founder's brother, whose arrival the port officials were expecting. Campion was able to state, without equivocation, that he was not their man and after an agonising few hours was released.

He hastened to London and this time Gilbert's men were ready. Several had been posted at the wharves along the bank to watch the incoming boats. The records do not state if Henry Vaux was one of the lookouts, but as Campion's former student he would have been an obvious choice. In the event, though, it was the honour of Thomas James to pick up Campion and take him to the safe house. 'Young gentlemen came to me on every hand,' Campion wrote, 'they embrace me, reapparel me, furnish me, weapon me, and convey me out of the city.'[29]

Before he was secreted out of London, Campion attended a number of meetings with Catholics who wanted clarity on various issues. On 29 June 1580, he defended the papal primacy at a house in Smithfield. Soon afterwards, at the so-called 'Synod of Southwark', he and Persons attempted to reassure a group of influential laymen and priests that they had not come to meddle in Irish affairs or any other matters of state. They had been sent 'to treat of matters of religion in truth and simplicity' and they read out General Mercurian's instructions to that effect. But what was religious and what was political? To the question of whether it was ever permissible for a Catholic to attend a Protestant service, even if only for the outward display of temporal loyalty to the Queen and the avoidance of penalty, the Jesuits responded in the negative. Attendance at the parish church, token or otherwise, was an act of 'great impiety'.[30]

By allowing themselves to be drawn into the debate, Campion and Persons strayed into an area where the line between religion and politics was decidedly blurred. It could be argued that the English government, by not questioning the motives of attendance and by resisting Puritan calls for severer penalties against non-attendance, had tried to temper the issue. In insisting upon absolute recusancy, Campion and Persons showed no such restraint. Indeed, they seemingly went further than Pope Gregory XIII himself, who had hinted that accommodations might be made as circumstances dictated.

This was not overt sedition. The Jesuits were not inciting armed rebellion or debating the deposing power of the Pope, but nor were they shying away from controversy. In assuming the determining authority over what was conscientious objection and what was political dissent, Campion and Persons had not employed the prudence demanded by their General.[31]

A few days later, Campion and Persons moved up to Hoxton, then a village north-east of London. Thomas Pounde, who was on day parole from the Marshalsea, paid a visit. He was concerned, Persons later explained, about the 'false rumours' given out by the Council that 'our coming into England was for rebellion and matter of State'. He feared that the Jesuits would be further impugned when they began their tours of the shires. Above all, he and his fellow prisoners in the Marshalsea were worried that if either priest was captured or killed, he would not be able to refute the government's allegations, 'whereby many well-meaning people might be deceived and the Catholic cause not a little slandered'.[32]

It was decided, therefore, that Campion and Persons would write short statements defending the mission. They would take the originals with them on their travels and leave back-up copies with Pounde, who would only release them in the event of mishap. In their texts, both priests stressed the spiritual nature of their apostolate and insisted upon the purity of their motives. 'My charge,' Campion declared, 'is of free cost to preach the Gospel, to minister the sacraments, to instruct the simple, to reform sinners, to confute errors.'[33]

'Religion not politics' was the refrain. But both priests also laid down the gauntlet of a public disputation before the Queen and issued fairly inflammatory challenges to her Council. 'If,' Persons wrote,

> your intentions are bloodthirsty (from which evil may God defend you), there will be no lack of scope for them. For you are persecuting a corporation that will never die and sooner will your hearts and hands, sated with blood, fail you, than will there be lacking men, eminent for virtue and learning, who will be sent by this Society and allow their blood to be shed by you for this cause.[34]

Persons sealed his statement. Campion did not and so his is more famous, Pounde being unable to resist what must have seemed like an invitation to read the manuscript and show it to his co-religionists. Soon Campion's 'Brag', as it became known, enjoyed a wide circulation and it was not long before a copy was in the hands of the government. It made for unsettling reading:

> And touching our Society, be it known unto you, that we have made a league – all the Jesuits in the world, whose succession and multitude must overreach all the practices of England – cheerfully to carry the cross that you shall lay upon us, and never to despair your recovery while we have a man left to enjoy your Tyburn, or to be racked with your torments, or to be consumed with your prisons. The expense is reckoned, the enterprise is begun; it is of God, it cannot be withstood. So the faith was planted, so it must be restored.[35]

These statements can be read in two ways: either, as the authors maintained, as spur-of-the-moment, last-resort *apologiae*, only to be issued in the event of capture or death; or, as their enemies insisted, as jingoistic manifestos, designed to rally the Catholic community and declare war on the Protestant establishment. Campion claimed that Pounde had acted 'without my knowledge', but suggested that the 'mistake' could be exploited to put pressure on the government.[36] It has been queried whether such careful strategists could really have been caught unawares by the leaking of such sensitive material. Perhaps, as they had shown on their journey towards England and during the preliminaries in London, they were so keen to argue the disputed issues – especially at a time when the Anjou match made Catholic prospects more hopeful – that they conceived a way of airing them while still being able to maintain 'plausible deniability'.

It is impossible to know for sure – arguably all Jesuit conduct before and after the release of the 'Brag' was reactive to the peculiarities of time and place – but one thing is certain: the moment the 'Brag' and its invitation to a disputatious showdown were released, the mission outlined by the Jesuit General in Rome mutated. Whether Campion and Persons ever meant to court publicity, it is what they would get. Their persistent cry of 'religion not politics' would be matched by the plangent government charge, 'politics not religion'. The louder and longer this counterpoint was played, the harder it became to separate one part from the other.

Campion was in the countryside when his 'Brag' was released. He and Persons had left Hoxton early in August 1580, equipped by Gilbert and his men with horses, money, disguises and massing equipment. The Jesuit superior headed for Gloucestershire, then Herefordshire, Worcestershire and Derbyshire. 'Although all conversation with us is forbidden by proclamation,' Persons reported, we 'are yet most earnestly invited everywhere; many take long journeys only to speak to us and put themselves and their fortunes entirely in our hands.'[37] But there was always the threat of unwanted guests. Persons vividly described the nervous tension in the houses of his hosts:

> Sometimes, when we are sitting merrily at table, conversing familiarly on matters of faith and devotion (for our talk is generally of such things), there comes a hurried knock at the door like that of a pursuivant. All start up and listen – like deer when they hear the huntsmen. We leave our food and commend ourselves to God in a brief ejaculation, nor is word or sound heard till the servants come to say what the matter is. If it is nothing, we laugh at our fright.[38]

Campion began his ministry in Berkshire and continued through Oxfordshire and into Northamptonshire, where, after an absence of

more than a decade, he returned to Harrowden Hall. He was
welcomed back by Lord Vaux, 'by whom I am dearly loved and whom
I particularly revere'.[39] In a letter written to the Society General in
November, Campion reported on his ministry:

> I ride about some piece of the country every day. The harvest is
> wonderful great. On horseback I meditate my sermon; when I come
> to the house, I polish it. Then I talk with such as come to speak with
> me, or hear their confessions. In the morning, after Mass, I preach.
> They hear with exceeding greediness and very often receive the sacra-
> ment . . .
>
> I cannot long escape the hands of the heretics. The enemies have so
> many eyes, so many tongues, so many scouts and crafts. I am in apparel
> to myself very ridiculous. I often change it and my name also. I read
> letters sometimes myself that in the first front tell news that Campion
> is taken, which noised in every place where I come, so filleth my ears
> with the sound thereof that fear itself hath taken away all fear.[40]

Due in no small part to the efforts of hosts and helpers like William
and Henry Vaux, Campion managed to evade the authorities. 'I find
many neglecting their own security to have only care of my safety,'
he wrote. Lord Vaux imperilled his liberty and property by giving
Campion a place to sleep and preach.[41] The congregations at Harrowden
may not have numbered as high as the sixty-strong gathering at Lyford
Grange in Berkshire the following year, but any extraordinary comings
and goings were a risk, especially in a county where there was a
preponderance of Puritans, and to a house where the famous Edmund
Campion had once taught in the schoolroom.

'Threatening edicts come forth against us daily,' wrote Campion.
In August 1580, in the wake of the conflict in Ireland, many prominent
Catholic gentlemen were rounded up and confined. Close associates
of Lord Vaux, including his brother-in-law, Sir Thomas Tresham, were
placed on Burghley's list of untrustworthy recusants.[42] On 13 November,
Ralph Sherwin, one of the seminary priests who had accompanied
the Jesuits on their journey from Rome, was captured mid-sermon
only two days after sharing a fire with Persons against the 'extreme
cold' of the November night.[43] 'The persecution rages most cruelly,'
Campion wrote in his dispatch from an unknown location that month.

'The house where I am is sad; no other talk, but of death, flight, prison or spoil of their friends. Nevertheless, they proceed with courage.'[44]

With the coming of the Jesuits, the rules of engagement between the government and the Catholic community changed. In the face of such a public challenge, and with recusant numbers increasing, the Queen and Council could no longer maintain the unofficial 'don't-ask-don't-tell' position of the past twenty years.[45] 'The expense is reckoned, the enterprise is begun,' Campion had trumpeted in his 'Brag', but he had only reckoned the expense of the mission for himself and his fellow Jesuits. He knew that it might lead to the rack and the rope. It was a price that he, already 'a dead man to this world', could pay 'cheerfully'. But for those English Catholics trying to balance their civil and religious obligations, the accounting procedure was more complicated. They had not vowed to be poor or chaste or obedient only to the Pope. They rather enjoyed the 'wealth, honour, pleasures and other worldly felicities' that Campion had renounced.[46] They had families to support and houses to run. They had, in short, more to lose than their lives.

Campion was not concerned with household accounts or worldly attachments. He left Harrowden Hall and continued on his circuit, all the while insisting upon absolute recusancy and agitating for a public debate. Back in Northamptonshire, on 22 September 1580, Lord Vaux signed a certificate of musters at Rothwell.[47] Christmas came and went and as the New Year approached, he dusted off his parliamentary robes and prepared to journey to Westminster. Twenty-five miles away at Apethorpe, the Chancellor of the Exchequer, Sir Walter Mildmay, polished a speech that would set the agenda for a new bill. Once passed, the lay Catholics of England would have to reckon new expenses. They were about to realise quite how much the enterprise was going to cost.

2

To be a Perfect Catholic

Parliament met on 16 January 1581. Lord Vaux took his seat four days later and was in regular attendance till the close of session on 18 March.[1] On 25 January, Sir Walter Mildmay rose in the Commons and delivered an excoriating speech against the 'implacable malice of the Pope', the insolence of the 'stiff-necked Papist', and the 'hypocrites naming themselves Jesuits, a rabble of vagrant friars newly sprung up and coming through the world to trouble the Church of God'. He depicted the Jesuits' antics – 'creeping into the houses and familiarities of men of behaviour and reputation' – as part of a strategy 'to corrupt the realm with false doctrine' and 'under that pretence, to stir sedition to the peril of her Majesty and her good subjects'.[2]

The Queen's 'favourable and gentle manner of dealing' with her Catholic subjects had failed. Indeed, the Jesuit mission had spawned 'many, yea very many' more recusants. New legislation was required to meet the renewed threat. The result was 'An Act to retain the Queen's Majesty's Subjects in their due Obedience'.[3] Also known as the 'Act of Persuasions', it increased the scope of the 1571 law against Catholic conversions. From thenceforth, anyone attempting, 'by any ways or means', to 'absolve, persuade or withdraw' any of the Queen's subjects from their 'natural obedience' to her or, *'for that intent'*,* to persuade them to forsake her Church for 'the Romish religion', would be committing high treason. Anyone who was reconciled to Rome would also be adjudged a traitor. Anyone who assisted in, or had any

---

* The phrase 'for that intent' is ambiguous. It could be read to mean that any recon-ciliation to Rome was necessarily a withdrawal of allegiance from the Queen and therefore treasonous, or it could provide defendants with a loophole: their 'intent' was purely religious and not related to treason. In practice, the courts tended to apply the former interpretation.

knowledge of, a treasonable act of reconciliation and failed to report it within twenty days was to be found guilty of misprision (non-disclosure) of treason.

The saying and hearing of Mass would be punishable by fines of 200 marks and 100 marks respectively; both offences also incurred the sentence of a year's imprisonment. Anyone over the age of sixteen who refused to go to church would be charged £20 a month. If they persisted in their 'obstinacy' for a year, they would have to post a bond of £200 'at the least' for good behaviour. This amounted to a massive £460 per annum.* Failure to pay within three months of conviction would lead to imprisonment until conformity or the settlement of the account. Further sections of the Act concerned the recusant schoolmaster (banned from teaching, imprisoned for a year, his employer fined £10 for every month of service retained) and against the conveyancing of property for the 'covinous purpose' of evading the fines. This was meant to prevent the common recourse to trusts. Any such transactions made since the beginning of Parliament were declared void. Another clause dealt with the owners of private chapels. They were exempted from the penalties of nonconformity if they used the right service book and provided they put in an appearance at church four times a year.

The provisions of the Act had been hammered out in eighteen meetings by a joint committee of Lords and Commons. Early drafts had been a great deal harsher, but that was small comfort to the Catholics of England who faced an unprecedented onslaught on their social and financial standing. The maximum penalty for a year's recusancy was roughly equivalent to the annual income of a landed gentleman.[4] If successfully enforced, the Act would confront all but the wealthiest recusants with a stark choice: conformity or ruin.

In May 1581 Lord Vaux was cited as a recusant. It was a sign of the government's determination to enforce the new legislation. A more discreet approach to the problem of the recusant nobility had been attempted the previous year. In a dispatch to Rome in November 1580, Robert Persons had mentioned an offer, 'lately proposed to certain noblemen', that required just one church outing a year with 'a previous

*By the common law there were twenty-eight days in a month and thirteen such lunar months in a year. Thus the yearly sum of a recusant's fines was £260.

protestation that they came not to approve of their religion or doctrines, but only to show an outward obedience to the Queen'. Persons had been delighted to report that 'all most constantly refused'.[5]

The recusant grandee presented a particular problem to the authorities, not only because people looked to his example for guidance in their own conduct, but also because of the protection he could afford his dependants. That is why the Jesuit General had instructed Campion and Persons to target the upper classes. The 1581 Act aimed to close the umbrella of protection held by influential recusants by threatening to undermine their personal standing in society and strike at the heart of their household.

The entry for Harrowden in the Visitation book of the Archdeacon of Northampton provides a case in point:

> We do present the right honourable William Lord Harrowden, his household and familiars and divers servants not to frequent the parish church of Harrowden aforesaid, nor receive the holy communion in the parish afore rehearsed . . . Also we present my Lord's schoolmaster.

Further down the page, which has been invaded by damp, one of Lord Vaux's yeoman servants is mentioned:

> Item, we present Athony [sic] Carrington's child, being born before Shrovetide last, not to be baptized nor presented to the congregation, nor the said Athony's wife churched* nor repaired to the church since the said deliverance.[6]

Lord Vaux defended himself and his household by claiming that Harrowden Hall was 'a parish by itself'. Men like Mildmay may have regarded such insularity as contempt for the Queen's authority, but others, including the churchwarden who 'affirmeth' Lord Vaux's statement, may have preferred to view it as a harmless matter of private devotion. We know that Campion the Jesuit had been welcomed through the gates of Harrowden Hall 'sundry times' the previous summer, but it cannot be told whether this was a factor in Vaux's

---

* Churching was the ceremony that marked the return of a mother to the congregation after the birth of her child.

citation. However his defence was construed, it was no longer adequate in the law. Gone were the days when he could pay lip service to the regime and then entrench himself at home. Private worship was still permitted at the family chapel – provided, of course, that the correct service was used – but thenceforth Lord Vaux, along with his recusant servants, his recusant schoolmaster and the rest of his recusant household, would also have to be seen to attend the Queen's Church.

The presentment for recusancy was a singular humiliation for a peer who stood on his honour as much as Lord Vaux, but it would be eclipsed by the loss of two stalwarts of the English mission. At the end of June 1581, George Gilbert was smuggled across the Channel to France. He had encouraged his friends 'to imitate the lives of apostles and devote themselves wholly to the salvation of souls' and he had led by example, putting himself 'and all that he had, even his very life, to frequent hazard in defence of the Catholic faith'.

Since Father Persons' arrival in England, Gilbert had been his 'good angel'. Not only was he the funder-fixer of the mission, but he had also performed the roles of 'counsellor, companion, servant [and] patron' to the Jesuit superior. 'If we have done any good,' Persons wrote in a letter of recommendation to Rome, 'a great part of it is to be attributed to this youth.'[7] By mid-summer 1581, however, 'the rarest spectacle to all England' was too prominent. 'We had more trouble and anxiety in protecting him than ourselves,' wrote Persons. No longer able to operate in England 'without plain peril of his life', Gilbert was finally persuaded to flee his homeland and 'keep himself for happier times'. Having hidden in a cave until his ship came into view, he escaped to Rheims and thence to the English College at Rome.

His exile would not last long. On 6 October 1583, having commissioned a series of thirty-four paintings celebrating past and recent English martyrs for the College chapel, he caught a fever and died. In his last moments, the 31-year-old reportedly asked, 'Why are you weeping? You, who have the chance of martyrdom – while I am lying on a soft bed.'[8]

Gilbert bequeathed the English mission a Latin memorandum entitled *A way to deal with persons of all sorts so as to convert them and bring them back to a better way of life* – based on the system and methods *used by Fr. Robert Parsons and Fr. Edmund Campion.* It was, as its title suggests, a proselytiser's manual for future missioners to use, as applicable, on 'heretics', 'schismatics' and 'lukewarm Catholics'. In his practical, tactical advice and complete understanding of what conversion entailed, Gilbert showed just how closely he and his lay companions had worked with the Jesuits in England and what a debt they were owed.[9]

George Gilbert's absence was keenly felt by all involved in the English mission, but for the Vauxes the loss of Edward Brooksby was more affecting. The exact date of his death is unknown, as is the cause. It deprived Eleanor Vaux of her husband, their two small children of their father and Henry Vaux of a brother-in-law, who, according to Persons, had been his 'great admirer and follower'. Edward had been Robert Persons' first escort in London and had also been involved in the secret Jesuit printing press at Greenstreet House, his father's place in East Ham about six miles from London.[10]

The press was, perhaps, the mission's greatest asset. Not only did it clank out devotional works that provided spiritual sustenance to the lay community, but it also enabled the Jesuits to launch a propaganda campaign that was every bit as sophisticated as that of the government. 'They are publishing most threatening proclamations against us, as well as books, sermons, ballads, libels, fables, comedies,' Persons groused, but once the press was up and running, the Jesuits gave as good as they got. In August 1581 Persons gloated that 'the heretics should not be able to publish anything without its being almost immediately attacked most vigorously'.[11]

A sixteenth-century printing press, even a small one like the mission press that could only print half-folios, is a cumbersome contraption, not easy to hide. It was carried to Greenstreet House 'with much charge and peril'. Printers were needed to operate it – Persons mentions 'seven men continually at work' – and they had to come and go without attracting attention. Once, on his way to the Brooksby house, Persons was 'stayed by the watch'. Another time, one of his printers, 'going about to buy paper in London', was arrested, sent to the Tower and racked. The press was expensive to maintain and there was always the risk that 'the noise of the machine' would betray it.[12]

The chief overseer of the press was Stephen Brinkley, who had translated and published *The Exercise of a Christian Life* back in 1579. He was forced to move it several times, which required dismantling, carriage and reassembly. From Greenstreet House, the press went to the home of Francis Browne, and later to the estate of Dame Cecily Stonor near Henley-on-Thames, where it was eventually discovered. Once printed, a work had to find an audience and here a slick, but spectacularly risky, distribution system came into play:

> All the books are brought together to London without any being issued and after being distributed into the hands of priests in parcels of a hundred or fifty, are issued at exactly the same time to all parts of the kingdom. Now, on the next day, when according to their wont the officials begin to search the houses of Catholics because these books have been distributed, there are plenty of young men of birth ready to introduce these books by night into the dwellings of the heretics, into workshops as well as into palaces, to scatter them in the court also and about the streets, so that it may not be Catholics only who are accused in the matter.[13]

The most outrageous publicity coup, one that immediately intensified the hunt for Campion, was the dissemination of his *Rationes Decem* or *Ten Reasons* on 27 June 1581. The tract itself, concerning ten points that Campion wanted to make in debate, was provocative – 'Listen, Elizabeth, mighty Queen, the prophet in speaking to thee is teaching thee thy duty'[14] – but not especially novel. What rendered it so offensive was the illegality of its publication and the audacity of its distribution. Printed at Stonor Park, copies were found strewn across the benches of the university church of St Mary in Oxford on the morning of Commencement. Persons and Campion, both Oxford alumni, knew that the church would be full of students and dons gathering to hear the supplicants for degrees defend their theses. Campion had failed to meet this requirement in 1569. Twelve years later, he wrote in his tract, 'it is tortures, not academic disputations, that the high-priests are making ready'.[15] In fact, it was both.

Campion was taken on 17 July 1581. It is a wonder, if the more celebratory accounts of the mission are to be credited, that he had not been caught sooner. People had reportedly flocked to his sermons, even suffering the discomfort of a night in a neighbouring barn in order to guarantee entry. There had been a number of close shaves. Once, at the home of the Worthington family in Lancashire, Campion was saved from arrest by a plucky maidservant, who disguised his priesthood by the irreverent act of pushing him into a pond.[16]

The authorities finally caught up with him at Lyford Grange in Berkshire, tipped off by a spy among the large crowd that had gathered at the home of the Yate family to hear him preach and celebrate Mass. In the ensuing search, Campion and two other priests were found in a concealed chamber above the stairwell. (Not until 1959, however, would electricians working on the house discover an Agnus Dei blessed by Pope Gregory XIII in a wooden box nailed to a joist under the floorboards of the attic.)

On Saturday, 22 July, Campion rode into London under armed guard. He was trussed up securely with his elbows tied behind him, his wrists in front, and his feet fastened by a strap under his horse's belly. A sign on his hat announced to the market crowds that he was *Campion the seditious Jesuit*. He was incarcerated in the Tower of London and spent his first few days in a tiny cell known as 'Little Ease', where he could neither stand nor lie straight. He was interrogated* and tortured, but refused to recant any of his writings or beliefs.

There was little chance that without apostasy he would be allowed to live. Everything that followed – the disputation that he was finally granted (though with no time to prepare, no say in the choice of topics and no books apart from the Bible[17]), the rumours, the tracts and the public performances – contested the reason for his death. For Campion, who had embraced martyrdom the moment he had accepted his mission, it was quite simple: he died for faith. 'I am a Catholic man and a priest,' he announced from the scaffold at Tyburn on 1 December 1581. 'In that faith have I lived and in that faith do I intend to die; and if you esteem my religion treason, then am I guilty. As for any other treason, I never committed, God is my judge.'[18]

For Burghley and the Council it was no less straightforward.

---

* Alas for Campion and for readers of Evelyn Waugh's sparkling biography, 'the vast red wig' never 'nodded acknowledgement' of the Jesuit, nor did 'the sunken, painted face' smile in recognition (Waugh, p. 171). The story that Queen Elizabeth was present at Campion's first examination is unfounded (Colthorpe, p. 199).

Campion was a traitor, tried and convicted, along with six other priests and a layman, under Edward III's treason statute for conspiring 'both at Rome and at Rheims and in divers other places in parts beyond the seas', to foment rebellion in England, procure a foreign invasion and kill the Queen.[19] The prosecution would have been on firmer ground – and less reliant on dubious testimony – had it stuck to the original plan of charging Campion according to the 1581 'Act of Persuasions', which clearly defined his activities as traitorous. The application of 'the ancient temporal laws of the realm' revealed the government's determination to condemn Campion for his politics rather than his priesthood.

The debate over whether Campion had returned to England, plough in hand, for 'the harvest of souls' or the 'tillage of sedition' glowed with white heat in England and throughout Europe for many years after his death. The chief protagonists, Lord Burghley (denouncing a political traitor) and William Allen (championing a religious martyr), both claimed victory and conceded nothing. Each wrote with perfect conviction. Burghley ended *The Execution of Justice in England* with the biblical line 'Great is truth, and she overcometh' (I Esdras 4:41). Allen began *A True, Sincere, and Modest Defence of English Catholiques that Suffer for their Faith* with 'Thy mouth hath abounded in malice, and thy tongue hath cunningly framed lies' (Psalm 49:19).[20] There was no middle ground.

For those without a passion for absolutes, the issue was more complex. There was no hard evidence to suggest that Campion had conspired to kill the Queen or encouraged her subjects to revolt. The 1351 statute under which he was charged was not clearly applicable to his activities. Campion had always been combative about the mission. He had set out from Rome 'to my warfare in England', but his weapons were faith and force of argument. He wanted to provide counsel and sacramental grace to England's Catholics and reconcile others by evangelical proselytising. 'We only travelled for souls,' he protested at his trial, 'we touched neither state nor policy, we had no such commission.'[21] And yet he returned to his homeland knowing that, by law, there was treason inherent in his mission.

Whether by accident or design, Campion and Persons did engage in matters of state. Indeed, they actively pushed for a free and public debate with the Elizabethan regime. Once denied, they

utilised illicit media to promote their arguments. They forbade
Catholics to go to church and justified disobedience by attempting
to redefine the boundaries between the temporal and spiritual
realms. Arguably this impugned the royal supremacy and challenged
the authority, and even the legitimacy, of the Elizabethan regime.[22]
It was not treason in the conventional sense, but it was inescapably
political. Considering the Jesuits' co-religionists at the Synod of
Southwark had queried their motives from the outset, it is hardly
surprising that, a year and a half later, Protestants regarded them
with suspicion.

For many folk, however, the religio-political wrangling was irrele-
vant. The issue was not so much what Campion did, but what he
was: a Jesuit priest and avowed servant of the Pope. No matter what
delaying tactics he was currently employing, the Pope was no friend
to the Queen. The papacy had been involved in the northern uprising
of 1569, the Ridolfi Plot of 1571 and the recent insurrection in Ireland.
It had also been instrumental, in 1576, in a plot to send Don John of
Austria into England with an army that would put Mary Stuart on
the throne. Spanish setbacks in the Netherlands meant that the plan
was not implemented, but it had been drawn up in some detail. A
lengthy memorial of advice had been prepared by William Allen, the
founder of the English Mission, the leader of the Catholic exile
community and Edmund Campion's great defender. At a time when
fears for national security were great and real, Campion's guilt by
association was enough to secure his conviction.

In a subsequent, highly partisan account of Campion's trial written
by Thomas Fitzherbert (later a Jesuit priest), the author recounted a
conversation that he had had at the time with a student of Lincoln's
Inn. The man, 'a familiar friend of mine (though an earnest Protestant)', had witnessed Campion's trial and had reportedly been surprised
by the verdict because the evidence was 'so weak'. Fitzherbert had
asked him how anyone of conscience could have condemned Campion.
'Content yourself,' his friend had reputedly replied, 'it was necessary
for the state.'[23]

On 1 December 1581, Edmund Campion was dragged on a hurdle
to Tyburn and executed with two other priests: Alexander Briant,
once known as 'the handsome boy of Oxford', who had been minis-
tering in England since 1579, and Ralph Sherwin, a graduate of the

English College at Rome, who had journeyed to England with Campion and Persons. It was reported (by a Catholic eyewitness at Tyburn) that when pressed by Sir Francis Knollys to acknowledge his guilt, Sherwin replied, 'If to be a Catholic, if to be a perfect Catholic, be to be a traitor, then am I a traitor.'[24]

As was the custom, each man was hanged on the gibbet, then cut down and eviscerated in front of the assembled crowd. Their quartered body parts were 'disposed of at her Majesty's pleasure', though one relic hunter managed to steal away with one of Campion's fingers. Another reportedly rescued his arm from the gate upon which it was nailed. Within five years, 'certain pieces of Father Campion's body', his girdle and one of Briant's bones had found their way into the Vaux household – a clear sign to where the family stood in the martyr–traitor debate.[25] In May 1582 seven more priests were executed.

Robert Persons had been Campion's superior on the mission and was grievously affected by his death. He fled to France soon after Campion's arrest and carried with him all the emotions of the survivor.[26] He left behind his elderly mother, Christina, who later joined the household of Eleanor and Anne Vaux. He would never return to his homeland, but he soon became embroiled in other, more militant schemes for its conversion. Indeed he would become the overtly seditious Jesuit that his subordinate had never been. Campion had sacrificed his life for the English mission, Persons would endanger his soul.

It should not be forgotten that Campion the saint (canonised in 1970), or Campion the traitor, was also Campion the scholar, poet, philosopher, historian, dramatist and, for the Vaux children, the school-master. He was as capable as any man of human frailty and as suscep-tible as any prisoner to torture.

Towards the end of 1580, the Privy Council had specially authorised the use of torture on Jesuit priests 'to make some example of them by punishment to the terror of others'. On 30 July 1581, with Campion then in custody and having undergone a preliminary examination, the Council had granted that he might be put to the rack.[27] This was a contraption that mechanically stretched the body, exerting excruciating pressure on the joints. Often it was enough just to give prisoners sight of it. William Allen, writing from the safety of exile, claimed that

Campion, when asked how his hands and feet felt after a session on the rack, had replied, 'not ill because not at all.'

> And being in that case benumbed both of hand and foot, he likened himself to an elephant, which being down could not rise; and when he could hold the bread he had to eat between both his hands, he did compare himself to an ape.[28]

At his arraignment, Campion could not raise his hand to make his plea without assistance. Inside the Spanish and Venetian embassies, it was said that he had also suffered another form of torture, 'the most dreadfully cruel of them all. This is to drive iron spikes between the nails and the quick', with the fingernails subsequently being 'turned back'.[29]

In the furore that followed, Thomas 'Rackmaster' Norton defended his treatment of Campion by arguing that torture was only applied carefully, not cavalierly or cruelly, and only on those 'known to the Council to be guilty of treason'. (He was also at pains to point out that although he may have interrogated Campion, he had not turned the ratchet himself.) Torture, Norton argued, was not a punishment, but a means of extracting the 'truth'.[30]

There has been much debate over the nature and extent of Campion's disclosures on the rack. He did not renounce his faith. Nor, he protested, did he reveal where he had said Mass or provide any information that the government did not already know. But in a reply to Thomas Pounde, who seems to have believed rumours of Campion's backsliding and sent him a letter of reproach, he did admit to having surrendered the names of some of the people who had sheltered him. He consoled himself that 'I never discovered any secrets there declared'. When it was put to him at his trial that the withheld secrets must have been treasonous, Campion protested that they only related to the confessional: they were 'such as surcharged the grieved soul and conscience, whereof I had power to pray for absolution. These were the hidden matters, these were the secrets' and he would never give them up, he said, 'come rack, come rope'.[31]

The summer of 1581 was a febrile, frightening time for all those who had given Campion hospitality. No one could be quite sure what truths or untruths he was providing. 'Rack't carcasses make ill anatomies,'

John Donne would write.[32] There were plenty of rumours: that Campion was about to recant, that he would buy his pardon by accusing friends of treason, that he had taken his own life. On 10 August 1581, Lord Burghley sent a message to Walsingham in Paris: 'We have gotten from Campion knowledge of all his peregrination in England . . . We have sent for his hosts in all counties.'[33]

Three days earlier, the Privy Council had ordered Francis Hastings to examine his elderly kinswoman Elizabeth Beaumont, and search her home. This was the house in Leicestershire where the Vaux children had lived for much of the previous decade. Their grandmother was suspected of having harboured Campion, but Hastings was frustrated in his commission, complaining to the Earl of Leicester on 18 August that 'our authority was hardly large enough in that we could minister no oath to her, nor examine any servant in the house'. Had he been given greater power, he wrote, 'we should have understood more than now we do'.

Undeterred, Hastings suggested that it would be fruitful to search a number of other places in the county, including 'the house of Mistress Brooksby, daughter to the Lord Vaux and wife to Brooksby's son, but now a widow'. This was Eleanor, Lord Vaux's eldest daughter, whose husband, Edward, had recently died. 'I like not to take upon me the office of a promoter in any thing,' Hastings wrote, 'but in this case love to the persons whose conversion I wish with all my heart, love to my country . . . and love to her Majesty . . . have moved me to presume to put your lordship in mind of these persons.' Hastings hoped that the Queen would 'soon be rid of such dangerous people (for subjects I cannot call them till they obey better)'. His belief that their 'obstinacy', if not checked, 'may happily infect the heart and mind of many a simple subject' was undoubtedly genuine; most of his letters are peppered with anti-Catholic statements. However, it seems that, in this instance, his love for Newark Grange, the reversion for which he petitioned in a postscript to his letter, may also have encouraged him in his civic duty.[34]

Lord Vaux was in no position to help his mother-in-law or his daughter. On 6 August 1581, the Privy Council issued Sir Walter Mildmay with a warrant:

to send for the Lord Vaux (at whose house Edmund Campion hath upon his examination confessed that he hath been) and to examine him touching the said Campion's being there, or if one Persons, or any other Jesuit or priest . . . and after that he shall have examined him in this sort, then to send him to the house of some honest gentleman well affected in religion in that shire, to remain for a time under his charge without having conference with any others.[35]

The storm clouds had gathered over Harrowden Hall. They would not disperse in Lord Vaux's lifetime.

3

Lying Lips

And yet, alas, full many a man we know,
    Whom fortune draws, will bear a friendly cheer,
While luck doth serve, and prosperous wind doth blow;
    As swallows swift in spring time do appear;
When storms arise, farewell, they will be gone,
    They leave him all to sink or swim alone.

             Henry Vaux, 'Of Friendship' (final stanza)[1]

Lord Vaux was an unlikely criminal. Apart from his citation as a recusant in May 1581 and a few minor episodes concerning unlicensed bear baiting and the unauthorised bailing of poachers, he had never been in trouble. As a peer of the realm, he was involved in the creation and enforcement of the law. He had defended his recusancy by claiming that his house was 'a parish by itself', but he did not otherwise segregate from the community. He may have preferred the company of his co-religionists, but he was happy to enjoy the noble pursuits with his Protestant neighbours. He was 'always welcome' at Boughton, the home of Edward Montagu, a six-mile ride from Harrowden, and he was on good terms with Lord Burghley, who had acted as his proxy in the Parliament of 1576. The Lord Treasurer may even have had his Harrowden neighbour in mind when he wrote in *The Execution of Justice* about 'men of good credit in their countries, manifestly of late time seduced to hold contrary opinions in religion for the Pope's authority'.[2]

    'Good credit' was important to Lord Vaux. Writing to Lady Montagu late in 1581, he announced that 'the preservation of my good name, and especially among my kinsmen, neighbours, and friends', mattered more than 'any worldly treasure'.[3] His apprehension and interrogation by his neighbour, Sir Walter Mildmay of Apethorpe, with whom only two years previously he had been working on cases of gaol delivery, was therefore acutely embarrassing.[4] The Chancellor of the Exchequer had his hands full that August, for he also received instructions to examine Vaux's brother-in-law, Sir Thomas Tresham, his kinsman Sir William Catesby* and another neighbour, Mr Griffin. He did not waste time querying Vaux's beliefs. He wanted details: times, places, names.

> How many or what priests do you know or have heard to report to any house, and what be their names?
> How do you know them or have heard them to be priests?
> What Masses have you heard since the beginning of the reign of the Queen, and where?

Above all, Mildmay wanted to know about Vaux's involvement with Campion and Persons. Had he ever known them? By what occasion and for how long? Had he ever given them or the seminaries any money or relief?

> Whether were they, or any such, or any seminary men or priests at your house, and at what time, & how often?
> Whence came they & who came with them & who were with you at that time?[5]

Lord Vaux batted back every question with a denial. No details are provided, but some of Sir Thomas Tresham's responses to the same questions were subsequently written down in a Catholic commonplace-book that was probably kept – and added to – by his daughter. The book was a recusant memorial, an alternative, secret (and selective) history of the time, written and compiled by Catholics for Catholics. Protestants – 'the very sons of Satan & forerunners of Antichrist' – are painted in an unrelentingly harsh light.[6] Had Tresham floundered in his interview with Mildmay, it is unlikely that his words would have made it onto the page. But they did, and

---

*Robert Persons ('Memoirs', p. 27) claimed Tresham and Catesby as early converts of the Jesuit mission, which is to say that their Catholicism was revitalised and raised to a new level of intensity. In practical terms it meant a renewed commitment to Rome and a renunciation of outward conformity.

although they may have gained something in the retelling, in tone and style they ring true.

Lord Vaux's brother-in-law, who claimed a friendship with him 'even from my cradle', and who wielded an overwhelming influence over the mild-mannered peer, was an extraordinary character. Quick-witted and charismatic, he could be wonderfully entertaining, but also fearfully intimidating. A priest would later describe Tresham as 'a wall of brass against the forces of hostile domination', and compare him to Moses: 'if thou hadst not stood in the breach against the violators of the Catholic faith, many . . . would not have battled so stoutly in the Lord.'[7] Depending on one's confessional bent that was either a very good or a very bad thing.

Tresham was well prepared for his interview – perhaps Vaux had managed to brief him – and he offered a string of facetious responses. To the question of whether he had heard any Masses in the reign of Queen Elizabeth, he admitted that he had, 'for he was married at a Mass . . . but it was in the first year of her Majesty's reign when the law did not forbid it'. Yes, he conceded, he knew some priests, 'for many were in prisons whom he knew [had been] priests in Queen Mary's time'. When asked if he had ever given alms to the mission, 'he thought if his estate were sufficiently known to them', they would have realised that 'he was not likely to give much'.

Mildmay had met his match. Even when Tresham was told by 'one Mr Flower dwelling in Northamptonshire' that Campion 'the caitiff wretch' had, 'for fear of the rack & torment', betrayed his hosts and 'specially named' Tresham, he refused to buckle. Priests were not in the habit of reporting lies, he said, much less of inventing them:

And if Mr Campion or his like should say it, as by reason of the untruth of the thing I will never believe it, yet am I to answer for the deeds of Sir Thomas Tresham & not for the words of Mr Campion, & therefore in this behalf I make no account what he or any other shall say of me, no not the least hair of my head: for he that pisseth clear needeth not the physician's help.[8]

After their examinations at Apethorpe, the prisoners were transferred to the homes of gentlemen 'well affected in religion in that shire'. Lord Vaux was sent a few miles south to Boughton House, the home of Sir Edward Montagu. Staunch Protestant though he was, Vaux's new keeper was also a friend and erstwhile colleague on the county bench. Indeed in 1579 the two had been allies in a quarrel over two poachers they had seen fit to bail without commission.[9] Lord Vaux's confinement at Boughton cannot have lasted more than ten days, but it was an awkward time for all concerned. Montagu was not required to examine his noble charge, but he had to keep him close enough to prevent 'conference with any others'. Under the circumstances, keeper and prisoner muddled along fairly well. Vaux praised Montagu's reputation for 'discretion and judgement' in knowing 'how to use one of my calling committed to his custody'. He referred to his 'good entertainment' at Boughton, though he did add somewhat archly that it was 'fit for a prisoner'.

There was one incident, however, that left the peer smarting – 'some unkindness which I conceived of you,' he later wrote to Montagu's wife, Elizabeth, 'which was your somewhat too zealous (I will not otherwise term the same) urging me in matters tending to religion'. Evidently Lady Montagu had thought it a good idea to lecture her guest on the errors of his faith and he had taken offence. The episode had threatened to sour relations between Vaux and the Montagus, but they had parted on cordial terms and he had nothing but praise for Montagu's son, who had the unenviable task of delivering him up to the Lords of the Council at Leicester House on the Strand.[10]

On Friday, 18 August 1581, Vaux and Sir Thomas Tresham were 'required whether they would swear to their knowledge and thinking that Campion the Jesuit was at their houses according to his confession or no'. Campion was still alive at this stage, battling the rack on the other side of town. He would be tried in November and executed the following month. The rumour mill was attempting to grind down his reputation, but nothing was confirmed. Tresham, and in all probability Vaux too, had been told at Apethorpe that the Jesuit had revealed 'not only all the places where & when he had been since his first arrival in England, but likewise what relief, what letters, yea & what messengers had been sent him by any'. Also that 'Campion had made a long accusation & was so timorous of torment, or specially of death, that he would do anything before he would endure either the one or the other & that most certainly he would recant & become a Protestant'.[11]

In this maelstrom of truth and lies, Tresham had preferred to believe – or at least maintain – that it was all slander. He and Vaux resolved to give nothing away that could have implicated or perjured themselves, or indeed could have prejudiced Campion's position. They refused the oath, neither confirming nor denying the presence of the priest in their houses, 'and thereupon were committed close prisoners to the Fleet'.[12]

The prison was a short ride along Fleet Street from Leicester House. If the prisoners were permitted the honour of arriving by boat, it was a quick journey down the Thames to Blackfriars and up the Fleet River, which marked the boundary between Westminster and the City. The river was the epitome of squalid London, its foul waters swallowed the waste of each street, its 'stinking lanes' welcomed disease and allowed it to linger. The prison was situated on the east bank and was surrounded by a moat that Londoners were inclined to use as an open lavatory. When the poet Earl of Surrey had been a prisoner there in 1542, he had feared contamination from its 'pestilent airs'. In the reign of Mary I, Bishop Hooper, imprisoned for his Protestantism, had complained that 'the stench of the house hath infected me with sundry diseases'.*[13]

Sir Thomas Tresham was quick to join the chorus of disapproval. A fortnight after their committal, he complained of the 'noisome and moist imprisonment'. He was furious that 'brawlers, fighters, unthrifty and loose people' were allowed the liberty of the prison, while he, Vaux and other gentlemen 'in for their consciences' had to suffer the indignity of close imprisonment. This was not solitary confinement, but as Vaux wrote in October, 'none may speak with me, but by warrant in the presence of the warden or his deputy'.[14]

Nevertheless, the Fleet was, by common consent, the best prison in London and for those who could afford them a few 'luxuries' were permitted. Vaux and Tresham both had bedchambers, if sparsely furnished, and each was allowed a servant. They clearly also had access to writing materials, even if Tresham had to scribble a hasty conclusion to one letter, 'hearing my jailor bustling at my door, who in no wise may be knowing hereof'. They could stretch their legs down their 'accustomed walking alley along the brick wall in the Fleet

---

* The river Fleet has long since been covered, but it can still be heard in Clerkenwell, coursing underground beneath a grate in front of the Coach & Horses pub on the corner of Warner Street and Ray Street.

garden' and they had the honour of dining with the warden, his wife, fellow prisoners and occasional guests from outside. On 3 September, in the presence of Vaux and some other prisoners, Tresham initiated an after-dinner debate on transubstantiation with a visiting Protestant theologian, Dr Lilly, Master of Balliol College, Oxford. It was a 'friendly controversy' and when 'jailor's restraint (to whose beck I now am taught without all gainsay servilly to bow)' ordered the prisoners back to their chambers, Lilly lent Tresham a book, which he returned a few days later with a long letter of thanks.[15]

The following month, Lord Vaux received distressing news from Northamptonshire. His kinsman Robert Mulsho, talking to his servant Carrington, had expressed regret that Vaux should have railed so lewdly and unfairly against the Montagus of Boughton. Apparently Vaux's cousin, neighbour and, until now, 'ever reputed good friend' William Lane had told Lady Montagu that Vaux was a 'backbiter and defamer'. He had, said Lane, been telling tales about the 'evil' treatment he had recently received at Boughton, protesting that he was 'almost famished for want of necessary relief of entertainment and diet'. Lady Montagu was understandably upset. As soon as the report came to Vaux in the Fleet, he went to Tresham, who drafted a letter for him to send to Lady Montagu disclaiming all the rumours.

'Good Madam,' it begins, it is 'a world's wonder' that Lane could 'so violate the rules of true Christian charity' as to 'contrive to add affliction to affliction' by his slanders 'against me in my present inexpected and deep disgrace'. Assuring Lady Montagu of his esteem, love and reverence, he asked her to

> mark withal the cunning couching of this shameless slander to be now raised in the time of my absence forth of the country, and in my restraint of liberty and close imprisonment here, when by all likelihood I should never have heard thereof. O wicked devise. O devilish drift. Better be the words of a true friend than a Judas kiss of a covert enemy.

The 'daily experience' of his adversity had taught Vaux to distinguish between fast and 'faint friends', yet he could not conceive a reason for Lane to have become 'so extreme an enemy to my honour and reputation, as vainly and loosely to suggest things neither spoken, nor once thought of by me'. He protests that he has never been 'a brabbling backbiter', as 'the testimony of all my neighbours' will confirm. The Montagus are 'dear' friends. 'I was always welcome' at Boughton, 'and so did I hold myself'. There was no truth in the slander: 'I never said so: nay further I say, I protest I never had any such thought, which I will aver to the face of him whosoever, to his utter shame and reproof, that dareth to gainsay it.'

Had the letter ended there, it would have been so much the better. But Vaux had been offended by Lady Montagu's credulity and he proceeded to offer a homily on the evils of detraction and the folly of listening to 'lying lips'. It was a 'necessary lesson fit for us to learn in these wicked days, that if we frequent the company of lewd and perverse [people], we also shall be perverted'.

The author acknowledged that his letter might be 'tedious reading', but felt compelled – now that 'all unkindness at once should be shuffled forth' – to lay one more card on the table. This was Lady Montagu's 'somewhat too zealous' attempt to discuss religion with him. Vaux had clearly not forgiven her for what he deemed untimely and inappropriate behaviour, 'and that in the presence of your husband'. One lecture deserved another:

> since St Paul admonisheth that women should learn in silence and in subjection, and that in their houses they themselves should learn by demanding of their husbands, who doth not permit them to teach in their presence but to be in silence. For silence extolleth womanly shamefastness and such comely shamefastness adorneth their age.

'At which time, Madam,' the letter finally concludes, 'if I anything, as haply in reply, I might offend you, I pray pardon thereof, for I had no intention to minister offence to you. And what then passed from you to me, God forgive me, as I therein forgive you.' Commending himself to the Montagus, Vaux signed off, 'not doubting but we shall many times meet and be merry'.[16]

We are none the wiser as to what had 'then passed' at Boughton between Lord Vaux and Lady Montagu – perhaps a hearty slanging match – but it was probably the seed of all subsequent rumour and the reason for Lady Montagu's credulity. Nor do we know if Lord Vaux ever sent this letter or even approved of it in this form. It was conserved among the Tresham Papers at Rushton Hall alongside another folio containing an alternative paragraph and some biblical extracts on detraction. There is no record of the letter in the Montagu archive. It was written in a very neat hand, possibly Tresham's. The tone, punctuation, vocabulary and style all bear Tresham's hallmark, and at the end of the page, under the heading 'The contents of this letter', is an outline of the main points. This is written in Tresham's usual hand and ends, 'if you think the letter too long, you may leave out any of these 5 points'.[17] There can be no doubt, therefore, that Tresham ghosted the letter for Vaux. He provided substance and his inimitable style to Vaux's sentiments. He may even have influenced those sentiments, but the final decision on what to include or omit lay with Vaux.

This was the first of many subsequent letters drafted by Tresham for his brother-in-law. Although Vaux was senior in age and superior in status, he allowed Tresham to dominate almost every aspect of his life, recognising in him a keener intellect, a sharper head for business, a better way with words and a more complex and combative mindset. Tresham was a leader – self-conscious and self-appointed; Vaux was a follower – unassuming and unspectacular, but no less committed a Catholic.

Their families went back a long way, beyond the Wars of the Roses, and their interests were tied up in a myriad of trusts, testaments, indentures and leases. Their shared faith – and shared suffering in that faith – created a bond that could never be broken. As Tresham would write in 1590, Lord Vaux had 'loved me longest, esteemed me dearest, and by the space of full twenty-seven years (in matters of greatest weight) most trust in me hath over reposed'.[18] In other words, ever since his marriage to Mary Tresham around 1563, Vaux had sought her brother's guidance. There is an implied weakness in his deference to Tresham. He was impressionable and it seems that imprisonment, poor health and financial hardship would diminish him. Sir John Roper, whose daughter would marry Vaux's son George, called him 'the simple Lord Vaux' in 1590, and there is an interesting reference by Tresham in 1594 to Vaux's 'deafness' – perhaps one reason for his over-reliance on his wife's brother.[19] But Vaux had heard Lady Montagu's lecture loud and clear in 1581 and his offence at her behaviour – even if subsequently ventriloquised by Tresham – was genuine. As contempt proceedings against Vaux and his fellow prisoners loomed, he may once again have sought Tresham's advice, but he knew that when the time would come, he would have to stand up in the Star Chamber and speak for himself.

The time came three months into his imprisonment. On Wednesday, 15 November 1581, the day after Campion had pleaded not guilty at his arraignment, Lord Vaux was tried in the Star Chamber.[20] He stood at the bar with Tresham, Sir William Catesby and three others. They faced a phalanx of dignitaries that included Lord Chancellor Bromley, the Earl of Leicester, Sir Walter Mildmay, Sir Francis Knollys and two Chief Justices. The prosecution was led by the Attorney General, John Popham. After an exordium on the Pope's seditious interference in the Queen's affairs, Popham accused the defendants of having received the 'renegade' Jesuit Edmund Campion into their homes. Further, they had contemptuously refused to swear on oath, or even upon their allegiance or honour, to the veracity of their testimonies provided during earlier interrogations.

According to an eyewitness:

the evidence read in that behalf was a confession of Mr Campion's at the rack the [blank] of August last etc. before the Lieutenant of the Tower, Norton & Hammon. The content whereof was that he had been at the house of the Lord Vaux sundry times, at Sir Thomas Tresham's house, at Mr Griffin's of Northamptonshire, where also the Lady Tresham then was, and at the house of Sir William Catesby, where Sir Thomas Tresham & his lady then was. Also at one time when he was at the Lord Vaux's, he said that the Lord Compton was there, but not mentioning conference with them or the like.

In corroboration, the letter that Campion had written to Thomas Pounde was produced, 'wherein he did take notice that by frailty he had confessed of some houses where he had been, which now he repented him, and desired Mr Pounde to beg him pardon of the Catholics therein, saying in this he only rejoiced that he had discovered no things of secret'. These were the secrets of the confessional that Campion would protest at his own trial on 20 November that he would never divulge 'come rack, come rope'. Campion's clarification of this point in his letter must surely be seen as an acknowledgement that he did indeed write it, even though it no longer survives. However, Lord Vaux and his fellow defendants were tried five days before Campion. They probably suspected, or hoped, that the letter and the confession, read aloud but not examined by them, were forgeries. The government could have received information about Campion's sojourn in Northamptonshire from someone else. Lord Vaux's experience with the Montagus had shown that there were men in the county who bore him ill will. Even if Vaux suspected that Campion had given his name away, the evidence presented here was vague and, as the Queen's Counsel admitted, extorted under torture.

As the highest-ranked defendant, Lord Vaux was tried first. Ordered to affirm or deny Campion's statement, he made 'an humble & lowly obedience', but the Earl of Leicester apparently discerned 'some want of duty or reverence therein' and pointed it out to the Chancellor.

Lord Chancellor: My Lord, doth it become you so unreverently to presume to make answer with only bowing of your leg in so high an offence as this is that you have committed against her Majesty? No, it little beseemeth you & greatly is to be disliked.

Lord Vaux: My Lords all, if I have failed in any part of my duty, I humbly pray pardon, for I had intention not to offend therein (God is my judge). And the rather I hope you will pardon it in me, who through ignorance hath committed this error, being erst never acquainted with the answering of any like cause in this court or any other court.

All this, the record states, 'he spake upon his knee, and so continued kneeling' for the rest of his hearing.

Lord Chancellor: Answer to the matter that her Majesty's attorney hath charged you withal. Do you confess it or deny it?

Lord Vaux: My Lords, I acknowledge all to be true that I am charged withal concerning my refusal to swear, and withal do affirm my examination taken before Sir Walter Mildmay to be true, offering now, as always heretofore I have done, to depose to any interrogatories that concern my loyalty to her Majesty or duty to the state, requiring all only to be exempted to depose in matters of conscience, which without

offending of my conscience grievously, I may not consent to do. With
further offer that if I be not a most true & faithful subject to her
Majesty, show me no favour, but cut me off forthwith, at whose
commandment my goods, my lands & my life ever hath been & ever
shall be most ready in all duty to be employed. And as to the receiving
of Mr Campion (albeit I confess he was schoolmaster to some of my
boys), yet I deny that he was at my house. I say that he was not there
to my knowledge, whereof reprove me & let me be punished with the
punishment I deserve.

Lord Chancellor: You have denied it unsworn. Why do you refuse to
swear it? Nay, you were but required to say it upon your honour and
withal but to your knowledge. And the favour you had also showed
you, that Campion's examination in that point was read unto you,
wherein he confessed to have been at your house.

'I had good reason for my denial,' Vaux replied, but he would not
swear to it or affirm it upon his honour – 'which to us noblemen is
[the] same that an oath is to others' – because, he said, 'I would not
hazard the same to be impeached by untrue accusation.'

Lord Chancellor: You see he hath said herein what he can. You may
proceed with Sir Thomas Tresham.

Lord Vaux: Thus much I humbly pray of your honours that if I have
committed any offence herein, that you would not impute it to
contemptuous obstinacy, but rather to fear of offending my conscience.

Tresham's defence was also mounted upon the rock of his
conscience, but it went a great deal further than Vaux's rebuttal. He
fell to his knees and began to question the prosecution's case: 'You
have charged me generally with sundry times receiving of Mr
Campion. I pray you limit the times & places [so] that my answer
may be particular & direct.' Tresham had already written to the Lords
and prepared detailed notes on the harbouring charge. His defence
essentially boiled down to this: he owned a large house and people
came and went all the time. Sometimes he had as many as a hundred
guests in his house, but he was not introduced to them all. Campion,

he was told, frequently went about in disguise and under an alias, so although Tresham had no recollection of his visit, he risked perjuring himself with an emphatic denial. 'Mr Campion might have been in my company, might have been in my house, and also might have had conference with me, and notwithstanding pass from me unknown.'[21]

The Lords in the Star Chamber were not at all keen to debate this point, choosing instead to focus on the contempt charge. Tresham responded with a long, sophisticated discourse on the true nature of an oath and the relative jurisdictions of the temporal and spiritual spheres. Drawing on 'learned schoolmen & deep divines', he put it to the court that an oath without judgement or justice was indiscreet and illicit. Every scenario open to him – confirming or denying Campion's true confession or confirming or denying his false confession – made him liable to offend the laws of nature or of God. Even if he attested on oath to the truth of Campion's confession, it would render him 'an egregious liar' according to his former denial. Moreover:

> I should greatly sin uncharitably to belie him, to make him and myself both guilty by my oath, who to my knowledge are most innocent, which I am by God's word expressly forbidden. Lastly, I should commit a grievous sin to swear against the knowledge of my own conscience.

The individual, Tresham maintained, had a duty to obey the laws of God as he understood them. He would be more than happy, just as Vaux had been, to swear loyalty to the Queen, but he could not be forced into making an invalid oath, no more than he could be coerced into committing a sin:

> Some things be proper to God, others to Caesar, which we may not confound. But in this, it being no mere temporal demand but a matter in conscience & thereby concerneth my soul, I am to have such special regard hereto in this my oath before your honours, as I may be able to make my account before the majesty of Almighty God at the dreadful day of judgement.

In other words, God trumped Caesar. This was the great ideological issue of the age: dual allegiance, religion or politics, conscience set against the state. Like the Jesuits at the Synod of Southwark, Tresham was challenging the legitimacy of state power. It had its limitations, he argued, and should be confined to the temporal sphere. In spiritual matters, the individual had the right to refuse to obey dictates that offended divine law. Tresham's case amounted, one historian has argued, to 'a slippery and compelling theory of resistance', albeit impeccably couched in the language of obedience.[22]

The judges were infuriated by Tresham and realised that he had used the trial to make a broader point. Lord Hunsdon accused him of having 'studied & premeditated his argument' in order 'to incense the ears of so great an assembly and thereby (as it were) to premonish all Catholics by his example how to answer and how to behave themselves in like cases'. The other defendants also claimed scruples of conscience in refusing to swear. Sir William Catesby and Tresham 'tell both one tale,' Hunsdon noted, so 'they have had both one schoolmaster'. Catesby retorted that indeed they had one schoolmaster, 'that is God, who teacheth us to speak truth'.

Before the court proceeded to judgement, Sir Walter Mildmay spoke. After rehashing the anti-papal, anti-Jesuit speech he had delivered in Parliament at the beginning of the year, he summed up the case against Vaux, Tresham and Catesby, noting two things in particular: one, that their refusal to swear to their previous denials 'manifestly' suggested that they had lied. 'The other (& that the greater)': their refusal was contemptuous and indicative of 'an utter failing in their duties' towards the Queen.

> Therefore, seeing the running about of these lewd Jesuits and priests is so dangerous to her Majesty and the realm, and seeing that my Lord Vaux & th'other[s] have refused to confirm by oath or otherwise their former sayings, as they were lawfully required by persons of the greatest authority under her Majesty, this doing of theirs cannot be but taken for a great offence & contempt to her Majesty and her government, and such as deserveth punishment answerable to so great a fault that others thereby may be warned not to fall into the like hereafter.

He recommended that they be fined and returned to prison. He posted Lord Vaux's fine at £1,000, Tresham and Catesby's at 1,000 marks (£666) apiece. The Lords in the Star Chamber put it on record that they deemed the sentence too light. Lord Chief Baron Manwood argued that the offence proceeded from 'malice & not ignorance or zeal', while Francis Knollys thought it 'participating of treason & little differing from treason'. Lord Buckhurst agreed, declaring it 'an odious act' that 'concerned the state greatly'. Lord Norris branded the defendants 'ungrateful & faithless subjects'. All the lords agreed that the fines were minimal. Lord Chancellor Bromley was the last to speak. He opined that the prisoners were 'guilty of receiving Mr Campion', and he noted 'obstinacy & undutifulness' in their refusal to swear:

> He urged against the Lord Vaux that he was at full years at her Majesty's coming to the crown, who at that time did his homage whereto he was sworn . . . [but now] in the refusing to swear, he had violated the same, which was a grievous offence.

He ordered the defendants back to prison, 'to continue there till they had sworn', and specified that they should not be released 'without her Majesty's special favour obtained first therein'.

'And herewith,' the report ends, 'the court did arise & the prisoners were carried away.'

A fortnight later, on 1 December 1581, Edmund Campion was hanged, drawn and quartered at Tyburn. From the scaffold, he begged the forgiveness of all those 'whose names he had confessed upon the rack', claiming that he had only revealed them 'upon the commissioners' oaths that no harm should come unto them'.[23]

4

Worldly Woes

... which future half-year, if it equal in sequel this now past ...
then shall I, wretched man, be so plunged in a sympathy of
miseries that my only comfort must consist in most desired
death ... wherewith I shall then give end to these my endless
worldly woes.

Draft letter of Sir Thomas Tresham to
Sir Christopher Hatton, 10 February 1582.[1]

The Catholic community was quick to rally round Mary, Lady Vaux,
who by a single verdict had been deprived of both husband and brother.
She removed with a small staff to Southwark, taking lodging at the
house of Francis Browne in St Mary Overy's. He was the younger
and more radical brother of Viscount Montague (not to be confused
with the Montagus of Boughton) and was a valuable asset to the
mission, having harboured priests and allowed the Jesuits to use his
house for their clandestine press.[2] Two priests, Stamp and Bayarde,
frequently visited the house, and over the Christmas of 1581 Lady
Vaux also benefited from the ministrations of Edward Osborne, a
seminary priest from Kelmarsh in Northamptonshire and a distant
kinsman. Assisted by the Vaux servant, Henry Tuke, he celebrated
three or four illicit Masses before the lady and her household.[3]

On Sunday, 7 January 1582, Osborne was secreted into Lord Vaux's
chamber in the Fleet where he said Mass before several recusant
inmates. The prisoners' 'close' confinement had evidently been relaxed
somewhat since their recommittal. The Spanish ambassador revealed
on 11 December 1581 that 'by means of priests' he was in 'constant
communication' with Tresham. He added that Sir Thomas was
'extremely prudent and circumspect in his actions'. The same could

not be said for Thomas's younger brother William, who abandoned England for France in January, leaving behind a pile of debts and a number of indiscreet letters to the Queen and the Lords of the Council. One parting shot to his former patron, Sir Christopher Hatton, accused him of being 'like a grasshopper who flourisheth in the summer's heat and yet is killed with the first Bartholomew dew'.[4]

More ominously, William Tresham was machinating with Robert Persons over a papal–Spanish invasion of Scotland, to be followed, after the conversion of the Scots, by an invasion of England and the deposition of Queen Elizabeth. All the usual suspects – Mary Queen of Scots, her cousin the Duke of Guise, Pope Gregory XIII, Philip II of Spain and William Allen – were involved in the scheme at varying levels of commitment, but it was aborted when Guise's Scottish ally, the Duke of Lennox, was overthrown. According to the Spanish ambassador in London, Bernardino de Mendoza, it was William Tresham *and* his brother Thomas who were 'the first people to broach this subject, and it is with them that I deal, in addition to the priests who have the matter in hand'.[5] It was less than circumspect and certainly less than prudent for Sir Thomas Tresham to be dabbling in overt treason from his prison cell. Such a blatant act of disloyalty should be borne in mind when considering his past and future protestations of allegiance to the Queen.

In February 1582 Edward Osborne was captured in London by a pursuivant called Richard Topcliffe and thrown into the Clink. The priest did not have the strongest disposition* and was soon talking about the secret Masses for Lady Vaux and her husband in the Fleet. Their servant, Henry Tuke, was arrested that month and imprisoned in the Counter in Poultry.[6] On 13 March the Warden of the Fleet was ordered to search the rooms of the recusant prisoners and have 'a due regard' to their close confinement. Two days later the Privy Council authorised the examination of Vaux, Tresham and others 'touching a Mass said there in the Lord Vaux his chamber'.[7] One of the interrogators was Topcliffe, the pursuivant who had claimed Osborne's scalp and would take so many more in subsequent years. His name would become synonymous

---

* Osborne had lasted seven weeks with the Franciscans, to whom he had resorted after being dismissed from Rome as unsuitable for the English College there. William Allen later alleged that Osborne was threatened with torture in the Clink.

with cruelty, but as no details of the Fleet interview survive, it is impossible to determine whether or not he gave Lord Vaux an exhibition of the corruption and brutality that would later distinguish his reputation. The man had, apparently, a 'most railing manner'.[8]

On Wednesday, 11 April, Vaux and Tresham found themselves once again in court. Instead of the Star Chamber, it was a session of oyer and terminer at the Guildhall. In place of Sir William Catesby, who had been released on bond the previous month, there was Mr Tyrwhitt, who had attended the Mass in Vaux's chamber. According to the Recorder of London, all three 'did stoutly deny' the offence, but after Osborne produced his 'lively evidence', they 'did most humbly submit themselves unto her Majesty'. Each was fined a hundred marks and returned to his cell.[9]

Lord Vaux's adherence to his faith was becoming incredibly expensive. A six-month recusancy fine (£120) dating back from the previous October came into effect at the same time as the Guildhall charge. There was also the £1,000 penalty imposed by the court of Star Chamber and the mounting costs of bed and board at the Fleet. Presumably he took responsibility for the bond when Henry Tuke was released from the Counter in July 1582 and sometime that year he also promised Jasper Heywood, the Jesuit uncle of John Donne, £100 towards his collection for the relief of Catholic prisoners.[10]

With four sons (Henry, George, Edward and Ambrose) and five daughters (Eleanor, Elizabeth, Anne, Katherine and Merill), it could be said that Lord Vaux was, to use a Tresham phrase, 'clogged with children'.[11] At the beginning of 1582, only Eleanor was of independent means thanks to the widow's jointure she had received from her short-lived union with Edward Brooksby. However, her father still owed Tresham for her marriage money. According to their 1571 agreement, Tresham was supposed to give £500 for each of the dowries of Eleanor, Elizabeth and Anne in return for a fifteen-year annuity of £100. Tresham had only stumped up £160 for Eleanor, but he had seen nothing from Vaux, 'nor any farthing thereof, nor jot of recompense'.[12] In 1582, the middle sister, Elizabeth, resolved to become a bride of Christ. She was smuggled across the Channel in March and entered the closed community of the Poor Clares in Rouen. Eleanor and Anne suspected that Tresham had put pressure on their sister to take the habit and 'under colour of religion abused her to gain her portion to his own use' – the entry cost of a convent being cheaper than marriage to a gentleman.[13]

The previous October, Lord Vaux had been confident he could keep 'misery from my door', even with an estate that was 'not in all respects as of late it was'. Despite his daughters' assertions, it was in no small part thanks to Tresham that it continued that way after the two trials. Tresham may have wailed in February 1582 that he would soon have to 'beg at the box', but he was a ruthless estate manager who strived to keep on top of his finances.[14] Vaux, by contrast, was careless with money and constantly in debt. Before the end of March 1582, under Tresham's guidance, he conveyed property to his eldest son, Henry. When the Sheriff of Northamptonshire attempted to levy the fines 'imposed upon my Lord Vaux', he found he could not 'by reason of estates and conveyances made by the Lord Vaux of his lands and goods to his son'. Lord Burghley ordered an enquiry, but no action seems to have been taken.[15]

According to the 1581 Act of Persuasions, it was illegal to convey property for the 'covinous purpose' of fine evasion, but it was not easy to establish motive. Long-term loans were hard to come by and mortgages were unpopular, so property transactions were fairly common and could be incredibly complex. In the National Archives and at the Northamptonshire Record Office, there is a seemingly endless catalogue of deeds, covenants, licences and trusts that spun the Vaux patrimony into a fairly impenetrable cocoon. The twenty-one-year lease of a farm in Isham, for example, which yielded an annual rent of three pounds, six shillings and four hens, passed through the hands of at least nine men between 1580 and 1594. The names read like a roll call of the Vaux/Tresham affinity – Richard Allen of Hoxton and Rothwell (Tresham's servant), George Robinson of Hackney (where Vaux would soon reside), Thomas Bawde (Tresham's cousin and lawyer), John Lee (yeoman of Harrowden), Francis Pettit (executor of Lady Vaux's will and witness of Lord Vaux's codicil) and so on.[16] Such arrangements could lead to complications, but they also helped deflect the levies.

On 30 January 1582, Sir Henry Cobham, the English ambassador in Paris, wrote to Sir Francis Walsingham, the Principal Secretary of State:

> It is given me to understand, Sir, how that Nicolson, servant to the Lord Vaux, is come over, passing at Dover, with a great packet of

letters, being gone hence to Rheims, from whence, as they say, he goeth to Rome with informations of the Lord Vaux's troubles and estate, together with new instructions of Campion's acts and others his confederates.[17]

Evidently prison and pecuniary pain had done little to dent Lord Vaux's enthusiasm for the mission. Nicolson may have gone about in London and Paris as a baron's servant, but when he arrived at Rheims on 25 January, he was able to drop his cover. He was entered into the seminary register as 'presbyter', that is, a priest. After two days at William Allen's college, he 'set out for Paris with the intention of returning to England'. The following year, in March 1583, he visited Rome.

In addition to information on Vaux's 'troubles and estate', Nicolson had also delivered, 'from his very lips, as truly as we live and breathe', the latest news on the missionary priests incarcerated in England. Robert Johnson (executed on 28 May 1582), who had been seized in London in 1580 during a search for Campion and Persons, was allegedly racked three times and 'suffered the pulling asunder and dislocation of all his limbs, with excruciating agony'. Luke Kirby, who would be hanged two days after Johnson, 'had his body twisted and was then thrown onto an iron ring, so that he endured pain beyond belief throughout his entire body'.* Thomas Clifton, meanwhile, was in chains at 'that most vile prison', Newgate, 'with his body held upright against the wall in such a way that throughout the whole of the day he has no opportunity whatever of sitting or of moving his position'.[18]

Nicolson's 'instructions', as Cobham called them, had a didactic purpose and propaganda value. He informed his brethren at Rheims that when Clifton was sentenced to life imprisonment, 'he went down on bended knees, raised his eyes and hands to heaven and repeated *Alleluia, Alleluia* as though he were exultantly triumphant'. Here for the missioners-in-training was an inspiring model of Christian fortitude. But the accounts were not unremittingly heroic. Fathers Johnson, Sherwin and Kirby, the Rheims registrar noted, were 'admirable priests', but reportedly

---

* Kirby seems to have tortured by a device known as the Scavenger's (or Skeffington's) Daughter – an iron clamp that compressed the body in contrast to the rack, which stretched it.

had such terrible punishments and such carefully contrived tortures inflicted on them that they revealed everything they knew about the soldiers sent to Ireland by our most Holy Lord, and during the actual torturing said that they had been sent by his Holiness to England to stir the English people under the seal of confession or by other means to treason and to the taking up of arms against the monarch.

According to one master at Rheims, accounts like Nicolson's only made the students more hungry for combat: 'Our brethren are so animated by those dangers that it is difficult to hold them back.'[19]

The traffic between Allen's seminary and the English Catholic community was increasing in both directions. Despite strict laws on unlicensed travel, the student body at Rheims had swollen from 55 in May 1578 to over 120 at the beginning of 1582. According to Allen, writing on 15 January 1582, 'gentlemen and others driven away by the persecution' were arriving 'every day' from England. Not all came with the intention of taking holy orders. Some sought a Catholic education and stayed on as lay students. Others paid shorter visits, 'to have cases of conscience solved, or for instruction or consolation'. Although money was always tight, Allen was proud of his open-door policy: 'And to show the heretics that we have not been tired out and forced by necessity to send away students, thirty of our number prefer to live on less than a crown a month with some fragments from our table rather than leave us.'[20]

In April 1582, the registrar noted new arrivals:

On the 18th two noble boys came to us from Rouen, Ambrose and Edward Vaux, the sons of the most noble baron Lord Vaux, who has been imprisoned in England for his most steadfast profession of the Catholic faith. They were at once admitted to our community.

Ambrose and Edward, around twelve and thirteen respectively, stayed for just under a fortnight. The registrar recorded their departure on the last day of April (New Style): 'The two Vaux boys left, whom I said above had flown to this city on the 18th of this month.'[21] They had flown (*advolasse*) from Rouen, the historic capital of Normandy, about 130 miles west of the seminary. The verb suggests some urgency. Rouen was the location of Elizabeth Vaux's convent.

Since she had left England the previous month, it is possible that her two half-brothers had provided an escort and then sped on to visit Allen's famous seminary. Perhaps they were on a tight schedule. But Rouen had also become a byword for Catholic intrigue. It harboured a sizeable community of disgruntled expatriates and was the current refuge of Robert Persons and his printing press. When William Tresham had fled there earlier in the year, it was made known to his brother that the Queen 'doth greatly dislike' the place and 'feared that he cannot long continue there a good subject'.[22] Persons was secretly housed in the city by its archdeacon, who was a future regional chief of the Catholic League, a militant confederation of zealots first formed in 1576 and reconstituted by the Duke of Guise in 1584. Persons' association with the Leaguers drew him into Guise's plans for the deposition of Queen Elizabeth. The latest scheme, over which the Spanish ambassador in London had liaised with the Treshams, was the invasion of England through Scotland. It would be abandoned upon the fall of the Duke of Lennox, but in May 1582, a month after Ambrose and Edward's speedy journey from Rouen to Rheims, Persons set off for Paris to discuss the proposal with Allen, Guise and others.[23]

Ambrose and Edward were almost certainly too young to know about any of this – even if they might perhaps have been asked to carry messages – but two days after their arrival at the seminary, Ambassador Cobham reported from Paris: 'The Lord Vaux sent hither a man with letters to Morgan, Copley and Doctor Allen who returneth with letters from the papists.'[24] A suspicious mind would have no trouble casting a sinister light on this report. Doctor William Allen, as we know, was not only the seminary founder, but also the effective leader of the English Catholics in exile. He, like Persons, was up to his neck in plots against Queen Elizabeth, though he tried to keep his intriguing separate from seminary business and claimed to have banned any discussion at Rheims of the papal bull of deposition.[25]

Thomas Copley was another prominent Englishman in exile. He had converted to Catholicism early in Elizabeth's reign and left the country in 1570. In May 1582, he would settle in Rouen. He consistently protested his temporal loyalty to Queen Elizabeth and begged to be restored to her favour, but he received a knighthood from the King of France and a pension from the King of Spain. In December 1582, the Jesuits paid him four hundred crowns 'towards his maintenance'.*[26]

The other recipient of a Vaux letter – 'Morgan' – is harder to identify. It is a common name and there could plausibly have been any number of Morgans who had briefly slipped unnoticed across the Channel. Two early contenders – the priest Polidore Morgan, who would soon accompany another Vaux boy to Rheims, and a singer called Nicholas Morgan, who was a 'gentleman sometime of the [Queen's] Chapel' – were both reported by a spy to have visited Copley in Rouen in the autumn of 1582, but they can be discounted here since the former was in a London prison in April 1582 and the latter, it seems, had not yet left England. Two other Morgans were living in France at this time. Roland Morgan had arrived at Rheims on 18 October 1581 and was ordained at Laon on 18 May 1583. His older brother Thomas was the Paris agent of Mary Queen of Scots and her go-to man for plots against Queen Elizabeth. According to government sources, he was one of the men 'known to her Majesty and her Council to be notorious practisers, very inward with the Duke of Guise, and contrivers of the treasons and devices for the invasion intended'. If Thomas Morgan was Vaux's correspondent – or even if Vaux was simply the middleman who provided a courier – it seems more than possible that our baron was on the fringes of something shady. However, this is to speculate; the contents of the letters are not known.[27]

This was a febrile time. England's relations with Spain had deteriorated. Philip II, having annexed Portugal and its colonies at the start of the decade, was more threatening than ever. His representative in the Low Countries, the Duke of Parma, seemed to be gaining ground over William of Orange and the rebel provinces. But it was the forces of Catholic zeal in France that Walsingham feared most at this juncture. Suspecting 'some great and hidden treason not yet discovered', he placed moles in the French embassy in London.[28] In the event, a plot to overthrow the Queen would be discovered, the so-called Throckmorton Plot that involved, once again, Mary Stuart and Morgan, the Duke of Guise, the King of Spain and the papacy. The

---

*Sir Thomas's son, Anthony Copley, would be involved in the Bye plot to seize James I in 1603. Banished from the realm, he would undertake a pilgrimage to Jerusalem with Ambrose Vaux.

conspiracy's linkman in England was a young gentleman called Francis Throckmorton, a kinsman of the Vauxes and the Treshams.* He was arrested in London in November 1583, put to the rack and executed the following summer. There is no hard evidence to suggest that the Vauxes were involved in the Throckmorton Plot, or in any of the intrigues swirling round the exile communities in the early 1580s, but it was definitely not a sensible time to be communing with the Queen's enemies.

In the autumn of 1582, Lord Vaux's second son, George, who had just turned eighteen, was smuggled into France with the help of one Persall of Rye, 'a common conveyer over of papists'. A spy in Thomas Copley's household reported that George visited the exile in Rouen 'now and then'. (Another visitor was 'Mr Ffrogmorton' from Paris, probably Francis Throckmorton's brother and co-conspirator, Thomas.)[29] Accompanied by Polidore Morgan, George then made his way to Paris, where Ambassador Cobham noted his arrival. 'The English papists,' he wrote to Walsingham on 17 October 1582,

> say that one of the Lord Vaux's sons will become a religious man and receive the orders of their priests. It is to be thought the coming over of Englishmen should be now as good a trade as in other times the passing over of geldings, or else it is not to be imagined they should resort hither so easily and in such great number.[30]

A few days later, George and Father Morgan left Paris for Rheims. George stayed at the seminary for four months, taking his leave on 3 March 1583 (New Style).[31] It is not known if he left upon his own initiative or was summoned home by his father, but by the spring of 1583 it had become apparent that his older brother, Henry, was the more likely candidate for holy orders. Lord Vaux had hoped that his eldest son would marry a rich heiress and thereby discharge his debts and revive 'my poor estate'. He had 'a very worshipful match' lined up 'and no small portion of money', but Henry 'flatly refused to

---

* Francis Throckmorton's grandmother, Catherine, was the daughter of Nicholas, first Baron Vaux of Harrowden. Sir Thomas Tresham had been a ward of Francis's uncle, Sir Robert Throckmorton of Coughton, Warwickshire, and married Sir Robert's daughter, Meriel, in 1566.

marry'. He was 'no less resolutely determined (though such resolution till then kept secret to himself) to live a sole life'. According to Sir Thomas Tresham, 'this came to be debated among priests concerning his retiring from the world and refusing to marry wherein he fully satisfied them'.

It took two years to draw up a formal settlement. Tresham, as always, was the facilitator. Henry took a small annuity and relinquished his inheritance. On 20 April 1585, George formally replaced him as Lord Vaux's heir. It was 'peremptorily provided' that he would not be able to marry without the consent of his parents and elder brother.[32] Henry, released from the burden of his birthright, was free to train for the priesthood, but he was in no hurry to cross the Channel. There was still much work to be done in England and he believed that he was the man who should carry it out.

5

Refuse of the World

> Above twenty seminary priests of reputation and best learning now
> in London . . . They walk audaciously disguised in the streets of
> London. Their wonted fears and timorousness is turned into mirth
> and solace among themselves . . . My instruments have learned out
> sundry places of countenance where sometimes these men meet
> and confer together in the daytime, and where they lodge a-nights.
> Richard Topcliffe to the Lords of the Council, *c*.1584[1]

It is not known exactly when Henry Vaux became one of the leaders
of the Catholic underground movement. By 1585 he was the mission's
chief lay contact and fund manager, but perhaps the spring of 1583
was the watershed, the moment when he committed body and soul
to mission England.

He moved north-east of London, to the village of Hackney, where
in April 1583 his father was placed under house arrest. The peer's
release after twenty months of the 'noisome and loathsome' Fleet
owed a great deal to Lord Burghley, who interviewed him on
6 February and drafted a 'submissive declaration' for him to transcribe
and send to the Queen. It stressed Vaux's loyalty and contrition. He
was a 'most obedient subject', who now realised how 'grievously' he
had offended in refusing to answer on oath about Campion. Never
again, Vaux protested, would he 'offend in any like case'. He beseeched
the Queen for forgiveness and compassion, especially regarding 'the
great fine' – still unpaid – 'set upon me for the said offence'. Further-
more, he pleaded 'most humbly to be forborne to be compelled to
come to the church'. This was a matter of conscience, Vaux declared,
not contempt, and he was open to instruction 'whereby my conscience
may be better informed and satisfied'.[2]

It was a fairly remarkable request, especially as it was guided by Burghley, a determined anti-papist who was not known for putting sentiment before the interests of the state. Burghley respected noble rank and shared county connections with Lord Vaux. He may have been moved by his fellow peer's plight – in future years, he would assist Vaux 'in relieving my distressed, my else desperate estate'[3] – but it is still surprising that he should have engaged in special pleading of this kind, especially at a time when his fears for the security of the realm were growing. His sympathetic intervention serves as a reminder that no one was predictable in Elizabethan England and nothing was ever quite what it seemed.

Lord Vaux's 'submissive declaration' was partially successful. He was relocated from the Fleet to a large house in Hackney. Sir Thomas Tresham was released at the same time and was eventually allowed to live in his house in Hoxton, but only after an intolerable few months confined to a chamber 'over a noisome, smoky kitchen' in the next-door house, where the air was blue with expletives and thick with 'noise, smoke, heat [and] loathsome savours'.[4]

The laws on church attendance were not relaxed for Vaux and if he submitted to instruction and conference with 'learned persons' according to his pledge, it had no discernible effect on his conscience. Between October 1583 and January 1587, he was regularly indicted 'for not going to church, chapel or any other usual place of Common Prayer'. Sometimes Henry Vaux was also named in the indictments and sometimes George, along with several household servants: William Hollis, William Worseley, John Parker, William Cheney, Valentine Kellison, William Vachell.[5] These names recur in the Vaux records: witnessing wills, leasing land, harbouring priests, delivering messages. They were loyal servants to their master and no less, it seems, to their faith.

Lord Vaux's youngest daughter, Merill, seems to have been brought up in the Hoxton household of her uncle Tresham. She was certainly there at the time of a raid on 27 August 1584. The pursuivants failed to find any priests, but they confiscated a hoard of Catholic books and images. One 'popish painted crucifix' was found on a tablet hanging by Lady Tresham's bedside. There was also 'a new fashioned picture of Christ in a great table and a tabernacle of sundry painted images, with leaves to fold, serving as should seem for a tabernacle or screen to stand upon an altar'. That the picture of Christ should be described as 'new fashioned' shows that Tresham was not just preserving the old, but commissioning new objects of worship. A large plaster relief of the crucifixion, dated 1577, can still be seen at Rushton Hall, his seat in Northamptonshire (now a very good hotel). For those who knew where to look, there was a thriving black market in 'popish trash'. According to an informant in 1595, Mr Bentley of Little Oakley, near Rushton, 'had an old man named Greene, a carpenter and mason', who not only turned his hand to the construction of elaborate priest-holes, but also 'maketh all the beads that lie in little boxes' – for rosaries, presumably.[6]

Much of the information on Vaux activity in the mid-1580s derives from spy reports. In August 1584, the same month as the raid at Hoxton, one James Hill, an erstwhile Catholic who had spent time at the court of the King of Spain and the English College in Rome, wrote to Sir Francis Walsingham with information on 'such persons, with the places of their resort, as was enjoined me by your honour'. In London, he wrote,

> lodging at the sign of the White Hart in Holborn, I there grew acquainted with one Hugh Yates, sometimes servant to the Lord Vaux his son. This Yates had one Alfield repairing to him, with whom I was acquainted, who had his stuff for the purpose commonly carried with him in a box.* He lodged ordinarily in inns, but would not be known of the place. His custom was to repair (as he found himself requested) to gentlemen's lodgings.
>
> Likewise here in this inn by means of this Yates, I know one Ballard, sometimes called Fortescue. He had his abode chiefly in Hampshire, and at the house of an old lady called the Lady West: there repaired hether to this Yates another named Stamp, but I never knew his common abode.[7]

---

* That is, the equipment Alfield needed to celebrate the Mass. As the Jesuit John Gerard explained,

'At first I used to take round with me my own Mass equipment. It was simple, but fitting, and specially made so that it could be carried easily with the other things I needed by the man who acted as my servant. In this way I was able to say Mass in the morning wherever I happened to lodge.' (Gerard, *Auto-biography*, p. 40)

Thomas Alfield, the brother of the servant of Robert Persons who had helped Elizabeth Vaux escape to the convent in Rouen in 1582, was a priest. He would be hanged at Tyburn on 6 July 1585 for importing and distributing copies of William Allen's *A True, Sincere, and Modest Defence of English Catholiques*, a tract that defended the power of the Pope to depose heretic rulers. Ballard and Stamp, who had said Mass for Lady Vaux at Francis Browne's house in 1581, were also priests. Their acquaintance with the Vauxes would continue.

Hugh Yates was described in a 1583 conveyance of Vaux property as a yeoman 'late of Harrowden Magna'. The Tresham Papers reveal that he received occasional payments from Sir Thomas Tresham. The report now in Walsingham's hand showed that he also served the Catholic underground movement in London. 'By means of this Yates' and others like him, safe houses were maintained, priests were introduced to laymen and the sacraments were administered to secret congregations.[8]

The question troubling the authorities was whether or not the priests went any further. Did they engage in clandestine activity of the more political kind and conspire in plots against the Queen and her realm? Burghley, Walsingham and the majority of the Privy Council were convinced that they did. Some well-placed Catholics seemed to concur. The Spanish ambassador in London had written in December 1581, regarding the Lennox Plot, that priests in England 'have the matter in hand'. The following year the papal nuncio in Paris reported that once an invasion was launched, 'the principal Catholics in England will be advised in time through their priests'. Whether they knew it or not, whether they approved of it or not, William Allen's graduates were expected to fulfil a role in England that would ultimately go beyond conventional devotions.

In 1585 Allen would inform the Pope that the English Catholics were 'much more numerous' and 'much more ready (*intenti*)' for invasion due to 'the daily exhortations, teaching, writing and administration of the sacraments of our men and priests'. Only fear made them obey the Queen, 'which fear will be removed when they see the force from without'. There were 'almost three hundred priests in the households of noblemen and men of substance,' he added, 'and we are daily sending others, who will direct the consciences and actions of the Catholics in this affair when the time comes.'[9] In light of these comments, the popular Protestant fear of a Catholic fifth column, primed for rebellion when 'the time' was ripe, does not seem entirely paranoid.

Whatever their intentions when they first arrived in England, some priests did become involved in subversive activity against the Elizabethan regime. It does not, of course, follow that all priests were rabble-rousers or potential assassins. Only a handful were directly involved in what would obviously be labelled treason, but there was a vast grey area that encompassed all kinds of suspicious activity – the circulation of tracts that defended the validity of the papal bull of deposition, for example, or the misprision of treason: the knowledge, but non-disclosure, of a treasonous act. 'I came into the realm, my native country,' Father Roger Dickenson protested, 'to give myself to study, to prayer and devotion and to use my function, and that, I hope, is no treason.'[10] But even if most priests shared Dickenson's outlook, even if they were scrupulously pastoral in their concerns and eschewed anything that smacked of politics, they were nevertheless feared for what they might do if there was ever a direct confrontation between the Queen and the Pope. The so-called 'bloody question' that was put to many Catholic prisoners was an attempt to discover their ultimate allegiance: in the event of a foreign invasion to enforce the bull of deposition, would they take the Pope's side or the Queen's?

Many tried to sidestep the issue – they did not bear arms; it was too high a matter; it would depend on prevailing circumstances; they would pray 'that God's will might be done in heaven and on earth'.[11] Such responses infuriated those individuals tasked with the assessment and management of potential threats. How could Burghley and his colleagues sift out the individuals who were ignorant of conspiracy from those who were complicit? How could they prevent potential treasons, but also uphold the rule of law? And what was the appropriate response to the laymen who publicly denounced political intrigue, but nevertheless housed, fed and funded priests, some of whom subsequently turned out to be subversive? These are, in many ways, timeless issues and they kept Burghley up at night.

On 9 October 1584, Ralph Miller, a twenty-year-old tailor from the Peak District, was hauled before the London magistrate Richard Young. A well-travelled Catholic before his arrest and imprisonment, Miller had spent time in the Low Countries, Rheims and Rouen, where he had been sent by a priest 'to work for all the papists there'. Now he gave a long statement detailing all the people and places he had seen in Europe and since his return. A recent encounter with Robert Browne, a theology student who had left Rheims in December 1583, had led to an introduction to Lord and Lady Vaux and their son George. Miller seems to have won their trust, for a fortnight afterwards he had been invited to Hackney to hear Sunday Mass, 'whereat were present about 18 persons, being my Lord's household'. The officiating priest was Robert Browne's uncle, 'a little man with a white head & a little brown hair on his face', who went about in an ash-coloured doublet and a gown trimmed with rabbit fur. Miller knew where the priest lodged – in a room beyond the hall left of the stair leading to the chambers – and revealed the location of the secret chapel – 'right over the port entering into the hall & the way into it is up the stair aforesaid on the left hand at the further end of the gallery, & there is a very fair crucifix of silver.'

Miller also gave away the names of other visitors: 'a young man named William Harrington', recently arrived from Rheims and lodging in Holborn with two other priests, had attended the Mass at Hackney. He was 'very desirous to be a Jesuit' and knew of priests 'lying about Kentish Town'. Also, 'Meredith the priest was at the Lord Vaux his house within this month.' This was Jonas Meredith, a flaxen-haired, Bristol-born seminarian described by an informant five years earlier as 'short of stature and well timbered, fat faced and smooth counten- ance'. He had accompanied Miller on the crossing from France and had, Miller thought, 'a brother that doth serve Charles Arundell* in

---

* Charles Arundell, a prominent supporter of Mary Stuart, had fled to Paris a month after the arrest of Francis Throckmorton. He was suspected of having had a hand in a scurrilous 'evil counsellor' tract that portrayed the Earl of Leicester as a power- and sex-crazed murderer, who kept bottles of erection-enhancing ointment at his bedside. More ominously, the tract anticipated the assassination of Queen Elizabeth and advanced the claims of the Scottish Queen to the succession. Compiled in Paris and printed at Robert Persons' press at Rouen, 'Leicester's Commonwealth', as it was popularly known, was circulating in London from September 1584. Writing to Leicester on the 29th of the month, Sir Francis Walsingham called it 'the most malicious written thing that ever was penned sithence the beginning of the world' (BL Cotton MS Titus B VII, f. 10r). Along with Allen's *True, Sincere, and Modest Defence*, also published in 1584, it marked a shift in Catholic polemic towards a more combative stance.

Paris'. This brother, John Meredith, had recently been accused of concealing crucial evidence regarding the Throckmorton Plot. He had subsequently fled, 'for in truth,' went the government line, 'he was privy to the treasons and a fellow practiser in them'.[12]

Ralph Miller further recalled that during one conversation at Hackney, Lord Vaux had asked him why he had come to England. 'You see how the world goeth,' Vaux had said, 'we are poor prisoners.' The priest had added that the family 'looked any day for search to be made for them'.[13] One recalls the words of Robert Persons four years earlier:

> There comes a hurried knock at the door, like that of a pursuivant; all start up and listen – like deer when they hear the huntsmen. We leave our food and commend ourselves to God in a brief ejaculation, nor is word or sound heard till the servants come to say what the matter is. If it is nothing, we laugh at our fright.[14]

It is surprising that the Vauxes were not targeted with the Treshams and the other recusant families whose homes were raided on 27 August 1584 in a major crackdown on Catholic centres in and around London.[15] Perhaps Burghley's friendly shadow was behind the omission, or perhaps a decision was made to observe the family from within. According to Thomas Dodwell, a renegade priest in the pay of the government, Henry Vaux was keeping 'in manner of a serving man one Bridge *alias* Gratley, a seminary priest'. What Dodwell did not mention, and probably did not know, was that Gratley was himself a government spy. It was, perhaps, on the recommendation of the unsuspecting Henry Vaux that he soon became chaplain to the Earl of Arundel, a recent convert to Catholicism. In April 1585, the Earl wrote to Queen Elizabeth explaining his decision to forsake his family, friends and property for a life on the Continent 'without danger of my conscience, without offence to your Majesty, without this servile abjection to mine enemies & without the daily peril to my life'. He did not make it beyond the Channel. He was captured in his boat and taken to the Tower of London, where, a decade later, he would die. Gratley had betrayed him and, unfortunately for the Vauxes, he was not the only spy in their midst.[16]

*

On 10 July 1584, William of Orange, the Dutch resistance leader and Protestant figurehead, was assassinated. He was shot in the chest by a Catholic fanatic, who said 'he had done an act acceptable to God . . . and that for so doing, he was confident that he should be sanctified and received into the heavens into the first place near to God'.[17] It transpired that Philip II of Spain had offered a bounty for Orange's death. Two months later the city of Ghent succumbed to Philip's general, the Duke of Parma. The grim spectre of Spanish victory in the Low Countries – and consequently of Habsburg control of the North Sea coastline – loomed large. The Duke of Guise's Catholic League looked set to dominate affairs in France and by the end of the year it had concluded an alliance with Spain to prevent the succession of the Protestant heir. The forces of international Catholicism were arguably more militant and menacing than at any previous time in Elizabeth's reign. Her government braced itself for war.

For many Protestants, 'the enemy within' was just as threatening. Catholic polemic had become noticeably more offensive and there was a steady stream of intelligence leading to further intrigues on behalf of Mary Stuart. Some plots were obscure: we may never fathom the true intentions of puffed-up William Parry, a government agent, turned Parliamentarian, turned freelance adventurer, who became ensnared in his own trap to expose disloyalty within the Catholic community. Other designs on Elizabeth's life were frighteningly simple: John Somerville seems only to have had a 'frantic humour' and a pistol in his pocket when he set off from Warwickshire to kill the Queen.[18] But as the fate of William of Orange highlighted, it only took one extremist, bent on martyrdom and blind to worldly consequence, to effect an assassination. The thread upon which hung the safety of the Queen, and that of her subjects, was frail indeed. In the autumn of 1584, Burghley and Walsingham discussed ways of making it a little stronger.

They came up with the 'Bond of Association', a national covenant to protect the Queen and defend the Protestant establishment. The signatories, who numbered in the thousands, pledged as members of 'one firm and loyal society' to pursue, 'as well by force of arms as by all other means of revenge', anyone who tried to harm the Queen or anyone 'for whom any such detestable act shall be attempted or committed'. In effect, the Bond turned subscribers into vigilantes, obliging them, if circumstance arose, to form a lynch mob against Mary Stuart or any other 'pretended successor', regardless of whether they had connived in a plot or not.

Elizabeth I disliked the Bond. She would never have survived her sister's reign had such a provision existed and, quite apart from the dubious ethics of slaying a potential innocent, she baulked (as she had in 1563) at Burghley's additional efforts to force through radical constitutional measures that would have interfered with her right to determine the succession. The Act for the Queen's Surety, which was passed in March 1585, enshrined a moderated version of the Bond in statute. In the event of a plot or assassination, intended beneficiaries could be killed according to the Bond, but only if found guilty of involvement or 'privity' by an official commission. There was no question of unsuspecting heirs being at risk (the nineteen-year-old James VI of Scotland was thus kept onside) and no revenge could be wreaked without a nod from on high. Nevertheless, the enthusiasm with which Englishmen from all backgrounds had subscribed to the Bond in its early form told of the strength of their devotion to their Queen and the national religion. The other side of the coin revealed a virulent strain of anti-Catholicism throughout the land.[19]

It was in this climate of fear and retribution that another major piece of legislation was introduced in Parliament. The bill 'against Jesuits, Seminary Priests and such other like disobedient Persons' was designed to annihilate the English mission. Any priest ordained abroad since the accession of the Queen and found in England after forty days of promulgation would automatically be deemed a traitor and face the death penalty. Anyone who wittingly harboured him would be 'adjudged a felon' and 'suffer death, loss and forfeit as in case of one attainted of felony'. The bill presented an impossible scenario for England's Catholics. Their one hope lay with Queen Elizabeth, 'our headspring and fountain of mercy'. In a long petition, probably drafted by Tresham, and endorsed by several prominent recusants, including Lord Vaux, they begged for a measure of toleration. 'O most lamentable condition,' they cried:

If we receive them (by whom we know no evil at all) it shall be deemed treason in us. If we shut our doors and deny our temporal relief to our

Catholic pastors in respect of their function, then are we already judged most damnable traitors to Almighty God . . .

Albeit that many ways we have been afflicted, yet this affliction following (if it be not by the accustomed natural benignity of your Majesty suspended or taken away) will light upon us to our extreme ruin and certain calamity: that either we (being Catholics) must live as bodies without souls, or else lose the temporal use both of body and soul.

'Suffer us not,' they begged the Queen, 'to be the only outcasts and refuse of the world':

Let not us, your Catholic native English and obedient subjects, stand in more peril for frequenting the Blessed Sacraments and exercising the Catholic religion (and that most secretly) than do the Catholic subjects to the Turk publicly, than do the perverse and blasphemous Jews haunting their synagogue under sundry Christian kings openly, and than do the Protestants enjoying their public assemblies under diverse Catholic kings and princes quietly. Let it not be treason for the sick man in body (even at the last gasp) to seek ghostly counsel for the salvation of his soul of a Catholic priest.

The petition stressed the apostolic nature of the mission and the loyalty of the priests to 'their undoubted and lawful Queen'. In the unlikely event that any hint of treason could be discerned in any priest, the petitioners pledged to turn him into the authorities. 'For our own parts,' they concluded, whatever the outcome of the petition, 'your Majesty shall find us such subjects as God requireth and your Majesty desireth, that is most obedient first to God and next to your Highness most loving, most loyal and most dutiful.'[20]

One of the petitioners, Richard Shelley, put the document in the Queen's hands as she took the air in Greenwich Park. His presumption was rewarded with a cell in Marshalsea prison. The petition evokes a great deal of sympathy for England's Catholics, stretched to breaking point by the uncompromising injunctions of rival authorities. At one level, they simply wanted to be allowed to receive the sacraments and purify their 'unclean souls'. Yet they were also aware of the politics of religion and the latest casuist teaching that allowed a certain amount of equivocation and 'mental reservation' in dealing with a persecuting body. One must wonder how sincere they really were when they offered to betray all treasonous priests. Reconciliation to Rome was categorised as treason, so official and Catholic interpretations of the crime clearly differed. While the petitioners' first allegiance was to God – a Catholic God who, through the Pope, had excommunicated Elizabeth I – their love, loyalty and duty to the heretic Queen would always be qualified. Burghley's confidant, Robert Beale, had expressed his concern years earlier: 'It is unpossible that they should love her, whose religion founded in the Pope's authority maketh her birth and title unlawful.'[21]

And yet so many of them did love her – despite the bull of excommunication and despite the repressive laws. When the 24-year-old Robert Markham resolved to flee abroad and convert to Catholicism, he wrote a desperately sad letter to his parents, craving their forgiveness and explaining 'the horror of my conscience'. He abhorred the 'odious name of traitor' and pledged never to fight against the Queen or have any truck with conspiracy. 'I am,' he declared, 'and will be as good a subject to her Majesty as any in England.' But there had to be a caveat: 'my conscience only reserve I to myself, whereupon dependeth my salvation.'[22] Fellows like Markham would have loved nothing more than to have been a good Englishman and a good Catholic. Parliament and the papacy conspired to make it impossible.

At the end of March 1585, royal assent was granted to the 'Act against Jesuits, Seminary Priests, and such other like disobedient Persons' (27 Eliz. c. 2). For all those priests ordained after 1559 it was now a capital offence just to be in England. They had forty days to leave the country.

Not long afterwards, a group of men gathered at a house in Hoxton. Lord Vaux, Sir Thomas Tresham and Sir William Catesby (our triumvirate of Fleet veterans, cousins and countrymen) were present, as were Henry Vaux, 'certain other gentlemen' and six priests, including the superior of the Society of Jesus, William Weston *alias* Edmunds.* The new law had rattled the recusant community and a fresh wave of raids was anticipated. Some householders felt that the risk of

---

* Weston's alias was a tribute to his late friend and Oxford contemporary, Edmund Campion, S.J.

harbouring was too great. It was decided that priests should approach their homes by invitation only. Otherwise, they would 'shift for themselves abroad, as in inns or such like places'.

There was no question, though, of leaving them exposed and destitute. The mission was a collaborative effort. Sometimes, as George Gilbert's handbook written just before his death in 1583 makes clear, it was the layman who took the initiative with conversions, assessing and priming potential candidates, briefing the priest on 'natural dispositions' and exploitable weaknesses, creating 'an opportunity for conversation suited to the occasion'.*[23] If the lay brethren did not live with the quotidian fear of the rack and the gibbet in the same way as their confessors, they nevertheless pledged lasting devotion to the cause and refused to abandon it in its hour of need.

It was 'concluded and agreed' at Hoxton to set up a fund. Lord Vaux, who later in the year would declare himself unable to pay a levy for the Queen's army,[24] pledged one hundred marks 'to the relief of priests that would tarry'. Tresham, Catesby and their Hoxton host, Mr Wylford, matched Vaux's donation and other unnamed gentlemen were 'assessed at lower sums'. They also decided to launch an appeal in the shires. Henry Vaux was appointed treasurer. It was a formidable role, one that Henry, now in his mid-twenties and officially free from the burden of the Vaux inheritance, was seemingly keen to undertake.

The meeting at Hoxton broke up and the participants melted back into the streets and alleys of north-east London. One man, who identified himself as 'A.B.', returned to his lodging and took out his quill. 'May it please your honour,' he began his letter to Sir Francis Walsingham, 'to be advertised that it is concluded & agreed among the papists that such priests as are determined to remain in England or hereafter shall come into England shall be relieved at the hands of Mr Henry Vaux, son to the Lord Vaux, or by his assigns.'

The spy proceeded to give a detailed account of the meeting and the proposed fund. 'All this money,' he continued,

---

* The weather was a useful opener: 'He should seize also any opportunity from the weather, which renders a man more apt to devotion – as, for instance, when the weather is fine to speak of elevation of spirit, in bad or rainy weather of graver things.'

is presently to be delivered to Mr Vaux before the 40 days to avoid the danger of the statute. And letters also directed into the countries abroad for the said collection & the money to be delivered to Mr Vaux. And he to take notice of all priests that shall remain or come into England & in secret by his servant Harris* (as is thought) to relieve them where they shall be heard of.

In the margin, the spy added an ominous note: 'The hope which the papists have to receive comfort by the Duke of Guise & his confederates is not little.' By the end of May 1585, the relief operation was functioning well. The spy reported to Walsingham that Henry was 'daily' collecting money for the fund.[25]

For several years, it seems, probably since at least 1580, Henry Vaux had been privy to a certain amount of sensitive information on the English mission. After Hoxton, he was in receipt of the intelligence and income needed to bolster the whole enterprise. Not only was he in regular touch with lay benefactors, but he also took 'notice of all priests that shall remain or come into England'. From the late spring of 1585, he liaised with priests and sustained their work. According to Robert Persons, he was a 'blessed gentleman', who presented 'a rare mirror of religion and holiness unto all that knew him and conversed with him'.[26] According to Elizabethan law, he was a felon, who 'wittingly and willingly' mixed with traitors and abetted their treason. He had become a person of very great interest in the ongoing investigations of Lord Burghley and Sir Francis Walsingham.

---

* The following year, another spy reported: 'There is one Thomas Harris, a trusty servant to Mr Henry Vaux; much matter might be found out in him if he were apprehended.' Around the same time, one 'Harris, servant to Henry Vaux', headed a list of 'knaves & papists & harbourers of priests'. (PRO SP 12/195, ff. 36r, 184r)

6

Flibbertigibbets

In Shakespeare's original version of *King Lear*, Edgar, disguised as the madman Poor Tom, claims to have been tormented by the fiends Obidicut, Hobbididence, Mahu, Modo and Flibbertigibbet, 'who since possesses chambermaids and waiting-women'.[1] As fantastical as these names sound, they are not the product of Shakespeare's imagination. He was inspired by real events. They occurred over a period of about eight months around twenty years before he wrote his great tragedy and the most extraordinary episode, 'the prime grand miracle', was performed at Lord Vaux's house in Hackney towards the early autumn of 1585.

It involved the Jesuit superior Weston and Nicholas Marwood, a servant of Henry Vaux's friend Anthony Babington. In attempting to expel the devil from the unfortunate Marwood, Weston utilised several 'fresh green new relics', including 'certain pieces of Father Campion's body', which 'did wonderfully burn the devil, all the organs of all his senses seeming to be broken and rent asunder'. Marwood's screeching was witnessed by various members of the Vaux household alongside a carefully selected audience, which was reportedly put into 'such astonishment as there was a confused shout made of weeping and joy for this foil of the devil'.[2]

The exorcism was the talk of the town in smart Catholic circles. It must have been a welcome diversion for the Vauxes, who were reeling from the death at home of the baron's third son, Edward,* and the 'unfortunatist mismatching' of his second son, George, to Eliza Roper.[3] No one in the family seems to have had a good word for the girl. George's uncle, Sir Thomas Tresham, questioned Eliza's motives – George had

---

* Little is known about the teenager's death beyond its date (25 July 1585) and place ('apud Hackney in com. Middlesex'). He was probably buried secretly.

formally become his father's heir in April 1585 – and her virginity. George ignored the warnings and on the very day of his younger brother's death, 25 July 1585, he defied the conditions of his inheritance and married without permission. By November, though, when a young man called Richard Mainy dined at Hackney with a son and daughter of Lord Vaux, there was not much talk of death or undesirable brides, nor even, it seems, of the imminent war with Spain (effectively declared the following month when Elizabeth I sent the Earl of Leicester to command an expedition in the Low Countries). Instead there was much excited chatter about 'the late possession and dispossession' of Nicholas Marwood.

Seventeen years later Mainy would inform an ecclesiastical court that 'the tales which were told of that matter seemed strange unto me, as what extraordinary strength he had in his fits, how he roared like a bull, and many other things were then mentioned, which now I have forgotten'. At the time, though, he was more receptive to his hosts' tale and, soon after the dinner, he too became 'possessed'. He later claimed to have feigned his 'pretended visions' to please Father Weston and 'to gain to myself a little foolish commendation or admiration because I saw how the Catholics that heard of them, and were present at many of my fond speeches, did seem to wonder at me'.[4]

Also exorcised around this time were four servant girls, including Lady Vaux's maid, Sara Williams. She was around sixteen years old and had previously attended the Peckhams of Denham in Buckinghamshire, where she had reportedly been possessed and 'dispossessed' of 'divers devils'. For a while the transfer to Hackney, a place considered 'more convenient for the health not only of her body, but also of her soul', seemed the perfect tonic. Sara acquired a 'sweet & comfortable manner' and displayed all the attributes that befitted the female servant of a devout household. Everything changed on New Year's Day, 1586. As the Vauxes celebrated the Feast of the Circumcision of the Lord, one priest perceived by Sara's 'behaviour & gesture that all was not well'. Upon further examination, he concluded that she had been repossessed. He sent for some of his colleagues, who 'prepared themselves, through the help of Almighty God & authority of his Church, to cast out & expel this troublesome devil from this young maid & virgin'.

A manuscript account of Sara's experience survives in the Bodleian

Library in Oxford, within a vast two-volume Catholic encyclopaedia that once belonged to the Brudenells of Deene.* The account was purportedly written by a 'true witness' and probably also appeared in the now-lost *Miracle Book*, a compendium of supernatural occurrences compiled to showcase the power of the Catholic Church.[5] According to this witness, the devil, through Sara, repeatedly cursed and threatened the exorcists: 'God's wounds! God's life! Six popish priests. Six popish priests. A pursuivant. A pursuivant. To prison with them & hang them. Hang them!'

The following morning, the Vauxes ushered more priests into their home to do combat with Sara's demon. He scoffed at their appearance and apparel, calling one 'red face' and 'other priests that were in vestments going to Mass, white coat & red coat, whooping and shouting, and all to disturb the company that were at devout prayers'. During Mass, at the elevation of the host, he 'would roar & screech in most terrible manner, saying: I will none of your God, turn away my face, turn away my face, turn me away!'

Prayers and priestly commands having failed, the proceedings entered a terrifying phase:

> Well, quoth the Exorcist, I will punish and torment thee for thy obstinacy, & with that called for fire and brimstone. First he hallowed the fire, and after scraping the brimstone upon the coals, the devil roared & cried in most terrible manner, cursing & swearing, saying: A pox on you, God's wounds, you will burn me.

'It was a wonderful sight,' our narrator assures us,

> to behold the pain & torment that the devil was put unto at the burning of the brimstone & holding the same before him at his nose, how he roared, tormented & screeched in most terrible manner, swelling in the face of the party, swearing & cursing so grievously that a man would have been afraid to have heard it.

---

* The Brudenells were co-religionists, friends and country neighbours of the Vauxes. In 1605, Sir Thomas Tresham's daughter Mary would marry Thomas Brudenell, later created Earl of Cardigan.

Another priest, 'holding the party possessed by the head', placed a relic under her nose: 'The devil raged & tormented, sniffing and blowing & winding away the face of the party from it, spitting & crying most strangely.' The Eucharist caused a similar reaction, as did a picture of the Virgin Mary, which led Sara's devil to threaten to 'hollow* out so loud that I will be heard a great way'. The exorcist then gave her a 'hallowed drink', which made her 'spew & spit . . . in most wonderful manner, sometimes crying out that the drink burned her'.

Sara's ordeal lasted from four o'clock in the morning till two or three in the afternoon. According to the Catholic narrative, her devil gradually began to succumb to priestly power. He gave his name as 'St Maho' and confessed to having lost Sara's heart. He even said that Alexander Briant, who had been executed for treason alongside Edmund Campion and whose bone was utilised as a relic towards the end of the ritual, was a saint who had never suffered purgatory. 'If this be not a sufficient testimony of the glorious martyrdom of our priests,' the narrator writes, 'I know not what we may believe.'

Still the devil refused to depart. With 'the whole company praying devoutly for the delivery of the maiden from the tyranny and power of Satan', he made her 'gape in most pitiful manner, and withal deformed so her face as any man's heart would have bled to have seen the same'. He then retreated into Sara's body. 'Oh, he will break my belly,' she cried, 'he will break my belly; he lieth in the bottom of my belly.' Indeed, so low did he descend, that:

> therewithal she called for the help of a woman. Then the priest, perceiving that the devil was gotten into the bottom of her belly, gave a relic unto one of the women, willing her to apply it unto the belly of the party, the which being done by the woman, it was wonderful to see how the devil was tormented.

Finally, with Sara 'calling upon the help of Almighty God and of our Blessed Lady', the devil departed:

> And the maid, coming to herself, gave thanks to God for her safe delivery, for I thank God and our Blessed Lady, quoth she, I am now

---

* *hollow/hollo*: yell out to attract attention. The American word 'holler' is a variant.

delivered; and being asked whether she saw him depart or no, she said, I did see him depart in the likeness of water. Whereat the exorcist and all the rest of the priests gave thanks to God.

Thus ended the exorcism of Sara Williams.

There are several ways of interpreting this episode. According to the 'true witness', it was a demonstration of 'the wonderful work of Almighty God', even 'in these days so full of wickedness & impiety, so full of heresy & infidelity'. In granting his priests 'such power and authority . . . to drive out & expel devils', God had revealed the true Church. And 'so would He have it done in the presence of many to give testimony of the same to the honour of His holy name & confirmation of the Catholic cause'. In an age when people noted supernatural phenomena as a matter of course, when they divined for treasure, executed witches and would have been hard-pressed to identify a precise boundary between religion and magic, the exorcism accounts in the *Miracle Book* were powerful propaganda. Here was the armoury of the resurgent Church of Rome in triumphant combat with the devil. 'The intervention of heaven was undoubted,' Weston later wrote in his *Autobiography*, 'and incredulous onlookers were astounded.'[6] Indeed, they became part of the ritual, the priest exhorting them to strengthen their devotion and redouble their prayers, so that when the devil was eventually repulsed, triumph was shared, faith was reinforced and the word was spread.

Although the spectators at Hackney, 'which were very many, respecting the dangers of the time and place', were hardly unsympathetic to the Catholic cause, the subsequent publicising of the event aimed at wider conversion. Indeed, it has been persuasively argued that the exorcisms were 'a crucial arm of the Tridentine missionary campaign to reconcile schismatics and evangelize Protestants'.[7] Throughout the account of Sara's exorcism, the devil is aligned with official religion. 'All Protestants and heretics are at my right hand near unto me,' he announces. 'The schismatics' – those Catholics who went to church – 'are at my left hand somewhat farther off, yet notwithstanding they are all mine.' He summons his pursuivant allies to capture the priests, but they are thwarted by the combined might of the Trinity and the Virgin Mary. When the devil is finally expelled, it is as much a triumph for Catholicism over the Elizabethan Settlement as it is for God over the devil. 'Be then assured,' the priests at Hackney proclaim, 'that we will all spend our lives to expel & drive out of England all heretical spirits, & that we will yield our lives to save the Queen's Majesty's soul.'

Here was a strain of post-Reformation English Catholicism that was muscular and ambitious. While many individuals preferred to lie low and wait, there were others – secular priests as well as Jesuits; laymen as well as clergymen – who were determined to effect change. The exorcisms of 1585–6 and their subsequent advertisement can be seen as part of the same evangelising impulse that stimulated William Allen to set up his seminary and Robert Persons his printing press; it drove Henry Vaux towards the Catholic underground and his father into communication with the Queen's enemies on the Continent. A similar fervour sent men and women scrambling under the scaffold for 'fresh green new relics' in order to make saints of their martyrs, even though Rome would not recognise them as such until the twentieth century. Here were English Catholics, in defiance of Elizabethan law and free from the strict regulations of Tridentine Europe, attempting to seize the initiative and reclaim their faith.

Not all of their co-religionists were delighted with their behaviour. According to Friswood Williams, who was 'dispossessed' soon after her younger sister Sara, the exorcisms divided the community 'in so much as divers ancient Catholics themselves did utterly dislike them, and the priests themselves grew to be afraid'. Sara herself later claimed that one priest, Father Yaxley, shook his head when she told him what had happened to her, and said 'he was very sorry for it, and that he hoped they had repented themselves for dealing so with her'. When pressed for his opinion as to whether or not Sara had actually been demonically possessed, he closed ranks and 'would give her no other answer, but shaking his head, will[ed] her to be contented, seeing all was now past'.[8]

Nor, it seems, were the exorcisms particularly effective in winning souls. Had the priest who boasted of five hundred conversions been remotely accurate, one would have expected a robust response from the authorities, but there was little evidence of immediate concern. According to Weston, Lord Burghley 'merely laughed' when informed of the practice and 'brushed it all aside as probable fraud and as a series of impostures devised by priests in order to deceive people'.[9]

At the turn of the century, however, the events of 1585–6 became interesting to the establishment and an investigation was launched. It may be that with time the popular appeal of spirit dispossession had grown, but there were also intersectarian rivalries at play. The enquiry was spearheaded by the Bishop of London, Richard Bancroft, and his chaplain, Samuel Harsnett, the future Archbishop of York. In 1603 Harsnett published his findings in a book entitled:

> A Declaration of Egregious Popish Impostures, to with-draw the harts of
> her Majesties Subiects from their allegeance, and from the truth of
> Christian Religion professed in England, under the pretence of
> casting out devils.
> Practised by Edmunds, alias Weston a Jesuit, and divers Romish
> Priests his wicked associates.
> Where-unto are annexed the Copies of the Confessions, and Examinations
> of the parties themselves, which were pretended to be possessed, and
> dispossessed, taken upon oath before her Majesties Commissioners, for
> Causes Ecclesiasticall.[10]

The full title betrays the churchmen's agenda. William Weston was only one of around twelve Catholic priests involved in the exorcisms of the mid-1580s, and he was the only Jesuit, but Harsnett gave him prominence in order to discredit the Society and capitalise on the divisions within the Catholic community at the time of publication. Harsnett and Bancroft insisted that the age of miracles had long since ceased. They had recently secured the conviction for fraud of John Darrell, a radical Puritan exorcist, and they extracted 'confessions' from some of the 1585–6 demoniacs in their ongoing campaign to expose all such practices as 'diabolical legerdemain'.[11]

Harsnett's retrospective commentary on the events at Hackney, Denham and elsewhere is no more reliable, therefore, than the heavily didactic accounts written by the Catholic eyewitnesses. Both are exploitative works of religious propaganda. Harsnett's latest editor has shown that he asked leading questions, suppressed information that did not suit his agenda and may even have tampered with witness statements.[12] Needless to say, his 'immodest style and lascivious pen' (as one Puritan divine described it[13]) attracted the playwrights of the day. The *Declaration* was a source for Ben Jonson's *Volpone* and supplied

Shakespeare with the names of the fake demons by which Edgar protected himself from unfair persecution.

In Harsnett's hands, the exorcism of Sara Williams is a sordid tale of mental, physical and sexual abuse. It may very well be the case that some readers have concluded as much from the Catholic account extracted above from the Brudenell manuscript. After all, a group of men in authority had fumigated a teenaged girl with noxious substances and forced her to imbibe a 'hallowed drink' that made her vomit. At one stage of the proceedings, Sara had suffered a 'beating . . . about the head with a maniple'; at another, she had been forced to wear an alb.* Her torture and humiliation before a conventicle of her superiors must have been terrifying. After complaining that the devil 'lieth in the bottom of my belly', she had also had to endure a relic being applied there by 'one of the women' in the Vaux household. After much torment, the devil had reportedly left her body 'in the likeness of water'.

According to Sara's deposition, taken sixteen years later on 24 April 1602 and published the following year in Harsnett's *Declaration*, the priests, 'when they were weary with dealing with her', would announce that:

> the wicked spirits were gone down into her leg, and sometimes into her foot, and that they should rest there for that time. And again, when they took her in hand the next time, they would begin to hunt the devil from the foot to bring him upwards, of purpose as they said to cause him, when they had him in her head, to go out of her mouth, ears, eyes, or nose. And the manner of their hunting of him was to follow him with their hands (as they did pretend) along all the parts of her body.
>
> At one time, when it began to be with this examinate according to the manner of women (as since she hath perceived), whereby she was much troubled, the priests did pretend that the devil did rest in the most secret part of her body. Whereupon they devised to apply the relics unto it, and gave her such sliber-sauces as made her (as she was

---

*A maniple was a Eucharistic vestment consisting of a strip of material worn suspended from the left arm, near the wrist. The alb was a white linen vestment reaching to the feet and bound at the waist with a girdle.

persuaded) much worse than otherwise she thinketh she should have been. At some times they would cause a maid that served the Lord Vaux to apply the relics unto the place: the which their dealing with her (she saith) she doth now loathe the memory of it.[14]

'Good God!' Harsnett exclaimed, 'what do we hear? Or is it but a dream? Or have we ears to hear such impious unnatural villainy?' He lambasted the 'fiery holy hands' of the priests, 'having a rank itch in their fingers to be fiddling at that sport'. He questioned why the devil would go anywhere near 'that nameless part' in Sara, since the priests had made it their 'quest and haunt which they had hunted sore, had crossed, recrossed and surcrossed with their holy hands'.[15]

It seems a tragedy that something as natural as the onset of menstruation could be interpreted as a sign of possession, but contemporaries were convinced of the ubiquity of the devil, who was known to delight in blood, and the 'monthly flux of excrementitous and unprofitable blood' was regarded with suspicion and hostility.[16] Menstruating women were polluted and polluting and if, like Sara and her fellow demoniac Anne Smith, they suffered from 'fits of the mother' – a condition that seems to have combined period pains and hysteria – then there might have been further cause to single them out for the exorcist's chair.* The intense drama of the exorcisms may also have encouraged over-credulity and the suspension of common sense. If Sara's stomach rumbled, the priests would make it a 'wonderful matter'. Likewise, another demoniac, William Trayford, was suspected of having a devil in his toe because he sometimes 'felt a spice of the gout'. Harsnett reacted at his sneering best:

* 'Mother' was a common word for the womb. One of the male demoniacs, Richard Mainy, also claimed to have suffered from 'the mother', though his symptoms reveal little more than headache and trapped wind. There is a remarkable correlation between the rituals of exorcism and contemporary remedies for irregular periods. To treat amenorrhoea (cessation of menstruation), it was thought that noxious fumes at the nose might drive the blood down. For immoderate menstruation, medicines, fumigations, injections to the womb, pessaries and the inducement of vomiting were recommended. Around the time of the publication of Harsnett's *Declaration* in 1603, the physician Edward Jorden produced *A Briefe Discourse of a Disease called the Suffocation of the Mother*, in which he diagnosed 'the mother' as a hysterical condition with natural causes. Both tracts were almost certainly commissioned by Bancroft's faction and can be seen as part of the campaign to destroy belief in spirit possession.

Now, what a woeful taking are all those poor creatures that have about them by birth, casualty or mishap any close imper, ache or other more secret infirmity? When a pain in a maid's belly, a stitch in her side, an ache in her head, a cramp in her leg, a tinkling in her toe (if the good exorcist please), must needs hatch a devil and bring forth such chair-work, fire-work, and devil-work as you shall hear hereafter?[17]

Although Sara later condemned the *Miracle Book* writers 'for their false and dissembling dealing with her', she was wary of accusing her own exorcists of fraud. At the time and during her subsequent exam-ination when she was encouraged to cast aspersions, she seems to have believed that they had acted in good faith. Indeed, she admitted that she would 'feed them with visions, saying she had seen this and that when she had seen no such matter, but only spake to content them'.[18] The priests saw and heard what they fervently wanted to see and hear: a terrified girl, susceptible to maladies and mood swings, inhabited by the devil and in desperate need of the miraculous cure that only the Catholic Church could provide. Harsnett, Bancroft and their faction were equally bent on concluding that Sara was a victim of 'egregious Popish imposture'. If both camps were guilty of sensa-tional writing, it might charitably be attributed to artistic licence: reality might have been heightened, but it was still reality, still the truth in the eyes of its beholders.[19]

It is not the historian's job to make lofty judgements. The rights and wrongs of the case depended, and perhaps still depend, very much on one's viewpoint. There were the inevitable few who acted in bad faith,* but most, surely, did not. William Weston was so certain of the miraculous and proselytising power of the exorcisms that he 'wished that the Queen had been present, or one of her Council, to witness the sights, or that they could have taken place in public'.[20] The Vauxes, for their part, not only hosted some of the sessions, but

---

* The apostate priest Anthony Tyrrell, for example, claimed that 'all was but coun-terfeit' and admitted to having written up events 'with the best skill I had to make them seem strange and wonderful' (*DEP*, p. 394). He did, however, threaten to revoke his confession should he ever reconvert to Catholicism. Regarding the demoniacs, Richard Mainy confessed to having feigned his visions and it is likely that Sara's sister, Friswood, 'one of nature's fablers' according to Harsnett's editor (Brownlow, p. 77), lied in her deposition against the priests.

also regaled guests with the details afterwards. The keynote was triumphalism. There is no reason to doubt that most spectators were indeed
'astonished' by the charisma of the priests and the miracle they believed
they had seen. Their pity for Sara – 'there was not one person which
beheld her distress whose eyes flowed not with tears for compassion
of her pains'[21] – was transformed into thanksgiving at her deliverance.
Harsnett may have mocked their credulity, but he did not question
the sincerity of their emotions.

On 8 October 1586, Sara's confessor and exorcist, Robert Dibdale
(born around thirty years earlier in the parish of Stratford-upon-Avon),
was executed at Tyburn. Shortly afterwards, Sara was imprisoned in
Oxford for recusancy, though there is no record of her being questioned about exorcism. It took fourteen weeks of 'earnest suit' and a
great deal of venison 'bestowed upon the scholars' to secure her
release. She was sheltered by the recusant community and 'conveyed
from place to place for almost four years'. In the early 1590s, she was
examined about the exorcisms, but refused to disclose anything and
it was only in April 1602, after her sister had informed on her, that
Sara gave a deposition. By then she was in her thirties, married and
a mother of five, despite the fears of the priests at Hackney that 'the
devil had torn those parts in such sort as that she could not conceive'.[22]

It may be no coincidence that Sara's married name, Cheney,
belonged to 'a house of great worship in Northamptonshire' that was
intimately associated with the Vauxes. Lord Vaux's mother had been
a Cheney and there are several relatives – Mary, Giles, Lawrence,
Thomas, Ursula and John Cheney – cited in the wills of the baron
and his wife. John Cheney was Lord Vaux's solicitor and knew his
secrets; Lawrence was listed as a Catholic prisoner at the Counter in
Wood Street for a brief summer spell in 1586; Giles, 'gent. of Irthlingborough, Northants', was convicted of a year's recusancy from May
1586. Another Cheney, William, 'yeoman . . . of Hackney', was indicted
'for not going to any usual place of Common Prayer' in 1585 alongside
his master, Lord Vaux.[23] If Sara was ever married to one of these
Cheneys, or another from the family, it would be interesting to discover
if it was to secure her protection or her silence, or was simply a matter
of love.

In the course of her semi-conscious ravings, Sara had vented her

frustration at the intense piety, oppressive secrecy and uncompromising tenets that governed the lives of the Vauxes and their servants.
Her taunting of the priests and threat to raise a hue and cry against
them gave expression to latent hostilities and a siege-like mentality
within the household. Her ventriloquised expletives – 'God's wounds!',
'A pox on you!' – and the references to her as a 'poor wench' give us
a flavour of the language of the time.* She even provides a snapshot
of a Hackney Christmas: one vision she had of the devil coming in
'with a drum and seven motley vizards, dancing about the chamber'
was directly influenced by the 'gaming and mumming at the Lord
Vaux his house'.[24]

When Vaux had first been cited as a recusant in May 1581, he had
defended himself by claiming that his home was 'a parish by itself'.
As the years went by and the laws against nonconformity grew in
number and severity, Elizabethan recusants increasingly closed ranks.
They continued to engage with institutions and people beyond their
immediate community, but, as much for the sake of their Protestant
neighbours (most of whom had no desire to inform on their friends)
as themselves, the inner sanctum of the recusant household became
harder to penetrate. Whatever the rights and wrongs of the exorcism
of Sara Williams, whatever the truths, half-truths and untruths, it
affords a fleeting glimpse into that shuttered world and the hopes,
fears, mores and mentality of those who lived and served within it.
Sara's voice was hijacked by demons, Catholic propagandists, Establishment churchmen and playwrights. It is manifestly artificial and,
paradoxically, a deeply authentic expression of its time.

Before we leave Sara drugged by 'sliber-sauces' with a face 'blacker
than ever I saw a chimney sweeper's', there is one final aspect of this
strange series of events to be noted. Nicholas Marwood, the subject
of 'the prime grand miracle' at Hackney, was the servant of Anthony
Babington, a young gentleman from Derbyshire. Babington had
attended the exorcisms 'oftentimes' with 'divers of his company'.[25]
The previous spring he had stood surety for George Vaux, who was

---

* Alongside a passage containing one of Sara's blasphemous outbursts, the Catholic
narrator has written in the margin of the Brudenell Manuscript (p. 185): 'The devil
sweareth & speaketh as Protestants use to do.'

bound to keep the peace after an unspecified incident in London. This was no small matter as it meant forfeiting twenty pounds if George defaulted on his bond.[26] Two days later, on 26 May 1585, Babington had called at Hackney and presented Lady Vaux with a silver and gilt basin and ewer 'for her friendship'. He and Lord Vaux had talked for 'about three hours'. According to the goldsmith's apprentice who accompanied Babington, their discussion concerned 'the sale of a lordship which the said Babington was in hand to purchase of the said Lord'.[27]

The Hackney exorcist and Jesuit superior, William Weston, who claimed to have talked 'intimately' and 'very frequently' with Babington, described him as young, not yet thirty, good-looking, charismatic and witty. Babington was well travelled, well mannered and well read. 'When in London, he drew to himself by the force of his exceptional charm and personality many young Catholic gentlemen of his own standing.' These men were 'gallant, adventurous and daring in defence of the Catholic faith'. They were 'ready,' wrote Weston, 'for any arduous enterprise whatsoever that might advance the common Catholic cause.'[28]

According to the servant of a friend of Babington, 'the Lord Vaux's son' was one of a dozen men whose company 'Mr Babington did usually or otherwise frequent'.[29] On the face of it, therefore, Anthony Babington was a man whom the Vauxes liked and trusted. On 14 August 1586, he was arrested for conspiring to kill the Queen.

7

Atheistical Anthony Babington's Complotment

Madam, I stand charged by you to have practised something
against you. I call God and all the world to witness I have not
done anything as a private man unworthy of an honest man, nor
as a public man unworthy of my calling. I protest before God
that as a man careful of my mistress's safety, I have been curious.

Sir Francis Walsingham to Mary Queen of Scots at her trial,
Fotheringhay, 14 October 1586

The Babington Plot was a conspiracy to assassinate Queen Elizabeth
and replace her with Mary Queen of Scots. Like its predecessors, it
relied for success on papal sanction, foreign aid, internal Catholic
support and government incompetence. Like its predecessors, it
failed. Indeed, the plot was probably most welcome to Burghley and
Walsingham, who had been patiently waiting for a foolish young
firebrand to come along and put the 1585 Act for the Queen's Surety
to the test.

The Babington Plot is the most notorious of the schemes to overthrow the English Queen because it precipitated the destruction of
her Scottish cousin. Rocked by the 'enormous ingratitude' of her son
James, who had decided that the defence of his mother's dynastic
interests was not necessarily compatible with his own, Mary Stuart
had grown desperate and reckless. She had been a prisoner in England
for eighteen years, latterly at Chartley Manor in Staffordshire under
the beady eye of Sir Amyas Paulet, who crowed that nothing and no
one could be conveyed to her without his knowledge. He was quite
right. When a local young Catholic called Gilbert Gifford turned up

with a warm recommendation from Mary's Paris agent and an offer to serve as her secret postman, Paulet knew all about it. As did Walsingham, for Gifford was in the spymaster's pay, a double agent primed to win Mary's confidence and secure her destruction.

Unsuspecting Mary was delighted to resume contact with her friends in the French embassy. She passed on spying tips: alum was unreliable as a secret ink, messages might be hidden in books or the soles of shoes. She even sent the ambassador the key to a new cipher. Walsingham and his chief intelligence officer, Thomas Phelippes, intercepted everything and when Gifford used a new way of smuggling letters in and out of Chartley – via a watertight container slipped through the bung-hole of a beer keg – these too were seized, copied, resealed and only then delivered to their intended recipients. By the time Anthony Babington emerged with a 'desperate truculent' plan to lay 'violent hands upon her Majesty's sacred person',[1] the trap to catch Mary was perfectly poised.

There has been much debate over the architecture of the so-called Babington Plot. The eponymous conspirator was not its chief designer, though it was Babington's letter of 6 July 1586 that floated to Mary the plan for 'the dispatch of the usurper'. Babington wrote that there were 'six noble gentlemen, all my private friends', who were willing to undertake 'that tragical execution'. He claimed to have been approached in May by a priest called John Ballard, 'a man of virtue and learning', who had liaised in Paris with several English exiles and the Spanish ambassador there about the viability of an invasion to deliver England from 'the extreme and miserable state wherein it hath too long remained'.[2] Other men, including Gifford (with Walsingham pulling his strings), were on board from an early stage.

Babington seems to have been something of a fantasist. As vain as he was charming, he was attracted to the potential glamour of the plot and the romanticism of rescuing a Catholic damsel. There were moments – when he was not penning quixotic letters or commissioning portraits of himself and his accomplices – when doubts crept in, but Ballard and Gifford were on hand with resolve-stiffening pep talks. When, in early August, Babington finally realised that the game was up, he cut his hair, smeared his face with walnut juice and made for the country in the guise of a farm labourer. He was captured in a barn, a rather bathetic showdown for a man who liked to be seen in 'ostentatious splendour'.[3]

Babington might have been arrested much earlier. His letter was proof enough of his treason. But Walsingham wanted Mary. Her reply, drafted in French, then translated and enciphered by her secretary, was slipped into the beer keg on the morning of 18 July. The following day Phelippes deciphered the text and sent a transcript to Walsingham. Ten days later, the original was delivered to Babington, who destroyed it. A postscript had been added by Phelippes, asking for the 'names and qualities' of the six assassins. It was an audacious forgery, but the main substance of the letter, which commended Babington and gave advice on how to 'ground substantially this enterprise and to bring it to good success', was most likely genuine. Babington and Mary's two secretaries would later attest its contents. Mary's approbation for the assassination of Elizabeth is obvious, if not explicit:

> The affairs being thus prepared and forces in readiness both without and within the realm, then shall it be time to set the six gentlemen to work, taking order, upon the accomplishing of their design, I may be suddenly transported out of this place, and that all your forces in the same time be on the field to meet me in tarrying for the arrival of the foreign aid, which then must be hastened with all diligence.[4]

Phelippes sensed Mary's death knell in these words and sketched a gallows on the outside of his transcript. The Vauxes and their friends thought Elizabeth would not dare put her cousin to death 'for fear of afterclaps'.[5] They were wrong. Mary was tried not far from Harrowden, at Fotheringhay Castle, and, despite much hand-wringing by Elizabeth I, was beheaded there on the morning of Wednesday, 8 February 1587.

Anthony Babington had ascended the scaffold the previous September along with John Ballard and twelve others. He was in the first batch of executions that were undertaken 'not without some note of cruelty'. That is to say, the hanging was kept brief so that the victims were still conscious when cut down, castrated and disembowelled. The Queen had called for an even worse form of punishment, according to Burghley, something that would inflict 'further extra-ordinary pain', but he had assured her that 'the manner of the death would be as terrible as any other new device could be'.[6]

'In the midst of our calamities,' William Weston recalled, 'the bells were rung throughout the city, sermons and festivals [were] held, fireworks set off, bonfires lit in the public street – a customary and unmistakable manner of manifesting public joy – and with one cry the whole people exulted and clapped their hands over the wretched-ness of the papist traitors.'[7]

It was an uncomfortable time for the Vauxes, whose links to Babington appeared suspicious. On 9 August 1586, 'the Lord Vaux his son' was noted in a list, now in the British Library, of 'persons to be sought after'. His name appeared alongside several plotters, including Robert Barnwell, whose servant had fingered 'the L. Vaux's son' as a member of 'the company which Mr Babington did usually or otherwise frequent'. Of those identified in the manuscript as 'familiarly acquainted with Barn-well', two names – 'French, gent.' and 'Humfrey Wheeler of the Inner Temple' – recall an undated informer's report in the State Papers:

> There is one Mr Wheeler that dwelleth behind St Clement's Church towards the fields that hath resort unto him the Lord Vaux and his son and divers other papists very often and, as it is thought, they have Mass said there, or some lewd practices. The accuser: Mr French, Gentleman of the Temple.[8]

Anthony Babington had helped bail out George Vaux on 24 May 1585. A couple of days later he had spent three hours with Lord Vaux at Hackney negotiating a property sale. We only know about the meeting because Vaux's servant, Walter Wolsley, subsequently got into trouble for some loose words uttered in praise of the imprisoned Earl of Northumberland, a prominent supporter of Mary Stuart. He also championed another Catholic, John Talbot of Grafton, whom Ballard would attempt, without success, to draw into the plot. Wolsley was reported by the goldsmith's apprentice who had accompanied Babington to Hackney.* Upon examination, he protested that he had

---

* The apprentice seems to have resented Wolsley's clumsy attempt to convert him: Wolsley had taken out an old devotional manual 'and of purpose laid it open in the window'. The apprentice recalled that it contained advice on confession and fasting,

'meant no evil at all', but his indiscretion earned him a spell in the Counter prison in Wood Street. In 1592 Sir Thomas Tresham would describe him as Lord Vaux's 'chief servant'.[9]

Although Vaux's business with Babington had commenced a full year before the conspirator claimed to have been recruited by Ballard, it nevertheless brought him unwelcome attention. There is an intriguing document in the records of the Exchequer entitled:

> Interrogatories to be ministered to Edward Smythe of Loughborough in the county of Leicester for the finding of John Smyth of London, grocer, to which John and one John Palmer, Anthony Babington, attainted of treason, caused lands to be conveyed upon trust to his own use by the Lord Vaux.[10]

Trusts were a common recourse for landowners in danger of fine or forfeiture and were particularly popular with Catholics. Smythe and Palmer were known recusants and were listed, along with 'the Lord Vaux his son', in the British Library manuscript detailing persons of interest in the Babington investigation. Both are described there as 'very inward with Babington', with Smythe 'said to be gone into Derbyshire with the sisters of Babington'. Smythe had earlier accompanied Babington to Hackney. He is sometimes described as a grocer, sometimes an apothecary (useful professions for someone wanting people and packages to come and go without suspicion). When Babington had travelled to France, he had put Smythe in charge of 'all that he had'.[11] The other trustee in the Babington–Vaux transaction, John Palmer, was arrested in Loughborough in his home county of Leicestershire a few days before Babington's execution. His chambers were searched, but no 'writing or letters concerning her Majesty or the Estate' were found.[12] Lord Vaux, it seems, was untouched, though it wasn't just Babington with whom he had links.

The priest John Ballard *alias* Fortescue, upon whom Babington would lay 'all the blame . . . for bringing him to his destruction', had liaised with Hugh Yates, 'sometimes servant to the Lord Vaux his son', at the White Hart Inn, Holborn, in 1584. He was frequently attended by 'a man and a boy' and liked to dress 'in a grey cloak laid on with

as well as 'divers printed pictures of the Virgin Mary, of saints and other superstitious toys, which book this examinate [the apprentice] misliking threw aside.'

gold lace, in velvet hose, a cut satin doublet, a fair hat of the newest fashion, the band being set with silver buttons'. On 26 May 1586 he was identified as one of a handful of priests 'lodged in common inns about London', who received 'their relief of Edmunds the Jesuit [William Weston], who receives the same of Mr Henry [Vaux], that daily collecteth money for the same purpose'.[13] Unwittingly or not, therefore, Henry Vaux had helped to fund a priest who had been planning an act of terror. Whether this made him an accessory to the plot or simply a naïve idealist who wanted to do his bit for the mission, it certainly explains why the authorities wanted to talk to him.

Ballard was also named as one of the exorcist-priests who had prac- tised their 'devil work' at various Catholic homes throughout the autumn, winter and spring of 1585–6. Samuel Harsnett later tried to claim that the exorcisms, which he wanted everyone to think were fraudulent, were part of the Babington Plot. According to the dubious testimony of Anthony Tyrrell, an exorcist who quickly turned informant after his arrest in July 1586, the dispossessions 'procured unto ourselves very great favour, credit and reputation, so as it was no marvel if some young gentlemen, as Master Babington and the rest, were allured to those strange attempts which they took in hand by Master Ballard, who was an agent amongst us'. Tyrrell, who recanted his faith on several occasions, claimed that the exorcisms were part of the battle for 'the hearts and minds of Catholics', so that 'when such forces as were intended should have come into England, they might have been more readily drawn . . . to have joined their forces with them'.[14]

Sara and Friswood Williams were less keen on making a direct connection between the exorcisms and the plot, noting only that Babington and 'most of the rest that were executed' had sometimes watched. It is hardly surprising that in the small world of Catholic recusancy, Babington and his crew had heard about, and been attracted to, an aggressive counter-reforming initiative. It may even be the case that the spectacular scenes they witnessed contributed to the reckless optimism that would draw them into the plot some months later. This cannot be proven and even if it could, it would by no means follow that the Vauxes, as hosts to several exorcisms including that of Babington's servant Marwood, were party to the plot.[15]

Try as it might, the government could find no formal connection between the exorcisms and the Babington Plot. 'In all their most detailed examinations of the prisoners,' William Weston recalled, 'there was nothing they could find against me.'[16] Another Hackney exorcist, Thomas Stamp, whose 'flearing countenance' Sara would never forget, was, upon his arrest in September 1586, 'specially to be dealt withal and touched for this last conspiracy'. It was noted that he 'did much harm in the Lord Vaux his house', but he could not be implicated in the conspiracy and was soon carted off to Wisbech Castle in Cambridgeshire, where he joined several of his fellow exorcists, none of whom was brought to trial for involvement in the Babington Plot.[17]

If there was any hard evidence to substantiate Tyrrell's claim that the exorcisms at Hackney and elsewhere were deliberately staged to win 'hearts and minds' in advance of invasion; if it could be proven that Lord Vaux and Anthony Babington had ever discussed treason during their property negotiations; if it could be stated with any kind of certainty that Henry Vaux had known about Ballard's plans when he had given him (via Weston) some of the mission's funds, then a case linking the Vauxes to the Babington Plot might be more substantial. As it stands, all is suspicion and circumstance. It is little wonder that Babington, Ballard and several of their accomplices had crossed paths with members of the Vaux family. George and Ambrose had mingled with exile communities on their travels abroad and Henry had worked alongside several conspirators in the early days of the Jesuit mission. Indeed, Lord Vaux's eldest son was such a crucial cog in the machinery of the Catholic underground that the real shock would have come from finding no link. One can hardly be deemed guilty of plotting for knowing a conspirator, still less for knowing the associates of a conspirator. While the Vauxes clearly hung from the fringes of the Babington Plot, they cannot, or at least not now unless new evidence comes to light, be woven convincingly into its fabric.

Nevertheless, the assumption certainly existed in some exile circles that Lord Vaux could be relied upon 'if any foreign power should come to invade this realm'.[18] His brother-in-law, Tresham, was also claimed as a potential insurgent. In August 1586 Bernardino de Mendoza, the Spanish ambassador in Paris, who had liaised with the plotters earlier in the year, reported to Philip II that Vaux, Tresham and three other recusant gentlemen, 'have not been informed of the business, as they are declared Catholics and are consequently held prisoners by the Queen and under very heavy money penalties, but it is confidently assumed that, as others far less interested are joining the design, they certainly will do so'.[19]

Mendoza was misinformed. Ballard had attempted to recruit Tresham the previous month and not only had Tresham refused to hear him, but he had also 'threatened to discover him'.[20] Perhaps Tresham really was the loyal Elizabethan that he always claimed to be, or perhaps he had suspected '*latet anguis in herba* [a snake in the grass]'. If not at the time, then certainly seventeen years later, he was of the opinion that 'atheistical Anthony Babington's complotment' was a 'cursed Machiavellian project' of the government's making.[21] Whatever Tresham's motives, he was wise to stay out of the conspiracy and so, it seems, were his Vaux relations. 'Of all the plots they have hatched these many years past,' Mendoza informed his master in August, 'none have been apparently so serious as this.' Let God 'dispose as He will,' he continued, 'but if for our sins He should decree that it shall not succeed, there will be much Catholic blood spilt in England.'

'Yes,' Philip II scribbled on the letter, 'that is what is to be feared.'[22]

*

> The day is gone and yet I saw no sun,
> And now I live and now my life is done.

Thus wrote Babington's accomplice, Chidiock Tichborne, just days before his execution. Once again, youth and talent had fallen at the feet of fanaticism. It seems a terrible waste:

> The spring is past and yet it hath not sprung,
> The fruit is dead and yet the leaves are green,
> My youth is gone and yet I am but young,
> I saw the world and yet I was not seen.
> My thread is cut and yet it was not spun,
> And now I live and now my life is done.[23]

8

Lambs to the Slaughter

> It was a period of very great confusion for us all. Every road, cross-way and port was watched night and day, and sealed off so effectively that no person could pass without the most rigorous examination. Lodging-houses, private homes, rooms were searched and examined with minute thoroughness; neither friend nor acquaintance could escape without being forced to give an account of himself. In this way many priests were captured, and Catholics filled the prisons throughout the country.
>
> William Weston, S.J., *Autobiography*

Just before sunrise on 7 July 1586, a Kentish shepherd stood on a bluff and looked out to sea. His eye fixed on a small boat sailing smoothly towards the shore. It was a strange place to land, so far from the harbour. At length, one of the sailors alighted and, taking a passenger upon his back, waded ashore. He set him down, returned to his vessel, conveyed a second man over the water, then struck sail. The shepherd continued to stand and stare. 'He was scrutinising us carefully,' one of the travellers recalled, 'and was obviously asking himself who were these people who landed at this unusual place.'[1]

They were Henry Garnet and Robert Southwell, Jesuit emissaries from Rome. By putting priestly foot to English sand, they were committing high treason. Derbyshire-born Garnet was in his early thirties and possessed of a fair complexion, a 'comely' gait and a hairline that might already have begun to recede. He was the son of a schoolmaster and had been a scholar at Winchester and an employee at Richard Tottel's famous printworks* before going abroad to study

---

*Richard Tottel was the publisher of the first anthology of English verse, popularly

for the priesthood. At Rome, where he became a Jesuit priest, he was known as the 'poor sheep' on account of his shyness.[2] It had been eleven years since he had seen his homeland.

Robert Southwell was six years younger than Garnet and more striking, both physically and temperamentally. He had auburn hair, the bearing of a gentleman and the jagged intensity of a poet. One admirer called him 'the rarest & most eloquent Ciceronian of our age'. He had left England at the age of fourteen and just before his seventeenth birthday had entered the novitiate of the Society of Jesus, 'that body,' he wrote, 'wherein lyeth all my life, my love, my whole heart and affection'.[3]

They had been travelling for two months, having left Rome at the beginning of May. The Society General, Claudio Aquaviva, had initially been reluctant to give his blessing to this new phase of the English mission. Garnet, in particular, he had thought 'more suited to the quiet life rather than the unsure and worrisome one that must be lived in England'.[4] But even as he lamented that he was sending 'lambs to the slaughter', Aquaviva was persuaded of the need for reinforcements in England. 'Pray send men to help us and someone to take charge,' Weston had begged in April, 'then we shall gather in sheaves on sheaves with laden arms.' Under pressure from Allen and Persons, Aquaviva had relented. Garnet was appointed the senior member on the journey and successor to Weston should the Jesuit superior ever lose his life or liberty. 'The need for prudence is very great,' Weston warned.[5]

Writing 'from death's ante-room', just before his passage to England, the 24-year-old Southwell veered from bullish defiance to blanket fear:

> I know very well that sea and land are gaping wide for me, and lions as well as wolves go prowling in search of whom they may devour. But I welcome more than fear their fangs. Rather than shrink from them as torturers, I call to them to bring my crown. It is true that the flesh is weak and can do nothing and even now revolts from that which is proposed . . . I do not dare to hope what I so violently desire, but

---

known as *Tottel's Miscellany*. It included several poems by Thomas, second Lord Vaux, and was an extremely influential text. Shakespeare owned a copy. When Henry Garnet worked at the printer's in 1574, the book was in its seventh edition.

if I reach, God willing, the lowest rank of happy martyrs, I will not
be unmindful of those who have remembered me.[6]

The government knew that they were coming, but not where they
would land. A special watch had been placed on the ports. 'I must
say,' Garnet admitted, 'we felt a thrill of fear' under the shepherd's
gaze. 'However, the die was cast, and we must try our luck.' So they
marched up to the man with as much outrage as they could feign and
began to rail against their boatman for depositing them in this unlikely
spot. The shepherd was 'a very honest fellow', Garnet wrote, and
'most indignant at the wrong done to us'. He pointed out their location – not far from Folkestone – and 'described to us at length the
places round about, and the right way to get to them'.

After this 'merry' encounter, the priests received more good fortune.
It was the feast day of St Thomas of Canterbury and amidst the
crowds flocking to the fair, no one was suspicious of the two Jesuits
with oddly cut clothes and slightly strange accents, who 'made our
confessions to each other as we walked along'. They decided to separate and reunite in London with Weston. Southwell found himself a
horse and made good progress. Garnet began on foot and avoided
the coastal towns 'like the plague'. Both found the capital safely and
hailed each other in the street. 'For five or six hours,' Garnet recalled,
'we walked about the city, but we did not see a single friend. Then,
by chance, we met the man we were looking for.'[7]

It had been agreed at Hoxton the previous year that any priests
'determined to remain in England, or [who] hereafter shall come into
England, shall be relieved at the hands of Mr Henry Vaux, son to the
Lord Vaux, or by his assigns'.[8] If Henry was not the Jesuits' first
contact, then in all likelihood it was one of his men. They were given
breakfast, escorted to an inn and asked to wait for their superior. On
13 July 1586, Weston came and dined with his new recruits. He was
delighted to see them, but fretful. As the evening drew in, they changed
location. A few hours later, Anthony Babington (under suspicion, but
not yet under arrest) arrived and spoke to Weston.[9] The following
day the three Jesuits, presumably with the help of Henry Vaux, rode
out of the city gates and made for the Chilterns. 'The news of our
coming has already spread abroad,' Southwell wrote in his first letter
from England, 'and from the lips of the Queen's Council my name

had become known to certain persons. The report alarms our enemies, who fear heaven knows what at our hands, so nervous have they now become.'[10]

The priests and their lay assistants settled in a house, thought to be Hurleyford in Buckinghamshire, where they enjoyed a week of relative calm. On the banks of the Thames, to music by William Byrd,* the company sung Mass, heard confessions, prayed, preached and worshipped together. But this was no summer retreat. The fear of arrest hovered in the air and the practicalities of the mission intruded upon spiritual exercises. Weston briefed his juniors on the strategy for survival in Protestant England. He provided them with the names of friends and the locations of safe houses. He told them about the fund that he had set up with Henry Vaux at Hoxton the previous year. And he directed their onward journeys, Garnet to the country, South-well to the city. The Vauxes were to be their first hosts, entrusted with the crucial task of keeping them alive long enough for them to make a difference.[11] The decision speaks volumes for the Society's faith in the Vaux family and vice versa.

The missionaries were buoyed by their reception. 'We have had the happiest possible arrival in England,' Southwell enthused on 25 July. 'Things would be terrible here,' Garnet opined five days later,

> if we had only our enemies to think of, and wonderful if there were only the Catholics and their fervour. They show no fear of sheltering us at any time; and so great is our friends' opinion of the Society that we are forced to conceal that we are of it lest the whole of Jerusalem be disturbed.[12]

Within a few days, though, Babington was captured and the plot that bore his name was revealed to an outraged public. There were persistent rumours of a Spanish invasion. 'All highways were watched,' wrote Southwell, 'infinite houses searched, hues and cries raised, frights bruited in the people's ears, and all men's eyes filled with such

---

* Despite indictments for recusancy (sometimes alongside Lord Vaux and his sons), Byrd retained his position in the Chapel Royal. Queen Elizabeth was known, on occasion, to put talent before faith. It is conceivable that Shakespeare's 'bare ruined choirs, where late the sweet birds sang' (Sonnet 73) is a play on the composer's name. (Jeaffreson, I, pp. 163, 167; also pp. 127, 129, 143–4, 150, 158)

a smoke as though the whole realm had been on fire.'[13] The prisons overflowed with suspected conspirators and priests. Many Catholics were 'broken', Weston recalled:

> All men fastened their hatred on them. They lay in ambush for them, betrayed them, attacked them with violence and without warning. They plundered them at night, confiscated their possessions, drove away their flocks, stole their cattle.[14]

On 3 August 1586, just outside Bishopsgate, Weston was captured. Garnet automatically took over as Jesuit superior. For the next twenty years, while Weston was detained at Her Majesty's pleasure, Garnet headed the Jesuit mission in England. He would receive considerable assistance from two formidable ladies.

Robert Southwell, meanwhile, had returned to the London area, where he described the pursuivants prowling, 'lynx-eyed'. He quartered with the Vauxes at Hackney and worked closely with Henry for the relief of the missionary priests. 'Hemmed in by daily perils, never safe for even a brief moment', he also heard confessions, prepared sermons and carried out 'other priestly duties', including absolving three seminary priests of their sins as they hung from a Tyburn gibbet. 'Such is the multitude of spies,' he informed General Aquaviva, 'that we cannot set foot out of doors, nor walk in the streets, without danger to our lives.'[15]

The greatest jeopardy, however, was closer to home. Sometime the previous July, a priest called Anthony Tyrrell was arrested, interrogated and turned. He had been involved in the Hackney exorcisms and, in the autumn, gave up 'the names of divers priests where I understood they did haunt or lie'. On 5 November the Vaux house was raided. Richard Young, a notorious priest-hunter,* led the search

---

* Tyrrell described him as 'a most cruel bloodsucker', Southwell as a 'butcher of Catholics'. He was apparently so closely associated with the rack that it was known as 'Young's Fiddle'. According to the Jesuit John Gerard, Justice Young was 'the devil's confessor', who met a fitting end: 'Day and night he toiled to bring more and more pressure on Catholics, drawing up lists of names, giving instructions, listening to reports. Then one rainy night, at two or three o'clock, he got up to make a search of some Catholic houses. The effort left him exhausted; he became ill, contracted consumption and died.' Of course, none of these statements is without bias. Confessional writers (from both camps) seldom missed an opportunity to attribute divine wrath to the death or mishap of their enemies. (Gerard, *Autobiography,* p. 92; Kilroy, *Edmund Campion,* p. 93)

in person. He swooped first thing in the morning in an attempt to catch the family at Mass. His prime target was 'one Mr Sale, a priest that for certain,' said Tyrrell, 'did lie at the Lord Vaux his house'.[16] This may have been Southwell, who gave an account of a raid around this time:

> The pursuivants were raging all around and seeking me in the very house where I was lodged. I heard them threatening and breaking woodwork and sounding the walls to find hiding places; yet, by God's goodness, after four hours' search they found me not, though separated from them only by a thin partition rather than a wall. Of truth, the house was in such sort watched for many nights together that I perforce slept in my clothes in a very strait, uncomfortable place.[17]

Young was frustrated. He was certain there were priests in the house, 'conveyed away so that they could not be found'. Henry Davies and his wife, who were operatives in the underground movement and had ridden 'to my Lord Vaux and to Sir Thomas Tresham about secret causes', pretended that she was the sister of Mr Marbury of the Pantry. (One of the pursuivants, 'being greatly beholden' to this Marbury, 'passed them over with friendly speeches'.) According to a spy known as 'II' (real name: Maliverey Catilyn), Lord Vaux managed to distract another pursuivant long enough for his wife to squirrel away 'her little casket, which she would not for five hundred pounds had been searched'.[18] Indeed, the entire fruits of Young's fossicking boiled down to some letters, found in a bag belonging to Henry Vaux. They were written in Latin and signed 'Robert'. Initially thought to signal the return of Robert Persons from Rouen, the letters were subsequently recognised as Southwell's.[19] Henry was taken in for questioning. He refused to give anything away and was committed to the Marshalsea.*

That evening Lady Vaux sent for her brother, Sir Thomas Tresham, and his lawyer 'to give advice what course was best to be taken in the cause and behalf of her [step]son Henry'. The two men hurried over from Hoxton and 'after long talk' agreed to leave him 'to his own

---

* The Marshalsea prison in Southwark kept a substantial number of Catholic inmates. Depending on confessional bias, it was either 'a school of Christ' (Father Gerard) or 'a college of caitiffs' (Bishop Aylmer). (Gerard, *Autobiography*, pp. 4, 215)

answers', hoping that he would frame them 'so wisely . . . as he shall not need any other means of deliverance'.[20]

Half a year later, Henry was still languishing in prison. On 22 May 1587, Walsingham granted him three months' leave, probably on compassionate grounds.[21] He rode up to his sisters Eleanor and Anne in Leicestershire, the county where they had spent much of their childhood. He did not return to the Marshalsea in August 'according to the tenor of his bond'. His burial was recorded in the parish register of Great Ashby on 19 November 1587.[22] According to Garnet, who almost certainly attended him at the end, Henry suffered from a wasting disease brought on by his imprisonment. Robert Persons wrote that he died 'most sweetly and comfortably'. Another Jesuit, John Gerard, claimed that Henry's only deathbed regret was that he could not, 'there and then', be admitted into the Society of Jesus. He had been 'most anxious' to enter the Society and had, Garnet recalled, made a vow to that effect, telling Eleanor and Anne that he recognised God's favour and providence in men of the Order. 'I have no doubt,' he said to his sisters, 'that He will be propitious to them, that they in time will reap in this kingdom the same fruit from their labours as they have done elsewhere, for they are not excepted here from the injuries that they suffer in other countries.'[23]

The English mission lost a valuable asset when that 'boy of such great promise', as Campion had called Henry, died. Sir Thomas Tresham thought his young cousin a 'gentleman of rare worth'. For Garnet, he was 'a shining example of learning, innocence and piety'. Robert Persons even took it upon himself to play pope, declaring Henry Vaux a 'blessed gentleman and saint . . . whose life was a rare mirror of religion and holiness unto all that knew him and conversed with him'. The Queen's ministers would have vehemently disputed any notion of Henry's 'innocence', but even hostile sources acknowledged his significance. Walsingham's agent, Maliverey Catilyn, witnessed 'great lamentation' amongst the Catholics of Clerkenwell when Henry was arrested, for they had esteemed him 'a most singular young man'.[24]

Apart from a well-stocked library and eighteen extant poems (he considered himself an 'unripe yet rotten poet'), Henry left behind little of substance, having liquidated most of his assets and resigned his interest in the Vaux patrimony 'in order to devote himself entirely to God and to his studies'.[25] His chief legacy lay in the relief operation for Catholic priests that he had helped found and run. With his team of fixers, he had 'daily' handled money, intelligence and communications on behalf of the English mission. It helped that he had a 'pleasant demeanour', was 'accurate and quick at figures' and 'diligent in application'. Edmund Campion first spotted those traits in his nine-year-old pupil and they had served Henry well until his death nearly twenty years later. His pivotal role in the Catholic underground also required courage, self-sacrifice and a steely, single-minded belief in the cause. Small wonder that admirers thought Henry 'rare' and 'singular'.

But Campion had also recognised a match for Henry in the family. 'Your sister is your rival in study and in work,' the tutor had informed his charge in the summer of 1570: 'She shares the same intellectual interests and I warn you that if you underrate her now, even a little bit, and take things easy, she will achieve renown before and triumph over you.' Campion was almost certainly referring to Eleanor, the eldest of Henry's three sisters. He predicted that they would make 'a matchless pair' and 'shine with marvellous lustre'.[26] Fortunately for all those who relied upon her brother, Eleanor would not disappoint. Nor would her younger sister, Anne, who readily stepped into the breach.

The next phase of the English mission was an altogether different enterprise to that inaugurated by the seminary priests in 1574 or to the first Jesuit mission of 1580. The law had changed several times and was less frequently winked at. An Act 'for the more speedy and due execution' of the penal legislation (29 Eliz. c. 6), which came into force in March 1587, made fines cumulative and allowed the Crown to seize two-thirds of a defaulting recusant's estate. To be a practising Catholic in England was increasingly expensive, hazardous, stifling and demeaning. Homes were regularly raided. Rosaries, images, devotional books and treasured heirlooms were deemed unpatriotic, at best. Being a seminary priest was illegal; sheltering a seminary priest was illegal; both crimes courted the scaffold. With the Scottish Queen dead, the odds on a Catholic succession – and the restoration of the old faith by peaceful means – lengthened considerably. And England was at war with Spain, the Catholic Spain of Philip II, who still held his 'messianic vision' of world domination in sharp relief.

Focus shifted from attempting to debate the law (Campion's oft-declared objective) to finding the most discreet ways of breaking it. Catholic carpenters busied themselves with false walls, swinging beams, trap doors, loft conversions, 'chimney conveyances' and other tiny spaces in which priests and their kit could be stowed at a moment's notice. Resolutions were sought, and given, to allow priests and laymen to 'equivocate' (Protestants called it lying) to avoid incrimination. Casuist handbooks guided Catholics through what had become an ethical minefield. As Garnet put it, 'we forged new weapons for new battles.'[27] The Hoxton fund and the early ad hoc arrangements for incoming priests were regularised. The mission became bigger and slicker and, perhaps inevitably, plagued by infighting. Towards the end of 1586, Southwell warned future missioners to 'gird themselves for heavier trials than their companions have hitherto suffered, for the sea is more boisterous than usual and swept by fiercer storms'.[28]

In 1586 Philip II turned down the plan of the Council of the Indies to strengthen the defences of the Caribbean. Two years later he refused a request for extra reinforcements made by the Viceroy of India for an attack on the Sultan of Acheh. It was the same story in East Africa – a fortress at Mombasa could not be built – and in South East Asia, where the Spanish colonists of the Philippines were frustrated in their plan to launch an invasion of China.[29] The ruler who famously presided over an empire on which the sun never set had his eyes – and resources – fixed firmly on England. There were, assuredly, rough waters ahead.

PART TWO

ELEANOR AND ANNE

Spell 'Eva' back and 'Ave' shall you find,
The first began, the last reversed our harms;
An angel's witching words did Eva blind,
An angel's 'Ave' disenchants the charms.
    Death first by woman's weakness entered in;
    In woman's virtue life doth now begin.
     Robert Southwell, 'The Virgin's Salutation',
                   first stanza[1]

9

The Widow and the Virgin

Eleanor was the elder sister, the 'very learned and in every way accomplished lady', who had so impressed Edmund Campion in his tutoring days. Her husband, Edward Brooksby, had been a 'great admirer and follower' of Henry Vaux and a keen supporter of the Jesuits, but he had died sometime between the summers of 1580 and 1581, leaving her with two small children.[1] Soon afterwards, she adopted her late aunt's five-year-old daughter. Early widowhood and the responsibilities of raising William, Mary and Frances in the forbidden faith had taken their toll. In the parish register recording her brother's burial in 1587, Eleanor is described as 'old M^{ris} Bruxby', though she was probably not yet thirty.[2] Her widow's weeds doubtless enhanced the ageing process, but it is unlikely that she cared. Her life was dedicated to God, 'her second spouse'. Forty years after her husband's death, she was presented with a little book called *The Widow's Glass* in which the translator praised her 'long, constant & most exemplar profession of that noble and worthy state of chaste widowhood'. No doubt Eleanor heeded the book's advice to live modestly, dress plainly and avoid bejewelled or frizzled hair, 'for these be the true signs of hell-fire'.[3]

Eleanor was fiercely intelligent, forceful and resourceful, but not always brilliant in a crisis. Garnet thought her 'rather timid' and noted that she struggled to cope with 'the threats and evil looks of the searchers' who frequently raided her home.[4] Not so Anne, who was emboldened by their presence. She was the youngest child from Lord Vaux's first marriage, the one whose birth might have caused her mother's death.* With no children of her own, and no husband either, Anne could afford to take risks. She was happy to impersonate her sister

---

* Modern calculations suggest that just under 1 per cent of mothers died in childbed in Elizabethan England. (Cressy, *Birth, Marriage, and Death*, p. 30)

and become the lady of the house when the pursuivants came knocking. She was equally comfortable as 'Mistress Perkins', riding up and down the country with strange young men. There were the inevitable rumours, but Anne was a virgin and determined to stay that way. And the men were not that strange; they just happened to be priests.

Henry Garnet called them 'the widow and the virgin' and for two decades they would be his mainstay, providing practical, financial and emotional support as he attempted to steer the mission out of troubled waters. His arrival did not mark the beginning of their service – Eleanor had already been flagged as a probable priest-harbourer and one of the sisters (unnamed) had been happily endorsing the exorcisms over dinner at Hackney in 1585.[5] But once Garnet took over as Jesuit superior, the preservation of his life and work became their vocation.

Their dedication was phenomenal. They would rent property for Garnet and his brethren, sometimes 'diverse houses at once', and provide cover for the sacraments that were administered within. They would handle the 'continual resort' of priests and penitents – and the pursuivants that so often came in their wake. Twice a year they would host the Jesuit conferences, where vows were renewed and resolves hardened. They would visit, supply and occasionally bail out imprisoned priests. They would make significant contributions to the Jesuit fund and provide a fence for their fiendishly complex finances. They actively promoted the Counter-Reformation in England, not only by maintaining the liturgical rhythms of the Catholic calendar, but also by catechising the young, patronising devotional literature, preserving relics, championing home-grown 'martyrs', and myriad other ways that were not always popular in Rome. They would be outspoken defenders of the Society of Jesus, attracting a considerable amount of misogynistic vitriol in the process, and they, particularly Anne, were there for Garnet when the pressures of leadership threatened to overwhelm.

It was a brave man who tried to cross these sisters. 'In God's cause and in the protection of His servants', Anne could be quite magnificent. Despite an unidentified but 'chronic weakness' that she 'nearly always' suffered and which could render her speechless, she would spend many hours arguing with her adversaries. In 1594 the Master of the Rolls would describe her as 'stomachful', by which he meant that she was stubborn. 'She is really quite funny and very lively,' another contemporary observed, and she had a good line in sarcasm, often mocking her interrogators as if they were ignorant schoolboys.[6] Eleanor was no pushover either, especially when it came to defending the interests of her family. Indeed, Sir Thomas Tresham (her stepmother's brother), against whom she would 'ungorge herself' of some imaginative insults in 1594, considered Eleanor the dominant sister. Even their beloved brother Henry had been 'powerfully terrified' of the two when he had bypassed Eleanor's children in his plans to resign his birthright.[7] They were sisters in blood and sisters in faith – 'seeing virginity and widowhood have ever been accounted sisters and betrothed to the same eternal spouse Christ Jesus'[8] – and they made a formidable pair.

Garnet did not refer to them in every missive to Rome. Indeed he hardly mentioned them. The need for circumspection had been drummed into him and Southwell at the onset of their mission. 'Be more on your guard,' Southwell was admonished in February 1587:

> Do not say so much in plain and open terms, lest (if what you write fall into others' hands) danger should thence arise either to others and to yourself . . . Things, especially when of importance, should be somewhat veiled in allegory (for the receiver will grasp the sense) and when persons are in question, they should be merely alluded to indirectly.[9]

Thus, when Garnet wrote of 'creditors' and 'debtors', he was referring to persecutors and persecuted. 'Merchandise' stood for souls, 'merchants' for priests; 'prentices' were novices and 'engagements' were religious vows. By 'places of much trading', he meant sites of execution, and instead of prisons he wrote 'credit-houses'. He was vague on location – 'the great house', 'my former dwelling', 'our places of abode' – and careful not to incriminate his hosts – 'my 2 ostesses', 'the two sisters', 'the widow and the virgin'. From 1594, he used a numerical code for particularly sensitive information.[10]

The sisters were not always at his side. Advising Anne on her future in 1606, Garnet expressed his wish that she and Eleanor live 'as before in a house of common repair of the Society, or where the superior of the mission shall ordinarily remain'.[11] Eleanor, it seems, often kept to the headquarters, but Anne frequently escorted Garnet on his travels. At the time of the Gunpowder Plot, almost twenty years after Garnet's return to England, a servant testified that 'Mrs Anne Vaux doth usually go with him whithersoever he goeth.'[12] In 1598, an angry husband whose wife had attached herself to the Jesuits challenged a priest to ask Garnet 'with what face he can carry a gentlewoman up and down the country with him and thereby give such bad example to his subjects to take my wife from me'.[13]

There was mutual respect, reliance and affection between Garnet and Anne. He was her senior by seven years and her 'ghostly father'. She was his penitent and protector. She had vowed to obey him, but if necessary would order him down a priest-hole. *In extremis*, she feared she could not live without him and he would call her 'my ever dearest in Christ'. It was an intensely familiar relationship. Some contemporaries, even some Jesuits, suspected it might be too familiar.[14] But those looking for scandal tend to overlook Garnet's last two words: *in Christ*.

Garnet and his colleagues were heartened by the support they received from the recusant women of England. Wives, widows and spinsters, even young girls, took to the missionary field with considerable flair. 'The work of God,' Southwell reported six months into his apostolate, 'is being pressed forward, often enough by delicate women who have taken on the courage of men.'[15] The Catholic clergy had a great deal of admiration for these women, but there was also an underlying discomfort at having to rely upon them for succour. Most men, and indeed women, shared the sentiments of Lord Vaux, who had chastised Lady Montagu in 1581 for her 'somewhat too zealous (I will not otherwise term the same) urging me in matters tending to religion'. Citing St Paul, he had argued that 'women should learn in silence and in subjection . . . for silence extolleth womanly shamefastness, and such comely shamefastness adorneth their age'.[16] Women should be meek and decorative; that was the natural order of things. If they started to show signs of rationality or courage or other virtues traditionally associated with men,* then they were circumventing the order, and that could be dangerous for anyone who liked order and hierarchy in their lives – notably Catholic clergymen.

---

* Virtue (*virtus* in Latin, deriving from *vir*: man) was originally a male preserve. It is not known how many contemporaries believed the (quite wrong) assertion in the 1486 witch-hunter's handbook, the *Malleus Maleficarum*, that *femina* (woman) was a derivation of *fe* + *minus* (less faith).

On the other hand, there was an acceptance that these were not ordinary times. English recusants, like Christ's followers in the early days of the primitive Church, believed they were answering a call to arms; peacetime rules need not apply. Nor could the usual structures of patriarchal and ecclesiastical authority be strictly maintained. Many fathers, husbands and brothers had been taken out of action – either by death or by imprisonment or because they had been so browbeaten by fines and forfeiture that they had surrendered (as recusants saw it) to conformity. The missionaries were fledglings operating 'amidst bird lime and traps', one priest wrote.[17] They needed protection wherever and however they could get it. The mission was fluid, fragmented and necessarily flexible. There was no coherent leadership. The Jesuits had their superior, though visitors were carefully vetted – 'I know not where to come to you,' one priest groused to Garnet.[18] Members of the secular clergy (those priests who did not belong to a religious order) might look to William Allen for guidance, but he was in Rheims and, from 1587, a cardinal in Rome, and would in any case die in 1594 with no obvious successor. The Pope's attempt to establish 'perfect love and union' among the clergy by appointing an archpriest in 1598 backfired spectacularly and would have only the opposite effect.[19]

Through the fissures and fractures, the recusant women slipped; not many – a minority of a minority of a minority – but their influence was disproportionate. They undertook whatever role was required of them and adapted to circumstance. On the ground, where resourcefulness and spontaneity were essential, common sense might prevail over canonical procedure. A quick-witted lady could be the difference between the capture and concealment of a priest. Or, indeed, the salvation and damnation of a soul, if, like Dorothy Lawson from Newcastle, she was instrumental in conversions and played the catechist to the extent that her chaplain had 'no other share in the work but to take their confessions'. In emergencies, she even performed baptisms 'with her own hand'.[20]

Catholic women were conduits and fixers. John Donne had a childhood memory of going to the Tower of London with his mother to visit her imprisoned brother, Jasper Heywood. He was the senior Jesuit in England in 1584 and another visitor was his successor, William Weston. Elizabeth Donne had provided the first contact between the two priests and arranged for their eventual meeting, perhaps even helping to allay Weston's 'great trepidation as I saw the vast battle-ments, and was led by the warder past the gates'.[21]

Women with autonomy at home were the custodians of household religion, and of the young, and of the priests they decided to take in. Then, as now, the 'gatekeeper' was in a privileged position and that made Anne Vaux and Eleanor Brooksby very influential indeed. The priest who had griped at the lack of access to Garnet also vented his spleen at 'the elder gentlewoman', who had 'refused to take notice' of him and treated him as 'a person justly to be mistrusted'. He identified Eleanor so closely with the Jesuit superior that he considered her snub a reason to take offence at him.[22] Other Catholics sought Anne's advice. Garnet would convey instructions and even appoint his temporary successor through her.[23] The sisters knew where the bodies were buried – figuratively and, in the case of 'fresh green new relics', quite literally.[24]

The special conditions of the English mission presented women like Anne and Eleanor with opportunities for influence and action that would have been unthinkable in the more disciplined countries of Tridentine Europe. The Yorkshire Catholic, Mary Ward (1585–1645), would realise quite how different those conditions were when her attempts on the Continent to establish a female religious institute outside the cloister were met with suspicion and derision.*

Contemporary portraits of recusant women were not always flat-tering. Alongside all those edifying reports of perfectly pious ladies – like Mary Gifford, who wore her dresses out at the knees from so much praying[25] – are ones where they were depicted as either too much of a woman, or not quite a woman at all. A staple of anti-Catholic, especially anti-Jesuit, discourse was to lampoon the recusant woman as a silly slut,

---

* Ward and her society of English Ladies (later known as the Institute of the Blessed Virgin Mary) settled their first house in St Omer (then in the Spanish Netherlands) in 1609 and expanded throughout Europe. The superior of the house in Perugia was Lord Vaux's granddaughter Joyce. The English Ladies sought an active apostolate in imitation of the Society of Jesus, but in defiance of the Council of Trent, which insisted upon female claustration. They were branded 'Jesuitesses', 'chattering hussies', 'galloping girls' and 'wandering nuns'. According to the papal bull that suppressed them in 1631, they were guilty of 'arrogant contumacy' and 'great temerity', and their work was 'by no means suiting the weakness of their sex, intel-lect, womanly modesty and above all virginal purity' (Lux-Sterritt, p. 50). The Insti-tute finally gained papal approbation in 1877 and on 19 December 2009 Pope Benedict XVI declared Mary Ward 'Venerable', thus progressing the cause for her canonisation.

who sated her lust by keeping a priest in her closet. Richard Sheldon, author of *A Survey of the Miracles of the Church of Rome, proving them to be Antichristian* (1616), suggested that cosy households were not good environments for chastity. 'Is it not a miracle,' he asked,

> that so many of your priests, Ignatians* and monks feeding here in England daintily, arrayed gallantly, lodging softly, should be very domestically and privily conversant with ladies, dames, matrons, maids of all sorts, and yet none of all these be scorched?[26]

At the other end of the scale was the image of the virile woman: the exceptionally heroic lady who could, in special circumstances, assume the qualities of a man (strength, aggression, fortitude, rigorism, rationality and so on) and thereby transcend the perceived limitations of her gender. 'Though she has all a maiden's modesty and even shyness,' Garnet wrote of Anne, 'yet in God's cause, and in the protection of His servants, *virgo* becomes *virago*.'[27] The image was neither new, nor confined to England. Like Martha, the New Testament hostess who was transformed in medieval legend into the dragon-taming hero of Provence, or Teresa of Ávila (1515–84), a patron saint of Spain, who 'ceased to be a woman, restoring herself to the virile state to her greater glory', it seemed that some women could only be privileged with a man's praise if safely stripped of their femininity.[28] Queen Elizabeth would work the same prejudices with her heart-and-stomach-of-a-king wartime rhetoric. It was made clear by the priests who wrote about them that these women were not typical. They were temporary aberrations in a patriarchal world and only impressive because, like Dorothy Lawson, their 'masculine spirit' had been inflamed by 'divine fire'.[29]

If the thought of a divinely administered shot of testosterone was one way for a man to bestow acceptance upon a recusant woman, often it was better for the woman to go the other way: to make a great show of her femininity and play up to the Pauline stereotype. 'Oh! put up your swords!' cried Eleanor's eleven-year-old adopted daughter Frances, when pursuivants crossed the family threshold, 'or else my mother will die, for she cannot endure to see a naked sword.'

---

* *Ignatians*: Jesuits, after their founder, Ignatius Loyola.

At the sight of the little girl and her swooning 'mother' (who could have been Eleanor or Anne impersonating Eleanor), the men were momentarily abashed and under the guise of fetching some wine, off trotted Frances to see the priests safely hidden.[30]

Distraction, delay and feminine outrage were deployed on another occasion when Anne accused a pursuivant of indecorum. 'Do you think it right and proper that you should be admitted to a widow's house before she or her servants or children are out of bed? Why this lack of good manners,' she enquired, 'why come so early?' Breakfast and a bribe could not prevent a thorough search of the house, but in those vital seconds Garnet, Southwell, three other Jesuits, two secular priests 'and all other signs of our religion' were stowed away.[31]

Not all women succeeded in hiding behind feminine modesty. When the wife of Mr Bentley of Little Oakley, Northamptonshire, stayed in bed during a raid in 1595, the pursuivants searched her bedchamber and found 'near the bed' a small coffer containing a 'chalice of silver, a crucifix of jet, a surplice, a Mass book, and divers other vain things belonging thereto'. Mr Bentley was promptly declared a 'true prisoner' and bound by a one thousand-pound recognisance to present himself at the sign of the Swan in Kettering the following morning.[32] The husband was punished for the contents of his wife's bedchamber because he was their legal owner. Upon marriage, he assumed her property and, so it was commonly believed, responsibility for her conduct. Such inequality in the law gave a recusant wife a degree of immunity from prosecution. Elizabeth Moninge of Kent, questioned in 1591 about her refusal to go to church, claimed that 'as a wife under subjection, she had no ability to give an answer'.

There seemed little point in going to the trouble of securing indictments and convictions for recusant wives if there could be no pecuniary pain or, indeed, no financial reward for the state. Some women, especially the poor, were imprisoned. Of the twenty-five recusant prisoners in Ousebridge gaol in York in 1598, eleven were women. But this was not considered viable in the long term as few female prisoners could afford the upkeep.

In 1593, Parliament tried to solve the problem of the recusant wife by making her husband pay for her nonconformity, but it was not a popular measure – not least because some members feared for their own purses – and despite an initial flurry of prosecutions, there remained a general awkwardness at state intrusion of family life. Even in the aftermath of the Gunpowder Plot, there would be 'much dispute' and dilatoriness in Parliament over the question of a husband's exact liability.[33]

Of course, not all wives were safe and not all women were wives. Spinsters and widows could own property and were theoretically liable for prosecution. In practice, however, a great many of them also seemed to slip through the net. Eleanor had her widow's jointure, a portion of the Brooksby estate in Leicestershire, while Anne was, for a time, cash rich, her brother Henry having 'dealt very bountifully with her' just before his death. She could also draw on an allowance from her father (twenty pounds a year) and, soon, the 'great plenty of wealth' bequeathed by her grandmother.[34] We know this because Sir Thomas Tresham wrote about it in a letter to his wife, detailing a financial dispute he was having with Anne. It is unlikely that the authorities charged with collecting recusancy fines knew much about it. Indeed, only in the aftermath of the Gunpowder Plot and only after torture would one of Anne's servants admit that he had heard that 'she had a stock of money of some five hundred pounds and an annuity out of Leicestershire by the death of her grandmother.'[35]

The crisis of the Gunpowder Plot would also lead to the revelation that Anne had donated what seems to have been a substantial part of her fortune to the Jesuit mission. Indeed, because the Society's rules forbade the mission from having a regular source of income, Anne seems to have handled the money herself, parcelling it out in loans and investments and giving the incoming annuities as alms. There is a vague reference to these investments in an intercepted letter from Garnet to Anne that under normal circumstances he would never have risked writing.[36] The point here is that with no obvious fixed assets and no neat paper trail linking Anne to her money, it was very difficult for the authorities to assess her wealth, let alone get their hands on it.

Tracing the sisters was almost as challenging. Both used aliases: Anne was sometimes Mistress Perkins and Eleanor, in homage to her late husband, was Mrs Edwards. Independent women, if they had the means and the stamina, could live peripatetically, moving their households and crossing counties whenever they sensed danger. When, in 1592, Eleanor ('Mrs Elizabeth Brookesbye *alias* Edwards' of the parish of Tanworth) was presented in Warwickshire as 'a most wilful and seditious recusant', she ought to have appeared at the county assizes for judgement. Instead, a note was added that she had 'removed from thence: it is thought she is gone into Leicestershire'.[37]

Even with very little notice, recusants with good contacts and deep pockets could often make good their escape. In 1588 the Sheriff of Leicestershire admitted that some of those he had been ordered to detain had 'removed & gone from their habitations before the coming of the sheriff his men & officers (though with great secrecy & speed they were sent)'. He reported that most of the women 'rest unapprehended until your honours' pleasures be further known'. The Sheriff of Cambridge and Huntingdon, responding to the same command, admitted that he 'durst not presume to apprehend' the women without further direction.[38] It was no ordinary year, 1588, and yet even at that time of heightened security, the thought of dragging women away from their families made some officials squeamish.

So, some recusant women enjoyed a degree of latitude in the law and there seems to have been a vague but quite deeply ingrained feeling in society that private women and their private consciences should not be exposed to public prosecution. However, the exigencies of time and place, the peculiarities of character, tensions from within and pressures from without could all combine to blow a vapid generalisation out of the water. On 25 March 1586 a butcher's wife from York was pressed to death by the hand of the law. For her general defence of the recusant cause and, specifically, her refusal to plead to the charge of priest-harbouring, Margaret Clitherow was sentenced to the gruesome medieval penalty *peine forte et dure*. In the tollbooth on the Ouse Bridge in York, she was stripped and ordered to lie down. A large sharp stone was placed under her back and 'seven or eight hundred weight' was piled on top of her. Her ribs shattered and 'burst forth of the skin'.

Clitherow's gender could not save her. On the contrary, her overt defiance of male authority almost certainly contributed to her fall. Contemporaries and historians have discussed the Clitherow case and the 'remarkable confluence of circumstances' that produced it.[39] Some hailed her as a selfless martyr, others denounced her as a showboating suicide. Quite a few thought she was just plain mad. She was the first of three women put to death in Elizabeth's reign for allegedly giving aid to outlawed priests. The others were Margaret Ward, executed in 1588 for helping a priest escape from prison, and Anne Line, hanged for harbouring on 27 February 1601. None was the daughter of a peer. None could boast in her corner a Burghley or a Beaumont or any of the connections that seem to have afforded the Vauxes a measure of protection. The nobility, regardless of faith, tended to view the molestation of their own as 'a common insult to their grade'. Anne and Eleanor would never have 'kissed the gallows tree' like Anne Line, or had their ribcages crushed on the Ouse Bridge.[40] Their commitment was unswerving and they made hard sacrifices, but they were undeniably more secure in their activities than the unfortunate butcher's wife from York.

In the early hours of 29 July 1588, Anne and Eleanor's grandmother Elizabeth Beaumont died at home in Leicestershire. It was apposite that she expired on the feast day of St Martha because, Garnet noted, she had been a great hostess herself, tending to the needs of the priests in her house and even cooking and cleaning for them 'so that their presence might be kept more secret'. The sisters had spent their formative years with their grandmother and they continued to live nearby, often visiting with Garnet, to whom she had showed 'great devotion'. Indeed her deathbed request was to see him. Garnet said Mass every day for ten days until 'her death agony began'. He read the commendation of her soul to God and 'in the space of four or five *Misereres*'* she died 'with the name of Jesus on her lips'. In the evening, the obsequies were performed and the following night, in accordance with her wishes, she was buried in the parish church 'without the ministers saying their prayers over her body'. In death, if not in life, consecrated ground was consecrated ground, irrespective of the Reformation.†

* The recitation of Psalm 51 beginning *Miserere mei Deus* ('Have mercy upon me, O God').

† In principle recusants were not entitled to parish burial because they died excommunicate, but in practice a sympathetic (or bribable) minister might permit a quiet bending of the rules, especially between dusk and dawn. This is probably what happened with Henry Vaux, whose burial was recorded in the register of Great Ashby on 19 November 1587. It was advisable to bury the dead with the connivance of the vicar or one of his wardens: one widow from Edmonton was indicted in the next reign 'for her misdemeanour about the interment of her dead husband, who was a recusant, whom she caused to be carried to the cemetery of Hornsey and there to be buried not one foot deep in the soil whereby his head and feet remained uncovered and exposed.' (Jeaffreson, II, p. 236)

There was one notable absentee: Elizabeth's elder son, Francis, who had conformed to the 'new religion' for the sake of his career. That was, in any case, the family's view. Francis was only informed of his mother's death after Garnet had sung the Requiem Mass and made good his exit. A few months later he organised a memorial service at which his mother's virtues were praised, but her 'popery' was decried. Thus, wrote Garnet, the minister 'ruined the soup with one ill-chosen herb'. The following year, Francis Beaumont accepted promotion to the degree of serjeant-at-law and on 25 January 1593 he was appointed a Justice of the Common Pleas.[41] He seems to have been on good terms with his Vaux nieces, despite their different paths. Perhaps he recognised that ignorance of his mother's dying days had spared him any career-compromising questions about fugitive priests. Anne and Eleanor, for their part, would have occasion to be grateful for the legal muscle of Justice Beaumont.

Lord Vaux had not been able to attend his mother-in-law's obsequies either. In December 1587, after more than six years of confinement, he was transferred to the custody of the Archbishop of Canterbury. The reason was soon clear. 'Her Majesty,' the Privy Council informed the county lieutenants, 'being advertised sundry ways of the great preparations that are made abroad of shipping and men' was willing to do 'all things necessary' for the defence of the realm. Among other things:

> considering how of late years divers of her subjects, by the means of bad instruments, have been withdrawn from the due obedience they owe to her Majesty and her laws, insomuch as divers of them most obstinately have refused to come to the church to prayer and divine service

it was thought appropriate that 'those bad members that already are known to be recusants' should be 'so looked unto and restrained as they shall neither be able to give assistance to the enemy, nor that the enemy may have any hope of relief and succour by them'.[42]

After years of having his coastlines harried, his ships plundered, his rebellious subjects aided and, to paraphrase Francis Drake, his beard singed by Elizabeth's privateers, Philip II of Spain had decided to call time on his erstwhile sister-in-law and launch the 'Gran Armada' that he had long threatened. Pope Sixtus V promised indulgences and a million gold ducats (about £250,000) for a successful invasion. On 25 April 1588, the expedition standard was blessed at a special service in Lisbon Cathedral. By the end of the following month, it was billowing atop the flagship *San Martín* off the west coast of Portugal. It bore the words: 'Arise, O Lord, and vindicate thy cause.'[43]

10

Fright and Rumour

A thousand years after the virgin birth
and after five hundred more allowed the globe,
the wonderful eighty-eighth year begins and
brings with it woe enough. If, this year,
total catastrophe does not befall, if land
and sea do not collapse in total ruin, yet
will the whole world suffer upheavals, empires
will dwindle and from everywhere will
be great lamentation.

The fifteenth-century prophecy of
'Regiomontanus'[1]

La Felicissima Armada: the most fortunate fleet – 130 ships, 19,000 troops, 60,000 tons of shipping. When the captain of a Hamburg-bound cargo ship came across this great behemoth in the Atlantic, he thought he heard the ocean 'groaning' under its weight. That was before the planned embarkation of the Duke of Parma's 27,000 veterans and a further 300 small ships waiting in Flanders.[2] On 19 July 1588 the first sails were sighted off the Scilly Isles. The following morning, in its awesome crescent formation, the Armada beat slowly up the Channel.

Lord Burghley was confident that if the Spanish could be kept at a distance, the English would better them at sea: 'Her Majesty is of her own proper ships so strong as the enemy shall not be able to land any power where Her Majesty's navy shall be near to the enemy's navy.'[3] The problem lay in intelligence: everyone knew the Armada was on its way, but no one could agree on its precise destination. The Queen did not have a standing army and her veteran troops were stuck in the Netherlands or on the Scottish border. Recent research suggests that the 'trained bands' upon whom she was forced to rely were better prepared than previously thought, but whether these raw recruits could match up to Parma's professionals was another matter.[4]

The great dread was that if the Spaniards could gain a foothold and wave their banner, all the Catholics in England – the quiescent as well as the notorious – might see it as their one chance of salvation and start to mobilise. The spectre of a fifth column of unquantifiable Catholics lined up alongside their Spanish co-religionists haunted many Englishmen, or at least it haunted the Puritans, to whom, at times like this, Englishmen lent an ear. A bloodbath was feared, a repeat of St Bartholomew's Day, 1572, when French Catholics had massacred thousands of their Protestant compatriots and the Seine had run red with blood. The Spanish were held to be the most savage race of all. According to the Protestant polemicist John Ponet, there was 'no nation under the cope of Christ like them in pride, cruelty, unmerci-fulness, nor so far from all humanity'.[5] Flemish and Dutch refugees told lurid tales of Spanish cruelty, while those old enough to remember the last time that Philip II was king in England found it convenient to blame him for the burning time. Should he succeed now, they feared their womenfolk would be ravished, their children slaughtered and the faggots at Smithfield would glow again. Protestants who usually muddled along fairly amicably with their Catholic neighbours now imagined the horns of Antichrist under their hats. The philoso-pher Thomas Hobbes, born in the spring of Armada year, believed that his mother 'fell in labour with him upon the fright of the inva-sion'.[6]

The Privy Council was taking no risks. 'It is hardly ventured to repose that trust in them which is to be looked for in her [Majesty's] other good subjects,' it had reasoned. So the orders had gone out to the lieutenants of each county to commit their 'most obstinate and noted' recusants to prison. Lord Vaux – categorised as a substantial recusant, but 'not so obstinate' – was placed in the custody of the Archbishop of Canterbury.[7] In mid-July, 'the chief recusants' were transferred to Ely, 'until it be known what will become of these Spanish forces'. Vaux, however, was left in Lambeth, 'in respect only', it was thought, of 'bad health'.[8] He was lucky. His brother-in-law Tresham and cousin Sir William Catesby were two of the fifteen gentleman prisoners 'bloodily threatened' at Ely by locals who had deduced from their detainment that they were enemies of the state. The Catholic prisoners begged to be allowed to give 'undoubted spectacle' of their loyalty by presenting themselves 'unarmed' in the vanguard, but then came the news that 'the powerful enemy's navy had passed the ocean' and was entering the narrow seas.⁹

The 'Armada Portrait' of Elizabeth I shows what happened next. In the picture behind her on the left, the two fleets prepare to engage. In the picture on the right, the storm-struck Armada struggles to return home. The Queen, looking remarkable for fifty-five, taps the Americas on a globe. Her eyebrows are just slightly raised; her dominance is assured. The Spanish were never allowed to touch England's shore. They were repulsed and dispersed at sea and the relief among the English people was palpable. But someone had to pay for 'that time of fright and rumour', and, with few Spaniards to hand,* the

* Only about half the Armada would straggle back to Spain. The supplies had perished, the ships were leaking, the survivors were wounded, sick and starving. (The horses had long gone, thrown overboard to save on water.) Many of those forced ashore in their flight round Ireland were summarily executed. Perhaps as many as fifteen thousand men succumbed in the end.

Catholics at home inevitably bore the brunt. 'Our rulers,' Southwell reported on 31 August, 'turned their arms from foreign foes against their own sons and with inhuman ferocity vented the hatred they had conceived against the Spaniards on their own fellow citizens.' Seventeen priests, nine laymen and one woman were executed in the space of three months for alleged religious treasons. They were dragged in horse carts, flanked by a baying mob 'uttering all manner of harsh and savage abuse'. At the scaffolds, 'there was an extraordinary concourse of citizens and a crowd surging on all sides'. All the usual courtesies were withdrawn. One priest who tried to address the crowd had a cloth stuffed into his mouth 'very nearly suffocating him before he was hanged'. Bystanders on the lookout for sympathisers caught a man making the sign of the cross and had him arrested. Another, falling to his knees in prayer, caused 'a great outcry' and 'was hurried off to prison'.[10] This, at least, is what Robert Southwell, S.J., reported.

Lord Vaux was spared 'the enemy's barbarity'. By 20 February 1589, he was free and sitting in the House of Lords.[11] He was allowed to return home to Northamptonshire the following year, but he never really recovered his standing in society. His already fragmented estate had grown 'lamentable', two-thirds having been seized in the autumn of 1587 for recovery of arrears.[12] By the time he attended the Queen's next Parliament in 1593, he owed his creditors £2,800 and was forced to present a humiliating petition for a bill to allow him 'to sell certain lands for the payment of his debts'.[13] Having pawned his parliamentary robes, he appeared in the Lords 'without decent clothes to his back for such an assembly'. He was, he wrote to Burghley (in a letter drafted by Tresham), the 'infortunatest peer of Parliament for poverty that ever was'.[14]

Given the chance, would he ever have taken up arms against his countrymen? When he had drawn up an indenture in 1571, it had been a matter of course to include a provision for ransom money in the event of capture while serving 'in any of the Queen's warlike affairs'.[15] In 1585, though, when he was the Queen's prisoner, he pledged one hundred marks to the Hoxton missionary fund, but declared himself 'unable to furnish' a levy for the Queen's light horse serving against the Spanish in the Low Countries. (He did, however, offer his lands for review 'for payment of the money' and by the following March he had 'disbursed £50 for the setting forth of horses').[16] He was a fierce supporter of the mission to change his country's religion and this was undeniably damaging to the Elizabethan establishment. Yet in signing statements of loyalty and petitions for toleration, and in his attendance (albeit occasional) at Parliament, he also displayed a preference for peace and a desire to effect change from within the system of which he was a part.

He knew people on either side of the Armada divide. One of his trusted servants, Athony (*sic*) Carrington of Harrowden, took the oath of supremacy and marched for the Queen in the eastern division of the Northamptonshire militia only a few months after being convicted of recusancy. The Earl of Arundel, by contrast, prayed in his prison cell for the 'happy success' of the Spanish.[17] If we are to believe Burghley's propaganda, Viscount Montague of Cowdray, keen to display familial loyalty, presented his sons and almost two hundred horsemen to Queen Elizabeth at Tilbury, announcing his 'full resolution' to 'hazard his life, his children, his lands and his goods' in her defence. He could not, however, hazard one of his brothers, who had died aboard the *San Mateo* a few days earlier.[18]

Some very senior Catholic clerics, including Cardinal William Allen, urged the people of England and Ireland to 'join with the Catholic army' in the 'holy war' against the 'infamous, deprived, accursed, excommunicate heretic'.[19] But Sir Thomas Tresham, who always claimed to speak for his brother-in-law Vaux, indignantly trumpeted his patriotism as if it should never have been in doubt. A government spy writing in 1591 confirmed that the two were 'accounted very good subjects & great adversaries of the Spanish practises'.[20] Against these statements should be weighed the views of Catholics abroad. Some clearly claimed Lord Vaux as a potential, if not yet actual, collaborator. In 1571, he had reportedly been 'well disposed' to the Ridolfi Plot 'and ready to act'. In 1586, the year of the Babington Plot, he had appeared in 'a catalogue of such men in England as the papistical fugitives make account to be assured if any foreign power should come to invade this realm'.[21] And so again, on the eve of the Armada, 'Lord Vaux of Harrowden, a good Catholic, now a prisoner in the Fleet', was named a 'friend' of Philip II. Considering he had not been in the Fleet since 1583, the accuracy of the report is questionable, but there is no mistaking the sentiments of its Scottish author. In a reference to Queen Elizabeth's imprisonment in her sister Mary's reign, he comments: 'I wish to God they had burnt her then, as she deserved, with the rest of the heretics who were justly executed. If this had been done we should be living now in peace and quietness.'

The author, who also advised where the Armada should land (Kirkcudbright) and announced his willingness to die 'in defence of the Catholic faith under the protection of his Majesty', clearly had strong views.[22] What the Privy Council did not know, and in the absence of quantitative data could not know, was how many Englishmen secretly shared them. We will never know Lord Vaux's ultimate loyalty because it was never, ultimately, tried. He and his friends were immobilised before the Armada got anywhere near the English Channel. Tresham complained bitterly. There was, nevertheless, some justification in his accusers' assertion that 'while we lived her Majesty should not be in security, nor the realm freed from invasion'.[23] The Spaniards sailing aboard the *Rosario* had been told to expect support from at least a third of England's population.[24] Elizabeth's Privy Council had been 'certain' that an invasion would 'never' have been attempted, 'but upon hope' of internal assistance. It may very well have been a false hope, built on a house of cards by exiles desperate to see the old faith restored at home, but for as long as it was held and acted upon by backers powerful enough to do damage, Vaux, Tresham and the rest, whether 'faithfullest true English subjects' or not, were indeed a security risk.

There was no such thing as a random occurrence in the sixteenth century. Divine will determined all. God decided where to quake the earth and where to beam his sunshine. And so, in the minds of most contemporaries, England had repulsed the Spanish fleet, not because of strategy, supplies, seamen, ships or shot, not even because the Armada had failed to 'join hands' with Parma's expeditionary force. England emerged victorious because God had willed it. In the words sung at the thanksgiving service held at St Paul's Cathedral, 'He made the winds and waters rise / to scatter all mine enemies.'[25] Even messianic Philip, usually so sure of his status as the special one, was momentarily confounded by the mysteries of God's will.

In England, commemorative medals were struck and pithy mottoes captured England's gloating spirit of triumph: 'God blew and they were scattered'; 'It came, it saw, it fled.' The post-Reformation calendar gained a red-letter day – Armada Day – some recompense for all those lost saints' days. In pulpits all over the country ministers rhapsodised

over 'special providences' (they could hardly call them miracles) and
God's covenant with the children of England. Not only had Englishmen
defeated Spaniards, but the true Church had triumphed over the false,
Christ over Antichrist and freedom over tyranny. Elizabeth I was hailed
as Gloriana, the Virgin Queen who 'brought up, even under her wing,
a nation that was almost begotten and born under her, that never
shouted any other *Ave* than for her name'.[26]

So the myth was forged, the Protestant identity of the nation was
reinforced and Vaux, Tresham and their friends were left to ponder
quite how they and their 'true English hearts' were to fit into this
predestined, Protestant version of English history.[27]

The year 1588 might indeed have been the 'climacterical year' pres-
aged by the astronomers, but England's victory was neither inevitable
nor conclusive.[28] The fleet of 1588 has come down to us as *the* Spanish
Armada, but Philip II would send two further (failed) fleets against
Elizabeth I and there were rumours of more. The war would continue
for fifteen expensive years and at every whisper of invasion, every
'time of fright and rumour', the screw would be turned on the 'obstinate and noted' Catholics of England. Ely would become a 'familiar
prison' for Thomas Tresham. Ordered there again in March 1590 amid
renewed fears of invasion, he penned a heartfelt lament to Archbishop
Whitgift: 'We are disgraced, defaced, confined from our native countries, imprisoned, impoverished, forsaken of friends, triumphed upon
by foes; scorned of all men.'[29]

Spanish aggression in France the following year prompted an inflammatory proclamation ordering householders to be specially vigilant
against the priests and papists, who were spreading 'treasons in the
bowels of our Realm'.[30] Another scare in 1593 called for another
measure: the 'statute of confinement', which forbade all recusants
over the age of sixteen from travelling beyond five miles of their
homes without a licence. It was adhered to by some more than others:
Lady Tresham would address a letter to her niece Merill Vaux on
8 May 1593, 'assuring myself that you stir not above five miles from
Irthlingborough, whatsoever your mother dareth or doeth'.[31]

There was a gulf between the law and its enforcement. The abstract
language of anti-popery nearly always exceeded the lived experience
of anti-Catholicism and there were lulls when international pressures
would relax and life might seem tolerable. Nevertheless, it must have

been profoundly alienating and psychologically draining to be told, at every critical juncture, that one was an 'unnatural subject' and 'bad member' of the commonwealth. Tresham likened it to being 'drenched in a sea of shameless slanders' and foretold that for as long as the hostilities between England and Spain continued, there would be no end to the recusants' 'quotidian kind of imprisonment'.[32] It would prove, for many, a more accurate prophecy than that of 'Regiomontanus', the fifteenth-century astronomer of Königsberg.

Henry Garnet was circumspect over the summer of 1588. He wrote to Rome from London on 9 June and again on 11 July, but knowing that Southwell was reporting 'the still unfinished story of what wickedness is being planned against us', he resolved to 'write of pleasant things instead'. In late July, he spent ten days at Elizabeth Beaumont's bedside and thereafter seems to have toured the Midlands. By the end of October, he was back in London, anxiously awaiting the arrival of two young Jesuits from Rome. 'Unless we have urgent business,' he wrote, 'we dare not go about the city save at night.'[33]

If Anne and Eleanor were with Garnet in London, it is not recorded. All that is known is that they were no longer at Great Ashby. On 12 February 1588, the Sheriff of Leicestershire, William Cave, wrote to the Privy Council admitting that he had failed to detain all the 'undutiful' recusants of the shire. 'Mrs Helline Brookesbye, widow' and six of her servants had 'fled from Ashby and escaped apprehension'. Cave was at pains to point out that his officers had operated 'with great secrecy & speed'. If he suspected his fellow commissioner Henry Beaumont of tipping off his nieces, he did not inform the Council. But he certainly regretted their flight. It was not common to make presentments to the Privy Council of children under the age of sixteen, but Sheriff Cave did just that, citing Eleanor's son William ('about the age of x years') and daughter Mary ('about the age of viii years'), as well as a fourteen-year-old boy called William Hutchinson. 'These are of Mrs Brooksby's household also,' he informed the Council, 'where these youths receive evil instruction as we fear.' They had also fled, 'whereby,' the Sheriff concluded, 'we are confirmed in opinion that it is most dangerous to the state where there is a recusant mistress'.[34]

II

Mrs Brooksby's Household

Why was Sheriff Cave so agitated? How could a widow's household constituting six servants 'of small ability' and three children be considered a threat to state security? We know, of course, as Sheriff Cave must also have done, that Anne and Eleanor were priest-harbourers. More often than not, one of those priests was the superior of the Society of Jesus in England. 'Since the coming of the Spanish fleet into these waters,' Garnet would write, 'far more than any other priest in the country I am suspect of stirring sedition and raising the Catholics to support the King of Spain.'[1] His presence in Eleanor's house would have been reason enough for Sheriff Cave to sense danger, but what seems to have troubled him more was the 'evil instruction' of the children there, something for which the 'recusant mistress' was as responsible as the holy men under her roof.

Great Ashby lies in the south of Leicestershire, conveniently close to the borders of Northamptonshire and Warwickshire. The sisters knew the area well and probably escaped Cave's jurisdiction with ease. Northamptonshire was the seat of the Vaux barony, but it was Warwickshire, 'Forest of Arden' country, where they settled, taking a house that would be Garnet's 'ordinary abode' for the next three years. The new place was large enough to accommodate upwards of a dozen visitors. It was near a copse and had stables, a courtyard and some 'very safe and close' hiding places, including a damp but 'very cleverly built sort of cave'.[2]

It may well have been Baddesley Clinton with its sewer-turned-priest-hole in the west range* and an owner, Henry Ferrers, who shared the Vauxes' religion as well, it seems, as some of their business

---

* This can still be seen. Baddesley Clinton, near Knowle, is a National Trust property open throughout the year.

contacts. (Two names in a 1601 Baddesley Clinton conveyance crop up as witnesses in three Vaux-related leases of 1599; in February 1596, the manor would be conveyed to George Shirley of Staunton Harold, Leicestershire, a fellow recusant, kinsman and trustee of Eleanor Brooksby.) Or it could have been neighbouring Rowington Hall, another moated manor and the home of the Skinner family, who were suspected priest-harbourers and also had links with Vaux associates (one of Anne's most trusted servants, John Grissold of Rowington, would be hired on Robert Skinner's recommendation; William Skinner of Rowington Hall later acquired a manuscript copy of Southwell's *A Short Rule of Good Life*).[3] Or the sisters may have chosen somewhere else in the region. They covered their tracks well and no direct documentary evidence pins them down for the 1588–91 period. What matters more than its site is what actually happened in Mrs Brooksby's house and why it was thought to have such a pernicious effect on the commonwealth.

It was, by all accounts, deeply pious. The informer George Snape mentioned that there was 'commonly a priest or two' resident, frequently more. One of them, Oswald Tesimond, wrote that 'sometimes there might be more than twenty or thirty priests in her house at one time', though this was extraordinary. Henry Garnet thought the house *'angelica'* on account of the 'many holy women consecrated to God' there.[4] The sisters were clearly not cloistered. They moved about more than most women, but inasmuch as circumstances allowed, they strived towards 'the highest & most perfect' manner of living: that of a convent. In 1621 the priest and Staffordshire man John Wilson would dedicate his translation of *The Treasure of Vowed Chastity in Secular Persons* to 'the honourable and right virtuous gentlewoman, Mrs Anne Vaux' in recognition of 'the constant report of your virtuous life in the state whereof this little book entreateth'. To this Jesuit-authored work, Wilson appended another, *The Widow's Glass*, in which he paid tribute to Eleanor's 'long, constant & most exemplar profession of that noble and worthy state of chaste widowhood'.[5]

Such women, striving to live 'in the world' until the coming of their 'heavenly spouse', were expected to exist wholly for God, 'contemplating him and meditating on him day and night'. The books prescribed daily fasting, prayer, spiritual reading and 'handiwork'. The women

were to wear 'decent and grave' clothes, 'without any kind of vanity
or curiosity, without pride also, or any secular ornaments'. They were
not to squander their money on frivolities, but invest it in 'the succour
& relief of the poor, and of such as are servants of God'. Their
companions must be 'modest and devout women', ideally widows and
virgins, and they should shun 'the conversation of secular persons (as
much as they may)'. Leonard Lessius, the author of *The Treasure of
Vowed Chastity*, did not even attempt to disguise his revulsion of family
life. 'The irksome slavery of marriage' bound women to violent
unfaithful drunks, and husbands to vain jealous shrews whose birthday
'must be made a holy day'. Sex was 'unclean, as a thing wherein we
differ not from a beast', and 'the sluttishness [filthiness], the ill savour,
the weeping, crying & brawling' of babies was quite beyond the pale:

> How many times a day must it be made clean, fed, made up, apparelled,
> laid to sleep, rocked in the cradle, taken out again to give it suck and
> be held out? How many times must it be flattered and entreated with
> fair speeches & with a thousand pretty hypocrisies and flatterings to
> make it leave crying, or to sleep?
>
> These are the continual exercises of such as be mothers and in such
> they are employed, not only all day long, but also most part of the
> night, so that they can scarce take any rest but with often interruption.

Chastity, by contrast, produced innumerable profits to which Anne
Vaux had shown 'good proof these many years'. There was some
sacrifice: anyone seeking to emulate Anne 'must first kill all carnal
affections in herself' and thereafter dwell 'as it were mentally and
spiritually with the Blessed, in community of heavenly things'.[6]

Quite how a woman of the world could achieve this on a day-to-
day basis was the subject of Robert Southwell's *A Short Rule of Good
Life*, which he wrote for Anne's friend the Countess of Arundel. It
described best practice for a heavenly life on earth and offered guide-
lines, 'which may be, as it were, a lantern unto thy feet & a continual
light unto thy steps', as the writer of the 'Preface to the Reader'
(probably Garnet) put it.[7] An exemplary day for the recusant householder went something like this:

5 a.m. – Rise. Short silent prayer and meditation.

'I must procure to go neatly & handsome in my attire agreeably to my calling & to avoid all kind of undecency, which breedeth dislike and contempt and doth rather offend than please God.'

Morning Prayer.

'After prayer on working days I must go presently about some work or exercise that may be of some profit, and of all other things take heed of idleness, the mother of all vices.'

Towards 11 a.m. – Rosary.

'If company and other more weighty causes will permit, I may say my beads and call to mind how I have spent the morning, asking God grace to spend the afternoon better.'

11 a.m. on a flesh day (12 p.m. on a fasting day) – Dinner.

'I must learn my little children (if I have any) to say some short grace or at the least I must say grace to myself . . . At meals I must neither be too curious or doubtful of what I eat, neither too precise in the quantity, fineness or coarseness of the meat, but of that which God hath sent take a competent meal measureable to my need and not hurtful to my health.'

Give thanks to God and leftovers to the poor.

Keep obligations and appointments.

3 p.m. – Evensong: 'use the same order of my morning prayer'.

Household chores.

'It is good for me sometimes to go about the rooms of the house and to see that they be kept clean and handsome, thinking that God is delighted in cleanness both bodily and ghostly, and detesteth sluttishness as a thing which he permitteth as a punishment of sin and one of the scourges of hell.'

Read 'some part of some good book'.

6 p.m. – Supper (or if a fasting day, a drink at 7 p.m.).

'After supper I may talk as occasion shall serve, or walk for my health, or read some pleasant yet profitable book as Catholic histories or suchlike.'

Examination of the conscience 'touching the thoughts, words and deeds of that day'.

Bedtime prayers.

9 p.m. – Bed.

'When I lie down to rest, my intention must not be so much for sloth and contentment of the body as for necessity of keeping my health & that I may rise fitter to serve God. Also, when I lie down I may imagine to lie by the pillar, cross, manger or some such place where Christ was present, that when I wake in the morning he may be the first that shall come into my mind.'

Sundays and feast days required earlier starts and 'greater devotion', with preparation for communion (beginning with confession the previous evening) and meditation after it. Although Southwell acknowledged that the householder was more likely to be 'troubled with company' on these days, he expected 'godly exercises' to take priority.[8] In the absence of processions, shrines and the great spectacles of the medieval parish, Catholics were encouraged to look inwards and use their homes as commemorative and devotional aids. Thus:

> I must in every room of the house where I dwell imagine in some decent place thereof a throne or chair of estate and dedicate the same & the whole room to some saint, that whensoever I enter into it, I enter as it were into a chapel or church that is devoted to such a saint and therefore in mind do that reverence that is due to them.

In big houses with many rooms, that meant a lot of saints, but Southwell had a solution for the forgetful householder, suggesting that the room and the saint could be matched according to function. So, 'saints of spare and regular diet, of sober and virtuous conversation', could go in the dining room or parlour, while those saints 'given to short sleep and watchfulness' might be better suited to the bedchamber. Certain spots in the garden or orchard could also be linked to particular saints, so that walks could become, 'as it were, short pilgrimages'. The technique could be deployed throughout the meditative exercises, a visit to the dining chamber, for example, prompting thoughts of the last supper.[9]

Frequent confession and communion were recommended. Many recusant women, including Anne Vaux, took private vows of obedience to their spiritual fathers, 'taking his words when he counselleth, commandeth or forbiddeth me any thing, as the words of Christ'. Some women wore a hair shirt; others preferred fasting and flagellation. Southwell approved of all three, but counselled moderation.[10] The point was to subdue one's own passions in order to focus on Christ's Passion, to confront the devil, the world and the flesh with a heart surrendered to God.

An occasional 'exercise' recommended by Southwell and based on his training as a Jesuit highlights the centrality of the Passion in Counter-Reformation thought:

> I may take occasion of other creatures to remember God's mercies: as by money the selling of Christ, by meat his last supper, by water the water of his eyes & side and washing of his disciples' feet, by drinking his easel and gall,* by wood his Cross and thorns, by stone, his grave.

None of Southwell's 'rules' were meant to be easy. 'He that entereth into the way of life,' he wrote, 'must remember that he is not come to a play, pastime or pleasure, but to a continual rough battle & fight against most unplacable & spiteful enemies.' He was following in the footsteps of Christ:

> who from his birth to his death, was in a restless battle, persecuted in his swaddling clouts by Herod, annoyed the rest of his infancy by banishment, wandering and need; in the flower of his age slandered, hated, pursued, whipped, crucified and most barbarously misused.[II]

These were images with which England's recusants could identify, but if they were to become soldiers of Christ, they required rigorous training; they had to learn about discipline, obedience, self-control and self-sacrifice; they needed *ascesis*.

The Vaux sisters were ready for the fight, mentally and physically primed by exemplary, near-monastic living, and armed by the contents of their household. It is known from various accounts that they possessed books, pictures, crosses, rosaries, plate, vessels, vestments and massing equipment. An inventory, taken early the next century, lends a thicker description to the materials kept in the house:

> Two gold reliquaries of two of the thorns.
> A great relic of gold with leaves to open.

---

* *easel and gall*: this is how Thomas More described the vinegar given to Christ on the cross. In 1535, on the way to his own execution, he reportedly rejected some wine that was offered to him, saying: 'My master had easel and gall, not wine, given him to drink.' (R. W. Chambers, *Thomas More*, 1935, p. 348)

Father Ignatius* picture of gold.

St Stephen's jawbone in gold and crystal.

A bone of St Modwen of Burton set in gold.

A piece of a hair shirt of St Thomas of Canterbury set in gold.

A thumb of Mr Robert Sutton† set in gold.

A gold cross full of relics that was Mrs Anne's grandmother's.

A gold crucifix bigger than that full of relics.

A cross of gold without a crucifix that hath little crystals.

A reliquary of silver, of silver and gilt.

For church stuff: A vestment of cloth of silver and embroidered cross of gold upon it, stole and maniple of the same.‡

A vestment of cloth of gold, stole and maniple.

A cope of the same.

Two tunicles of purple.

A taffeta vestment with an embroidered Jesus.

An altarcloth to that with letters about: these two things were Mr Page's the martyr.§

A great reliquary of silver and gilt without relics with Mr Blu[nt].¶

A great deal of brass and pewter that were Mrs Brooksby's and Mrs Anne's.

There should be 12 feather beds with their furniture.

A tawny rouge mantle that was Anne's grandmother's, which she must have.

A great brass pot to boil beef for a college.[12]

This was quite an arsenal. As monuments to martyrs and reposi-tories of numinous power, relics were a crucial aspect of traditional

---

* Ignatius Loyola (1491–1556), the Spanish founder of the Society of Jesus.

† Robert Sutton, seminary priest, executed at Stafford, 27 July 1588.

‡ *Vestment* in this context usually denotes the chasuble, the sleeveless, sometimes very ornate, outer garment worn by the celebrant at Mass. The *stole* is a long strip of material worn over the shoulders. The *maniple*, which hung from the left arm, was another Eucharistic vestment. Further down the list, the *cope* was a long cloak; the *tunicle* went over the alb; the *altarcloth* was placed over the altar during Mass and the *reliquary* was a box, often of precious metal, containing relics.

§ Francis Page, S.J., executed at Tyburn, 20 April 1602.

¶ Probably Richard Blount, S.J., later Jesuit Provincial in England.

The Lady Vaux.

1. and 2. Thomas Vaux, second Baron Vaux of Harrowden (1509–1556) and his wife Elizabeth, Lady Vaux (d.1556).

3. Harrowden Hall, now Wellingborough Golf Club. It was sold by the family in 1694 and almost entirely rebuilt.

4. and 5. William Vaux, third Baron Vaux of Harrowden, and his second wife Mary née Tresham. Vaux's adherence to his faith cost him his freedom, his fortune and perhaps also his sanity.

6. Catholic atrocities like the Massacre of St Bartholomew's Day in France, 1572 (*above*) shaped the popular Protestant impression of Catholic bloodlust. 7. In the woodcut below, the Pope is depicted as Antichrist riding the seven-headed beast of the apocalypse. Demons are fired from his mouth as he orders a monk, a priest and a layman to 'go kill your prince'.

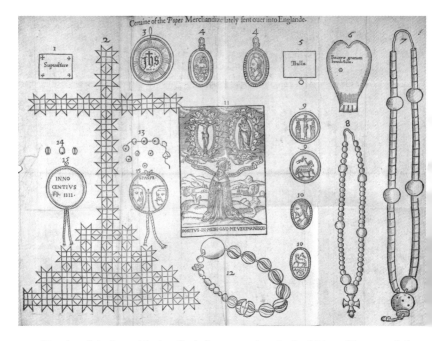

8. 'Certaine of the Popes Merchandize latly sent over into Englande', issued in 1579 to help officials identify devotional objects banned by Elizabeth I. They include rosaries, crucifixes, Agnus Deis and (object 1) a superaltar. 'These stones are portable,' explains the accompanying text, 'and serve to say Mass on in any secret place where there is no altar, and to that purpose are they sent over into England.'

9. Young missionaries pray with Pope Gregory XIII before being sent to England 'to the defence of the faith against the treachery of the enemy'. Seminary priests started arriving in England in 1574 and the Jesuits six years later. After March 1585 they were deemed traitors for being on English soil and their harbourers also risked the death penalty.

10. Edmund Campion, Jesuit missionary priest, hanged, drawn and quartered on 1 December 1581.

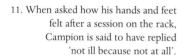

11. When asked how his hands and feet felt after a session on the rack, Campion is said to have replied 'not ill because not at all'.

12. Part of the rope purportedly used to bind Campion to the hurdle upon which he was dragged to Tyburn.

13. The pressing to death of Margaret Clitherow, York, 25 March 1586. The butcher's wife wa
the first of three women put to death in Elizabeth's reign for helping outlawed priests.

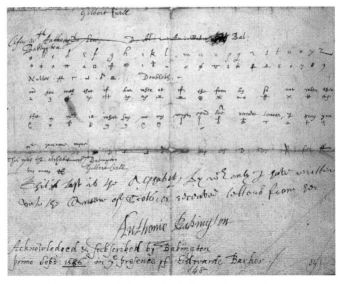

14. Mary Queen of Scots' cipher 'acknowledged & subscribed'
by Anthony Babington, 1 September 1586.

15. Sir Thomas Tresham (1543–1605) whose sister Mary was married to the third Lord Vaux. A prominent recusant spokesman, Tresham was a prickly character who frequently clashed with the Vaux women.

16. Tresham's Triangular Lodge at Rushton, built in honour of the Trinity.

17. Lyveden New Bield, devised in a cross formation as Tresham's tribute to the Passion.

18. Engraving of the Catholic plots against Queen Elizabeth.

Christianity. Formed at the juncture of heaven and earth, they were the conduits of God's wonders and were believed to emit 'a kind of holy radioactivity', charging anyone or anything that touched them.[13] Prayers said in their vicinity were more likely to be answered, fires might be quenched, the sick healed. Relics could not bestow sacramental grace like a priest, but set into an altar or pressed against the flesh of a demoniac, they might assist him in his work. At times of clerical scarcity, moreover, their function and value might rise to a quasi-sacerdotal level. Just as books and manuscripts became, for want of regular pastoral direction, the recusant community's 'domme preachers',[14] and 'sacramentals' (rosary beads, medals, crucifixes, holy water and the like) could offer penitents temporary relief until they received formal absolution, so relics came to be regarded, to some extent, as supernatural stand-ins, affording a household a measure of protection until normal priestly service could be resumed.

As memorials to the suffering of Christ and his followers, they also reminded those labouring under the cross that they were not alone. When they appeared efficacious, like during the exorcisms of the mid-1580s, they validated faith and encouraged constancy. Sometimes the relic itself was the miracle. Robert Sutton's right index finger and thumb (named in our inventory) were the only parts of his quartered body 'preserved from decay' after a year 'pinned up to be eaten by birds'. These were the two digits 'anointed with sacred oil at ordination' and 'sanctified by the touch of the Blessed Sacrament' – so wrote the Jesuit John Gerard, who was later housed by the Vauxes.*[15]

To the dismay of their superiors in Rome, who favoured strict, centralised regulation, the Jesuit missionaries did little to discourage,

---

* Contemporaries had a jolly time mocking 'popish credulity'. One 'merry jest' doing the rounds in East Anglia in the mid-seventeenth century centred on a query posed by a Royalist to a prominent Catholic convert:

'A gentleman that had drunk of many waters and tasted variety of flesh, conversed at last with a holy nun; she grew pregnant upon it, was handsomely delivered and soon after died. The father (formerly extreme dissolute) came to a sight of his sins, repented, proved a serious convert. The child was carefully educated, proved a profitable member of the church and after death was canonised for a Saint. Now, Sir, since this gentleman's prick was at last a means of his salvation, and brought so much honour to the Rubric of the Catholic Church, why are not they bound in conscience to keep it for a relic?' (Lippincott, Merry Passages and Jeasts, no. 228)

and much to foster, English lay enthusiasm for the 'fresh green new relics' of the recently departed. In part, this was a simple matter of supply and demand. No official shrines and fewer priests meant a greater recourse to portable relics at the very time when their supply was dwindling through confiscation and export. The shortage in clerical manpower must surely also have enhanced the perceived charisma of the few priests that were left, so that when one was captured and eviscerated, his remains were pounced upon as the precious remnants of a heroic martyr. Then the hagiographers set to work. Knowing that they could not hope to control the wave of popular saint-making (had they even been so inclined), the missionaries chose to ride it for all its didactic and proselytising potential, stressing in particular the righteousness of recusancy and the sacred powers of the priestly caste. Conversely, God's fury at conformists and persecutors was allegedly manifested in slow death and swift decay. In stark contrast to Robert Sutton's miraculous thumb, for example, the rotting corpse of Francis Walsingham (d. 1590) allegedly emitted such a 'noisome smell' that it gassed one of the pall-bearers.[16]

Relics were not always gathered with the dignity in which they were subsequently held. Thomas Garnet (Henry Garnet's nephew and fellow Jesuit) complained of being fleeced of his possessions while awaiting execution in prison in 1608.[17] A gun battle nearly broke out between rival camps of body-snatchers after the execution of John Almond at Tyburn in December 1612. On that occasion, a Spanish noblewoman called Luisa de Carvajal claimed the spoils. 'There are two instances,' she informed Don Rodrigo Calderón that month, 'in which I always find England to be very sweet, and forget about it being a sea of bile.' One was when she triumphed against Protestants in debate. The other

is when I receive these joyous corpses and spend the whole night exhausted from dressing them with aromatic spices, having first cleaned them of mud and caught the blood that still springs from some of the veins. I kiss their hands and feet many times, binding the severed limbs in new white holland,* keeping vigil over them and putting them in their sepulchre of lead, so that they might be preserved should Our Sovereign Lord so choose.[18]

---

* A linen fabric.

It is not known if Anne and Eleanor ever became quite so involved, but relic traffic certainly passed through their house and, looking ahead to 1606, Anne would help propagate the most notorious miracle tale of all, that of 'Garnet's Straw'.

Another prominent item in the aforementioned inventory is the vestment, the ritual apparel of the Catholic clergy. The most significant and symbolic were the Eucharistic vestments, those worn by the priest at Mass. They could be works of art: sumptuous textiles, exquisitely embroidered and sometimes (like the Vaux set at Harrowden Hall) embellished with gold and pearls. They helped the priest represent Christ at the Sacrifice of the Altar and they presented the laity with a 'living picture' of the Passion. A priest celebrating Mass without the right vestments – that is, the alb, amice, stole, maniple and chasuble – was committing a mortal sin, even in England, it was ruled, despite the high risk of detection.[19]

Recusants became adept at replacing confiscated vestments. One gentleman, a Knight of the Bath, offered up his investiture robes to be 'turned to use at the altar'. Others converted dresses, gowns, blankets, even cushions (permissible as long as they were blessed afterwards). Some vestments were designed to be reversible, others were disguised as ordinary domestic items. Unfurled in all its glory, a dalmatic at All Saints Chapel, Wardour, displays a cross; folded up with the linen, it could have passed for a patchwork quilt.[20] In households like Anne and Eleanor's, pious ladies were supposed to work the needle in sober, straight-backed devotion. It was a commendable pastime 'in which the mind is little or nothing at all busied' and could focus on edifying thoughts. And as they sat and sewed and meditated, these ladies also produced altar-cloths and chalice veils, silk panels, appliqué hangings, monogrammed handkerchiefs and even – in one house in Samlesbury, Lancashire – a 'gown without a pocket and yet devices secretly to keep letters in'.[21] It is a testament to their industry that John Gerard, S.J., only had to carry around his own Mass equipment for a few years after his arrival in England in 1588. 'In nearly every house I visited later I would find vestments and everything else laid out ready for me.'[22]

Only the most privileged families could afford – both in terms of cost and risk – to have much 'church stuff', that is: chapel plate and furnishings, altarpieces, crucifixes, candlesticks and other holy objects

and images. These were encouraged, but not required, for the legitimate celebration of the Mass. A priest would need his missal, however,
even if he could remember all the words, and consecrated vessels for
the bread and wine. Chalices were sometimes made to a small scale
and unscrewed at the stem for portability and concealment. Traditionally, they were cast in precious metals, but hard times called for hard
measures. To the question, *May a tin chalice be used for saying Mass in
England at the moment?*, came the sensible resolution:

> There is no difficulty at all for we have the express decision of a canon,
> where it is laid down that the chalice of the Lord and the paten should
> be made of gold, or, if that is not possible, of silver. In cases of great
> poverty, a chalice should at least be made of tin. But chalices should
> not be made of bronze or brass because they react with the wine to
> form a mould, which can cause vomiting. No one has dared to sing
> Mass with a wooden or glass chalice. Lo, there you have every material
> of which a chalice may or may not be made, and it may be made from
> tin, especially in England where the most perfect tin is to be found.[23]

The casuist texts that pronounced such rulings were written by
senior clerics in exile to help seminarians adapt the inflexible institutional mandates of Rome to the conditions on the ground in England.
In certain circumstances, rules could be relaxed for the greater good
of the mission. Thus, on a fast day, a recusant might serve meat to
an Elizabethan magistrate or even break the fast herself to avoid
detection on the road. 'Gambling games' were acceptable and even
preferable to excessive abstinence, which could be 'more dangerous
than useful'. Church property could be rented from Protestant landowners and 'a blind eye' might be turned to servants who attended
divine service.[24]

But the casuists could only bend so far. When it came to the Mass,
the central observance of their faith, there was a basic minimum
requirement. Hence the need for vestments, vessels and, above all, an
altar for the sacrifice. A vast stone edifice of the kind used before the
Reformation was clearly impractical, so a portable altar (or 'superaltar',
or altar-stone) was used. This was a slab of natural stone, about the
size of a placemat, into which a relic was usually set. In theory, it had
to be consecrated, but in cases of extreme necessity the stipulation

might be waived.* One altar-stone used at the time and now at Stony-hurst College in Lancashire was found in a 'pedlar's chest' hidden behind the wall of a nearby house. The chest also contained a lady's bonnet (intended to dupe the casual searcher), vestments and a chalice and paten (see Plate 27). This was the field kit of the missionary priest and it allowed him to bring his Church – and his God – into almost every place that he visited.

The Mass could happen anywhere, the texts ruled, 'except at sea or on a river'. It could be said outside, within a gentleman's wardrobe, behind bars, even in 'a bridal chamber'. Some of the grander, more protected residences like Harrowden Hall or Battle Abbey still enjoyed the use of traditional altars in private chapels, but this was exceptional.[25] For Anne and Eleanor, trying to maintain secrecy on the move or in rented accommodation, the Mass would often have been celebrated on an altar-stone slotted into a frame built into a tabletop or the surface of a sideboard or bureau. The diminutive carpenter Nicholas Owen *alias* 'Little John' often travelled with the sisters and may have created bespoke furniture or adapted existing items for this purpose.

Security mattered more than status in the room or rooms selected for the Mass. It had to be private and quiet, and have as many stairs and lockable doors in the way as possible. Attics and withdrawing rooms were favoured. Once the sisters decided to settle somewhere, they would have established the 'chapel' on a more permanent, but still convertible, basis, introducing a range of vessels, vestments and images, as well, no doubt, as their grandmother's 'gold cross full of relics'. At Stanley Grange, a house that Anne would later run as a school in Derbyshire, a pursuivant discovered

> two chapels, one opening into the other, and in either of them a table
> set to the upper end for an altar, and stools and cushions laid as though
> they had been lately at Mass. Over the altars there were crucifixes set
> and other pictures about it.[26]

---

*On 21 December 1586, Southwell wrote to Aquaviva: 'I earnestly do beg your Paternity to have sent unto us those faculties we sought for, especially to consecrate chalices and superaltars. Of this there is very great need, for that by reason of these long searchings of houses, many such things have fallen into the hands of the pursuivants, so we are in great want.' (Pollen, *Unpublished Documents*, p. 314)

Raids were often timed to catch the priest in the act of saying Mass, but households grew wise to their tactics and soon developed their own. At the signal, a well-drilled priest would throw off his vestments, snuff out the candles, strip the altar, pop his stone in his pocket and scuttle into his hide. He often benefited from the cover of darkness, especially during the dawn raids of the winter months, when waking embers and candlelight failed to lift the gloom. Even in daylight a young pursuivant born after 1558, having no memory of Catholicism as the official religion, might struggle to distinguish a dalmatic from a dressing gown. Others may not have looked that hard or may have had the 'golden reason' to flinch from the task.[27] Not all officials enjoyed rifling through their neighbour's goods, especially those of widows, who traditionally warranted the protection of society. One contemporary, referring to the ransacking of Eliza Vaux's house in 1611, acknowledged 'the disgrace that is wont to accompany this kind of service'.[28] It seems plausible that some of the tales of miraculous deliverance from discovery might have owed as much to official discretion as divine intervention.

Some raids, though, were truly terrifying. Around February 1574, in Common School Lane, York, men raged through the house of the recusant doctor Thomas Vavasour

> with naked swords and daggers, thrusting and porring [prodding] in at every hole and crevice, breaking down walls, rending down cloths, pulling up boards from the floors, and making such spoil of their goods in such cruel manner that the gentlewoman his wife . . . thereupon lost her wit.[29]

Despite their best efforts, the pursuivants failed to discover Vavasour's 'politicly devised' hide. This was England's earliest recorded priest-hole, though the vast majority were constructed after the 1586 Hurleyford conference, when it was decided that certain households should become proper missionary posts. Before that time, most priests had been itinerant and too many had been stopped in their tracks. Of the three hundred-odd priests who had returned to England between 1574 and 1586, thirty-three had been executed, over sixty had gone into exile, around fifty were in prison and a few had died naturally.[30] By the 1590s, their chances of survival had improved, thanks in no small part to the masons and joiners who put their skills to the use of the mission. Chief of their number was Nicholas 'Little John' Owen, a young carpenter from Oxford who presented himself to Garnet around the time that the Vaux sisters removed to Warwickshire. Together they strived to keep Garnet – and the Jesuit mission – alive.

Examples of Owen's handiwork survive, some so well hidden that they have only been found by accident. In 1894, a boy exploring a derelict part of Harvington Hall in Worcestershire chanced upon a loose brick that exposed a tiny room, eight feet long, three feet wide and five feet high. Its entrance, past a swinging beam at the back of a panelled cupboard, had not been tried for almost three hundred years (see Plate 26). The uninformed observer, looking at a wall or fireplace or staircase, might never suspect an Owen-built hide in the vicinity, but know where to look, lift the right step, tread on a particular tile and his genius is revealed. Owen understood buildings intimately. He worked with them, using their features, exploiting every angle and space. He had to operate quickly and quietly, keeping his plans in his head. He never grew lazy; each priest-hole was different. He was generous with his advice, giving tips 'for the making of others', and he was discreet – he never gave up his hides, even under torture. He was Garnet's man and lodged with the sisters, but was often on secondment, chiselling away in 'the chiefest Catholic houses' in the land. His talent seems only to have been matched by his industry. 'He was so skilful,' wrote John Gerard, S.J., 'both to devise and frame the [hides] in the best manner, and his help therein desired in so many places, that I verily think no man can be said to have done more good of all those that laboured in the English vineyard.'[31] He must have infuriated his adversaries.

One justice of the peace, characterised in a play performed at the English College in Rome, was said to have

> brought in engineers by art,
> With mathematic and instruments to sound
> The depth, the breadth, and length of ev'ry room,
> To see what close conveyance may be found,
> Or secret place that might conceal a priest.[32]

Others took less care, hacking, ripping, smashing and stripping until the house was unrecognisable. In an attempt to brazen out a raid on Garnet's cottage in Finsbury Fields* around 1591, the caretaker, Hugh Sheldon, offered to provide the pursuivants with an axe, so they could 'break open, pull down, knock holes through or cut to pieces anything whatever'.[33]

Not all homes benefited from the expertise of an Owen or a Greene, who reportedly made 'all the secret places' in Derbyshire.[34] Dorothy Lawson ill-advisedly used her oven; the Lygons of Elkstone hid stuff in the loo.[35] Priests inevitably were caught and had to think quickly. Disguises helped, as did pseudonyms and cover stories. But could they lie? If directly asked about their priesthood, could they deny it? No, said some clerics, this was 'tantamount to denying Christ' and would always be a mortal sin. Others posited that when truth and justice were at odds – for example, when priests were unlawfully declared traitors – they were not obliged to incriminate themselves or, indeed, their harbourers. The burden of proof lay with the accuser and the priest could do 'anything he can – using equivocation, silence, returning the question, or any method he likes – to avoid making a reply, as long as he neither denies his faith nor lies'. This was the resolution of a casuist text produced under the supervision of William Allen and Robert Persons in the early 1580s. The two clerics endorsed the resolution with the more pithy: 'He may delude.'[36]

Just how far a Catholic could delude his examiner was a matter of discretion and some controversy. The practice of 'mental reservation', by which a respondent kept in his head a statement that contradicted or qualified the answer he had just given, could be taken to faintly absurd lengths. When, for example, Thomas Cornford was captured saying Mass for the imprisoned Eliza Vaux in 1612, he told the Archbishop of Canterbury that he was John Underwood, a married father of six who had visited Eliza in the hope of renting a farm on her son's

---

* The cottage, which was just beyond the London wall, had only three rooms and was used by Garnet 'when exceptional danger threatened the city'. By day, it was perfectly still and silent. No food was prepared, no conversations were had, no fires were lit 'even in the most bitter winter weather, for fear the smoke might be seen.' The cottage was only discovered when a careless priest hazarded a daytime visit. (Caraman, *Garnet*, pp. 68–9, 122–6)

estate. At his second examination, however, he admitted that he was a Jesuit priest:

> Whereas he affirmed himself to be a married man, his meaning was that his wife was his breviary and that he had been married unto it twelve years. As for his children . . . those were his ghostly and spiritual children . . . The reason why he called himself a farmer was because he was so to God, according to that text, *Redde rationem villicationis tuae: Give an account of thy farmership*. And the reason why he said that he went to Mistress Vaux to take a farm of the Lord Vaux was because he was ready to do them any service for their salvation and for the spiritual tilling of their souls. Whereas he had denied himself to have been beyond the seas, his answer was that he spoke that with intention that he had been there, but not that he was bound to tell His Grace so much.[37]

For many people, this was lying by any other name and it showed that whatever the armchair casuists might prescribe from the security of exile, equivocation was a tricky doctrine to apply – and justify – on the ground. Priests were roundly condemned for the practice, especially the Jesuits with whom it came to be closely identified.* The 29-year-old gentlewoman Anne Bellamy, who would betray the whereabouts of Robert Southwell in 1592, claimed at his trial that he had coached her to deny having seen a priest, keeping the true meaning in her head that she had not seen one with the intention of traducing him.

In 1598, Garnet would enter the fray with *A treatise against lying and fraudulent dissimulation*, in which he defended Southwell and the use of equivocation 'both to heretics and also to diverse Catholics', who think it 'seemeth strange'. According to the Protestant polemicist Richard Sheldon, Cornford had been a 'doltish' simpleton before Garnet had received him into the Society of Jesus. 'Well it may be observed herehence,' he surmised, 'how efficacious the Garnetian Academy hath been for training youth in lying, cogging and equivocating.'[38]

This was presumably the sort of 'evil instruction' that Sheriff Cave

---

* The second definition of 'Jesuit' in the *Oxford English Dictionary* is 'a dissembling person; a prevaricator'. (*OED* Online)

of Leicestershire had feared – youths studying 'equivocating tricks' alongside their (equally harmful) catechism, servants drilled to deal with raids, girls sewing vestments, boys gathering relics, children learning to read and write in invisible ink* and being exhorted 'from the very beginning to protect religion and the holy Church'; households turning inwards, celebrating different holidays and heroes from the rest of the country, shunning Protestants ('since they are more grievous enemies of Christ and much more to be hated' than 'Jews or Turks'): the very bonds of society being broken by the pernicious influence of the recusant mistress. 'If only there was some one place where they might be permitted to live in peace,' Garnet opined, 'they would consider themselves treated fairly enough.'[39] But the authorities had no truck with this line, especially as regards the Vaux sisters, who were hardly retreating into a quiet seigneurial existence.

Alongside Eleanor's children, the sisters raised and educated other youths, including William Hutchinson, the fourteen-year-old cited by Cave in 1588, who was listed as a recusant thirty-five years later.[40] There was also their little cousin Frances Burroughs, whom Eleanor had adopted around 1581 when the five-year-old lost her mother (Lord Vaux's sister Maud). According to the Chronicle of St Monica's, the convent in Louvain that Frances would join:

> When this child came first to the said widow, she took her in her arms with tears and said 'I will have Frances, I will have Frances', having before intended to have taken another of the sisters who was her god-daughter. 'For to this child,' quoth she, 'God will give a blessing which none of the rest shall have.' Which proved true, for she became a religious [i.e. a nun] and none of the rest so much as Catholic.[41]

---

*In his satire 'The New Cry', Ben Jonson revealed the popularity in England of *De Furtivis Literarum Notis* (1563) by the Italian cryptographer and polymath Giovanni Battista della Porta:

> They all get Porta for the sundry ways
> To write in cipher, and the several keys
> To ope the character. They've found the sleight
> With juice of lemons, onions, piss, to write,
> To break up seals and close 'em . . .
>   (Miola, *Early Modern Catholicism*, p. 230)

ceive#

Family legend had it that Frances had been destined for God's graces since infancy, for every Sunday when her (conformist) father took the family to church, she had fallen into a deep slumber,

> not waking till she was out of the church again, and this continued with her after she could go alone, and was so observed in her that they thought it bootless to lead her into the church, but would leave her in the churchyard to play during the time of service.

Eleanor would have enjoyed, and presumably had a hand in, that tale, it being just the kind of conformity-bashing story that the missioners encouraged. At least baby Frances only fell asleep. The moment Francis Woodhouse entered his parish church in Norfolk, he felt a fire in his bowels that not even eight pints at the local tavern could quench. The message was clear: since England's churches were 'polluted' with heresy, God disapproved of attendance.[42]

Although Frances Burroughs was 'sickly all her life long', she had a mischievous, indomitable spirit. Once, when an alms-seeker came to the house, she sneaked him a slice of pie when the butler, who had already provided 'a good piece of bread and meat', disappeared to fetch some beer. During searches, she was 'always let out to go up and down to answer the officers, because her courage was such as she never seemed to be daunted or feared of anything'. On one occasion, a pursuivant, 'holding his naked dagger at her breast', threatened to stab her in the heart if she would not tell him where the priests were hiding. 'If you do,' she cried, 'it shall be the hottest blood that ever thou sheddest in thy life.' The pursuivant was so taken by Frances's courage that he tried to buy her for a hundred pounds.

The chronicler of St Monica's was less impressed. Although she praised Frances's patience, humility and obedience, she was clearly needled, even after Frances's death, by her 'hasty words' and 'some small defects' in her character, 'which,' the writer suggested with superb disdain, 'perhaps were not so displeasing to God as to creatures'. Her last words on Frances were that she had 'but a weak voice for the choir', a mortifying shortcoming for a nun.

Frances joined the Canonesses Regular of the Lateran at Louvain around 1595, when she was about nineteen. Her escape from England was arranged by Garnet. His servant Richard Fulwood

favoured the route from Gravesend to Gravelines, later uncovered
by a spy:

> The priests of the country command such youths as they make choice
> of unto him [Fulwood], who placeth them in some blind alley near
> the water until the wind serves for passage, which fitting, the vessel
> (which is some old hoy or suchlike, to avoid suspicion) goeth down
> empty towards Gravesend, and he provideth a pair of oars and boats,
> the passengers and carriage, and so ships them into the bark, commonly
> beyond Greenwich, and conveys the money which belongs unto them
> afterwards himself. They ship them to Gravelines or Calais and take
> forty shillings for the passage.[43]

A passing reference in 1598 to 'the safe shipping of her maidservant'
confirms that Eleanor sent others abroad too. It was not a decision
that was taken lightly. Border guards were on the lookout for the
'crafty Catholic children abroad in every quarter or coast in England'.
Garnet deemed the services of agents like Fulwood, though 'unbeliev-
ably burdensome and fraught with infinite perils and anxieties', to be
'the most necessary and useful works we undertake'.[44] Although quite
a few of the boys who made it out to the colleges and seminaries
abroad would return home, most of the girls entering the convents
did not expect to see their country again.* Frances would die in

---

* In his sonnet 'Upon the Sight of Dover Cliffs from Calais', the famous convert, Sir
Toby Matthew (1577–1655), captured the pain of exile:

> Better it were for me to have been blind,
> Than with sad eyes to gaze upon the shore
> Of my dear country, but now mine no more,
> Which thrusts me thus, both of sight and mind.
> Better for me to have in cradle pined,
> Than live thus long to choke upon the core
> Of his sad absence, whom I still adore
> With present heart, for hearts are not confined.
> Poor heart, that dost in so high tempest sail
> Against both wind and tide of thy friend's will,
> What remedy remains that can avail,
> But that thou do with sighs the sails fulfil,
> Until they split and if the body die,
> 'Tis well employed; the soul shall live thereby.
>   (Miola, *Early Modern Catholicism*, p. 216).

Flanders in 1637. As a child in Eleanor's house, she had agonised over her vocation for ten years, searching for a sign and 'wavering in her mind, sometimes she would be a nun, sometimes not'. She was encouraged by 'daily' conversation with priests, and by Eleanor, who told her inspiring tales about her sister Elizabeth's life with the Poor Clares in Rouen.

There could have been few better places in England for Frances to prepare for her vocation. Under the influence of Garnet, the son of a grammar schoolmaster, and Eleanor, who raised her 'as her own daughter', Frances was

> taught to say her prayers, then instructed in the Catholic religion and admitted to be present at the exercises thereof, for this was a very Catholic house. As she grew in years, so did she in the constant profession of her religion.[45]

Eleanor's grandson, Edward Thimelby *alias* Ashby (possibly after Great Ashby), who went on to the Jesuit colleges at St Omer and Rome, similarly recalled that Eleanor 'took care that I should be instructed in the Catholic faith'.[46] This was recognisably the same faith that the old Lord Vaux had learned as a boy. It involved the familiar rote prayers and the commandments of God and the Church. But it was also something different: a faith regenerated by initiatives that were imaginative, combative and exciting. The rosary, for example, that traditional, seemingly benign devotion, became, after Henry Garnet's 'repackaging' in *The Societie of the Rosary*,* a pedagogical instrument for Counter-Reformation spirituality, a worldwide confraternity of mutual charity and, in its special veneration of a

---

* The title-page of the first edition (secretly published around 1593) is illuminating:
     The Societie of the Rosary. Wherin is conteined the begining, increase,
     & profit of the same. Also the orders & manifold graces annexed unto
     it, with divers other things therunto appertaining.
        A thing, which as it was at the first instituted by the Holy Light of
     God's Church S. Dominicke as a present remedy against the Albigenses
     certaine heretikes of his Age: So undoubtedly will be a necessary remedy
     for all Christians to embrace in this miserable time.
        Gaudo MARIA Virgo, cunctas haereses sola interemisti in universo Mundo.
     [Rejoice, Virgin Mary, since thou alone has crushed all heresies
     throughout the world.]

militant Virgin mother (in implicit competition with the temporal Virgin Queen, whose children never uttered 'any other *Ave* than for her name'), a potent symbol of Catholic defiance.[47]

Another Catholic house in another part of the country might have had a very different concept of the faith and how it should be preserved and taught. But the Vaux house radiated apostolic activity. Whether as a centre for the Mass, a theatre for exorcism, a shrine for green relics or a haven for a meditative and prayerful lifestyle, it evolved with its guests, reflecting their priorities, preoccupations and proselytising zeal.

One guest, in particular, took over their lives. If the 'Garnetian Academy' could have been sited anywhere in England, it was at Anne and Eleanor's house. The Jesuit superior's physical presence made it a magnet for lay folk and clergymen. People knew that confessions would be heard there and the sacraments given. Thomas Bates, for example, a future gunpowder plotter, was cited for taking 'a man child' to the Warwickshire house in 1592, presumably for baptism.[48] Messengers rode in with instructions from Rome and bulletins from the scaffold. Nicholas Owen set off for the shires with his toolkit; Richard Fulwood returned from Gravesend with a nod or grim head-shake. Coaches rolled in on holy days for masses and music. Pedlars and gentlemen pitched up and swapped their disguises for vestments – young priests, old Marians, Jesuits flocking to their superior for succour and advice. 'The place of my residence is like a little college, never without four or five,' Garnet informed Aquaviva. 'We were yesterday five of our own family, two being driven unto me for fear; and continual resort is of others unto me.'[49]

Anne and Eleanor welcomed and fed them all, seeing to their health, their horses, their provisions, massing equipment and laundry. And 'since both lay people and priests come in such numbers to see us,' wrote Garnet, 'they are compelled to stay some period of time: it is not safe for them to leave immediately, since constant arrivals and departures would be observed by the heretics.'[50]

Security was an unending concern. Parish constables and village gossips could be a fatal nuisance. Eleanor became 'Mrs Edwards' and Anne was 'Mistress Perkins', sometimes the sister, sometimes just a kinswoman of Mr Walley, or Roberts, or Farmer, or whichever name

Garnet was using at the time. His true identity and location were known to 'very few persons who could be thoroughly trusted', Oswald Tesimond, S.J., recalled. The hidden informer haunted their dreams, for they knew that the devil could infiltrate even pious homes. 'A pox on you all!' poor possessed Sara Williams had shouted at Hackney, 'I will cause you all to be taken & hanged.' Robert Southwell warned mistresses with servants to 'see that they lie not out in the nights, but . . . know what becometh of them'. Sensible advice, since the devil had vowed to revisit Sara 'in the form of a tall man' and 'now & then tempt her, sometime with money'.[51]

Some of Anne and Eleanor's guests were a pleasure. Everyone seemed to love Robert Southwell, who was 'so wise and good, gentle and loveable'. Also Edward Oldcorne *alias* Hall, the Jesuit who came to the Midlands soon after landing with John Gerard in Armada year. This straight-talking, no-nonsense Yorkshireman was as comfortable in a party of demobbed sailors, 'roughs that they were', as he was with Dorothy Habington, the spiky mistress of Hindlip, near Worcester. Indeed, he succeeded where Garnet and others had failed: the lady was converted, Hindlip was peppered with priest-holes and soon resembled, in Gerard's words, 'one of our houses in some foreign country – so many Catholics flocked there to receive the sacraments, or to hear him preach or to get his advice'. For the next sixteen years, Oldcorne used Hindlip to spearhead the mission in Worcestershire and the west of England. 'It was his work,' wrote Gerard, 'to bring many to the faith in this and neighbouring counties, to support the wavering and lift up the fallen, and to station priests in many places.'[52] It was a pattern that Garnet hoped to replicate throughout the country.

Oldcorne, like Southwell, was born in 1561, and was younger than Eleanor, and older than Anne, by about a year. Many of the priests coming off the boats were younger. During the 1586 Hackney exorcism, the devil in Sara Williams had scoffed at the 'little boy in the surplice'. Harsnett called them 'our puny exorcists'. Edward Coke would label them 'boy priests'.[53] Garnet was only thirty-three when he became the Jesuit superior. 'Hoary senses,' wrote Southwell, 'are often couched under green locks and some are riper in the spring than others in the autumn of their age.'[54] There were still Marian veterans around – 'one Hales, a very old massing priest', performed

marriages and baptisms in Warwickshire and 'resorted commonly to
Mrs Brooksby' in 1592*[55] – but the mission was a young man's game:

> Those who purpose to come to this country and to work profitably
> therein must bring along with them vigorous souls and mortified bodies.
> They must forego all pleasure and renounce every game but that of
> football, which is made up of pushes and kicks and requires constant
> effort unless one would be trampled under foot; and in this game they
> have to risk their lives in order to save souls. On my return to England
> I found that it was one huge prison for all who, like us, profess the
> true faith.

So wrote John Pibush, a Rheims-educated Yorkshireman, who had
come to Garnet after landing in 1589. He was a secular priest, not a
Jesuit, but Garnet 'supplied his wants and recommended him to certain
friends'. In July 1593, Pibush was captured at Moreton-in-Marsh,
Gloucestershire. He endured more than seven years in prison before
writing this letter to Garnet, thanking him for his continued support
and asking him to convey his gratitude to 'good Mrs Anne' for her
'golden token'. Despite Garnet's efforts to improve the reception and
transfer of seminarians in England, Pibush's experience was not
uncommon. 'The only keepsakes I can send you,' he wrote, are 'a
phial full of bitter smoke, a bundle of filth, lice and fleas.' He was
executed on 18 February 1601, his constitution 'shattered' and his
appearance 'so changed' that none of his friends could recognise him.
Before his death, he sent Anne 'a picture which a priest sent me'. Her
reaction upon its receipt, and to the news of his death, is nowhere
recorded.[56]

The previous year, another secular priest, the 26-year-old Thomas
Hunt *alias* Benstead, to whom Garnet had also given succour, both
before and after his escape from Wisbech prison, was rearrested and
executed. 'He hath found a better place,' Garnet wrote, 'he was our
very friend.'[57] Anne and Eleanor must surely have felt protective
towards their young lodgers, especially the 'prentices', like tennis-
loving Thomas Strange, who stayed with them before crossing over

---

* Priests from the reign of Queen Mary, although still law-breakers in the course of
their ministry, were in a safer position than the seminarians since they had been
ordained before 1558 and were not, therefore, *de jure* traitors.

for training.[58] It must have been nerve-shattering to wave them off, knowing that they might not fare well.

Impulsive adventurers like John Gerard, who visited 'several times in the course of the year', probably caused as many sleepless nights as Thomas Lister, a brilliant theologian, but rotten missionary, whose claustrophobia, headaches, mood swings and multiple neuroses made him unsuited to a life in hiding.[59] Garnet stipulated that incoming priests have 'good health', but there was not much he could do about Lister's fear of priest-holes beyond taking him in himself and absorbing the risk (along with the priest's incessant complaints). Nor could he prevent Oldcorne's throat cancer (although a trip to St Winifred's Well in Wales reputedly cured it), or Pibush's jaundice, or the fevered delusions that would transform Thomas Stanney, a benign guest in 1591, into a dagger-wielding lunatic fourteen years later.[60]

The sisters extended their hospitality to so many others. Two fugitive Portuguese Jesuits, who had survived 'in woods off roots and such things as they could get', would stay for 'several months' in 1602.[61] Robert Persons' octogenarian mother spent much of the 1590s in their care. 'We are constrained to shift often dwelling,' Garnet would report in the spring of 1598, 'and to have diverse houses at once and also to keep diverse houses at those times when we run away, for we cannot remove the old woman so often.' Garnet also assumed responsibility for Persons' nephew, 'a little wry-necked boy', even though his distinctive appearance could have brought unwelcome attention to the house.[62]

The Jesuit superior was no easy guest himself. Upon his modest shoulders rested the fate of the Jesuit priests in England, as well, unofficially, as many non-Jesuits. He was overburdened, overworked and taxed by 'various troublesome affairs'. His writings reveal countless pastoral and moral concerns – about admissions to the Society, the propriety of bribes, the seizure of shipwrecked property, equivocation, occasional conformity, the illicit printing press, the welfare of Catholic prisoners, missionary circuits, frictions within the Catholic community and – always – issues over funding: 'Whatever I have to give, I give; when I don't give, it is because I have not got it to give, not because I do not want to give it,' he wrote in exasperation in April 1596. He was 'tortured in mind' by problem priests like Lister and, at times of extraordinary stress, bleak about the future: 'We are men. We can fail. And I do not know whether we stand or fall.'[63]

For the greater part of Elizabeth's reign, Garnet's health stood up well to the rigours of the mission, but when it faltered, as in 1600 for instance, it was noted that 'the two sisters that he is with have such care of him that he is able to endure such pains as his office requireth'.[64] This despite Anne's 'chronic' infirmity and, as shall soon become evident, trials of her own. But there was always music to lift the spirits, especially on the big feast days, when recusant noblemen and 'many ladies' would arrive 'by coach or otherwise' to hear Garnet, and sometimes also his friend William Byrd, play spiritual motets. Garnet was said to be an 'exquisite' musician, especially on the lute, and his singing was 'so rare & delightful' that his listeners hailed the voice of an angel.[65] This, presumably, was some recompense for the vocal shortcomings of little Frances Burroughs.

Twice a year, nearly every year, the sisters also made their house available for Jesuit meetings. As many of Garnet's subordinates as could make it would converge, usually in the spring and autumn, to pray, confess and confer. Over a three-day period, they would make a general account of their conscience to their superior and renew their vows. 'We have sung the canticles of the Lord in a strange land,' Southwell enthused in 1590, 'and in the desert we have sucked honey from the rock and oil from the hard stones.' Gerard was similarly, if more prosaically, uplifted:

> I never found anything that did me more good. It braced my soul to meet all the obligations of my life as a Jesuit and meet all the demands made of a priest on the mission. Apart from the consolation I got from renewing my vows, I experienced – after renewing them – a new strength and an ardent and freshened zeal.[66]

Practical matters were also discussed at these meetings. Garnet briefed his colleagues on the houses that were still safe, those that had been compromised and those that might be won. He imparted new instructions and resolutions from Rome. 'In mutual exhortation', the Jesuits planned ways of creating, as well as consolidating, support for the Catholic Church in England. It was then, Garnet wrote, that 'we forged new weapons for new battles'.[67]

As edifying as these biannual meetings were for the Jesuits, they were also extremely risky. When Walsingham died in 1590, his espionage network also expired, but Burghley and his son Robert Cecil ran and funded their own agents and there were always local officials eager to expunge the popish menace from their shires. What better way to achieve this than to catch the Jesuit superior in the act of giving 'evil instruction' to a cabal of traitorous priests?

'On one occasion,' Gerard recalled,

we were all together in the house where Father Garnet was living – it was the time he was still in the country. We had held several conferences and the superior had seen each of us for a talk in private. Suddenly, one of us raised the question: what would we do if the priest-hunters broke in without warning? (There were many of us there and an insufficient number of hiding-places for all: we were nine or ten Jesuits and some other priests, besides a few laymen who were forced to live in hiding.)

'Yes,' said Father Garnet, 'we ought not to meet all at the same time now that our numbers are growing every day. But we are gathered for God's glory. Until we have renewed our vows, the responsibility is mine; after that, it is yours.'

Up to the day we renewed our vows, he gave no sign of being worried, but on the day itself, he warned us all to look to ourselves and not to stay on without very good reason.

'I won't guarantee your safety any longer,' he told us.

A number of the party, when they heard this, mounted their horses immediately after dinner and rode off. Five Jesuits and two secular priests stayed behind.[68]

12

Virgo Becomes Virago

Henry Garnet to General Claudio Aquaviva on the events of mid-October 1591:

This solemn meeting of ours was fixed for the three or four days before the feast of St. Luke, so that having finished our business we might adopt this evangelist as patron of all our work. We chose for this meeting the house which we had hitherto almost always used for this purpose, belonging to the two sisters, the widow and the virgin, illustrious by birth, fidelity and holiness of life, whom I sometimes in my thoughts liken to the two women who used to lodge Our Lord, or to those holy matrons, sisters also, who continually honour and succour your whole family, especially in Rome.

It was getting near the appointed day when, behold, a Queen's pursuivant came to the house and knocked at the door. And because he was kept waiting a little while outside until everything that betokened our religion had been put out of sight, this drunken fellow was filled with sudden fury and said that today he had come as a friend, but because they would not receive friends with civility, he would return within ten days with others and they would break open the doors and shatter the very walls of the house. What could be worse!

There was no time to let our friends know of the impending danger and they turned up as arranged. We were in two minds what to do. However, the Lord had already assembled us and everything connected with our gathering would be safeguarded. The only danger was from one filthy fellow, who spent his days snoring in taverns, and it wasn't likely that he would forewarn us if he really intended to return. If he did come, it was hardly likely to be during the only three days that we were there. Moreover, it was confidently reported that he had gone out of the county, and he couldn't cross any district near adjoining ours without our friends letting us know at once, and if we had warning, we had a most satisfactory hiding place in a very deep culvert. All things considered, we decided to carry on as usual. After all, we could hardly hope ever to hold a meeting of this sort without the devil issuing some such threats. He had always sent one of his henchmen on previous occasions, at the very time of our being together, and though he had never actually searched the house while we were all in it (in fact it was not known to him), we were about as much put out by his being in the neighbourhood as we should have been by his arrival at the door.

So we passed the whole of that time in peace and quiet, but when we began dinner on the very feast of St. Luke, having finished all our business, something prompted me to say to them that up to that moment I had risked every danger, but that I could no longer guarantee their safety and that those who wished should leave after dinner. My premonition proved to be sound. Four of the nine left straight after dinner. Two secular priests arrived that very day, making us seven in all, and if those four had not left, there would have been eleven 'merchants' spending the night there, and that would have led to great confusion, as the sequel will show.

Some spent the whole night, almost till dawn, discussing certain serious matters. When morning arrived the whole house had been surrounded without our having the slightest inkling of it and all the roads were guarded as well. Our horses were being prepared for our departure and the servants were busy about many things, some getting breakfast, some cleaning our hose, some airing our cloaks and everything else that was wanted for a journey. (In Catholic houses all these things, when not needed, are put out of sight, so as not to give away their owners or betray the presence of a greater number of men than it is wise should be seen in public). For some inexplicable reason, a gate in the courtyard had been left open. There was a young layman who has since joined our ranks, who was just leaving the house, quite unconscious of any trouble brewing, when he suddenly spied a stranger. He slammed the door after him, took to his heels and hid in a nearby copse. Meanwhile, two Catholic servants, having discerned the situation, came running from the stable armed with farm implements and threatened to use them on the pursuivants unless they moved away from the door. These men (who are so brave if you show fear, but so craven if you stand up to them) dropped their menaces and resorted to requests. One of them asked the lady of the house to open the door and that then he would deal gently with her.

Only one or two had yet said Mass (though later on in the day they all did so) when the news spread through the house that the pursuivant was there. Doors were bolted, everyone warned, books collected, pictures, rosaries, chalices, vestments and all other signs of our religion were thrown into the culvert together with the men. The mistress of the house was stowed away in a separate hiding-place of her own, both to prevent her being torn from her children and carried off to prison, and also because she is rather timid and finds it difficult to cope with the threats and evil looks of the searchers. On this occasion, as often before when this same pursuivant paid us a visit, her younger sister (the aforementioned virgin) posed as the mistress of the house.

At length, everything was disposed of with such dispatch that not a sound could be heard through the whole house. Then the pursuivant and a companion were admitted. He expostulated with the lady for keeping him waiting so long. She replied:

'Do you think it right and proper that you should be admitted to a widow's house before she or her servants or children are out of bed? Why this lack of good manners? Why come so early? Why keep coming to my house in this hostile manner? Have you ever found me unwilling to open the door to you as soon as you knocked?'

He turned to his companion and said:

'It's quite true. I've always had courtesy from this lady and you can take my word for it that she was not yet out of bed. But I want to know who that man was who fled from the house. I haven't much doubt he was a priest and if you don't hand him over, either we stay here or take you away with us.'

At this she was very frightened, supposing the fugitive to be somebody other than it really was, but regaining her composure she said:

'Oh, he's a relation of mine (and she glibly called him by a name that was unfamiliar in those parts), I'm starting on a journey with him today.'

She had to add this because they could see the food prepared in the kitchen and if they had entered the stables (which, however, God forbade), it would have been difficult to account for so many horses being saddled for the road.

Then they set about searching the house. Everything was turned upside down, everything was closely examined – storerooms, chests and even the very beds were carefully ransacked on the off chance of finding rosaries or pictures or books or agnus deis hidden in them.*

---

* The priests' mattresses were still warm, but as Gerard recalled in his *Autobiography* (p. 42), 'some of us went off and turned the beds and put the cold side up to delude

I've no idea with what patience ladies in Italy would put up with this. Here we have been sold into slavery and have become hardened to this sort of barbarity. But on top of all this is the endless altercation with these uncivil fellows. The virgin always conducts these arguments with such skill and discretion that she certainly counteracts their persistence and their interminable chatter. For though she has all a maiden's modesty and even shyness, yet in God's cause and in the protection of His servants, virgo becomes virago. I've often seen her so exhausted by the chronic weakness that she nearly always labours under, that she finds it painful to speak even two or three words, yet on the arrival of the pursuivant she suddenly rallies to such an extent that she has been known to spend as much as three or four hours arguing with him. If there is no priest in the house, she is full of apprehension, but the very presence of one so heartens her that she is convinced that the devil can have no power there.

She had every reason to feel secure from the devil during this particularly rigorous search. She says the pursuivants behaved just like a party of boys playing blind man's bluff, who in their wild rush bang into the tables and chairs and walls and yet haven't the slightest suspicion that their playfellows are right on top of them and almost touching them. So it was with the searchers. One of them, she says, was banging on the walls with furious energy, shifting sideboards and upsetting beds, and yet when his finger or foot touched the very place where some article was hidden, he was completely blind to the most obvious significance of what he had touched. One instance was quite miraculous: a pursuivant picked up a silver pyx for containing the Blessed Sacrament and put it down again at once as though it were the most ordinary thing in the world. Before the eyes of another lay a folded dalmatic of great value and yet though he unfolded everything else, he never even touched this. I should never finish this letter if I put down everything that happened in this and similar searches, all worthy of our admiration. All I will say is that the zeal and courage of Catholics is never more in evidence than at times like this.

The pursuivants soon grew tired of their fruitless search and were invited to breakfast. Then they wanted to interview that brother of ours who had fled. He was a priest and they couldn't turn a blind eye to that. Having first

---

anyone who put his hand in to feel them.' He added that the pursuivants, or 'leopards' as he called them, 'pried with candles into the darkest corners.' It was October. The raid commenced at 5 a.m. and took four hours, so about half of it was conducted in near darkness.

extracted a promise that if he proved to be no priest, he would be suffered to have his liberty, she ordered him to be called in from the copse. He denied that he was a priest and his word was accepted, for at that date the heretics were certain that no priest could deny the fact without grave sin. Now we gather from the replies of your theologians that it is lawful to do so. Many accept this opinion at once, but there are some that are scrupulous because it is laid down in the canons of the apostles that a priest, who out of fear denies his priesthood, may be deposed. They are in doubt whether this new opinion is sanctioned by human law or is deduced from the divine.

After breakfast the whole house was thoroughly searched again, but when they saw they had no hope of success, they accepted a bribe for the lady herself, and for the man who fled, and they departed . . .

You can imagine our joy and mutual congratulations when we were brought out after their departure. There could be no lack of angel guardians in a house so angelic, and where so many holy women were consecrated to God. I had such confidence in their devotion and loyalty, which I had experienced over a period of many years, that I went to the hiding place with about as much apprehension as I should have felt in moving from one room to another at a time when there was nothing whatever to fear.[1]

13

Hurly Burly

'We were all saved that day,' John Gerard recalled – himself, Garnet, Southwell, Oldcorne, Stanney, 'two secular priests and two or three laymen' – all standing ankle-deep in water for four hours as the pursuivants 'tore madly' through the house above them. Anne did not give the signal to come out until the officials had gone some distance, 'so that there was no danger of their turning back suddenly as they sometimes do'. Eventually 'not one but several Daniels' emerged, blinking from their den.[1] There is no account of the raid from the pursuivants' perspective. They would, no doubt, have had other words for Anne's 'discretion', 'loyalty' and 'courage'.

The strength of official feeling against the mission was made very clear the following month when a royal proclamation was issued from Richmond, lambasting all Jesuits and seminarians as 'seedmen of treason'. These 'fugitives, rebels and traitors', it pronounced, had trained abroad 'in school points of sedition' and returned 'by stealth' to incite rebellion. Two years earlier, a Dominican monk had fatally stabbed his king, Henri III of France (on his close stool). Now, with the Spanish occupying French ports and again threatening the Channel, the Queen was determined, 'by execution of laws and by all other politic ordinances', to safeguard the realm. A general muster was ordered and subjects were enjoined to defend 'their natural country, their wives, families, children, lands, goods, liberties and their posterities against ravening strangers, wilful destroyers of their native country and monstrous traitors'. Special commissioners were appointed in every shire, city and port town to investigate suspicious behaviour. Householders were charged to assist by making a 'particular inquisition' of all newcomers and, if necessary, handing them over for further interrogation. Only with 'very diligent and continual search' and 'severe orders executed' could the 'secret infection of treasons in the bowels of our realm' be prevented.[2] Had the pursuivants in Warwickshire conducted a 'very diligent and continual search' at Anne and Eleanor's house on the day the proclamation was written, 18 October 1591, instead of the following day, they might have captured every Jesuit active in the country and saved themselves some work.

It was time to 'shift dwelling'. A seminarian turned informer called Snape had heard 'for a truth' that one of Lord Vaux's daughters was in Warwickshire. He wasn't sure which one, or the exact 'situation or state of the house', but it was said that priests did 'lurk' there.[3] On 11 February 1592, Garnet informed Aquaviva that he was living in London in order to give Southwell, who was currently based there, 'time to breathe'.[4] Southwell had just completed his defence of Catholic loyalism, *An Humble Supplication to her Maiestie*. As a response to the proclamation, it was a great deal more measured than the vicious output of the Continental presses,* but Southwell's description of the proclamation as 'so full farced with contumelious terms as better suited a clamorous tongue than your Highness's pen' was never going to go down well. Nor were the vivid passages detailing the tortures being carried out in the Queen's name, nor, indeed, the contention that the late Francis Walsingham had 'plotted, furthered and finished' the Babington Plot.[5]

The *Humble Supplication* was already circulating in manuscript when Garnet bemoaned, in his February dispatch, that 'the latest storm we are being tossed by is the worst we have yet suffered in this ocean'. He warned that no further missionaries should be sent to England, 'unless they are willing to run straight into the direst poverty and the most atrocious brigandage, so desperate has our state become and so close, unless God intervenes, to utter ruin'. The strains of leadership were telling. Four months earlier, Garnet had begged Aquaviva, in vain, for a chance to 'hand over the torch to someone more expert than myself' and to be allowed 'to learn rather than teach, and to run, not by my own discretion, but under the guidance of others'. Now in the

---

* Robert Persons, Joseph Creswell, Thomas Stapleton and Richard Verstegan all wrote 'evil counsellor' tracts in response to the proclamation. Persons' rejoinder, popularly known as 'Philopater', was funded by Philip II and appeared in several editions in 1592–3. His argument that Catholics could use violence to remove a heretical ruler did his co-religionists in England no favours.

throes of what his Antwerp contact Richard Verstegan called 'the new Cecillian Inquisition', Garnet was close to despair: 'More often than not,' he scribbled, 'there is simply nowhere left to hide.'[6]

In the spring of 1592, Anne Bellamy, the 29-year-old daughter of a notable recusant, Richard Bellamy of Uxenden, fell pregnant. She was unmarried and in prison. Her family, from whom she tried to conceal her condition, had 'hoped that she should have been kept undefiled, being the queen's prisoner'. They were sure that the man on whose estate she gave birth and whose crony she married was responsible. In an appeal to the Privy Council, Anne's brother Thomas formally accused the sexagenarian pursuivant Richard Topcliffe.[7]

'Old and hoary and a veteran in evil', Topcliffe (b. 1531) had been around for a while, long enough to remember the Marian burnings and to have served, so he claimed, in Princess Elizabeth's household. In 1582, he had interrogated Lord Vaux in the Fleet. In the ensuing decade, he had been busy gathering intelligence, conducting searches, inflicting tortures, cross-examining defendants and sometimes also gloating over their deaths at the scaffold.* He chased priests for zeal and recusants for money and he revelled in their suffering for the simple pleasure of watching pain. (He was happy to torture thieves, murderers, gypsies and vagrants too.) Henry Garnet labelled him *homo sordidissimus* – most sordid man. He had a strange relationship with the Queen, who seems to have indulged his little fiefdom of terror. She apparently let him have a torture chamber in his house at Westminster. With the authorisation of conciliar warrants, he made extensive use of it. His behaviour was so notorious that he spawned new words at court – *Topcliffizare* (v.): to go recusant hunting; *Topcliffian* (adj.): related to torture, as in Anthony Standen's comment about the Earl of Essex: 'contrary to our Topcliffian customs, he hath won more with words than others could do with racks.'[8]

Topcliffe was the arch-villain of Catholic literature, who spoke, Gerard wrote, 'from the cesspool of his heart'. The demonisation

---

* At the execution (for harbouring) of the recusant gentleman Swithin Wells on 10 December 1591, Topcliffe's taunt that papists 'follow the Pope and his Bulls; believe me, I think some bulls begot you all', was parried by Wells with: 'If we have bulls to our fathers, thou hast a cow to thy mother.' Wells immediately apologised, but his unguarded swipe at the Queen might have been more representative of private recusant opinion than the formal protestations of loyalty would suggest. (Questier, 'Elizabeth and the Catholics', p. 73)

of 'persecutors' was a key component of martyrology. Just as the missionaries were represented as descendants of the earliest Christians, so their enemies, in their 'barbarous cruelty', were likened, or even said to surpass, 'the old heathen persecutors of the primitive church'.[9] Catholic propagandists often caricatured Protestant officials unfairly, but in Topcliffe's case there was no need to exaggerate. He revelled in his notoriety and was proud of his excesses. Writing to the Queen, 'this Good, or Evil, Friday 1595', upon a brief imprisonment for maligning her councillors, he boasted that he had sent more traitors to Tyburn 'than all the noblemen & gentlemen about your court, your counsellors excepted'. Since his committal, he continued,

> wine in Westminster hath been given for joy of that news & in all prisons rejoicings . . . And now at Easter, instead of a Communion, many an Alleluya will be sung of priests & traitors, in prisons & in ladies' closets, for Topcliffe's fall, & in farther kingdoms also.[10]

To John Gerard – admittedly a lively witness – Topcliffe would allegedly snarl as he slammed his sword on the table, 'You know who I am? I am Topcliffe. No doubt you have often heard people talk about me.'

It will hardly be a surprise to learn that Topcliffe was also a bad husband and, like many psychopaths with the means, a sharp dresser.[11] Aside from assassination, which was never attempted,* there was not much that Catholics could do about him. The 'foul spider' that was dropped into his milk as he breakfasted in one recusant house was a feeble, if telling, protest. 'It was not a spider but a humble bee,' he was informed. It is not known if the gentleman thief who broke into his house and stole his fine clothes in December 1571 was a Catholic with a grudge, or an opportunist with a sartorial bent.[12] The ultimate revenge was had by the seminary priest, Thomas Pormont, who issued an account of his interrogation by Topcliffe following his arrest in September 1591. Topcliffe, he claimed, had offered to release him if he declared himself the bastard son of Archbishop Whitgift. Topcliffe also allegedly boasted

---

* Perhaps there weren't quite as many Catholic assassins out there as the government feared; or perhaps Topcliffe was, perversely, too good an asset, in terms of negative publicity, to lose.

that he was so great and familiar with Her Majesty that he many times putteth his hands between her breasts and papps [nipples] and in her neck.

That he hath not only seen her legs and knees, but feeleth them with his hands above her knees.

That he hath felt her belly and said unto Her Majesty that she had the softest belly of any woman kind.

That she said unto him: 'Be not these the arms, legs and body of King Henry?' To which he answered: 'Yea.'

That she gave him for a favour a white linen hose wrought with white silk.

That he is so familiar with her that when he pleaseth to speak with her, he may take her away from any company; and that she is as pleasant with every one that she doth love.

That he did not care for the Council, for that he had his authority from Her Majesty.

That the Archbishop of Canterbury was a fitter counsellor in a kitchen among wenches than in a Prince's court.

And to Justice Young the said Topcliffe said that he would hang the Archbishop and 500 more if they were in his hands.[13]

Pormort may, of course, have made it all up – Topcliffe reportedly tried, unsuccessfully, for almost two hours to get him to admit as much on the scaffold – but, if not, the timing is interesting. Pormort was executed on 21 February 1592. In a matter of days, Anne Bellamy conceived her child. Whatever happened to her in the Gatehouse prison and whatever fantasies may or may not have been swirling round Topcliffe's head at the time, he certainly took advantage of her plight.

In exchange for her freedom and a promise (not kept) that her family would be untouched, Anne provided information. On the basis of that information, her family home at Uxenden, near Harrow, was surrounded. In the early hours of 26 June 1592, Topcliffe stormed the house and announced that he knew where the priest was hiding and that he should give himself up or he would come and get him. A slim, auburn-haired thirty-year-old came out of his hide and entered the hall where Topcliffe was waiting. Thus, Robert Southwell later wrote, 'I fortuned to fall under his ungentle hands.'[14]

'A priest and a traitor!' Topcliffe allegedly spat when Southwell refused to identify himself. In his fury Topcliffe ran at Southwell with his sword and had to be restrained by his men. Southwell admitted to nothing more than being 'a gentleman'. He challenged Topcliffe to prove his assertion. At first light, Topcliffe took him to his 'strong chamber' in Westminster. 'My body trembled,' Southwell later wrote, 'and my tears bewrayed grief through the horror and expectation of my painful agonies.'[15] Before he set to work, Topcliffe wrote to the Queen, congratulating himself on his prize and detailing his intention to hang the prisoner by his wrists, 'his feet standing upon the ground & his hands but as high as he can reach against the wall'. Topcliffe promised that, 'if he be rightly used', Southwell would 'tell all'.[16]

But Southwell did not tell all. On 28 June he was transferred to the Gatehouse prison, where several high-ranking officials continued the interrogation. A month later he was placed in solitary confinement in the Tower of London. As he wrote in a letter to Robert Cecil on 6 April 1593, he was living 'as one enclosed up in an anchorite's cell, having had no more part of the whole world but the scope of a few paces, no more use of life but to expect and behold my death, no more comfort of mankind but the recourse of a keeper and sometimes of Her Majesty's Lieutenant'. Finally, after two and a half years in the Tower, he was taken to Newgate prison and, on 20 February 1595, he was tried before the Queen's Bench for the treason of being a priest ordained overseas during Elizabeth's reign and practising in her realm. He reportedly claimed to have been tortured ten times, 'so extremely that the least of them was worse than ten executions'.[17] Anne Bellamy gave evidence. Topcliffe railed a lot. Much was made of Southwell's advocacy of equivocation. He was found guilty. The following day he was hanged, drawn and quartered at Tyburn.

Much of what was written about Southwell at this time flowed from Garnet's pen. The moment he had heard the news of his friend's arrest, he had ridden post-haste to London from Warwickshire, whither he and his 'family' had returned and Southwell himself had been headed. 'Father Garnet had to move' to the capital, John Gerard explained, 'so that he could keep in touch with us all, scattered as we were up and down the country, and in this central position be more accessible when we wanted to see him.'[18] He also wanted to be the first to discover the news of Southwell. If he could do nothing to alleviate his friend's suffering, he was at least determined to tell the world about it. 'We will be no less persistent in writing to you than they are in persecuting us,' Garnet informed his General when he suspected that one of his letters had been intercepted:

> All the cruel, barbarous and bestial acts perpetrated under the noonday sun, these I shall make known on the summit of the Capitoline hill. Therein is our triumph, our crown and our laurels. Have they intercepted my letter about my dearest Robert? If so, I shall write again. His valour, constancy and devotion are not such as will be lost to memory if a single letter falls into the enemy's hands, unless there is obliterated at one and the same time everything that is written with such splendour in the hearts of all who knew him.[19]

Garnet's information was not always accurate. He stated, for example, that Southwell had acknowledged his priesthood before his transfer to the Tower, when in fact he only 'unveiled' himself in his letter to Cecil of 6 April 1593. On the other hand, before a manuscript copy of this letter was discovered in the Folger Shakespeare Library in Washington, its existence was only known because Garnet, solely of all reporters, mentioned it.[20] Clearly he was privy to a unique, if not always reliable, channel of information. He also mingled with the crowds when Southwell was moved. He was determinedly constructing a martyr's tale. He wrote for dramatic effect, but he also professed to tell 'the sole truth as far as I could any way learn'.[21] His reports reflect the news, and often his own mood, as the Vaux sisters would have experienced it. They provide snapshots of suffering:

> It is reported by some, and very credibly, that he hath been tortured: as by being hanged up by the hands, put in irons, kept from sleep and such like devises to such men usual, but hereof there is no certainty.
>
> (16 July 1592)

> He asked his gaoler not to be too far away in case some accident might happen, or he might need something. As a result of his severe torture, his sides were not strong enough for him to call out aloud.
>
> (Reported, 22 February 1595)

'God forgive me, Mr Topcliffe, but I do not think that there can be another man like you in the whole world.'

(Southwell, as reported by Garnet in his letter of
22 February 1595)

I have a rosary, which he threw from the scaffold and also the bone of one of his knees: and these I shall send to your lordship when I conveniently can.

(1 May 1595)[22]

In his dispatch of 22 February 1595, Garnet wasn't sure if he should be 'sorry' or 'glad' of Southwell's death. He was sad that he had lost his 'most dear and loved companion', who had also been his confessor, but decided that it was 'more fitting to rejoice' in Southwell's ascension to heaven. During his novitiate in Rome, Southwell had written:

If God, who knows man's misery, still wishes to lengthen my life . . . and to exercise me still further in this valley of tears, then let toil come, let come chains, imprisonment, torture, the cross of Peter and Andrew, the gridiron of Lawrence, the flayer of Bartholomew, the lions of Ignatius, all things in a word which can possibly come. Indeed, my dearest Jesus, I pray from my heart that they may come, and by Thy wounds and the sufferings of Thy Saints, by Thy merits and by theirs, I most humbly beg that they may begin now at this very moment when I am writing and last until the very end of my life. For Thy sake allow me to be tortured, mutilated, scourged, slain and butchered. I refuse nothing, I will embrace all, I will endure all, not indeed I, dust and ashes as I am, but Thou, my Lord, in me.[23]

Robert Southwell was hardened by years of ascetical training, primed for the rigours of the mission and ready, indeed eager, to die for his faith. From his first days at Hackney to his last in prison, he had kept 'the supreme goal of martyrdom in view'. It was said that his face had once lit up at the sight of human remains on London Bridge and he had exclaimed to his companion, 'If God grants it, you will see my head sometime on one of those.'[24] It is tempting, perhaps, to regard someone so intensely committed to his faith, and fixated on death and the afterlife, as somehow sub-, or super-, human. But South-well was also the 'boy-priest', who loved to write poems, good poems,* and whose family worried about him. 'Even from my infancy,' he wrote to his father, 'you were wont in merriment to call me Father Robert.' That Richard Southwell was eventually confirmed in his prophecy gave him no pleasure and when he heard that Robert was 'much troubled with lice' in prison, he obtained the Council's permission to send him fresh clothes.[25] In his letter to Cecil, Southwell wrote of his readiness to accept 'that happy destiny, which is commonly made the salary of priests' labours'. It is good to remember that in the same letter, he also wrote: 'I was the child of a Christian woman and not the whelp of a tiger.'[26]

'London is like a whirlpool,' Garnet wrote; 'every day it sucks Catholics into prison and throws them out again.' They tended to lodge in the capital for the autumn and spring assizes, keeping 'two or three houses there at the same time', but it was extremely risky and whenever they could, they would escape the 'watchers', the plague and the ubiquitous London mud ('rich and black as thick ink'†) and head for the shires.[27] Travelling entailed its own risks and could be a fairly wretched experience. Most roads were just well-worn tracks, often impassable in the winter and perilously rutted in the summer, which was also peak season for the high lawyers, rufflers, whipjacks, clapperdudgeons, dummerers, counterfeit cranks and priggers of prancers.‡ Fair weather also brought out the pursuivants, 'much worse', Southwell had written, 'than any rainstorm or hurricane'.[28] Since the 1591 proclamation, which required householders to enquire

---

* Ben Jonson is said to have stated that had he written Southwell's poem 'The Burning Babe', 'he would have been content to destroy many' of his own works. (*ODNB*)

† Horatio Bussino, the Venetian ambassador's chaplain in 1617–18, thought the city 'better deserves to be called Lorda (filth) than Londra (London)'. (Razzell, *Two Travellers*, pp. 116, 177)

‡ *High lawyer*: a full-time highwayman. *Ruffler*: a beggar claiming to be a discharged soldier seeking employment. *Clapperdudgeon*: a beggar born. *Whipjack*: a beggar claiming to have suffered losses at sea by shipwreck or piracy. *Dummerer*: a real or pretended mute. *Counterfeit crank*: a vagrant pretending to be epileptic. *Prigger of prancers*: a horse thief, usually at fairs and markets. (Salgādo, *The Elizabethan Underworld*, pp. 122–30)

after the 'condition and country' of newcomers, and the 'statute of confinement' of 1593, which forbade recusants from travelling beyond five miles of their homes without a special licence, the hamlets and highways of Elizabethan England had become even more hostile.

But static priests did not win souls and missionaries could hardly complain about travelling. It was particularly important for Garnet, as Jesuit superior, to encourage his colleagues in their lonely postings and persuade the authorities in Rome of the urgent need for more men. It is often impossible to trace Garnet's steps – or to ascertain whether he was accompanied by one, or both, of the Vaux sisters – but we do know that he visited the north of England over the winter of 1592–3 and was appalled by what he saw and heard. He was told that throughout Yorkshire, Durham and Northumberland the post-proclamation searches and rumours had been so intense that many recusants had forsaken their homes for the mountains and woods. He heard the story of one man and his heavily pregnant wife, who had spent six weeks enclaved under an oak tree: 'The entrance was invisible in a cleft root, just large enough for a man to pass through, and it was kept covered with a thin layer of sods. When the rain came and the snow melted, it collapsed on them.'[29]

Increasingly, since the loss of Southwell, Garnet was haunted by the prospect of his own arrest. He had visions of his quarters impaled on London Bridge. 'For me and for no other man,' he wrote, 'tortures are already prescribed; death itself would indeed be a delight.' He feared the manacles and the rack: 'I distrust myself, as well I might.' He begged, again, to be relieved of the superiorship. Aquaviva was sympathetic, but firm: Garnet was the best man for the job: 'You must retain this burden yourself, and with keenness.' But he could have a deputy: Henry Walpole, a priest since 1588 and an erstwhile chaplain in Sir William Stanley's rebel regiment supporting Philip II in the Low Countries (a standard-bearer of this regiment was a certain Guy Fawkes). 'We are daily waiting for Father Walpole,' Garnet enthused on 12 November 1593.[30] The following month Walpole landed and, within hours, was arrested.

He was dealt with, according to Topcliffe's written request, 'in some sharp sort'. According to Catholic reports, this sharp dealing occurred fourteen times. At Walpole's execution in York in April 1595 – just two months after Southwell's – sympathisers noted that his fingers appeared dislocated. He had given up some information before he died. The authorities now knew that Garnet used 'Verstegan in Antwerp' to convey his letters and that he 'kept at M^ris Vaux her house in London'. Walpole had also heard that Garnet had stayed at Braddocks Manor in Essex, but he 'never knew where he was'.[31] This was probably true. Garnet was well protected, his lodgings 'known to a very few persons who could be thoroughly trusted'. Thus wrote Oswald Tesimond, S.J. Another priest was commended to John Gerard by Robert Persons 'by token that he gave him his breviary at his departure, and by that token he should direct me to Garnet, otherwise called Walley, being a private man only to papists known'.[32] But Topcliffe and his colleagues had caught the scent of this private man and his private family and they were not prepared to give it up. As Garnet had written in July 1592, 'we can never be safe, never free from danger'.[33]

*

'The Friday night before Passion Sunday,' Garnet informed Robert Persons in September 1594,

> was such a hurly burly in London as never was seen in man's memory, no, not when Wyatt was at the gates: a general search in all London, the Justices and chief citizens going in person, all unknown persons taken and put in churches till the next day.

To Aquaviva, who may not have heard of Thomas Wyatt's 1554 rebellion against Queen Mary, Garnet suggested that 'the uproar was such that Hannibal himself might have been at the gates or the Spanish fleet in the river Thames'.[34]

The year had begun with the revelation of two assassination plots. The first involved the royal physician, Roderigo Lopez, a Portuguese Jew who had converted to Christianity. He had allegedly been paid by the King of Spain to poison Queen Elizabeth. Arguably the Spanish link made it a Catholic plot, but its disclosure at this time, indeed its very existence, had more to do with the political rivalry of the Earl of Essex and the Cecils. Keen to prove his security credentials, Essex announced his discovery of this 'dangerous and desperate treason' in January. Burghley, who had known about Lopez's Spanish connections much earlier and even used him as a double agent, was compromised and so had to lend his weight to Essex's vigorous investigation.

The following month Burghley was quick to make his own discovery: another murder plot, this time involving several Irish soldiers from the renegade regiment of Sir William Stanley (the same unit of which Henry Walpole had been chaplain). As far as Garnet was concerned, this plot was ominous because an English Jesuit in exile, William Holt, was accused of recruiting the assassins. One of the Irishmen also claimed that Walpole had known about the plan and had advised him in Calais to cross the Channel in secret. Again, though, all was not quite as it seemed: the confessions of the assassins-designate – so swift, so voluntary, so many of them – kept changing. Two of the Irishmen had been known to Burghley for nearly two years. One he had not deemed a significant threat; the other was an informant and probable plant. Whatever this was, it was not a state of emergency.[35]

It is an axiom of 'spiery' (as the Elizabethans called it) that if one presses hard enough for a certain kind of information, and pays sufficiently well, it might be received. Prejudices and political ambitions have no place in intelligence work,* but in the sixteenth century they sometimes intruded and the result was an occasional – and occasionally deliberate – blurring of perception and reality. Yet it must always be remembered that amidst the wild rants and inchoate posturing of angry young men, which was a fair constant for much of Elizabeth's reign, there were indeed real plots to kill her and invade the realm. There were Catholics, and not just from Stanley's regiment, who were prepared to kill as well as die for their faith, and as events elsewhere in Europe had shown, assassins were not bound to fail. The recent performance of Christopher Marlowe's *The Massacre at Paris* at the Rose Playhouse in Southwark reminded Londoners of Catholic capability. It is hardly surprising, therefore, that the consequence of the revelations of early 1594 was a closer watch on the ports and a strike on suspicious targets,

---

* Under section 2(2)(b) of the Security Service Act 1989, the primary legislation which put MI5 on a statutory basis and acknowledged the agency's continued existence, the Director General is required to ensure that 'the Service does not take any action to further the interests of any political party'. A similar provision applies to MI6 by virtue of section 2(2)(b) of the Intelligence Services Act 1994, although such provision does not prevent MI6 from taking action to further the interests of political parties outside the UK, providing such action is in accordance with the UK national interest.

the most suspicious being the recusant community in London and, within that community, the English superior of the Society of Jesus. It should not be forgotten either that one of the Queen's most determined enemies, Robert Persons, S.J., was Garnet's regular correspondent at this time, as well as the son of 'the old woman' who lived under the Vaux sisters' roof.

On Friday, 15 March 1594, teams led by Justice Richard Young descended on all known recusant properties in and around the capital. They were quick to proclaim the night a success – a haul of Catholic materials and manuscripts were seized along with several laymen in a house in Golden Lane, Clerkenwell. Garnet had recently stayed at this 'notorious den of priests' and John Gerard had been on his way there that night until Garnet had 'importunately stayed him' at his suburban retreat four or five miles from London. The priests remained safe, but some of their 'friends and chiefest instruments', including Richard Fulwood, who ran Garnet's smuggling operation, were taken. 'Some of them have been tortured,' Garnet wrote.[36]

Gerard moved on to Braddocks, the home of William Wiseman in Essex, but before daybreak on Easter Monday he heard galloping hooves. His narrative of the raid, even translated from the original Latin, shows what a fine storyteller he was:

> I was hardly tucked away when the pursuivants broke down the door and burst in. They fanned out through the house, making a great racket. The first thing they did was to shut up the mistress of the house in her own room with her daughters, then they locked up the Catholic servants in different places in the same part of the house. This done, they took possession of the place (it was a large house) and began to search everywhere, even lifting up the tiles of the roof to examine underneath them and using candles in the dark corners. When they found nothing, they started knocking down suspicious-looking places. They measured the walls with long rods and if the measurements did not tally, they pulled down the section that they could not account for. They tapped every wall and floor for hollow spots, and on sounding anything hollow they smashed it in.[37]

Throughout the four-day search for him, Gerard hid in an Owen-built priest-hole beneath the chapel fireplace. He had a couple of biscuits and the quince jam that Mrs Wiseman had thrust upon him at the last minute. On the final evening the officers lit a fire over the false hearth, sending a shower of hot embers into the hide, but Gerard remained silent and undiscovered. Three weeks later, having returned to London, he was captured with Nicholas Owen. This time, 'there was no escape'.[38]

The summer brought more grief for Garnet – a priest and three laymen executed in Dorchester; several youths bound for the Continent taken from their boats. 'One danger followed close on the heels of the next,' he reported,

> so that from that time hardly a week passed without some great hazard or some exceptional loss. And along with these hardships were the watches kept on the ports, the continual opening of letters, the searching of private houses, so that we were scarcely permitted to breathe.[39]

They were, at least, free. John Gerard, on the other hand, was taken to the Counter prison in the Poultry and placed in a cell next to the privy. The stench was 'not slight' and kept him awake at night. He was examined by Justice Young and Richard Topcliffe and put in irons. 'When the prisoners below started singing lewd songs and Geneva psalms,' he related, 'I was able to drown their noise with the less unpleasant sound of my clanking chains.' After about three months he was transferred to the Clink, where, for now, we leave him. 'He will be stout,' wrote Garnet, 'I doubt not.'[40]

14

Hot Holy Ladies

If we are to believe John Wilson's dedicatory epistle in *The Treasure of Vowed Chastity in Secular Persons*, Anne Vaux was honourable and virtuous and absorbed by 'pious and devout exercises'. She embraced chastity with a 'sincerity of heart and virtuous manner of life' and was as close to perfection as was possible for a laywoman. Her 'virtuous disposition' was also lauded by Michael Walpole, S.J. (Henry Walpole's brother), who dedicated his translation of the life of the Jesuit founder, Ignatius Loyola, to Anne, 'before all others', because she had 'deserved so well of his children living in our afflicted country'.[1]

Anne's allegiance to the Jesuits also inspired criticism, even in priestly circles. In his *Quodlibets, or, Decacordon of Ten Quodlibeticall Questions Concerning Religion and State* (1602), a secular priest called William Watson launched a vicious attack on the women who 'mightily dote and run riot after' Jesuit priests. Such 'hot holy ladies', he argued, were seduced by their confessors and turned into 'parrots, pies or jangling jays, to prattle up and down all that they hear and see'. Watson claimed that there was 'a whole brown dozen' of these 'silly gentle-women' about London. Earlier in his tract he identified three of them:

> Here a Lady *A.* (otherwise truly religious and honourable), there a Mistress *A.V.*, a seeming saintly votary, and every where a whipping Mistress *H.* (whose tongue goeth like the clack of a mill), so very unwomanly, much more so uncatholic-like do taunt, gibe and despise the secular priests.[2]

There was more to this than misogyny. 'Mistress A.V.' and her friends had involved themselves in the intra-clerical factionalism that threatened to implode the English mission. With no clear leadership or defined structure, and one group of priests who favoured episcopacy having to work alongside another whose activities cut across parochial boundaries, there were bound to be rivalries and disputes. The Jesuits had arrived after the secular priests and immediately ruffled feathers. They were accused of being provocative, publicity-seeking and aggressively uncompromising. Their refusal to allow any kind of conformity to the established Church (reinforced by Garnet's *An Apology Against the Defence of Schism* and *A Treatise of Christian Renunciation*, both of 1593) was subversive and counter-productive. Their initiatives were flashy, theatrical and morally questionable. They poached all the plum chaplaincies, diverted communal funds into their coffers and, in seeking to appropriate traditional devotions like the rosary, sought to dominate every aspect of the mission. They were proud, patronising and rather too comfortable in their gentleman's disguises. They meddled in politics and knew Machiavelli's works better than their breviaries. Their founder was a militant Spaniard and their 'chief firebrand', Robert Persons, pushed for a Spanish invasion and favoured a Habsburg over a Stuart succession. 'In their hearts and practices' they were 'altogether Spanish'.[3] They were traitors to their country.

The Jesuits hurled many of the same calumnies at their secular critics.* By condoning occasional conformity and seeking compromise with the government (which sensibly took full advantage of the dispute), they had become politicised. They lived lushly and lazily, languishing in their livings and not doing enough to reconcile the wider community. They were cowardly, cynical and small-minded. Jealous of Jesuit successes, they made the Society the scapegoat of all the Catholics' ills. They lacked proselytising zeal and all too often apostatised. They pandered to heretics and were morally turpid. They were traitors to their faith.

Much of the invective spewed out after the death, in 1594, of William Allen, who had commanded respect from all sides and somehow managed to prevent the principal factions from behaving too abominably. Troubles at the English College in Rome and at Wisbech Castle,

---

* Watson and the appellants did not represent the views of all the secular priests in England, of whom, in the 1580s and 1590s, there were between 120 and 150 in any given year. The Jesuits, by contrast, only ever comprised a handful, but they made a lot of noise and put a great deal on record. This can lead to a magnification of their role in the wider mission. For the Vauxes, however, their influence was immense. (McGrath and Rowe, 'Harbourers and Helpers', p. 209)

near Ely, where many priests were detained, were followed in 1598 by Rome's appointment of an archpriest to assume authority over the secular clergy in England. The Jesuits readily accepted archpriest George Blackwell, unsurprisingly, since the Pope required him to consult Garnet on major issues. A group of secular priests who saw Blackwell as a Jesuit puppet refused to accept 'the foisting of that poor simple fellow Master Blackwell into an office and authority about whose meaning he knew little'.[4] They appealed to Rome for a bishop free of Jesuit influence. Thomas Lister, S.J., labelled them schismatic. William Watson, prominent among the 'appellants', called the Jesuit faction a 'lewd brood' – and so the controversy rumbled on to the amusement of the government and the edification of none.*[5]

Although legitimate concerns were aired, not least about the government of priests in England and the relationship between Catholics and the state, much ink was spilt on unseemly squabbles like the competition over who had the most martyrs. There were also some petty personal attacks. Watson, playing on Robert Persons' name, accused him of being the bastard son of a country parson. (Garnet quietly investigated the charge and declared it unfounded.) Persons retaliated by calling Watson, who had a squint, 'so wrong-shapen and of so bad and blinking aspect as he looketh nine ways at once'.[6]

As Jesuit superior, Garnet was naturally a target of what he called 'the lash of a scorpion's tail'. Students who resented the Society's management of the English College at Rome branded him 'a little wretch of a man, marked out to die, who day and night thinks of nothing save the rack and gibbet'.[7] It transpires from Watson's tract of 1602 that Anne Vaux and her 'foolish virgin' friends were apt to defend their confessors aggressively. For every critic of a Jesuit, he wrote, 'you shall have a young Jesuitess ready to fly in his face' and accuse him of being 'a spy, an heretic, or at least an unsound Catholic, attainted in his good name ever after'. There was the usual misogynistic paradox here, for while Watson dismissed such 'women tattlers' in stereotypical fashion – 'they know not what a faction means, but as I said before like parrots speak as they be taught' – he also acknowledged their influence: they were 'a stain to that sex and a dishonour to womanhood'. Likewise,

---

* In October 1602 a papal brief ratified Blackwell's appointment and removed the clause regarding consultation with the Jesuit superior. The appellants were exonerated from charges of schism.

Christopher Bagshaw, in *A Sparing Discoverie of Our English Jesuits* (1601), mocked the 'poor souls' who had been flattered into fondness for the Society. At the same time, he divulged that some had been admitted into the Jesuits' secret councils and likened them to 'sirens' with powers of enchantment and destruction.[8]

★

'Lawsuits between Catholics for any cause whatever are scarcely ever heard of,' an idealistic young priest had written in 1582. 'If a controversy arises, it is left wholly to the arbitration of the priests.'[9] Someone neglected to show Anne Vaux and Sir Thomas Tresham this roseate image of Catholic harmony. In Michaelmas term, 1593, Anne sued Tresham for her marriage portion.

It will be remembered that Tresham, whose sister was Anne's stepmother, had stood trustee for the dowries of Anne and her two sisters in 1571. According to the agreement, he was to provide each girl with £500 upon her marriage in return for instalments of £100 every year for fifteen years. The eldest daughter, Eleanor, had married Edward Brooksby and received just £160 of her share. The second sister, Elizabeth, had become a nun and seems to have received £300. The youngest sister, Anne, in need of cash for rents, bribes, travel, prison costs and everything else that she contributed to the mission, decided it was high time she received her dues. Presumably she thought it not unreasonable, as an effective bride of Christ, to request the sum that her father had intended for her future; if she could not receive it, she at least wanted it returned.

Tresham refused: theoretically Anne was only entitled to the money upon her marriage or her father's death; practically, she could not have it because Lord Vaux had failed to pay the full and regular instalments. Tresham nevertheless claimed that he would have dealt 'bountifully' with Anne had she not resorted to 'her clamorous bill of complaint'.[10]

It is difficult to get to the bottom of the dispute because the evidence is one-sided. Only Tresham's notes survive and, as his letters and more than twenty other lawsuits reveal, he was very good at being aggrieved. He liked to be in control of Vaux affairs and was irked by the ingratitude of the next generation, who inevitably pulled away from his 'kinsmanliest counselling'.[11] (Anne was not the only one, as we shall

see.) He also resented the intrusion of Anne's 'uncle judge', Francis
Beaumont, who stoutly defended the interests of his late sister's children in this and other respects.

Anne's challenge was also offensive to Tresham because she was a
relative and a woman and a Catholic – or at least, in a sentence loaded
with spite, he wrote that she was 'reputed a zealous and virtuous
catholic maiden, in exterior show renouncing (as it were) the world,
to live a Christian virgin life'.[12] There are shades here of William
Watson's 'seeming saint' jibe at Anne and it is true that she pursued
Tresham with the same ruthlessness with which she defended the
Jesuits. Her resort to the Court of Chancery, a public institution of a
persecuting Protestant state, was, Tresham opined, just about the most
ignominious and 'irreligious' action that one Catholic could take
against another. Worse, she had paid her lawyers with money that he
had lent her and she had persisted in her suit even after he was made
a close prisoner in the Fleet, 'she joying whereat true Catholics ought
to have had Christian commiseration'. This 'too too passionate and
scandalous course', wrote Tresham, revealed Anne to be 'senseless',
devoid of charity and cut off from the body of the Catholic community. 'I sooner would have begged my bread,' he protested, 'than in
such sort have my fellow's bane.'[13]

While the lawyers were arguing and Tresham was stewing in his
cell, Anne and Eleanor travelled up and down the country threatening
and abusing him with 'ingrate, injurious, and infamous speeches'.[14]
The most dangerous allegation, which was presented in court, was
that Tresham had married the middle Vaux girl off 'to a monastery
instead of a man, and there relieved and maintained her in a seminary
beyond the seas'. Anne's point was that Tresham had duped her sister
to gain her marriage portion, but in exposing his contempt for the
Queen's proclamation against the maintenance of children beyond
the seas, she embroiled him in 'a matter of state'. Thus, he accused
her of 'bloodily' seeking his life.[15]

There was certainly no love lost between Tresham and Anne, but
he believed that the 'malignity' stemmed primarily from Eleanor,
'with whom she liveth and by whom she is speciallest directed'. He
traced it back to the help he had given their brother Henry in resigning
the patrimony to George Vaux, and not to 'widow Brooksby's children'.[16] At the end of a letter to his wife of 23 November 1594, Tresham

scribbled some notes that reveal a different side of 'Mrs E.B', to the timid creature portrayed by Garnet. She had apparently calumniated Tresham 'in intolerablest terms . . . in many companies and diverse countries', including at Harrowden Hall, when Lord Vaux had been seriously ill. Among other insults of which she 'ungorged herself' were:

> That [Tresham] was a mere Machiavellian. That he had a face of brass. That his fingers were like lime twigs, for what money he got into his clutches could not thence be gotten forth. That he had wrongfully many, and many years, withheld her sister's marriage money from her to her infinite hindrance. That he had deceived her father of a thousand pounds by many years since receiving a thousand pounds for the preferment of his two nieces. And, notwithstanding, covinously causeth her said father to sell land to levy money again to that self same use. That her uncle J[ustice] B[eaumont] should course* TT [*tear in manuscript*] . . . Lastly that TT was a scandal to the Catholic religion and to all Catholics and should also speedily be scoured up for it by them that had authority to do it, and should do it.[17]

The dispute reached its denouement on 2 November 1594. 'This present weeping All Souls Day,' Tresham reported late that night, 'which exceedeth all the extreme wet days of this long matchless wettest season, here arrived (as my petty Hoxton common was coming for my dinner) my now kind, former unkind, cousin.' The court had ruled for Anne, but on the condition that she go to Tresham, apologise for her behaviour and ask nicely for the money. She had tried to wriggle out of the meeting, arguing that it was 'an unseemly action for a gentlewoman', especially a Lord's daughter, but the Master of the Rolls said that 'if she was so stomachful as to refuse to do it', she would not get her money. Her friends begged her to yield. Her own counsel apparently threatened to ditch her. Even Justice Beaumont grew weary. 'She held out till the last hour,' Tresham wrote, but finally pitched up at Hoxton with her entourage. Despite her fragile constitution, Anne had rejected Tresham's offer of a more convenient venue, preferring to brave 'the furthest and foulest journey' in order to catch him alone

---

* *course*: literally, to pursue with hounds. It is not clear whether Eleanor meant that her uncle should chase Tresham in the courts or give him a beating.

and have her submission 'swallowed up in secret, as near neighbouring to auricular confession' as was possible. After about four hours of 'verbal combat', she fulfilled her obligation and was assured of her money. Tresham was satisfied on all points, if still seething. He noted pointedly that Anne had kept him from his dinner just as his malicious keeper at the Fleet had used to do.[18] It does not seem to have occurred to him that she might also have been hungry.

Quite apart from what the case might reveal about the sisters' characters, it confirms a few truisms: that co-religionists do not necessarily get on (even, or perhaps especially, during oppressive times), that Christians are more than capable of unchristian conduct and that a professed virgin need not be a saint.

'The extreme wet days of this long matchless wettest season' continued beyond the winter, seeping into the spring and summer months. The harvest failed that year, and the next, and the next. Prices rose, plague struck and, in 1596–7, there was famine. The 1590s were hard years of war, dearth and death, especially in the north and west, where there was little poor relief. For once English Catholics could agree with the future Archbishop of Canterbury George Abbot: 'He is blind who now beholdeth not that God is angry with us.'[19]

No priest was executed in London for four years after Southwell's death in February 1595, though bodies continued to swing in the regions. Between 1590 and 1603, fifty-three priests and thirty-five laypeople were executed. Compared to the seventy-eight priests and twenty-five laypeople between 1581 and 1590, this was an improvement.[20] Some captive priests were not executed. John Gerard was one. William Weston, Garnet's predecessor, was another. An informal alliance with France between 1595 and 1598 strengthened England's hand for a time, but there was always 'noise from Spain'[21] and concomitant chatter about Philip II's (after September 1598, Philip III's) sleeping allies in England.

With hindsight Queen Elizabeth's last decade (1593–1603) appears more settled in terms of religion than previous years, but Anne and Eleanor are unlikely to have seen it that way.[22] They were still harbouring the Jesuit superior and his brethren, still on the run, still jumping at shadows. We glimpse them only occasionally – visiting their sick father at Harrowden Hall in the summer of 1594; bailing

William Baldwin, S.J., out of prison in 1595; bumping into a surpris-
ingly upbeat Countess of Arundel in London in 1598 a day or two
after her teenage daughter had succumbed to tuberculosis: 'Ah cousin,'
she said to Anne, 'my Bess is gone to heaven and if it were God
Almighty's will, I wish the other were as well gone after her.'[*23]

In March 1598, Oswald Tesimond, a slender, rubicund Jesuit from
York, found Garnet and his family at a house called Morecrofts, 'about
twelve or thirteen miles from London near a village called Uxbridge'.
He had walked there from the capital and arrived just before sunset,
receiving 'the warmest welcome and the greatest imaginable charity'.
A couple of evenings later, a messenger galloped in from London
with news that the house, which belonged to Anne and Eleanor's
cousin Robert Catesby, was to be searched that night. Tesimond was
astonished by Garnet's equanimity, though he would soon witness it
'on some ten other occasions' of greater danger. 'In truth,' he wrote,
the Jesuit superior 'proved himself to be an old soldier and experienced
captain, accustomed to such assaults'.[24]

Garnet and his hosts were indeed veterans now, not only at running
away, but also at covering their tracks and managing their next steps.
Wherever they stayed, they had to keep in mind the planned itinerary
as well as multiple alternatives for themselves and their guests. 'We
are constrained to shift often dwelling,' Garnet explained a month
after their flight from Morecrofts, 'and to have diverse houses at once
and also to keep diverse houses at those times when we run away.'[25]
Tesimond was directed towards a halfway house at Brentford, where
Garnet caught up with him and took him, by boat, to a place that
the sisters kept just outside the city in Spitalfields. The following year

---

[*] Anne Howard, Countess of Arundel (the 'Lady A.' disparaged by William Watson
in 1602) was a great patroness of the Society of Jesus in England. Southwell wrote
his *Short Rule of Good Life* for her and she harboured him, and the Jesuit printing
press, at one of her houses in London for several years. According to her biographer
(and chaplain for the last fourteen years of her life), she had only meant for Southwell to be an occasional visitor, but he had assumed a more permanent arrangement
and she had been too polite to put him straight. Her husband, Philip Howard, Earl
of Arundel, who died a few months after Southwell in 1595, had prayed in prison
for the success of the Spanish Armada. The Countess's biographer wrote admiringly
of her charitable works, relating one instance when she walked three miles from
Acton to assist a poor woman giving birth 'in the common open cage of Hammer-
smith'. (Fitzalan-Howard, *Lives*, pp. 308–9)

that house was discovered, but again the tip-off arrived just in time, courtesy of John Lillie, Garnet's imprisoned lay assistant, who managed to smuggle out a message that the Lieutenant of the Tower knew all about the house 'of Mrs Anne Vaux and her sister Mrs Brooksby' and was planning a raid.[26]

Every captured priest and layman was now 'asked for Henry'.[27] In 1600 they removed to White Webbs, a large house in Enfield Chase about ten miles north of London. John Grissold *alias* James Johnson from Rowington, Warwickshire, acted as caretaker. He arrived in February and had the house ready for 'Mrs Perkins' (Anne) by Whit-suntide. One of the first guests was her 'kinsman', Mr Measy, 'an ancient well set gentleman, but plain in apparel'.[28] This was Henry Garnet. Around the same time, Eleanor's son, William Brooksby, and his bride, Dorothy Wiseman, moved in. Soon the patter of two little girls' feet could be heard.

There were other joys: Henricus Garnettus professed his final vows as a Jesuit on 8 May 1598, the anniversary of the day that he had set out from Rome with Robert Southwell twelve years earlier. To General Aquaviva he wrote a heartfelt letter of thanks.[29] To the Vaux sisters, who had protected and defended him all those years, he would surely also have expressed his gratitude. And still there was music and holy days and those supremely risky Jesuit meetings – 'I cannot keep them away, but they will flock to such feasts,' Garnet wrote on 25 November 1600. And still there were the sacraments, with their life-breathing properties for the ailing faith. Notwithstanding the dawn raids and the midnight runs, notwithstanding the spies and fallen friends, 'notwithstanding all our troubles,' Garnet wrote on 30 June 1601, 'we sing Mass.'[30]

PART THREE

ELIZA

Great Harrowden is a village in a million. Why? Because – so I am assured – there is no gossip, no scandal, no backbiting.

Tony Ireson, *Wellingborough News*, Friday, 21 March 1958

Thus this Harrodian hatred hath in Hydra-wise me in restless chase, ended with one, assailed by another, and multiplied in one stem of brothers and sisters: that as it seemeth neither determined with death, nor ought pacified in long process of years, yet all these religious and virtuous Catholics.

Sir Thomas Tresham on the Vaux family, summer 1599

15

Brazen-faced Bravados

Harrowden Hall is now Wellingborough Golf Club. Rolling fairways and smooth greens have replaced the pastures and meadows once trodden by forbidden priests. The drama of the final putt is the talk of the clubhouse, not the events of four hundred years earlier when Eliza Vaux's house was stripped bare, her plants and trees were uprooted and 'the charming shaded enclaves and summer houses' that she had raised in the grounds were flattened in a frenzied dawn raid.[1] The mansion was largely rebuilt in the early eighteenth century, but one Tudor wing might have survived and, with it, a priest-hole.

When the twenty-year-old Eliza* Roper came to the house in the summer of 1585, it was in some disrepair. Lord Vaux, confined to Hackney and overwhelmed by debt, was in no position to keep it up. Just over a decade later, some wings were 'quite dilapidated, almost in fact a ruin'.[2] Eliza was the controversial bride of Lord Vaux's newly instated heir, George. Thomas Tresham wrote of her 'creditless carriage when she went for a maiden', though he was hardly a disinterested observer.[3] As George's uncle and Lord Vaux's adviser, he had gone to great lengths to ensure the transfer of the inheritance to George from his half-brother Henry. 'Many, and many years, I much more busied my brains on your behoof than did I on my eldest son's,' he would later remind his nephew. Although George's 'adopting' was supposed to redound to his benefit, the 'original intention', Tresham explained, was 'to repair the ruins of Harrowden baned barony and to relieve your father's pitiful distress plight'.[4] It was agreed that Lord Vaux, who had a habit of making 'thriftless bargains' (as well as a wife who was 'a much better hand at spending money than saving it'), would only – and only with his heir's

---

*I use the abbreviated form because this is how she signed her name and also to avoid confusion with all the Elizabeths.

permission – be able to sell certain lands for the maintenance of his children. He would not be allowed to sell any for the payment of his, or George's, debts. George was to marry a suitable girl with a suitable marriage portion; that is to say, he was to be 'ruled in his marriage by the advice of his honourable parents and eldest brother'.[5]

But George would only be ruled by his heart. Three months later, on 25 July 1585, without the necessary consents, indeed plain against Tresham's 'oft reiterated' warnings, he 'heedlessly and headlessly' married his sweetheart and forfeited his inheritance. It was a double blow to the family, since on that very day Edward Vaux, the next son in line, died at Hackney.[6] The new heir was Lord Vaux's youngest son, Ambrose, who was under twenty-one and thus could not authorise any sale of land.

Tresham seems to have taken it all much harder than Lord Vaux. 'You well know,' he huffed to George, 'that I should have been one of them whose consents you must have had.' (If true, this was only an informal arrangement.) He threw a spectacular tantrum and refused to see George for two years. The match was 'brainless', he steamed, 'far-fetched'; George was 'inconsiderate' and 'over distaffly awed'. The 'track of time,' he warned, would completely unveil 'the guileful mask of blinded fleshly affection'.[7] Except that it did not. George and Eliza had six children in quick succession and seemed perfectly happy with each other. This only enraged Tresham further.

On paper, Eliza did not seem such a bad match. Granted, she was no great heiress, but her father, John Roper of Lynsted, Kent, paid £1,500 and an additional £400 in jewels and apparel, which does not seem ungenerous considering the state of the Vaux barony.[8] Moreover, the Ropers had an excellent Catholic pedigree: Eliza's great-uncle had married Sir Thomas More's favourite daughter, Margaret, in 1521. The memorial of Eliza's mother at Lynsted parish church bears the words: 'She led her life most virtuously and ended the same most catholicly.' Those of Eliza's brother and sister likewise celebrated their *constantissimo* Catholicism. John Roper's 'my hope is in God' was more circumspect, as befitted an ambitious patriarch, but his epitaph proudly celebrated his family's union with the baronial Vauxes. Indeed Roper, who was knighted in 1588, would eventually realise his dream of a peerage. Courtesy of £10,000 in King James's coffers, he would end his days as Lord Teynham, first Baron of Teynham.[9]

Eliza's younger sister Jane, Lady Lovell, was another strong character. She would found an English Carmelite convent in Antwerp and provoke the lines: 'she is as forward in her monastery as she was four or five years since, being a person humorous and inconstant, not only as she is a woman but as she is *that* woman the Lady Lovell.' Witness too her affronted letters to the Earl of Salisbury after being 'disquieted' by pursuivants: 'If your Lordship did rightly understand their abuses, you would not permit that gentlewomen of my sort should be subject to the authority of so base persons.'[10]

Eliza shared Jane's forcefulness, but seems to have had more charm. She may have been beautiful – her daughter Katherine inherited looks which, it was suggested, would have found favour with Henry VIII.[11] Eliza was probably the dedicatee of the composer John Dowland's *Mrs Vaux's Jig* and *Mrs Vaux Galliard*.[12] She was certainly beguiling. Tresham made constant swipes at her 'irresistible feminish passions'. George was utterly enchanted and soon so was Ambrose – 'scandalously', thought Tresham. Even Lord Vaux seems to have been charmed. Uncharacteristically, he warned Tresham that if he continued in his 'self-willed and obdured refusing' to see George, 'no mean part' of the blame for his predicament would be placed at Tresham's door. For a while, Rushton Hall was deprived of the baron's visits. 'Commend me to the captive Lord,' Tresham despaired to Vaux's solicitor on 6 January 1593, 'that dare not while the sign is in the predominating Virago to look upon poor Rushton.'[13]

Tresham had good reason to suspect Eliza of trying to dominate Lord Vaux. Around Shrovetide 1592 she allegedly read him a letter, 'as written from her father', that promised an end to all his debts and an easy life with his musicians, hounds and hawks on the condition that he 'renounce amity' with Tresham 'and be ruled by her father'. Clearly knowing the way to Vaux's heart, Eliza sweetened the offer with 'a cast of choice sore falcons, which purposedly was kept for him'. Vaux 'greedily swallowed' the 'baits and hooks', but when he signalled his willingness to discuss terms, Roper 'utterly disavowed' the letter, 'protesting that he never wrote any such and that it was lewdly devised' by George and Eliza.[14] Be that as it may, Roper clearly shared his daughter's view that Tresham was a pernicious influence on Vaux and should be 'severed' from future negotiations. As he explained to Lord Burghley on 4 July 1590, 'Sir Thomas Tresham hath intruded himself as the disposer of all my Lord Vaux his estate & the commander of him & all his, who dare no more offend him than a child his master having a rod in his hand.'[15]

Eliza claimed that 'the world thinketh what my Lord doeth is by his Lady's setting on, and what she doeth is by [Tresham's] setting on'. Tresham said this was a 'feminine feeble induction', but it is clear from his papers that his influence was powerful and pervasive. Vaux did sometimes act independently of his brother-in-law, making the 'thriftless bargains' that so jeopardised the patrimony, and letting land 'at Robin Hood's pennyworths', but more often than not Tresham's shadow can be glimpsed.[16] Whether it was friendly or not is debatable. Eliza accused him of 'cozening' Vaux. Lord Burghley, who was briefed by Roper, publicly denounced him as 'covetous, covinous and godlessly treacherous'. Lord Keeper Egerton, who had grown to dislike Tresham's religion as much as his character, declared in Chancery that he was 'a bad man every way'.[17] Tresham's response to the critics was glorious in its pomposity: 'My innocency and justifiable dealings is to me a brass wall of defence against these brazen-faced bravados.'[18]

Sir Thomas Tresham was undoubtedly an aggressive estate manager. He ruthlessly exploited his tenants and his practices would spark agrarian riots.[19] Regarding the Vaux estate, though, he seems, mostly, to have acted in the family's (or at least his sister's) best interests. His 'kinsmanly care' advanced him neither socially nor financially. He complained of being 'lugged and worried' like a baited bear and exposed to 'splenish censure'. In 1593 his brother-in-law's exorbitant borrowing on his credit cost him £2,400.*[20] One wonders why he bothered.

He claimed to be defending the patrimony from Roper, 'his darling daughter and her damnable drifts'. They claimed to be protecting it from fragmentation. Tresham sometimes behaved as though he had power of attorney over Lord Vaux. Eliza allegedly had him posthumously registered as an 'idiot'.[21] In the savage battle over the body

---

*Until the mortgage was properly established in the following century, landowners found it very difficult to borrow money, especially for a long term. In this instance, Tresham fell into forfeiture for Vaux's debt because he was 'fast fettered to my five miles tie at Rushton'. He had the money in London, but because he failed to secure a licence to travel beyond the five-mile limit prescribed by the 'statute of confinement', he did not get there in time. Thus, he informed the Bishop of Lincoln on 6 May 1593, 'my house is the cause of this my present hell; Rushton, I may say, is my ruin.' (TP, pp. 74–5)

and mind of the increasingly senile baron were these two determined personalities for whom being Catholic was just one – and sometimes seemingly the very least – of their attributes.

We have, of course, met Sir Thomas Tresham before: furious with Anne Vaux for taking him to court (1593–4); penning protestations of loyalty to the Queen (throughout the 1580s); scheming with the Spanish ambassador (1581–2); on trial in the Star Chamber alongside Lord Vaux and Sir William Catesby (1581); implicated in the assault of a Crown informant at Kettering market (1576). We know that he owned hundreds of books, kept Latin and Spanish dictionaries in his closet and liked his servants to read to him for an hour after supper. We know that he was a workaholic, even in prison, even on Easter Day, and that he was interested in mysticism. We know that he lost fifteen pence at cards on 19 April 1586 and that his wife spent money in 1588–9 on lute strings, virginal wire, barbers, wax lights and books for herself and the children.[22] We also know that he would die £11,500 in debt, that he paid almost £8,000 for his recusancy and that the marriages of his six daughters cost him at least £12,200. He increased his income to perhaps £3,500 per annum and spent less than £2,000 on his building works, largely because he could supply his own materials. We know that he loved his orchards and preferred the Windsor pear to the Norwich variety, which tended to give him colic.[23] We know all these things because Tresham kept meticulous records and, by a happy accident in 1828, they were found.

Builders removing a lintel over a doorway at Rushton Hall were surprised when an old, beautifully bound book came down with the rubble. They decided to investigate and knocked through 'a very thick partition wall in the passage leading from the Great Hall'. This exposed 'a very large recess', about five feet long and fifteen inches wide. Inside was 'an enormous bundle' of papers and books wrapped up in a large sheet.[24] They had held up remarkably well to the damp. The latest recorded date in the collection is 28 November 1605, two months after Tresham's death and sixteen days after the arrest of his son Francis for complicity in the Gunpowder Plot.[25]

The treachery of the son is often contrasted with the loyalty of the father, as if the one never touched on the other, but Francis was not quite the plotter he was made out to be, nor was Sir Thomas a paragon of loyalism. His papers expose a complex situation in which resistance to the state and its policies (if not always the person of the monarch) could be articulated and effected in myriad ways. Tresham's nephew, Ambrose Vaux, threatened, allegedly at Eliza's instigation, to have him hanged for matters with which he could charge him, 'yet these,' Tresham added pointedly, 'are accounted Catholics'.[26] Spy reports reveal that when Henry Vaux was arrested at Hackney in 1586, one Henry Davies and his wife, who both gave false names, had ridden there to talk to Tresham (and Lord Vaux too according to one informant) 'about secret causes'. Their next destination was France for a meeting with the Earl of Westmorland, the only surviving leader of the 1569 rising and one of the Queen's key opponents in exile. While this kind of intelligence rarely provides enough detail for firm assessment, it does suggest a seaminess to any perceived loyalty/resistance divide.[27]

Only at the Queen's death would Tresham's mask slip. Before a crowd wilting at his two-hour monologue on the history of the royal forests, he expressed resentment that he had been 'kept from the face of his country and had not been in any commission these 24 years'. He spoke of the late Queen with 'small reverence' (in contrast to his praise of Mary I), claiming that she was 'but a woman and one that was spurblind'. Tresham was ostensibly referring to Elizabeth's lack of hunting prowess, but his 'vain discourses' touched on wider commonwealth themes and caused much muttering. There is also a document in the Tresham Papers, probably dating from 1603, in which he stated that English Catholics had harboured 'a settled hatred' for Anne Boleyn and her daughter, and that Mary Stuart's claim to the English throne had been far superior to that of the 'bastardized' Elizabeth.[28]

Eliza Vaux's adversary was a devoted husband and a protective father and master. The Market House at Rothwell and the many books still lining the shelves of St John's College library in Oxford testify to Tresham's generosity and sense of civic duty. His architectural projects – most famously the unfinished cross-shaped New Bield* at Lyveden (which honoured the Passion) and the Triangular Lodge at Rushton (celebrating the Trinity) – were monuments to

---

* 'Bield', deriving from the Old English *byldo*, meaning variously: boldness, courage, sustenance and (in Scotland and the north of England) a place of shelter. (*OED* Online)

his faith, as well as a fairly monstrous ego (see Plates 16 and 17). Much was made by Tresham of the connection between his name (he and his wife called each other 'Tres') and the Trinity. The biblical inscription at the entrance to the Triangular Lodge, for example, bore the words: *Tres testimonium dant* (Three bear witness). No one viewing Tresham's buildings could have been in any doubt as to who was the loudest, proudest Catholic in the land.[29]

Then there were his grievances. He claimed to be 'inclinable to remit injuries', but was clearly a terrific grudge-bearer. He railed at 'pettifogging' solicitors and 'dosser-headed clowns', 'the man of Kent' (Roper), 'the Baron of Rye' (Lord Morley) and John Tufton, his son's father-in-law: potentially 'more impious than a Jew'.[30] Above all, he railed at the Vauxes, who had behaved 'ingratefully, unconscionably, perfidiously, treacherously, perjuredly, and bloodily' towards him. He saved his bilious best for Eliza, 'in whom malignity more than modesty, and covetousness more than conscience reigneth'.[31]

In fairness to Tresham, by the time he came up with that bit of alliteration – the summer of 1599 – Eliza had given him sufficient cause for complaint. Since her 'brainless match', there had been the 'godless goggling' of Ambrose in 1589, whereby she and George had managed to persuade the new heir to revert the inheritance to George. This was achieved with the help of Roper's lawyers and a 'secret sinister' fine, which Tresham, try as he might, could not undo. When the 'foul fraud' was discovered, the happy couple was unrepentant and flatly refused to allow any land to be sold for the relief of George's 'moneyless and creditless' parents.[32] In July 1590, the matter was referred to the Privy Council for arbitration and it was 'at the Council Table in the public presence of many standers-by and suitors' that Lord Burghley denounced Tresham as 'very a varlet', who had defrauded his brother-in-law Vaux. Tresham complained bitterly about the 'venomous and viperous drifts' of his enemies, especially Roper, who was briefing Burghley, but the damage was done, the 'Oracle' had spoken.[33]

In the end, Lord Vaux had to appeal to Parliament for permission to sell some land. It was a broken baron that turned up in London 'raggedly suited', his parliamentary robes at pawn. At Hoxton on the evening of 15 January 1593, Tresham saw him 'woefully distressed . . . with tears trickling down his cheeks'. But the Act was passed (Private

Act, 35 Eliz. I, c. 5) and Lord and Lady Vaux were afforded some respite in their 'hoarheaded old age'.[34] Recourse to Parliament was a humiliating expedient, especially for a peer, but William, third Baron Vaux of Harrowden, had lost his pride, his credit, his home (George and Eliza had turfed him out of Harrowden Hall[35]) and, perhaps also by then, his mind. Despite a brief flirtation with conformity over the autumn of 1592, he refused to surrender his faith.[36] 'Farewell my golden, gilded Lord, in [MS torn], not in purse,' Tresham ended a letter to his ailing brother-in-law on 22 July 1594. Vaux had become, like one of the papists in John Donne's second satire, 'poor, disarm'd . . . not worth hate'. He died at Irthlingborough on 20 August 1595 and was buried in the local parish church.[37]

The title passed to Eliza and George's six-year-old son, Edward, for George, like his half-brother Henry and his younger brother Edward, had predeceased his father. He had died of a sudden illness at Harrowden on 13 July 1594 and was buried the following day.[38] Eliza was 'completely overwrought' and, in as much as was possible with six young children, kept to her room. But she persisted in her pursuit (or protection as she would have termed it) of the Vaux patrimony and continued to snarl like a lioness whenever she sensed danger to her 'fatherless and penniless' cubs.[39]

On 1 November 1594, Tresham informed his wife about a quarrel over 'a petty portion of winter grass' on the Harrowden estate. Eliza, having been allowed to stay on at the Hall, was refusing to let her father-in-law graze his cattle on a small close nearby. The situation had grown ugly and her 'saucy servants', like 'Actaeon's dogs',* had 'violently withstood' the old baron and subjected him to 'menacing & braving speeches'. This was not appropriate behaviour for a lady whose husband was 'scant cold in his grave', wrote Tresham. He might have been right, but there was a hint of *Schadenfreude* to the message that he now asked his wife to give Eliza:

Tell her from me that it behoveth her to have more care in managing like actions now than when her husband lived. For then what error

---

* 'Aptly may he say that Actaeon's dogs he fostereth, who while he mindfully feedeth them, they monstruous mercilessly would devour him.' According to Greek myth, the Theban hunter Actaeon was transformed by the beautiful Artemis into a stag and then torn apart by his own hounds.

soever was committed Mr Vaux bare the blame (though the world reputed him but her instrument therein), where now she is not to mask under such a vizard, but barefaced will appear whence it floweth.[40]

Always quick to accuse his fellow Catholics of lacking compassion, Tresham showed none for Eliza or 'her sweet little ones'. He never forgave her for his estrangement from 'pliant uxorious' George and he was probably right in thinking that the couple harboured an inviolatable hatred against him. It was, however, presumptuous to suggest that George might have 'died impenitent'. Eliza, he assured himself, 'will hardly be reduced therein to any Christian terms, what profession of Catholic religion soever she to the world maketh show of.'[41] This echoes Tresham's comments on his other 'unkind kinswoman', Anne, by whose display of 'unchristian turpitude' he claimed to be equally appalled.[42]

In 1596, Eliza initiated a suit against Tresham in her son Edward's name in the Court of Wards. Presenting forty pages of evidence (now lost), she accused him of 'cozening' the late Lord Vaux of 'very great sums of money (in the thousands)' and of deceiving him 'of all, or of the greatest part, of the possessions of his barony . . . to the utter disinheriting of her son'. She requested that the late baron's actions be invalidated on the grounds of 'impotency (*non compos mentis*) of mind'. Some of Tresham's depositions have survived, showing that he was charged, among other things, with appropriating the manor of Houghton Magna, receiving money from the sale of Vaux lands and getting the baron, in his final illness, to change his will so that property in Irthlingborough would be held by his executors – one being Tresham – 'for certain years after the death' of Lady Vaux.

A codicil, made just two days before Vaux's death, confirms the change to the Irthlingborough inheritance, but Tresham protested that it had been made according to the baron's written instruction for the payment of his debts. Tresham denied ever having received any money that was not owed to him and he vigorously fought Eliza's 'truthless and detestable infamous bill'. Indeed he later claimed that he had defended himself so thoroughly, in the process exposing the 'sinister drifts' of Eliza and her lawyers, that they 'turned all their suit' to having his answer struck off the record.

They may have succeeded, for half a page of his 1597 examination has been cut out and another part redacted, though his accusation that Eliza had 'forcibly withheld' Lord Vaux's estate papers at Harrowden Hall remains on record, as does his tale of 'a mischance of overthrowing an oar', which led to a desk full of documents falling into the river.

Two years later Tresham was still livid at what he called Eliza's 'rabble of railing, lying inventions'. 'Where,' he asked,

> hath the like malignity been heard of as to bring my name into public hatred, to register of record the Lord Vaux her son's grandfather (from whom all their advancement was to grow) to be an idiot, my sister the child's grandmother to be a monstrous conspirator against him . . . myself, [great-]uncle to her son, to be arrantest knave, and treacheror . . . And that nothing should be wanting what sinfullest malice might excogitate, she would not forbear thus to stultify the Lord Vaux when he was dead, but in his lifetime thus frontlessly to record him for a witless seely creature. A worthy work of this virtuous wise woman it will be for her son to behold when he cometh to years of judgement.[43]

Another year brought another scandal, this time from a wholly unexpected quarter: Merill Vaux, Tresham's youngest niece, the only one, he had thought in 1593, who was 'worthy the saluting'.[44] Not so in 1597 when she eloped with his servant, George Fulshurst. They did not go far, only to Rushton Hall, which made Tresham appear collusive when in fact he was apoplectic. Merill's dowry (£1,700) was a good sum, more than three times Anne and Eleanor's portions, and Tresham claimed to have been 'the principal means' of getting it for her, indeed partly 'without her parents' privity' – a telling admission. A lucrative and 'worshipful' match with one Mr Lovell (presumably a kinsman of Eliza's sister Jane Lovell) had been lined up around 1590, but proceedings had stalled and Merill had cast herself away on Fulshurst, 'a land-lopper, a very beggar and bankroot base fellow'. Tresham had withheld some of the marriage money, they had sued him and he had wound up in the Fleet.[45]

Thus it was that Tresham became 'close prisoner' again, spending the whole 'contagious, hot and most dangerous' summer of 1599 in 'but one little chamber of fifteen foot long and twelve foot broad'. His wife and daughter came up from the country and were denied access. It was the last incarceration of Tresham's 'moth-eaten term of life' and the one (not being for religion) that most stung.[46] These were the circumstances under which he fired a volley of excoriating missiles at the ladies of the 'Harrowden stable'.

'Not unlikely,' he wrote to an unknown correspondent,

> but you will marvel whence this huge mass of malice and filth groweth. And why these 3 sisters [Anne, Eliza, Merill], reputed of others so virtuous and religious gentlewomen, should thus more like furies than fitting for a feminine sex, without due cause, sinfully and incessantly to outrage me in highest degradation . . . As it is said *nihil fit sine causa*, so is it likewise said that no malice [is] comparable to the malice of a woman.[47]

Tresham opined that Merill's 'so wicked mismatching herself shortened my said sister's life with extreme anguish'. Lady Vaux had died at Oxford on 29 December 1597 and Eliza had promptly seized property in Irthlingborough, which, according to Lord Vaux's contested codicil, was to be reserved for the payment of outstanding debts. Much to Tresham's disgust, 'fondly affected' Ambrose had sided with Eliza (allegedly upon the promise of 'one suit of costly apparel') and the two had attempted to overturn Lady Vaux's will – as well as Tresham's powers of execution – on the grounds of 'excommunication for recusancy'. The corpse of Ambrose's mother – just as well it was winter – had consequently lain unburied for three weeks.[48]

The next few months saw violent assaults on a barn in Irthlingborough, which Eliza and Tresham were both determined to possess. On one occasion Ambrose and some sixty men converged on it with swords, pike-staves, pitchforks, pistols and any other weapon they could find. When night fell, they 'made great outcries and shouts & shot of guns & pistols . . . to the terror of the neighbours'. Both parties sought restitution in the law and eventually came to a settlement, though Tresham had not seen 'any pennyworth' by the summer of 1599. The feud with Eliza had gone on for fourteen years by then, long enough for even a prize fighter to begin to flag. Tresham's letter from the Fleet was his parting shot to 'that house which is most beholden to me'. As for Eliza, he wrote, 'all the harm I wish her is, I wish she had lived in more credit before marriage, in marriage, and since marriage.'[49]

16

Assy Reprobateness

One positive outcome from all the spats with Sir Thomas Tresham was a truce between Anne, Merill and Eliza. According to Tresham, the Vaux women did not get along – 'notoriously every of them disagreed one with the other' – until their common enmity for him engendered a 'moody atonement' amongst them. 'What Christian charity could not effect in many years,' he exclaimed, 'sinful rancour brought to pass in a moment of time.'[1]

Tresham was, when it suited him, an eager subscriber to the ideal of 'Christian charity', insisting that Catholics, as 'fellow members of self same body' and labouring under the same cross, should suffer and heal together.[2] 'Look,' he announced in one inscription on the Triangular Lodge, 'I have not worked only for myself' (*Respicite non mihi soli laboravi*). The purity of Tresham's motives may be questioned, but not his industry, nor his value as one of the most articulate Catholic spokesmen of the time. It is, however, unsurprising that 'sinful rancour' sometimes got the better of 'Christian charity', for the same bond of suffering that brought Catholics together put strains on their relationships that could lead to some very unsympathetic behaviour.

Recusants were fined heavily, often irregularly and, from 1587, cumulatively, while some, like Lord Vaux, forfeited two-thirds of their estate to the Crown. It was hard for them to get credit, harder to keep it, difficult to travel and therefore to repay loans and honour obligations. Those imprisoned or 'fast-fettered' to their five-mile cordons found it difficult to exert the personal authority needed to resolve disputes and command respect. Estates became so tangled in fines and 'uses' and trusts, drawing in third parties, and 'pettifogging' solicitors, that confusion abounded and, with it, litigation, which cost more money.[3]

The indirect consequences of recusancy are impossible to quantify.

Did Merill Vaux run off with Tresham's servant because the lucrative match she had been promised for seven years did not materialise? Or did her claustrophobic, insular lifestyle (she was apparently a strict adherent to the five-mile rule[4]) encourage her to look below stairs for company? (If so, she was at least being true to the casuist texts that pronounced it better to marry beneath oneself than a heretic.[5]) Did a recusant culture emerge – secretive, nonconformist, necessarily duplicitous – and instil bad habits in Merill, making her more prone to clandestine, rebellious behaviour? Perhaps she simply fell in love. And perhaps Lord Vaux would have died in poverty, and Tresham and Eliza would have clashed, and Anne would have chased her marriage portion anyway, regardless of faith. They were their own agents and their temperaments determined their behaviour, but the state's attempts to repress their beliefs and practices forced them down avenues that they might not otherwise have contemplated.

At least the older generation could cling to a memory. They could recall a time when priests were revered and not reviled, when the Mass was celebrated and not suppressed. They might be patient (if not passive), knowing that orthodoxies changed with the passing of monarchs, for that had been their experience. It was different for their children, who had no living memory of easier, better times. It was perhaps hardest of all for the younger sons, boys like Ambrose Vaux, who would traditionally have been destined for the Church or the law or a military career. If they refused to take the oath of supremacy, they could not graduate from university or take up arms for the Queen or work for the state. Many grew up wandering and aimless, lacking skills and a sense of purpose. Ambrose received a seminary education in northern France.[6] He left England as the fourth son of Lord Vaux and returned as his heir, a teenager propelled into a situation with which he was not remotely equipped to deal. He had no training in estate management and, having spent his formative years in an all-male environment, was easily bowled over by the enchanting Eliza.

It is a picaresque and cautionary tale: the youngest son, adopted as heir, signs away his inheritance, spends the rest of his life getting into scrapes, in and out of prison, never out of debt. On the night of 10 February 1591, Ambrose and his cronies stole forty loads of barley from a barn (leaving the rest out to spoil in the rain). The Privy Council noted that he was of 'such disorderly disposition as

hardly can be brought to any good conformity'. The following year
he and his brother George were cited for ordering a revenge attack
on a local pursuivant who had prosecuted 'some of their friends for
recusancy'.[7] March 1593 saw Ambrose on the run from creditors, of
whom there were many. Tresham offered him temporary refuge in
London along with some stern words about his 'loose, riotous &
sinful misgovernment'. Ambrose was in danger of becoming 'a right
younger brother, having neither wit, credit, land, nor money. Yea, I
think I truly may say, scant clothes to put on your back.'[8]

Avuncular advice unheeded, Ambrose continued to borrow and, it
seems, speculate, with reckless abandon. He raised £320 in London in
the summer – half from a haberdasher, half from dyer – which he
promised to start repaying within six months of the return of a
gentleman from Venice.[9] It does not appear that he honoured any of
his obligations. In 1597, Peter Roos, from whom he had borrowed £200
in 1588, had him imprisoned. Despite 'sundry complaints' to the Privy
Council, Ambrose remained a prisoner, though Eliza was able to enter
a bond for his temporary release in the New Year. (This gave him just
enough time to contest his late mother's will, terrorise the good people
of Irthlingborough and 'return to the said prison'.)[10] On 27 March 1599,
Ambrose witnessed two Northamptonshire leases and seven months
later, under escort from his keeper, he visited the Fleet, where he tried
in vain to extract an annuity from Uncle Tresham.[11]

In 1605 he cropped up in the Low Countries, in an English company
fighting for Catholic Spain against the Protestant United Provinces.
Military service abroad was a popular path for angry young recusants
and, as far as the English were concerned, a more productive outlet
for their aggression than the shires. It was presumed to be remu-
nerative, in this world and the next, and fostered a spirit of camara-
derie. Eliza's son, Edward, who would enlist later in life, reportedly
swaggered about town with his unit like the Jacobean version of a
university drinking society.* Ambrose's comrades in 1605 included

---

*When the men came home, their association caused great concern, but investiga-
tion revealed little more than the donning of coloured ribbons, the adoption of silly
nicknames and a copious amount of drinking. 'What mischief may lurk under this
mask God knows,' John Chamberlain wrote from London on 6 December 1623, 'but
sure they were very confident and presumed much of themselves to carry it so
openly.' According to Chamberlain, one fraternity called themselves 'Titere-tu'.
Brewer's Handbook reveals that Tityre Tus (a pluralised version of the opening two

several other younger brothers, as well as a certain 'Mr Faukes of Yorkshire', a much-admired soldier who would be found later in the year in a vault under the House of Lords with a slow match and eighteen hundredweight of gunpowder.[12]

By the close of 1609, Ambrose had transformed himself into a Knight of the Order of the Holy Sepulchre. In Jerusalem he vowed 'to defend the honour of God' and, since he was able to show 'sufficient proofs of noble extraction', he was dubbed a knight by the Guardian of the Franciscan convent. (He would have had to pay for the privilege; one wonders how.) His choice of companion on the pilgrimage from Rome to Jerusalem suggests that Ambrose had not undergone a radical metamorphosis.

Anthony Copley, the son of an exiled friend of Lord Vaux and a cousin of the late Robert Southwell, S.J., was an erstwhile seminarian who had reputedly disgraced himself in Rome by appearing at the pulpit with a rose between his teeth. By the time he had linked up with Ambrose, he had fought for the Spanish in the Low Countries, turned coat, thrown a dagger at a parish clerk in Horsham church, abused the Jesuits in their dispute with the appellants, conspired against James I and then turned King's evidence. In a poem vaunting his loyalty to Queen Elizabeth, Copley had depicted himself as an 'Elizian outcast of Fortune'. Richard Topcliffe rather saw him as 'the most desperate youth that liveth'. Robert Persons, S.J., thought him 'idle-headed' and 'light-witted'. Copley's trial recorder noted his 'whining speech'.[13]

He was banished from England in 1604 and, according to his charitable kinswomen at the convent of St Monica's, gave himself up to 'devotion'. In 1609, he voyaged to the Holy Land with Ambrose 'and, coming to Jerusalem, they were both knighted at our Lord's Sepulchre'. Devotions performed, sights seen and souls cleansed, the two blades returned home. Copley died on the journey – it is not recorded how, but the passage was dangerous – and Ambrose conveyed the news to his family. On 10 December 1610, Lionel Wake in Antwerp heard from

---

words of Virgil's first *Eclogue*) was 'the name assumed in the seventeenth century by a clique of young blades of the better class, whose delight was to break windows, upset sedan-chairs, molest quiet citizens, and rudely caress pretty women in the streets at night-time'. (PRO SP 14/155, ff. 31v–32r; Brewer, *The Reader's Handbook*, 1880, p. 1011)

a contact in Marseilles that 'Mr Ambrose Vaux is returned from Jerusalem, but in very poor estate, and was there in prison, but now
escaped and upon his journey hitherward.'[14]

By 1612, Ambrose had made it back to England, but only as far as the
debtors' prison, where he borrowed money from at least one inmate.[15]
He was out before Easter and on 'about the third or fourth of April'
– he could not quite remember – he married Elizabeth Wyborne, the
widow of William Wyborne, a recently deceased recusant from Kent.
Ambrose, then in his early forties, was under the impression that his
bride was fabulously wealthy. In fact she was 'destitute of jointure or
any other means to live', having transferred all her property to her
late husband's executors. Ambrose contested the 'fraudulent deed' of
conveyance, claiming that it had been sealed after his marriage and
backdated by the executors to 2 April. They contended that it was
authentic and made of Elizabeth's own free will for the satisfaction
of her late husband's debts. Elizabeth subsequently separated from
Ambrose and lodged at 'one Billyes house in Fleet Street'. She was a
regular guest at the family home of her kinsman Dudley Norton, who
was one of the executors and a former secretary of the Earl of Salisbury. Ambrose was left wifeless, penniless and seething.

   One afternoon the following summer, the jilted husband learned
that Elizabeth and Norton were going to a play at the Globe theatre
in Southwark. (Norton was later at pains to point out that he was not
a regular patron of Shakespeare's playhouse, having only been 'four
or five times in his whole life'.) Ambrose raced over and tried to
reclaim his wife. Voices were raised, then fists. 'God's wounds,' Norton
reportedly swore, 'thether he brought her . . . and from thence he
would carry her again away.' Ambrose claimed that he was held down
and assaulted by twelve of Norton's men, armed with rapiers, daggers,
pistols and other weapons. Norton denied 'the pretended misdemeanour and riot', insisting that he had only touched Ambrose's wrist
to prevent him from drawing his own dagger.[16]

   Elizabeth, apparently in 'great fear and perplexity', was spirited
away and little more is heard of her until almost a decade later when
she was at the centre of another affray and another Star Chamber
suit. This one involved a broken-down door, some rearranged furniture
and an injured landlord. Elizabeth's 'near kinsman' Sir William

Windsor, an old comrade of Ambrose from Flanders, had found her rooms in the same building in St Mary-le-Strand that he and his wife occupied. A contract was signed with Robert Collins, the landlord, and Elizabeth – styling herself 'Lady Elizabeth Vaux' – moved in towards the end of January 1620.

She immediately found fault with the lodgings, bedding and furniture and asked the Windsors for help. Collins was duly summoned and he arrived at eleven at night, not happy about being dragged from his cups and, allegedly, somewhat the worse for wear. An argument ensued, with both parties claiming that they had been reasonable and the other 'uncivil & provoking'. There was, to use Elizabeth's phrase, 'some buslinge betwixt them'. Sir William sent Collins away with a box on the ear. The landlord regrouped, allegedly broke down the door, ordered his servants up the stairs with 'a great fire fork and a pair of tongs made of iron' and threw a stool at Lady Windsor. Further violence was prevented by a passing constable. Throughout the whole 'hurly burly and brabble', Sir William Windsor had been dressed 'in his pantables and ready to go to bed'.

There is no hint of farce in Collins' testimony, just a disturbing account of a man set upon by a gang of aristocratic rowdies. Thus: Sir William, refusing to hear the landlord out, felled him with his first blow and punched and kicked him on the ground. Collins found his feet, but Sir William's 'confederates, servants and acquaintances', including Lady Vaux *and* her husband, Ambrose:

> did most furiously, fiercely, cruelly, riotously, routously and unlawfully assault [Collins], some of them holding [him] by the arms and body, while other some did in terrible and cruel manner beat, wound and most grievously hurt [him]. And other some of them (at such time as [he] did call and cry out for aid and help to release him and to save him from being murdered) did hold and keep shut the door of the said dining room, not suffering those people, being very many that came to aid . . . to come into the room.

Apparently Sir William then charged at Collins with 'a stiletto or pocket dagger'. Collins fended him off with a stool. Sir William drew his sword. Collins parried the thrusts with more furniture until the constable finally came to the rescue.

Elizabeth Vaux pleaded not guilty to the charges and denied having seen Windsor box Collins' ear, even though Windsor confessed it. She sounds like a different person to the widow cowering at the Globe a decade earlier.[17] The case also suggests that her estrangement from Ambrose – such as it was – had ended. Although Collins named Ambrose in his bill, he gave no particular details and there is no deposition from Ambrose on file. Sir William maintained that 'there was no other person with him but his own lady and the said Lady Vaux' and their servants. Someone was lying, but even if it was Collins, it is telling that he chose to cite Ambrose. London parishes were close communities. The main actors in the scene all belonged to St Mary-le-Strand and it was there, five years later, on 25 April 1626, that Ambrose was buried. It is not known how he died.

As early as 1593, Sir Thomas Tresham had esteemed his nephew 'a world's wonder for assy reprobateness'.[18] If a satirical verse penned by Henry Shirley in the early seventeenth century is anything to go by, the intervening years had not improved Ambrose's reputation or, indeed, his physique.

The Battle
The combatants:
Sir Ambrose Vaux, knight, and Glascott the bailey of South-
    wark.
The place:
the Rule of the Kings Bench.

No amorous style affects my pen,
For why? I write of fighting men:
The bloody story of a fight
Betwixt a bailiff and a knight.
Let him that therefore writes the story
Of Warwick's Guy or Bevis' glory,
Sir Tristram's hurts and Lancelot's wounds,
Or otters hunted with great hounds,
Confess the story doth excel
With best of any I can tell,
Who was a witness of the fray
Which thus my muse 'gins to display.

Sir Ambrose strooke the first great blow,
Which did the bailiff overthrow,
That he lay tumbling in the dirt,
From which he took his greatest hurt,
Save that the knight away did tear
A handful of the varlet's hair.
The knight for teen,* the knave for fear
With roaring did their chopses tear,
Whilst all the women loud did cry:
'Sir Ambrose let the villain die!'
The bailiff then cried out for help,
With that another marshal's whelp
Did from his foe's devouring paws
All in the dirt his fellow draws.

The knight not with all this content,
A scornful kick at Glascott sent,
But then the dirt in which he rolled
(I grieve at what must now be told)
So slippery was, in all our sight
Upon his back fell down the knight,
And being much enraged thereat,
Upon his feet in rage he gatt
And forth his sturdy corpes he launches
With quivering thighs and quaging† paunches.

About the dump the bailiff ran
And now the worst of all began.
The knight no longer could pursue,
Too well his bounds the bailiff knew,
But had he in his clutches come,
Methinks I see what martyrdom
The women and the knight had made
On him that now no longer stayed,
But home returned, not shamed to be
Sore kicked by true nobility.[19]

* *teen*: annoyance.

† *quaging*: soft, flabby, wobbling.

So is the life of our anti-hero just an amusing sideshow, a futile and somewhat grotesque diversion from the main story? Or does it highlight the tragic consequences of recusancy for 'right younger brothers' and 'noddy nephews' and, indeed, for any 'untoward and giddy-headed young man' of the time? The phrases are Tresham's. He early spotted the 'unskill and weakness in worldly drifts of Ambrose Vaux'.[20] It is not something that can be blamed on the environment. Ambrose's only real achievement was his knighthood, an honorific reward for venturing to the Holy Land. As the gift of a Roman Catholic order, it underwhelmed in Protestant England. His wife's lawyers refused to recognise it, insisting that Ambrose was 'but an esquire & no knight'.[21]

If Ambrose's undoubted energy and courage (proven in war, travel, even in his appetite for a brawl) could have been channelled more productively, if he had met with opportunities rather than obstacles and received proper parental guidance, he might have thrived, might – just – have redeemed himself. Or not. Ambrose Vaux was a brigand and a debtor, a prisoner and a pilgrim, a soldier and a knight. He was also a recusant and if every trait in his character pointed to failure, his recusancy sealed his doom.

17

Long John with the Little Beard

We last saw John Gerard in the Clink. It was the summer of 1594 and he had not yet been tortured. Indeed, 'for a while', he had 'a quiet and pleasant time' in prison. Compared to the noisy, foetid Counter, the Clink was 'paradise' – even if it shared space on the South Bank with brothels, bear pits, gambling dens and the only marginally more respectable playhouses. Security was extraordinarily lax and at the right price Gerard was able to receive visitors, hear confessions, celebrate the Mass, give the Spiritual Exercises and conduct missionary business. By his own account, he reconciled many people to Rome, including one of his gaolers. 'The work John does in prison is so profitable that it is hardly possible to believe it,' Garnet enthused on 17 January 1596.[1] But John was being watched. A priest in the Clink informed on him in October and when, the following April, the authorities received details about his handling of a packet of letters from overseas, they took him over the river to the Tower of London.

Gerard was shown the warrant for his torture on 14 April 1597.[2] He had denied that the intelligence he had received from abroad was political and he had refused to disclose Garnet's whereabouts. In his own words, he was led to the torture chamber,

> in a kind of solemn procession, the attendants walking ahead with lighted candles. The chamber was underground and dark, particularly near the entrance. It was a vast place and every device and instrument of human torture was there. They pointed out some of them to me and said that I would try them all. Then they asked me again whether I would confess.
>
> 'I cannot,' I said.
>
> I fell on my knees for a moment's prayer. Then they took me to a

big upright pillar, one of the wooden posts which held the roof of this huge underground chamber. Driven in to the top of it were iron staples for supporting heavy weights. Then they put my wrists into iron gauntlets and ordered me to climb two or three wicker steps. My arms were then lifted up and an iron bar was passed through the rings of one gauntlet, then through the staple and rings of the second gauntlet. This done, they fastened the bar with a pin to prevent it slipping, and then removing the wicker steps one by one from under my feet, they left me hanging by my hands and arms fastened above my head.[3]

'Long John' Gerard was aptly named, however.[4] He was too tall and the earth under him had to be scraped away until his toes hung clear. He turned down a last chance to talk.

But I could hardly utter the words such a gripping pain came over me. It was worst in my chest and belly, my hands and arms. All the blood in my body seemed to rush up into my arms and hands and I thought that blood was oozing out from the ends of my fingers and the pores of my skin. But it was only a sensation caused by my flesh swelling above the irons holding them.

He hoped for death. The attendants urged him to relent: 'You will be a cripple all your life if you live. And you are going to be tortured every day until you confess.' Gerard prayed until he passed out. It was just after one o'clock. 'The men held my body up or put the wicker steps under my feet until I came to. Then they heard me pray and immediately they let me down again.' This happened 'eight or nine times that day'. William Waad, clerk of the Privy Council, asked if he was ready now to obey the Queen and her Council. Gerard was uncooperative. 'Then hang there until you rot off the pillar,' Waad stormed. The Tower bell struck five. The commissioners departed. Gerard was taken down. On his return to the cell he announced within the earshot of several inmates that he had not betrayed his superior. Thus the message was conveyed to Garnet, Eleanor and Anne that they were safe, for the moment.

The following day, wearing a cloak with wide sleeves (his old gown was too small for his swollen hands), he was questioned again about

Garnet. Waad asserted that the Jesuit superior meddled in politics and was 'a danger to the State'. Gerard replied, 'I have lived with him and know him well, and I can say for certain that he is not that kind of man.' He was manacled and tortured again, but not the following day. 'The man needs physic,' the Lieutenant of the Tower would warn in June.[5] By then Gerard could move his fingers, but it took five months for him to regain his sense of touch, 'and then not completely'. Gradually he won the trust of his warder and received small kindnesses, like the oranges that he converted into orange-peel rosaries for his friends in the Clink. He was also allowed some paper to wrap them in and a pick for his teeth. 'All the time I stored the juice from the oranges in a small jar.'

Orange juice can be used as invisible ink. Words can be scratched on paper with, say, a toothpick and later exposed by heat (see Plate 36 for an example). The writing is then indelible, so interceptions cannot be concealed. (Lemon juice is less effective in this respect because water can also reveal it, but only temporarily, so that it will disappear again when dry. It would, however, be preferable for a letter that needed to be forwarded to multiple recipients.) So Gerard sent his messages via his former Clink prison mate, John Lillie, and his friends returned theirs on paper enclosing 'some sweetmeats and other delicacies', and the obliging warder obligingly passed everything on.

It was by means of his orange-juice letters that Gerard was able to correspond with another prisoner, John Arden, in the Cradle Tower. Arden came from Evenley in Northamptonshire some forty miles from Harrowden Hall. He had been implicated in the Babington Plot and confined to the Tower ever since.[6] From his cell in the Salt Tower Gerard could peer across a little courtyard garden into Arden's cell. With the help of his well-bribed warder, he was able to visit Arden and thanks to Mrs Arden, who smuggled Mass equipment in with the linen, he gave him communion. It was only at this stage, Gerard later wrote, that he realised quite how close Arden's cell was to the moat:

> I thought it might be possible for a man to lower himself with a rope
> from the roof of the tower on to the wall beyond the moat. I asked
> the gentleman what he thought about it.

'Yes, it could be done easily,' he said, 'if we only had some really good friends who were ready to run the risk of helping us.'

'We have the friends alright,' I said.

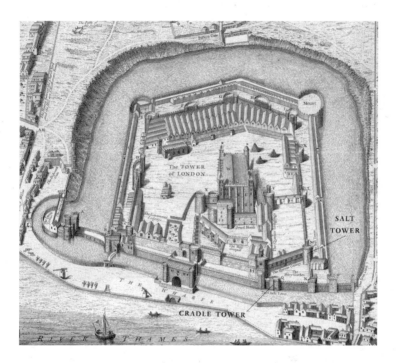

The Tower of London in 1597. The Salt Tower and the Cradle Tower are marked.

We do not know what Anne and Eleanor thought of Gerard's plan when John Lillie came to their house with it one day in September, but it received Garnet's cautious approval. On the night of 3 October 1597, Lillie, Richard Fulwood and Gerard's old warder from the Clink rowed up the Thames and looked out towards the Tower for two figures to emerge upon a roof. They had a rope in the boat and the plan was to tie it to a long weighted cord that Gerard would hurl down from the Cradle Tower roof. They would attach one end to a stake on the wharf and Gerard would gather up the other and affix it to a canon on the roof. He and Arden would then slide along the rope, over the moat and on to the wall, the wharf, the river and freedom.

'At midnight,' Gerard recalled, 'we saw the boat with our friends approaching.' They were just about to alight when 'a man came out from one of the poor dwelling-places on the bank' and chatted to them as if they were fishermen. The fellow soon retired for the night, but the rescue party 'paddled up and down' to give him time to slumber. The tide began to turn and the opportunity was lost. The boat turned back towards London Bridge, the old medieval bridge stacked with houses and underpropped by nineteen arches that could channel very dangerous currents at high tide. Gerard watched from the Tower as his friends' little boat was dragged towards the bridge and then driven against its piles. 'It stuck and it was impossible to move it forward or back,' he observed. 'Meanwhile, the water was rising and was striking the boat with such force that with every wave it looked as if it would capsize and the occupants be thrown into the river.' He heard their shouts, thought he could discern Fulwood's voice, though the distance was now about half a mile.

> Men came out on to the bank and we were able to watch them in the light thrown by their candles. They rushed to their boats and pulled off to the rescue. Several boats came quite near, but they were afraid to pull alongside – the current was too strong. Forming a semi-circle round them, they stayed like spectators watching the poor men in their peril without daring to assist.

A basket was lowered from the bridge in an effort to winch the men to safety, but then a sea-going ship powered through the current and drew up alongside them. Lillie and Fulwood were pulled on deck.

> Then immediately the small boat capsized before the third man could be rescued, as though it had only been kept afloat for the sake of the Catholics it carried. However, by the mercy of God, the man who was washed over into the river was able to grasp the rope let down from the bridge and he was hauled to safety. So all were rescued and got back to their homes.

The following day, which was Gerard's thirty-third birthday, he received a message from Lillie: 'It was not God's design that we should succeed last night but He mercifully snatched us from our peril. He has only postponed the day. With God's help we will be back tonight.'

And so they were. This time there were no interruptions. Lille and Fulwood made it to the wharf, tied the rope as instructed and waited for the prisoners. The rope was too thick, 'very difficult indeed to pull up', and Gerard had miscalculated the incline. Due to the height of the moat wall, the prisoners had to work their way along the rope rather than slide down easily. Careful not to alert the guard in the garden at the foot of the Cradle Tower, a nervous John Arden went first. He made it across without incident, 'but his descent slackened the rope', making it much harder for Gerard. Less than six months earlier, the Jesuit had been in 'an excruciating pain that distends the limbs unbearably'.[7] He said his prayers, gripped the rope with his arms and legs and began his descent:

> I had gone three or four yards face downwards when suddenly my body swung round with its own weight and I nearly fell. I was still very weak, and with the slack rope and my body hanging underneath, I could make practically no progress. At last I managed to work myself as far as the middle of the rope, and there I stuck. My strength was failing and my breath, which was short before I started, seemed altogether spent.

Gerard's friends could only watch and pray as he struggled to hold on. He drew strength, he said, from their prayers and the intercession of the saints. Slowly, painfully, he edged towards the moat wall. At last he could feel the stone against his toes, but the rope had become so slack that his head was no higher than his feet. He dangled lifelessly over the moat. But then John Lillie had his legs and pulled him onto the wharf. Gerard had to be given 'cordial waters and restoratives' before he could go on. The rope, untied and cut, swung back against the Tower wall.

'We rowed a good distance before we brought the boat to land.' Lillie escorted Arden to a safe house in the city run by Mistress Anne Line.* Gerard and Fulwood headed north to the Vaux sisters' house

---

* Anne Line *alias* Mrs Martha ran a boarding house for priests. The widow would be arrested on 2 February 1601. Charged with harbouring, she 'kissed the gallows tree' at Tyburn on the 27th of the month. Garnet's agent in London managed to procure some of her clothes as relics.

in Spitalfields. Nicholas 'Little John' Owen was waiting there with the horses and before dawn broke they were in the saddle. They rode a dozen miles flat out to Morecrofts, near Uxbridge, where Anne, Eleanor, Garnet and their household received them with dinner and rapture. 'The rejoicing was great. We all thanked God that I had escaped from the hands of my enemies in the name of the Lord.'

Gerard's *Autobiography* is one of the most thrilling sources of the period. Evelyn Waugh likened him to Buchan, while the publishers of Philip Caraman's 1951 translation compared him to Dumas. His prose is irre-sistibly swashbuckling and should be enjoyed, but with caution, for it is clearly partisan. He wrote in Latin around 1609 at the behest of his superiors and probably in the first instance for the edification of Jesuit novices. The initials of the Society motto, *Ad maiorem Dei gloriam* (To the greater glory of God), stud the top of his Preface page just as they have headed the homework of generations of Jesuit-educated children. Although writing from Louvain, Gerard never stopped being a missionary and his 'simple and faithful narrative' was forged, like the hagiographies of the time, in the furnace of the Counter-Reformation.[8] Thus, God was Catholic and Catholics were – mostly – good. Thus, God had carried Gerard through his torture and over the moat, and had chosen, during the first abortive escape attempt, to save the good Catholics, Lillie and Fulwood, before the 'schismatic' Clink gaoler. More controversially, Anthony Babington, 'a very dear friend' of Gerard, was executed 'in the cause of Mary Queen of Scots'. The gunpowder plotter, Sir Everard Digby, had a 'sincerity of purpose' and his accomplice, Ambrose Rookwood, 'died a martyr for the faith'. So too the 'saintly' seventh Earl of Northumberland, who was beheaded in 1572 for leading the northern rising three years earlier.[9]

Gerard was selective with his material, which is the preserve of any writer, especially of autobiography, and keen to tell a good story, but his primary objective was to elide the Jesuit mission with God's design. He gushed about his apostolic work in the Clink – 'so many Catholics came to visit me that there were often as many as six or eight people at a time waiting their turn to see me' – but he neglected to mention that he had once attempted to escape this 'paradise' on the South Bank.[10] His approach was probably not unlike the Jesuit line on equivo-cation: direct lies must not be told, but the truth might be embellished or partially withheld for the good of the cause – the greater truth.

The *Autobiography* abounds with marvellous pen portraits of Gerard's heroes and villains. Robert Southwell frets endearingly about blowing his cover; Richard Topcliffe swaggers about in 'court dress' and speaks 'from the cesspool of his heart'; Dr Abbot, later Archbishop of Canterbury, wears 'a silk soutane that came down to his knees' and talks 'volubly. It is all these men can do,' Gerard adds, 'they have no solid knowledge.'[11] This reveals as much about Gerard as it does about Abbot and, indeed, it is at self-portraiture that he often unwittingly excelled.

He tried to be modest, knowing that humility was a good thing, but the man who had been fast-tracked into the priesthood couldn't always keep the showboat off the page. He was particularly proud of the haul of aristocratic ladies that he won for his church. Lady Digby 'formed a flattering opinion of me that I did not deserve'. Two 'fashionable' and 'noble ladies, mother and daughter', bribed their way into the Tower and 'almost fought each other to be the first to kiss' his feet. Dorothy Rookwood, who was known as 'the saint' in the convent where Gerard directed her, 'was embarrassingly thankful to me for the little part I played in her vocation: she would sing my praises to the community, and so extravagantly, that when I came on a visit to Louvain, crowds pressed to see me'. One of the Flemish sisters apparently learned English 'merely to make her confession to me'.[12]

Gerard had clearly revelled in his Clink celebrity. He insisted on donning his Jesuit robes in examination (presumably over the hair shirt that he tells us he wore) and he insinuated that the priest who betrayed him was jealous of his popularity. Once, when the head warder banged on his cell door, Gerard had instantly known who it was, for 'the other gaoler would never have dared to treat me in this way'.[13] He could afford to be imperious because he had astonishing charisma. Good looks also helped. He was tall – 'Long John' – and well set. In contemporary parlance he was 'blackish'. He had dark curls, a 'hawk' nose and strong, angular features, 'somewhat hollow underneath the cheeks'. He kept his beard 'close' and had 'little mustachoes and a little tuft under his lower lip'. Topcliffe noted that he 'smiles much' and was 'somewhat staring in his look or eyes', which must have infuriated the interrogator, but didn't seem to bother the ladies.[14]

According to one informant, Gerard usually dressed 'costly and defencibly, in buff leather garnished with gold or silver lace, satin doublets and velvet hose of all colours, with cloaks correspondent, and rapiers and daggers gilt or silvered'. In 1603 he was 'very gallant in apparel'. His snipers observed that he did not dress like a man of the cloth and Gerard himself admitted that, as a gentleman born, he was 'at ease' in smart clothes, but they were also part of his disguise, along with apparent materialism and a fondness for worldly pursuits. Ladies were astonished when Gerard was unmasked: 'Why the man lives like a courtier,' they exclaimed, but by then they were hooked.[15]

Even on paper 'Long John with the little beard' is extraordinarily compelling. In many ways his flaws make him a more sympathetic character than cautious, self-effacing Garnet. It is an unfair comparison, for anyone would look square and stiff next to Gerard, but theirs was an interesting dynamic: the compassionate, scrupulous leader with the logical mind, and the dashing maverick who was not afraid to take risks and ruffle feathers. The men in Rome knew what they were doing when they sent both men to England; the mission required circumspection and chutzpah.

There was some tension between the two. Gerard irritated his superior by not following protocol when he landed in 1588. Nine years later, Garnet frustrated Gerard by insisting upon a thicker rope for the prison break, which actually 'increased the hazards'. When they wrote about each other it was with courtesy and admiration, but not the warmth that they bestowed upon a Southwell or an Oldcorne. Nevertheless, they earned each other's respect. Garnet valued Gerard as his 'most active and most useful' priest and Gerard seemed to appreciate that in 'this most modest of men' the English Jesuits had the right man at the helm.[16]

Garnet and Gerard may have had contrasting styles, but they had the same goal and were single-minded in its pursuit. It is tempting to think of Gerard as an Elizabethan gallant, but he saw himself as God's 'instrument'. There was certainly nothing romantic in his conversion of Francis Page, a handsome young man who was 'deeply loved by a lady' whom he hoped to marry. She was a 'good and devout' Catholic and introduced her sweetheart to the faith, and to Gerard, which was a mistake, since he spotted priestly potential in young Page and ground

20. Philip II of Spain. He may have lost the battle in 1588 (celebrated by 19: the 'Armada Portrait' of Queen Elizabeth, overleaf), but the war was far from over.

21. and 22. William Cecil, Lord Burghley, and his son Robert, Earl of Salisbury. Catholics complained of a 'Cecilian Inquisition', but the relationship between the Vauxes and the Cecils suggests a more subtle picture.

3. Kirby Hall, Northamptonshire, where Eliza Vaux planned to harbour the Jesuit missionary John Gerard before a pre-emptive raid forced her to change location.

24. The manacles: 'Such a gripping pain came over me,' wrote John Gerard after a session hanging from the iron shackles. 'It was worst in my chest and belly, my hands and arms.'

25. Baddesley Clinton, Warwickshire, probabl[y] home of the Vaux sisters between 1588 and 159[1]. The sewer hide ran along this side wal[l].

26. The swinging-beam hide at Harvington Hall, Worcestershire, discovered by a boy exploring a derelict wing in 1894.

27. The 'pedlar's chest' containing a portable church for the itinerant priest.

28. Recusant women at home, taken from *The Painted Life* of Mary Ward.

29. A chasuble embroidered by Helena Wintour, daughter of the gunpowder plotter Robert Wintour. Priests had to wear their vestments during Mass despite the high risk of detection.

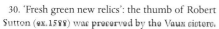

30. 'Fresh green new relics': the thumb of Robert Sutton (ex. 1588) was preserved by the Vaux sisters.

CONCILIVM SEPTEM NOBILIVM ANGLORVM CONIVRANTIVM IN NECEM IACOBI ·I·
MAGNÆ · BRITANNIÆ · REGIS · TOTIVSQ · ANGLICI CONVOCATI PARLEMENTI ·

Bates   Robert Winter   Christopher Wright   Iohn Wright   Thomas Percy   Guido Fawkes   Robert Catesby   Thomas Winter

31. Engraving of the main gunpowder plotters.

32. Sir Everard Digby: one of John Gerard's glamorous young converts and Eliza Vaux's 'great and tried friend'. He was one of the last recruits to the Gunpowder Plot: 'Oh how full of joy should I die if I could do anything for the cause which I love more than my life.'

33. St Winifred's Well, North Wales. It was on pilgrimage to this holy shrine in September 1605 th Anne Vaux noticed fine horses in her friends' stables ar 'feared these wild heads had something in han She implored Garnet 'for God's sake' to talk to Cates 'and to hinder anything that possibly he migh

34. Coughton Court, Warwickshire: home to the recusant Throckmorton family and rented by Digby upon the advice of Catesby. It was here that Garnet and the Vaux sisters first heard the news of the discovery of the Gunpowder Plot.

35. Henry Garnet, Superior of the Jesuit Mission in England. The Vaux sisters kept him safe for almost twenty years. (Inset: a representation of 'Garnet's Straw'.)

36. Anne Vaux's orange-juice letter to Henry Garnet in the Tower. The writing was invisible until exposed by heat.

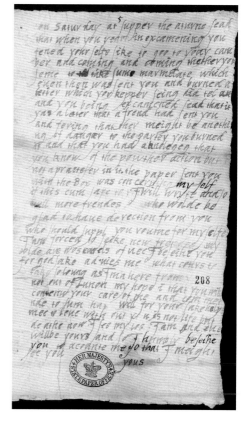

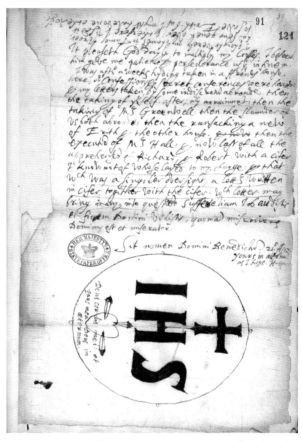

37. Henry Garnet's last letter to Anne Vaux, written from his cell in the Tower of London on Easter Monday 1606.

him down, 'pointing out', for example, 'that perhaps the girl's parents would not give their consent as she would be marrying below her station'. Soon all thoughts of marriage were abandoned. Francis Page, S.J., was executed at Tyburn on 20 April 1602; Anne and Eleanor kept some of his relics.[17]

John Gerard could be ruthless and, like many charming people, ruthlessly effective. According to one hostile source, he was the type of person 'in whose mouth a man would think butter could not melt'.[18] It was just the kind of comment that Sir Thomas Tresham might have made about Eliza Vaux. Henry Garnet had found the perfect hosts in Anne and Eleanor. His flamboyant junior with the good looks and brazen ways would find an equally suitable match with their sister-in-law Eliza.

18

St Peter's Net

'And so I happened, by God's good providence, to visit a noble household. I had often been invited there before and had been expected for a long time, but other business had always kept me elsewhere.'[1]

Following his escape from the Tower, Gerard laid low with Garnet and the sisters for a few days. When he attempted to resume work in London, word soon spread and his old city haunts were raided. It became so hot for him that Garnet considered sending him back to Europe. Gerard was 'much dismayed' by the prospect and managed to convince his superior to keep him on. 'I hope he will walk warily,' Garnet wrote on 31 March 1598.[2]

Meanwhile, Eliza and her six small children had moved into the Vaux house in Irthlingborough. It was 'old and tumble-down', but more suited to their needs than grand, derelict Harrowden. 'When I came to the house,' Gerard recalled,

> I found her completely overwrought by her husband's untimely death. So much had it affected her that she hardly moved out of her room for a whole year; and for three years after that (when I was visiting her) she had been unable to bring herself to enter the wing of the house in which her husband had died.

He added that she was 'worried by anxiety for the future of her son'. The barony was impoverished and Eliza was finding it hard to make ends meet. 'But,' Gerard concluded, with a nod to Proverbs 14:1, and also to Eliza's steel, 'a wise woman builds up her house and proves herself in it.'[3]

As the voluminous Tresham Papers reveal, Eliza had not just been sobbing into her pillow since George's death in 1594. She had been busy shoring up the Vaux patrimony and defending herself against threats of indictment and forfeiture. 'To her great costs and charges', she had also secured the wardship of her son Edward, fourth Lord Vaux. This had been achieved through the mediation of Sir Thomas Cecil, who had purchased the guardianship of the underage peer from the Queen and then sold it on to Eliza, who continued to look after Edward and the estate.[4]

A 'marked Catholic', Eliza was not afforded a completely free hand. As Gerard explained, 'the Lords of the Council wanted to keep in touch with her son the baron and watch where and how he was being brought up.' Although a bill for the seizure of the children of recusant parents had been dropped in the Parliament of 1593, the treatment of the Worthington boys – four brothers forcibly taken from a house near Warrington in 1584 – lived long in Catholic memory.* Recusant schoolmasters were illegal, so Eliza employed Thomas Smith, an Oxford graduate who was prepared to take the oath of supremacy and go to church. This made him a 'schismatic' in Jesuit parlance. 'He was the type of person,' wrote Gerard, 'who can say truthfully with the prophet "My belly cleaveth to the ground", and they are much more difficult people to move than heretics.'

The family chaplain did not fare much better. Although a Jesuit, 'a learned man and a good preacher', Richard Cowling of York was unpopular with the servants and had spent an ineffectual year in Eliza's house with his nose in his books. She claimed to like and reverence him, but she really wanted someone who 'mixed with men', someone who could advise on practical matters, someone, perhaps, like Gerard himself, who had previously strengthened the faith of her sister, Lady Lovell. During Gerard's visits Eliza's 'grief seemed to change to joy'. She let it be known that, if he came to live with her, she would 'put aside her long mourning – she would be a different person and all would be well'.[5]

On the basis of Tresham's testimony, John Gerard did not turn

---

* The fate of the four Worthington brothers became a cause célèbre in Catholic circles. The boys, aged between twelve and sixteen, were subjected to various attempts to make them apostatise. They refused and were flogged, separated and pronounced guilty of treason. All four eventually managed to escape overseas and become priests. Two of them returned on the English mission. (Beales, *Education under Penalty*, pp. 57–64)

'covetous, conscionless' Eliza into a saint.[6] In Gerard's prose, however, she is 'the gentle widow' and her life, hitherto 'good and holy', becomes exemplary. She learned 'to set cares of the next world before those of this'. She began to meditate, 'for she was capable of it – in fact she had intelligence and talents of a high order'. She embraced her widowhood, offering her chastity to God and promising to act as a 'handmaid' to His servants. Indeed:

> she was resolved to fulfil as nearly as she could the role of Martha and of other holy women who followed Christ and ministered to Him and His Apostles. She was ready to set up house wherever and in whatever way I judged best for our needs – whether, she protested time and again, it was in London or in the remotest part of England.[7]

This was a *vie édifiante*, an idealised version of the truth, but clearly changes were made in Eliza's household that were not to everyone's liking. One thinks of Valentine Kellison, for example, 'a well-willer, but no Catholic',* who was more used to raising hell with Ambrose Vaux than examining the state of his soul.[8] 'This lady had many servants in her house when I came to live with her,' Gerard recalled:

> A number were non-Catholics; others were Catholics of a sort, but all enjoyed too much liberty. Gradually I got rid of the abuses. By talking privately with them and by my sermons in public, I brought them slowly, with the help of God's grace, to better ways. Some I instructed and received into the Church, but there were a few I had to get dismissed, since there seemed no hope of their reform.[9]

Kellison, whose brother Matthew would become president of the seminary in Douai, was retained by Eliza and remained staunchly loyal to the family. But another, unnamed servant had to be let go when, on a visit to London in the train of his mistress, he carped at Gerard's reforms to 'a treacherous friend' and gave away their location. In the ensuing raid, Gerard hid in the gable, but his great

---

* This was the opinion of Gerard's predecessor, Richard Cowling, in a letter of 23 June [1599?] to Guilio Piccioli in Venice. The chief purpose of his letter was to entreat Piccioli for 'favour & friendship for my cousin germane Mr Guydo Fawkes', who was living on the Continent 'in great want'. (PRO SP 12/271, f. 56r)

stalwart John Lillie gave himself up and was reportedly tortured. Also seized were Gerard's meditation notes, his breviary, some devotional books 'and what I valued most: my manuscript sermons and notes for sermons, which I had collected together over the last ten years'.[10] Any notion of moving to London was abandoned. It was too dangerous for Gerard and too public for Eliza, who faced scrutiny as the fourth Lord Vaux's mother and estate manager: 'Officials and bailiffs would be constantly coming to see her', making it 'impossible for her to live near London under an assumed name as she would have to do if she was going to continue her good work for any length of time'.[11]

Having decided that Irthlingborough and Harrowden were shabby, inhospitable and ill-defended, Gerard and Eliza went house hunting. They combed Northamptonshire and finally came across Kirby Hall, a large remote Elizabethan manor with sprawling grounds. All it lacked were priest-holes. In the spring of 1599, they took the lease – or rather, the owner, Lady Elizabeth Hatton (whose late husband had inherited the property from his uncle, Sir Christopher Hatton), let it to John Wiseman, who let it to Henry Montagu, who let it to Francis Crisp and Thomas Mulsho, the last named being a trustee for Lord Vaux.[12]

There were already rumours of Eliza's plan in Puritan-run Northamptonshire when she and Gerard travelled to Kirby that summer with 'Little John' Owen and his carpentry kit. Pursuivants were posted at Kettering in a bid to intercept them on their return to Irthlingborough, but a servant fortuitously suggested an alternative route that was 'easier for the lady's carriage'. Back at Irthlingborough, Gerard and Eliza were not aware of the raid at Kirby the following morning, nor of the pursuivants galloping furiously towards them. They 'burst in on us at the dinner hour', but as the mistress and young master of the house were both ill and resting in their chambers, they stormed an empty room. Gerard was in his own chamber, about to dine with the gentleman convert, Roger Lee, who had come to take the Spiritual Exercises, and John Percy, a second Jesuit priest newly posted at Irthlingborough. 'Hastily I snatched up everything I wanted to conceal and made a dash for the hiding-place.' It was beyond the room where the searchers were gathered:

I heard them shouting out that they wanted to get on with their search without delay. One pursuivant actually pushed his head round the door to see who was passing and some of the Catholics in the room told me afterwards that he must have seen me as I went past. But God intervened, for how else can you explain it? There they were, straining and shouting to get through and search the house, yet they halted behind in an unlocked room just long enough to allow us time to reach the hiding-place and shut ourselves safely in. Then they broke out as though they had been let loose. They burst into the lady's apartment while others raged round the remaining rooms.

They searched the whole day, but found nothing and no one:

Undoubtedly it was the finger of God who did not want to cut at the roots of the lady's good works. Rather, by this manifestation of His providence, He wished to confirm her in her resolve and keep her for a future full of service and fine achievement.[13]

So Gerard wrote a decade later and so he must have told Eliza at the time, for she remained determined to risk all for the mission. She took 'very special precautions' and gave out that the Jesuit was going to 'quit the house altogether'. But he never left. Eliza shifted her household to Harrowden Hall and had an extension built for Gerard and Percy 'close to the old chapel where the former barons used to hear Mass when the weather was too wet for them to go to the village church'. Nicholas Owen probably constructed the new wing from which priests could 'pass out unnoticed into the private garden and through the broad walks into the fields'.*

There were other advantages to Harrowden, including an impressive library that had been enlarged by Henry Vaux and two sets of 'very fine' vestments – 'one for ordinary use, the other for greater feasts.' Several were embroidered with pearls and gold thread and

---

* This may be the present north wing, where a hiding hole remains. In 1694 Harrowden Hall was sold by Charles Knollys, the son of the fourth Lord Vaux's illegitimate son, to Thomas Watson, son of Lord Rockingham. It was substantially rebuilt in the Queen Anne style. The Gothic private chapel was erected by the seventh Lord Vaux, who returned the Hall to the family in 1895. It now houses Wellingborough Golf Club.

displayed 'exquisite workmanship'. Gerard was also delighted by the chapel plate:

> Six massive silver candlesticks stood on the altar and two smaller ones at the side for the elevation. The cruets, the lavabo bowl, the bell and thurible were all of silverwork.* The lamps hung from silver chains, and a silver crucifix stood on the altar. For the great feasts we had a golden crucifix a foot high. It had a pelican carved at the top and on the right arm an eagle with outstretched wings carrying on its back its little ones who were learning to fly; and on the left arm a phoenix expiring in flames so that it might leave behind an offspring; and at the foot was a hen gathering her chickens under her wings. The whole was worked in gold by a skilled artist.[14]

It was as if the past half-century had never happened. It helped, of course, that Harrowden was a baronial seat and that the Vauxes were tied, as the Jesuit, Oswald Tesimond, observed, 'by consanguinity or affinity . . . to practically every leading and noble family in the county'.[15] The old Lord Vaux had been well liked and there was good will towards his grandson. The Cecil connection continued into the next generations.[16] Sir Edward Montagu of Boughton, though a Protestant official, was not entrusted with a general search of Harrowden in February 1601 because it was suspected that he would not 'use the matter so strictly and circumspectly as is fit and convenient'. (It was further noted that Eliza had 'such places for the concealing' of a priest that unless 'a man pull down the house, he shall never find him'.)[17]

Thus, although Eliza was observed by the powers on high, she was also to some extent protected by them. As long as the altar furniture and ancestral vestments were kept out of sight, and on site, they might remain out of mind. Approaching danger usually came with a warning. Some local Puritans were outraged. Richard Knightley of Fawsley

---

* The elevation occurred at the sacring, the consecration of the Eucharistic elements. The priest held the host up for worshippers to see and adore. Extra candles were lit and the bell was rung to highlight the elements and call the attention of the faithful. The cruets held wine and the water that was used, along with the lavabo bowl, for washing the celebrant's hands. Incense was burned and distributed by means of the thurible.

would complain in 1625 about the family's apparent immunity from prosecution and their 'too daring and insolent' behaviour. Contacts and favours only went so far, however.[18] With the coming of Gerard and his colleagues, the noise and traffic from Harrowden began to increase. Eliza only had herself to blame for any withdrawal of privilege, the Earl of Salisbury (Burghley's son, Robert Cecil) would inform Lord Vaux in 1612, if, 'rather than content herself with one of the priests from Mary's reign, she chose to have two of those blood-soaked Jesuits'.[19]

*

During their first Christmas together in 1598, Eliza gave Gerard a 'precious ornament' depicting 'the Holy Name' in gold pins. Gerard estimated – or did he count? – 240 pins in total, each attached to a large pearl. There was another, smaller monogram at the bottom enclosing 'a heart with a cross of diamonds radiating from it'. Gerard was thrilled with his gift – technically a donation to the Society – if disappointed that the pearls weren't quite perfect. 'Had they been,' he wrote wistfully, 'the value of the ornament would have been fabulous, but as it was the whole thing was worth about a thousand florins.'[20]

The following Christmas, the children's 'schismatic' tutor, Thomas Smith, had an evangelical awakening courtesy of the edifying example of his young charges staying up for midnight Mass. Gerard observed that the pupils had taught the master 'by conduct and not by words a lesson which he should have been teaching them'. Smith departed for the English College in Rome and was replaced at Harrowden by another Oxford scholar, one Tutfield, who was not at all trusted by the Council and was later 'suspected to be a priest'.[21] The schoolroom was filled with Vaux children, the offspring of neighbours and servants and at least one child from further afield: Henry Killinghall, born of a recusant mother in York gaol, was educated at Harrowden and later became a priest.[22]

By his own account Gerard sent 'many young men to the seminaries' as well as several ladies to the convents. His conversion rate was extremely – perhaps suspiciously – high. Leaving Percy at Harrowden to receive visitors and administer the sacraments, he would go foraging for souls in the south Midlands. With introductions from the Vauxes and subsequent influential converts like Roger Lee and Everard Digby, he was welcomed into smart circles and offered generous hospitality. His disguise was crucial for it was often during card games* or out in the saddle that he would win the trust of his subjects. Only later, and with great delicacy, would he attempt to catch them in 'St Peter's net', a conversion that entailed not only a change of institutional allegiance, but also a complete reorientation of the self. Gerard taught his penitents how to examine their consciences thoroughly before confession and how to purify their souls through frequent prayer, spiritual reading and meditation. He utilised the principles and methods of the Spiritual Exercises and led some of his converts through the month-long meditative retreat. His goal was to reveal, 'by means of the Exercises, the straight road that leads to life with Him for guide, who is Himself the Way and the Life'.[23]

Gayhurst in Buckinghamshire, where the Digbys lived, soon resembled Harrowden Hall with its well-appointed chapel and priest-holes. There was even a pair of wafer irons for making altar breads. According to Gerard:

> what this family did, others did too. Many Catholic gentlemen, when they visited this house and saw the arrangements there, took it as a model. They founded congregations centred round their own homes, furnished their chapels and, designing accommodation suited to a priest's needs, maintained one there with reverence and respect.[24]

By 1609 the chief Jesuit 'churches' were known by code names. A surviving cipher list reveals that Lord Vaux and his mother belonged to A.P., the 'church' of their resident chaplain, John Percy, who was also responsible for Lady Digby in Buckinghamshire, Lady Wenman of Thame Park near Oxford, members of the Simeon family of Baldwin Brightwell, Oxfordshire, and the Fermors of Easton Neston.

---

* 'I should explain that whenever I was with Catholics and we had to stage a game in circumstances like these, we had an understanding that everybody got his money back at the end and that the loser said an Ave Maria for every counter returned. In this way I often played with brother Digby and others when there was occasion to act a part and make bystanders think that we were playing for money in good earnest.' (Gerard, *Autobiography*, p. 170)

All were related or affiliated to the Vauxes and it is evident that kin networks were as important as geography in determining the make-up of these 'churches'.[25] The Jesuits were often accused of elitism, but it was strategic elitism, designed for hierarchical England in order to open up as many mission fields and win as many souls as safely and as quickly as possible. The coverage could be wide, extending through tenants and other dependants to all levels of society.

Eliza turned her home, to use Alexandra Walsham's phrase, into one of the 'humid hothouses in which Tridentine spirituality seems to have flourished exuberantly'.[26] Indeed her contribution to the mission extended beyond her facilities. In his *Autobiography* Gerard told the story of the conversion of one of her kinswomen.[27] Eliza apparently loved this relative 'like a sister' and wept tears of frustration when she could not 'induce her to become a Catholic'. She refused to give up on the lady. Inviting her to stay, she introduced Gerard as a guest from London 'as we had previously arranged'. They kept the conversation light for a few days until Gerard chose a propitious moment for Eliza 'to open a serious conversation on religion'. He then took over and Eliza left the room. A few hours later, Eliza was accosted by her red-faced relative:

> 'Cousin,' she cried, 'what have you done?'
>
> 'What have I done?' asked my lady.
>
> 'Who's this man you brought to me? Is he what you said he was?'
>
> And she asked questions about me and spoke much too favourably about my eloquence and learning, saying she could not hold her own or answer back.
>
> The next day God confirmed what He had begun in her. She surrendered at discretion and I gave her a book to help her prepare for confession.

After her confession, the lady rushed to thank Eliza, 'who was the means of bringing her this happiness'. She stayed at Harrowden for about two years 'and during all that time she grew in devotion and read many ascetical books'. Although careful not to overstep the bounds of Pauline decency, Gerard gave his hostess due credit for her kinswoman's conversion, depicting it as a joint plan, jointly realised. Gerard was the exegete, but the initiative was Eliza's.

A later, extremely hostile source also portrayed Eliza in the proselytising process. A young clergyman called John Gee wrote a book,
New Shreds of the Old Snare, in 1624 in a bid to improve his Protestant
credentials after his attendance at a Catholic evensong was revealed
to his superiors. (The service in question was the 'fatal vespers' of 26
October 1623 when the floorboards of the gatehouse adjoining the
French embassy in Blackfriars collapsed, killing almost a hundred
worshippers. Gee saw God's hand in his deliverance from death and
the 'snare' of popery.) Written in the same intemperate vein as Samuel
Harsnett's exorcism-bashing *Declaration of Egregious Popish Impostures*,
Gee's tract sought to expose the 'legerdemaine tricks' of the Jesuits
and unmask them as a pack of actors so skilled 'that they should set
up a company for themselves, which surely will put down The Fortune,
Red-Bull, Cockpit, & Globe'.[28]

Gee seemed to be particularly incensed by the Catholic Church's
belief in miracles and its cultivation of the supernatural as a proselytising tool. Exorcisms, relics, signs, 'personated apparitions' and the
like were all, to Gee's mind, terrible cons designed to bolster conversion rates and extort cash from impressionable youths. He cited the
case of Mary Boucher, a London Protestant in the service of 'Lady
A., a Papist'.[29] The girl's mother had received assurances from Lady A
– presumably the Countess of Arundel – that no attempt would be
made to convert her. But three Jesuits, including 'Mr Fisher' (an alias
of John Percy), could not help themselves. 'We are God's prophets,'
Fisher reputedly told Mary, 'we can do miracles and we are inspired
with divine illuminations. It is revealed unto me that you must go
beyond the seas and become a nun.' When Mary protested that her
mother would never allow it, she was told that she should no longer
see her. Sick with confusion, Mary took to her bed,

where, after she had rested herself a while, there comes into the
chamber one M[ris] Vaux, a great recusant, and asked her how she did
and then came to her and did somewhat stroke or rub her forehead.
After which time Mary Boucher felt herself very ill at ease and distempered in her head. And about an half-hour after M[ris] Vaux was departed
from her, she heard her chamber door open and with that a great light
flashed into the room two or three times, which she thought somebody
did by way of jest or merriment to make her afraid.

Mary's dead godmother seemed to enter the room. She was dressed all in white, her hair was long and loose and her hand was 'cold as earth or iron'. She claimed to have come from purgatory and she admonished Mary of the perils of damnation. After the vision had disappeared, Eliza returned to help the girl make sense of it.

> 'Oh then,' quoth M^ris Vaux, 'it is time for thee to become a good Catholic, for assure thyself it was a special favour and mercy of God that thou shouldest have such a warning.' And so, giving her more instructions to this purpose, went away.

The ghost reappeared and reiterated the message (Gee noting in the margin that 'nimble actors know their Q'). Mary was visited over a dozen times and seemed keen to be 'nunnified', but in the end her mother's protestations were so loud that 'the voyage was stayed and her daughter restored'. Three years later, Mary was married and living near Baynards Castle in London and it was there that Gee claimed to have interviewed her 'to inform myself the better of the truth of these particulars'.

It is a classic tale of Jesuit duplicity. Gee was a plagiarist and a polemicist, determined to undermine the teaching of the Catholic Church. In an earlier work of the same year, he ridiculed Mary Boucher's 'ghastly ghost walking in a sheet knit upon the head'.[30] His modern editor was unable to trace Mary or her mother, but the story, though partisan, is not necessarily apocryphal.[31] It may have stemmed from a real event involving real people. Whatever the truth of the tale, Gee's inclusion of the 'great recusant' Eliza Vaux lent it an air of authenticity, for she was well known by then as 'one of the best friends the Jesuits have had in England'. So wrote her middle son, William, in a plea for special treatment from the Jesuits of Lisbon in 1612. This pallid redhead thought he deserved more respect from the brethren considering his mother 'hath harboured them and hid them in stone walls and furnished them with money'.[32]

Actually, it is easy to see why no one thought much of Eliza's foul-mouthed, volatile son. She did her sharp-elbowed best with him, sending him to the Jesuit colleges at St Omer and Valladolid, and imposing on friends for favours, but he consistently let her down. In October 1612 Eliza would petition Pedro de Zúñiga, Marquis of Flores

Dávila, who was in England on diplomatic business, to return to Madrid with William in his train. When Zúñiga refused, Eliza begged the intercession of Luisa de Carvajal, a Spanish noblewoman in London. Knowing that a refusal 'would have hurt her too much' and 'she would certainly have complained a great deal about it to me', Luisa reluctantly agreed. Zúñiga relented, but insisted that Eliza 'consider hard first' whether her son had 'the character and virtue for Madrid, because if he was not prepared to heed the advice of others and was not virtuous, he would be completely ruined there'. Eliza assured him that William was a good boy who 'neither gambled nor blasphemed'. Zúñiga took her at her word and William to Madrid, a decision that he would soon regret.

On the night of St James's Day, 1613, during the hot, Hispanic summer, William killed an English merchant called Copland 'in the street'. The English ambassador was so appalled by the 'odiousness' of the crime that he only gave William sanctuary for a day.[33] Writing from London a month later, Luisa, who was not a mother, blamed Eliza:

> Here everyone praises her for being a very wise woman, yet if she is indeed wise, I am astonished that she so deceived herself and brought dishonour on herself by sending that particular son to Spain; for the older one is a young man of considerable sense and good character.[34]

'The older one' would fare better. Indeed, it would seem for a short while in 1605 as though Edward, fourth Lord Vaux of Harrowden, might escape the recusancy rut, save the barony and marry the girl of his dreams. He was only sixteen then. Lady Elizabeth Howard, daughter of the first Earl of Suffolk and Lord Chamberlain of the Household, was eighteen. Certainly later, and perhaps already, their love was deep and mutual. Eliza promoted the match with characteristic vigour, securing the services of her 'great and tried friend', Sir Everard Digby, as well as the 'good will and gladness' of Robert Cecil, Earl of Salisbury, whose son was betrothed to another of Suffolk's daughters and whose intimacy with the pro-Catholic Countess of Suffolk was an open secret.[35]

Around Easter, 1605, Eliza sent her pregnant friend and kinswoman, Agnes, Lady Wenman, an update on her progress. Although 'chiefly concerning her son's marriage to my Lord of Suffolk's daughter', Eliza's letter also complained of Agnes's husband, Sir Richard Wenman, who had recently snubbed her in London. According to Gerard's searing pen, Sir Richard was 'a knight with a large estate, who hoped one day to become a baron, and is still hoping'.[36] He did not approve of Eliza, whom he accused, with some justification, of having 'corrupted his wife in religion'. In her letter Eliza acknowledged the 'disgrace' associated with Catholicism in her country. 'Notwithstanding, pray,' she urged Agnes, 'for Tottenham may turn French.' Or words to that effect. Agnes could not quite remember. Her husband, who also read the letter before his wife conveniently lost it, recalled that it 'concluded in this manner, or to the same effect: that she should pray, for that she did hope or look that shortly Tottenham would turn French.'[37]

The phrase, which may have had its roots in the heavy migration of French workers to Tottenham in the reign of Henry VIII, referred to a dramatic, but incredibly unlikely, change of circumstance and was usually used in the context of something unexpected or absurd. Witness the third Duke of Norfolk's reaction to a nasty rumour in 1536 that he should be in the Tower of London: 'When I shall deserve to be there, Tottenham shall turn French.'[38] Or the poet John Heywood's description of the end of the honeymoon period:

> The flowers so faded that, in fifteen weeks
> A man might espy the change in the cheeks,
> Both of this poor wretch, and his wife, this poor wench.
> Their faces told toys,* that Tott'n'am was turned French.
> And all their light laughing turn'd and translated
> Into sad sighing, all mirth was amated.[39]

On 14 July 1605, Edward, 'having lost the hope of my greater suit in another place', was granted a licence to travel abroad for three years.[40] It is not clear what had happened, but Eliza's father blamed her 'for refusing the match & offer of my La: of Suffolk'. A royal progress through Northamptonshire the following month, with the King bedding down at Harrowden Hall on 12 August, presented Eliza with the perfect opportunity to revive the suit. After bending the ear of the crypto-Catholic Earl of Northampton (Suffolk's influential

* *toys*: whims, fancies, jests.

uncle),* she was confident 'of the certainty of that match'.[41] Then months passed without word. In early November she decided to send Edward to London 'to make an end thereof one way or other'.

Between eight and nine o'clock in the morning on Wednesday, 6 November 1605, Agnes Wenman's father, Sir George Fermor of Easton Neston, received a request to visit his kinsman, Lord Vaux. He covered the twenty-odd miles to Harrowden Hall at an easy pace, arriving between four and five in the afternoon. Eliza greeted him and explained that she had sent for him in order to ask him to accompany Edward to London. While he had been in the saddle, however, news had arrived of 'some garboyl' in the city. Eliza had changed her mind, therefore, and would delay her son's trip 'until things were quieted'.[42]

It was some time – more than a quarter of a century – before Edward could conclude his suit, for the garboyl in London turned out to be the discovery of the Gunpowder Plot and no member of the Vaux family was untouched. Tottenham had not turned French. Along with the rest of the country it had remained English and Protestant and determined to find out what, in God's name, had been going on.

---

*Henry Howard, Earl of Northampton, was the second son of the poet Earl of Surrey (ex. 1547) and the brother of the fourth Duke of Norfolk (Suffolk's father), who was beheaded in 1572. Writing in the reign of Elizabeth, the Spanish ambassador noted that he 'completely rules his nephews and constantly keeps before them the need for resenting the death of their father, and following the party of the Queen of Scots, by whose means alone can they hope for vengeance' (Peck, *Northampton*, p. 11). Queen Elizabeth never trusted Howard, but James I made him a privy councillor, Earl of Northampton and, in 1608, Lord Privy Seal.

PART FOUR

POWDER TREASON

These late eclipses in the sun and moon portend no good to us. Though the wisdom of nature can reason it thus and thus, yet nature finds itself scourged by the sequent effects. Love cools, friendship falls off, brothers divide; in cities, mutinies; in countries, discord; in palaces, treason; and the bond cracked 'twixt son and father. This villain of mine comes under the prediction: there's son against father. The King falls from bias of nature: there's father against child. We have seen the best of our time. Machinations, hollowness, treachery, and all ruinous disorders follow us disquietly to our graves . . .

King Lear, Act 1, Scene 2
The play was performed at court on 26 December 1606

Fair is foul, and foul is fair,
Hover through the fog and filthy air.
Macbeth, Act 1, Scene 1
First performed in the months
following the Gunpowder Plot

19

This Stinking King

> I perceive there is no hope at all of amendment in this stinking
> king of ours. An ill quarter to look for righteousness: at the hands
> of a miserable Scot.
>
> Hugh Owen in exile, 1603[1]

Anne and Eleanor had a kinsman called Robert Catesby, or Robin to his
friends.[2] He was about a decade younger than the sisters and 'seldom
long from us', Garnet recalled, 'for the great affection he bore the gentlewoman with whom I lived & unto me'.[3] The Catesby family home,
Ashby St Ledgers in Northamptonshire, was just over twenty miles from
Harrowden Hall and even closer to Great Ashby, Eleanor's jointure house
in Leicestershire. Catesby, whose confessor, Oswald Tesimond, S.J., was
stationed with Garnet and the sisters, supported the mission and loaned
them houses. Morecrofts, near Uxbridge, where John Gerard had landed
after his flight from the Tower in 1597, was one. A house in Erith, 'in a
private back lane near the water', procured by Catesby late in 1603, was
another.* The arrangement seems to have been reciprocal: Catesby and
his friends 'often resorted' to White Webbs, the sisters' house in Enfield
Chase.[4]

---

* Once a naval dockyard, Erith on the Thames Estuary was the ideal place, not only
for a safe house, but also a smuggling operation. There may have been something
to the limerick:

> There are men in the village of Erith,
> Whom nobody seeth or heareth,
> And there looms on the marge
> of the river a barge,
> Which nobody roweth or steereth.
> (Monkhouse, *Nonsense Rhymes*, 1902)

According to Tesimond, Catesby was 'more than ordinarily well-proportioned, some six feet tall, of good carriage and handsome countenance'. Like Gerard, whom he knew, he was eloquent, charming and possessed of a mesmeric quality that inspired adoration and loyalty. Like Gerard too, he seems to have had the gift of making people feel good and important. To his kinsman Lord Monteagle (who was married to his cousin), he was 'the dear Robin whose conversation gave us such warmth' and 'the only sun that must ripen our harvest'. While Ambrose Rookwood 'loved' Catesby 'more than his own soul', Thomas Wintour vowed to follow him to the death.[5]

Of course, magnets also repel and the other side of Catesby was ugly, devoid of empathy and full of hatred. He had been 'very wild' in his youth according to Gerard, until he had properly committed to his faith, forsaken 'his swearing and excess of play and apparel' and taken up daily devotions. Thereafter a powerful zeal infused that extraordinary charisma and fired the restless spirit. 'He was beside himself with mindless fanaticism,' Tesimond later wrote, and he thought 'he was wasting time when he was not doing something to bring about the conversion of the country'.[6]

He realised too late that the botched political rising of the Earl of Essex was not the way. Along with his friends John and Christopher Wright, his kinsman Lord Monteagle and other Catholic malcontents who attached themselves to the reckless earl in February 1601, Catesby was imprisoned and heavily fined. His uncle (by marriage) Sir Thomas Tresham helped bail him out, which was generous considering Tresham also expended a year's income on the extrication of his own son, Francis, from 'the unfortunate action of the late Earl of Essex'.[7] Sir Thomas's earlier concerns that he had 'much more busied my brains' on the affairs of George Vaux to the detriment of his son – 'though otherwise Francis no less feared in those rather madding than gadding days' – now appeared justified.[8] (There had, however, been uses for Francis back then: in 1591, Sir Thomas had sent him out with men and crowbars to retrieve four hundred pounds from one George Ball. They had violently seized the septuagenarian debtor and thrown his pregnant daughter down the stairs 'to the very great danger of her life, being within one month of her time'. Ball's claim to have 'divers informations of very lewd matter against her Majesty and the State' regarding Tresham's servant,

George Fulshurst – he who later ran off with Merill Vaux – may also have contributed to his rough treatment.⁹)

Francis Tresham and Robin Catesby were 'near and dear'. Their mothers were sisters and the boys 'had been brought up from their childhoods together'.¹⁰ They may have also bonded at the end of the century over the deaths of their first-born infant sons, though this is to speculate.¹¹ Although Catesby's great-grandmother had been a Vaux, it was marriages to Treshams – Catesby's aunt to Sir Thomas Tresham; Anne and Eleanor's father to Mary Tresham – that brought Robert so close to the Vaux sisters. There was also their shared heritage in suffering: Lord Vaux and Sir William Catesby had, along with their 'brother' Sir Thomas Tresham, been tried together in 1581 for supporting Edmund Campion. They had petitioned the Queen for leniency four years later and, when ignored, they had met at Hoxton to set up the missionary fund. During the Armada crisis all three had been detained. Recusants to the last, each man had shouldered a pecuniary and psychological burden that their children had been quite unable to lighten.

Sir William Catesby had seriously considered exile. In 1582, the year after Campion, the trial and the exorbitant increase (from 12d to £20) of the monthly recusancy fine, he had backed a proposal to establish an English Catholic colony in North America. The scheme was promoted by Sir George Peckham and Sir Thomas Gerard (the Jesuit's father) and attracted several of Campion's erstwhile hosts.¹² It offered a possible way out, a haven where recusants could worship freely and thrive. Sir Francis Walsingham had endorsed it – with such enthusiasm that the Spanish ambassador thought it his design – and a list of articles was agreed in June 1582. In return for putting up a hundred pounds and ten men for the first voyage (forty for the next), 'associates' like Catesby would benefit from the lordship of ten thousand acres of virgin turf and election to 'the chief offices in government'. They would set up a legal system 'as near as they can' to that in England and extend 'special privileges to encourage women to go on the voyage'.¹³

The venture was undeniably risky – 'wild people, wild beasts, unexperienced air, unprovided land'¹⁴ did not inspire investor confidence – but it had some momentum in the summer of 1582. The Spanish killed it. Ambassador Mendoza argued that the emigration would drain 'the small remnant of good blood' from the 'sick body' of England. He was, however, far more concerned about Spain's interests in the New World. The English could not be allowed a foothold in the Americas. It mattered not a jot that they were Catholic, 'they would immediately have their throats cut as happened to the French'. Mendoza conveyed this threat to the would-be settlers via their priests, with the further warning that 'they were imperilling their consciences by engaging in an enterprise prejudicial to His Holiness' the Pope.[15]

So Sir William Catesby did not sail the seas or have a role in the plantation of what might have been the first English colony in America. According to Robert Persons, their attempt was soon mocked by the Protestants and scorned by the Catholics.[16] It does, however, posit some interesting counter-factual questions, for both sides of the Atlantic. From the Old World perspective, one thing is clear: had the venture succeeded and the Catesbys settled in America, there would have been no plot to blow up the Parliament house in 1605, no bonfire-night celebrations, and Guido – or Guy – Fawkes, a Yorkshireman soldiering in Flanders, would never have gained fame as the cloaked figure in the cellar that we burn in effigy every year.

Elizabeth I died in the early hours of 24 March 1603 'easily like a ripe apple from the tree' according to a law student of the Middle Temple. More hostile commentators dwelt on her decayed face and 'distempered' mind. John Chamberlain accused 'the papists' of spreading 'strange stories as utterly void of truth as of all civil honesty or humanity'.[17]

Sir Robert Cecil, who had once had his ears boxed by the Queen, made the observation that she had been 'more than a man and, in troth, sometime less than a woman'. She would have discerned the compliment. She had come a long way since 1572 when, dithering over the execution of the Duke of Norfolk, she had admitted to Cecil's father, Lord Burghley, that the 'hinder part' of her brain could not trust 'the forwards side of the same'. Hanging on the walls of her quarters at Hampton Court was a gold-embroidered tapestry depicting the murder of Julius Caesar – a salient reminder of the stalking threat of assassination in an age that had seen brother monarchs taken by bullet and blade. Country and duty had come first, masculine reason had prevailed over feminine passion, and 'justice', as Burghley termed it, had trumped natural clemency. Elizabeth's priorities were always more political than dogmatic. She would have preferred to have gained obedience 'without constraint', but 'when obedience was lacking', her godson John Harington observed, she 'left no doubtings whose daughter she was'.[18] Like her father, she made good use of the scapegoat and, like him also, she needed money.

To her credit, the statute book remained clean of the wilder anti-Catholic proposals that emerged during her forty-five-year reign. Nonetheless, it was manifestly the case that some priests were executed for being priests and a religious minority was punished for not attending the state church. Only at Elizabeth's death did recusants talk of a golden age and they were looking to the future. Henry Garnet reflected the mood in Anne and Eleanor's house: 'A golden time we have of unexpected freedom . . . Great hope is of toleration: and so general a consent of Catholics in the [King's] proclaiming, it seemeth God will work much.'[19]

The King was James VI of Scotland, now James I of England, the Protestant son of Mary Stuart, Elizabeth's nearest blood relative. There had been some anxiety before his accession because Elizabeth had refused to name her heir. Almost a decade earlier, Robert Persons, S.J., had produced a controversial tract in implicit favour of Isabella, the Infanta of Spain, whose hereditary claim through the house of Lancaster was weaker than James's, but apparently advantaged by her moral and religious position. In 1602 Garnet had received letters, or 'breves', from Rome insisting that Catholic support could only go to a successor who would promote the faith 'with all his might' and 'submit himself to the Sea Apostolical'.[20] During the Queen's final illness, her English-born cousin, Arbella Stuart, who was preferred by some Catholics, was moved closer to London. 'Some principal papists were made sure,' wrote John Chamberlain, and those with rebellious form, like Catesby and the Wright brothers, were 'clapped up'.[21] The nervous energy of the capital was captured by John Donne, who later teased the citizens for 'running up and down like ants, with their eggs bigger than themselves, every man with his bags, to seek where to hide them safely'.[22]

But there had been no need to panic. James's proclamation on the morning of the Queen's death was a work of neat choreography that had been years in the making. James and Rome, James and Madrid,

James and Brussels, and the English court, and the Privy Council, and latterly, above all, Sir Robert Cecil – the Scottish King had been playing a long and careful game, which ensured the smoothest of border crossings. To the Earl of Northumberland, acting on behalf of the English Catholics, he had promised: 'I will neither persecute any that will be quiet and give but an outward obedience to the law, neither will I spare to advance any of them that will by good service worthily deserve it.'[23] Either by accident or design, the Earl's messenger, his kinsman Thomas Percy, had returned from Holyrood with the impression that some form of Catholic toleration was in the offing.

On Friday, 25 March 1603, the day after the proclamation of the King at Whitehall and the morning after a night of hard riding in the rain, Thomas Tresham proclaimed King James at Northampton. The Puritans of the town were less than delighted. Tresham was surrounded by a hostile mob and one 'spleenish and peevish' fellow heckled him on the soundness of the King's religion. With glorious hypocrisy, Tresham lectured the man on the importance of 'civil loyalty and obedience'. The incident sheds light on Puritan hostility to Catholic confidence at the King's accession, in Northampton at least, though Tresham's abrasive personality probably accounted for some of the rancour and at least one Puritan, Lewis Pickering, was happy enough with James I to gallop to Edinburgh to seek his patronage.[24]

Sir John Roper was apparently 'the first man of note' to proclaim James in Kent, while back in Northamptonshire, at Harrowden Hall, his daughter, Eliza Vaux, and her priest, John Gerard, were soon celebrating the knighting of Gerard's brother, which was performed by James on his journey south with reference to his particular 'love' of Gerard blood on account of past support for Mary Queen of Scots.[25]

If recusant optimism was inflated, it was nonetheless sincere. Here was a King not a Queen, a Stuart not a Tudor, a peace-loving poet and family man with heirs and a recently converted Catholic wife. James had no record of religious persecution and no desire to create one, believing it to be 'one of the infallible notes of a false church'.[26] Above all, Gerard wrote later, 'the son of such a mother', who had died 'because she was a Catholic', would surely prove their friend. Exiles began to return home – Tresham's brother William with a French accent – and Garnet advised Robert Persons in Rome to muffle any noise about 'foreign competitors'. He even hoped that James the theologian-king might welcome a papal nuncio to London.[27] And because the papal breves on the English succession had become dead letters, he burnt them. Or so he later claimed, but not before Robert Catesby, his cousin Thomas Wintour and their friend Thomas Percy had all seen them. And so 'they made use of them', Garnet later admitted.[28]

In many ways, King James remained true to his word, at least the written word, verbal assurances being notoriously hard to prove. He gave places at court to prominent crypto-Catholics and he honoured his pledge, made to Tresham and others in July 1603, to remit the recusancy fines in return for dutiful conduct. He was apparently content to put up with the English Catholics as long as they were 'quiet and decently hidden'.[29] But for those who had hoped for some kind of formal toleration – perhaps even an English version of the French Edict of Nantes – James was profoundly disappointing.

Perhaps, for some, reality dawned at Easter, 1603, when the refusal of some court Catholics to attend divine service elicited the royal response: he 'who can't pray with me can't love me'.[30] For others it may have been during the summer when an official reply to a petition for toleration was not forthcoming. At least some of those involved in the 'Bye Plot' that summer claimed to have turned on James because he had reneged on his pre-accession promises. The conspirators included Eleanor's kinsman Bartholomew Brooksby, Anthony Copley, who would later expiate his sins on pilgrimage with Ambrose Vaux, and Sir Griffin Markham, who, in addition to a 'very great' nose, had use of the royal lodge in Beskwood Park, where Francis Tresham, Fathers Gerard and Percy and the young Lord Vaux had recently been hunting. The plot was headed by William Watson, an appellant priest whose idea to kidnap James and force him to grant full toleration was, even Copley conceded, 'without head or foot'.[31]

An attempt to draw Gerard into the conspiracy led to its disclosure: the Jesuit, his superior, Garnet, and Archpriest Blackwell tried 'to stay it what they could', but when Watson showed no sign of quitting, they leaked the details. Watson's rampant anti-Jesuitism – recall his tirade against the 'hot holy ladies' who supported the Society – had not aided his desperate cause. He was executed in November 1603, but most of his confederates were ultimately reprieved. A second

'Main' plot, involving Lord Cobham, Sir Walter Ralegh and the forcible enthronement of Arbella Stuart ('the King and his cubs' to be eliminated), also failed to ignite.

Sir Thomas Tresham, whom the Bye plotters had earmarked for the Lieutenancy of the Tower, was disgusted by the 'menstruous or rather monstrous filthiness' of the conspiracy. He half suspected it to be a put-up job (an erroneous view he had also held about the Babington Plot) and on the eve of his July meeting at Hampton Court, he blasted the Judas 'caitiffs' and pronounced them 'anathema among us'. Others were less perturbed. 'I hear much by private means of strange plots,' Sir John Harington noted in his remembrancer, but 'I have no concerns of this sort, save that my man Ralph hath stolen two cheeses from my dairy-house. I wish he were choked herewith.'[32]

On 26 November 1603, Garnet reported 'some contentment of toleration' in the south. He tried to remain positive despite reports of 'intolerable and continual searches' in the north, and the presence in the early autumn of 'restless men who even in our own name entice our most intimate friends to rebellion'. General Aquaviva urged prudence: 'Shun every species of activity that might make priests of our Order hated by the world and branded the instigators of tragedy or subverters of peace.' The message, which came 'in most grave and serious terms' from the very top, was to pray hard and trust in divine providence, which 'knows how to maintain its order in its own place and time'.[33]

That the time was not going to be 1604 was soon dismayingly apparent. Keen to get on with the union of England and Scotland and fed up with the Catholic clamour for toleration, James was seemingly happy in the New Year to clarify his position. Never, he assured his Privy Council on 19 February 1604, had he considered toleration for the Catholics, whose 'superstitious religion' he abhorred. By royal proclamation three days later, he reinstated the recusancy fines and ordered all priests out of the realm. His opening speech to his first Parliament on 19 March expressed his general hope for Christian union, but warned the Catholics against increasing in number. A bill confirming all the Elizabethan penal legislation on Catholic nonconformity received royal assent on 7 July. A few days later, a priest called John Sugar *alias* Sweet was executed in Warwick. His servant, who was hanged with him, was Robert Grissold, the brother of Anne and Eleanor's 'faithful man' John.[34]

For what it is worth, James I would turn out to be a relatively lenient monarch and his reign would see a marked reduction in the execution rate – 25 Jacobean 'martyrs' compared to an estimated 189 Elizabethans.[35] For what it is worth. For those Catholics who had been drunk with hope at James's accession and were now suffering the hangover, it is worth nothing. 'A flash of lighting,' Gerard explains, 'giving for the time a pale light unto those that sit in darkness, doth afterwards leave them in more desolation.'[36] There were some Catholics, however, like Robert Catesby, who had been sitting in the darkness for some time, waiting for his fellows to grow accustomed to the gloom. He was looking elsewhere for the lightning flash.

20

Desperate Attempts

Catesby looked first to Spain, for that is where his head was already turned. He wanted a Catholic England with a Catholic monarch, not a 'false Scots urchin' (the late Queen's phrase), who might just put up with Catesby and his ilk (if 'quiet and decently hidden'), but would never promote Catholicism in accordance with the papal breves.[1] Catesby believed that Spain was most likely to deliver his vision and in 1602, the year before the Queen's death, he and cousins Francis Tresham, Thomas Wintour and Lord Monteagle had begged financial and military aid from Philip III. Wintour had been the one to kiss the Spanish King's hands and his access had been facilitated by a letter of recommendation from Henry Garnet to Joseph Creswell, the mission's man in Madrid.

Wintour returned from the Continent with lots of promising, if procrastinating, noises: the Spanish would invade England in support of a Catholic claimant, but *mañana*. Then Elizabeth I had died, James I had succeeded and Philip III had sent official congratulations. An Anglo-Spanish ceasefire was declared and treaty negotiations followed. At this stage, Francis Tresham and his brother-in-law Monteagle turned into doves. They were 'resolved to stand wholly for the King' and wanted nothing more to do with the Spanish treason, as the various overtures to Philip would come to be known. Catesby, on the other hand, thought it worth pursuing. Within days of bringing Garnet and the sisters at White Webbs the first news of Queen Elizabeth's death and the popular 'applause' to James's accession, Catesby was sending another man to Spain to sound out Philip's true intentions.[2]

Unfortunately for Catesby the message from Spain really was peace not war. A soldier called Guy Fawkes pitched up at Philip's court around the same time and was equally disheartened to get the same response. Early in 1604 Catesby sent Wintour abroad for one last push, but it was no surprise when he returned at the end of April with 'good words', but a suspicion that 'the deeds would not answer'. Wintour sailed home with Fawkes. He told him that he and some friends were 'upon a resolution to do somewhat in England if the peace with Spain helped us not'.[3]

The peace with Spain did not help them. Despite Philip III's desire to secure toleration and Garnet's hope that 'some good will come out of it', the Treaty of London, eventually signed in August 1604, made no mention of England's Catholics. Catesby had been right to lose faith in Spain. The surprise, considering the defeat of his father's American Dream two decades earlier, is that he had kept it for so long. 'If the negotiations for toleration do not go well,' Garnet reputedly warned Rome that August, 'it will be impossible to keep the Catholics quiet. What can we do? The Jesuits will not be able to pacify them. The Pope must command all Catholics not to make a move.'[4]

*

Guy Fawkes was a stranger in London, albeit one with strong xenophobic tendencies. He had not seen his native country for over a decade. 'I can never yet hear of any man that knows him,' King James later remarked. Ambrose Vaux would have known him, for they had served in the same regiment, but Ambrose was still in the Low Countries. Eliza, too, might have heard of him, since her old chaplain, Richard Cowling, had entreated a Venetian for 'favour & friendship for my cousin germane Mr Guydo Fawkes' at the turn of the century.[5] Catesby's pals John and Christopher Wright certainly knew Guy Fawkes for they had been at school together in York. In May 1604, John and Guy were reunited in lodgings just off the Strand. Also present were Catesby, Wintour and Thomas Percy, John's hot-headed brother-in-law who had made those hopeful trips to Holyrood on the eve of James's accession and had since vowed vengeance. He had threatened to kill the King. 'No Tom,' Catesby had said, 'thou shalt not adventure to small purpose, but if thou wilt be a traitor, thou shalt be to some great advantage.' And he had told him that he was thinking of 'a most sure way', which Percy would 'soon know'.

Having taken an oath of secrecy and then, in a separate room, heard Mass and received communion, Percy and the others came to discover Catesby's 'sure way'. Wright and Wintour already knew the bare bones, having been entrusted with the secret earlier in the year. It was quite simple: they would 'blow up the Parliament house with gunpowder', for 'in that place have they done us all the mischief and perchance God hath designed that place for their punishment'. Wintour had been hesitant, but Catesby had persuaded him that 'the nature of the disease required so sharp a remedy'. The priest who administered the Mass at that May meeting in the Strand was Eliza Vaux's chaplain, John Gerard, S.J. He had, apparently, not been privy to the earlier conversation in the other room.[6]

Thus was the Gunpowder Plot hatched and reared. It evolved over time and adapted to circumstance. Percy had originally subleased a building next to the House of Lords from Henry Ferrers of Baddesley Clinton (the Warwickshire manor that Anne and Eleanor may have used as a safe house). They had planned to drive a shaft through the foundations, but when the lease for a ground-floor vault directly beneath the House of Lords came up, it seemed like divine providence. The gunpowder was initially stored at Catesby's lodging in Lambeth – a sixth man, Robert Keyes, was recruited to guard it – but it was subsequently ferried over to Westminster in order 'to have all our danger in one place'.

It was only confirmed in the autumn of 1604 that King James would be opening Parliament. The plotters assumed that his elder son, Prince Henry, would join him, but they were not sure about four-year-old Charles, so loose plans were made to capture him if necessary. Princess Elizabeth, who was nine and living at Combe Abbey near Coventry, would be proclaimed Queen. A rebel force gathered under the guise of a hunting party would take her to London and she would rule under the protectorate of an unspecified (or, at least, never disclosed) nobleman. Armour and weapons were stockpiled, and horses stabled, at key Midlands strongholds. Peers who were Catholic, or 'Catholicly affected', might be saved from the blow, but Catesby was vague about this when pressed and apparently held the 'atheist' Lords in such low regard that he thought 'dead bodies would be better for the commonwealth than they'.

Proclamations were drafted in order to lure disaffected Englishmen into the rebellion. Religion would be downplayed and they would march under the banner of 'Liberty and Freedom from all manner of Slavery'. They would protest against wardships and monopolies and the union with the parasitic Scot. With the extinction of the political, spiritual and judicial elite and the paralysis of local government, 'all the Catholics and discontented persons would take their parts and proclaim the Lady Elizabeth'.[7] That was the plan.

Parliament was adjourned on 7 July 1604 to reconvene in February. There was a further prorogation over Christmas due to plague. On 28 July 1605 'some dregs of the late contagion' lingered, so the date was pushed back again. The new and final date for the State Opening of Parliament was Tuesday, 5 November 1605.[8]

The delays were expensive and Catesby struggled to finance everything himself.[9] An August meeting in 1605 gave him the go-ahead to recruit a few men with deep pockets and fine horses. Their circle had already widened. Catesby's retainer, Thomas Bates (who had once taken 'a man child' to Anne and Eleanor's house in Warwickshire), had figured out what was going on and was formally entrusted with the secret towards the close of 1604. He was followed by John Wright's brother Christopher, Thomas Wintour's brother Robert, and John Grant of Norbrook in Warwickshire. Grant was married to the Wintours' sister, Dorothy. At the end of January 1605, he had received the following letter from Tom Wintour:

> If I may with my sister's good leave, let me entreat you, brother, to come over Saturday next to us at Chastelton. I can assure you of kind welcome and your acquaintance with my cousin Catesby will nothing repent you. I could wish Doll here, but our life is monastical, without women.[10]

Since Thomas had also asked John to 'bring with you my *Ragion di Stato*' (*Reason of State*) – a Jesuit work on the ethics of statecraft – it is clear that this was no ordinary weekend retreat.

Kinship ties were evident in the gunpowder ring, as they were in the wider recusant community. The Midlands connection was another strong bind. Most of the conspirators were gentlemen in their early thirties and the majority had wild pasts. They were frustrated men of action, 'swordsmen' the priests called them, and 'they had not the patience and longanimity to expect the Providence of God'.[11] Each had his own reasons for becoming what would today be termed a terrorist, but as Gerard's convert, Sir Everard Digby, warned Cecil:

> If your Lordship and the State think it fit to run another course and deal severely with Catholics, give me leave to tell you what I fear will happen, which in brief will be massacres, rebellions and desperate attempts against the King and State. For it is a general received reason amongst Catholics that there is not that expecting and suffering course now to be run that was in the Queen's time, who was the last of her line and last in expectance to run violent courses against Catholics.[12]

'Handsome', 'virile', 'affable and courteous', Digby was one of the last men to join the plot.[13] He was recruited in October 1605, late enough to have become thoroughly disillusioned with James I. Another in the outer ring was the dandyish, horse-mad Ambrose Rookwood, sworn in on 29 September 1605. He was from Suffolk, but had spent much of the year in the Midlands. Fifteen days later, on 14 October 1605, Francis Tresham took the oath of secrecy.

The Vauxes knew many of the plotters, some very well indeed, but they did not qualify for recruitment on several grounds: income (not enough), blood (too blue), age (Eliza's children were too young) and zeal (Ambrose was a bored and violent swordsman, but far too worldly for the 'monastical' plotters). Eleanor's son, William Brooksby *alias* Mr Jennings, might have been involved peripherally. The man with 'a bald head and a reddish beard' was known to officials, but though he would probably see Catesby at White Webbs just a few days before the scheduled blow, he would not be named or pursued as a plotter.[14] No one thought to ask the women, not even those toughened viragos Anne, Eleanor and Eliza. Which is not to say that they did not know what was going on.

21

Quips and Quiddities

While the gunpowder lay heavy in its vault and Catesby planned his final phase of recruitment, a royal hunting party blasted through the Midlands and the Vaux sisters prepared for a pilgrimage. With hindsight, the build-up to the November Parliament was a strange time. Not for everyone, of course: John Chamberlain had nothing to report in April beyond the tedious cycle of 'matches, marriages, christening, creations, knightings and suchlike, as if this world would last ever'.[1] But for those looking for signs, they could be found. An eclipse of the moon on 19 September, and of the sun a fortnight later, seemed to 'portend no good'.[2] Sick and sleepless Thomas Stanney, the Jesuit who had stayed with Garnet and the sisters in 1591, would stab a man after hallucinating phantom pursuivants and a town 'all in armour betwixt Catholics and heretics'.[3]

It seemed vaguely absurd that the King should stay at Harrowden Hall in August 1605, considering men who wanted to blow his heels to the sky would visit a few weeks later, but on the 12th of the month the royal hunting party rode in, and, after a night of Vaux hospitality, followed the horn and heralds out again. Earlier in the month the king had been at Lord Mordaunt's house in Drayton, where the plotter Robert Keyes had married the governess and where another plotter, Thomas Wintour, and soon-to-be-recruited Ambrose Rookwood had called the day before. The lord of the manor had reputedly wanted to murder his royal guest 'by way of a mask', but a priest had 'willed forbearance at that time because, said he, there is a course in hand that will cut up the very root & remove all impediments whatsoever can be alleged to hinder the cause' – a variation, perhaps, on Tottenham turning French.[4]

Eliza Vaux would soon try and recall that letter, the one, it will be

remembered, that she had written over Easter to her friend, Agnes
Wenman: *Pray, for Tottenham may turn French*. Agnes's mother-in-law,
Lady Tasborough, had intercepted it and broken the seal (it was apparently only lightly waxed). She had read treason in the letter and had
shown it to her son, 'saying it was a foolish letter and that Mrs Vaux
was a foolish woman to write so' to his wife. Either just before or
just after the King's visit to Harrowden, Eliza had met up with pregnant Agnes at her daughter Mary's house in Oxfordshire and had had
a good bitch about meddling mothers-in-law.[5]

A few weeks later, on 31 August 1605, another cryptic letter was penned:

> Jack, certain friends of mine will be with you on Monday night or
> Tuesday at the uttermost. I pray you void your house of Morgan and
> his she-mate or other company whatsoever they be, for all your house
> will scarce lodge the company. The jerkin man is come, but your robe
> of durance as yet not finished . . .[6]

Presumably John Grant knew how to interpret Thomas Wintour's last
line. Was he having a buff jerkin made up in anticipation of imminent
fighting? This is quite possible, since Catesby was using the war in
Flanders as a front for his martial preparations and some of the equipment was being stockpiled at Grant's house.[7] But might Wintour
also have been recalling a line from a play about rebellion written by
Grant's near-neighbour from Stratford-upon-Avon?

'Is not a buff jerkin a most sweet robe of durance?' Hal asks Falstaff.

'How now, how now, mad wag? What, in thy quips and thy quid-
dities?'

What indeed.*

One party visiting John Grant at Norbrook in the early autumn of
1605 was a group of pilgrims travelling to the holy shrine of St Winifred on the north coast of Wales. The patroness of virgins, St Winifred
and her well of healing waters had survived the Reformation and

---

I Henry IV, Act 1, Scene 2. Shakespeare's history plays were politically charged,
especially for those interested in the making and unmaking of kings. *The History of
Henry the Fourth* (as it was entered in the Stationers' Register on 25 February 1598)
was the sequel to *Richard II*, probably the play specially performed by the Lord
Chamberlain's Men for the Earl of Essex's allies the day before the 1601 rising.

attracted hundreds of visitors every year, 'especially,' noted the hostile John Gee, 'those of the feminine and softer sex'. The Jesuits actively promoted the cult and Edward Oldcorne, S.J., would pray to St Winifred on the scaffold in 1606 believing that she had cured him of cancer. The proof of the miraculous waters for John Gerard, in an age when beer was safer to drink than water, was that after taking several gulps from the well on an empty stomach, 'nothing happened to me'. Victory in war was another reason to make a pilgrimage. Writing for a catechism in the 1590s, Garnet explained that the saints and their shrines could be invoked for 'particular assistance in some special causes'. He also noted that the strangely sweet moss of St Winifred's Well contained 'a singular remedy against fire'.[8]

Much would be made of the Jesuit superior's pilgrimage to the well in September 1605 and an itinerary that was seemingly dusted in gunpowder. Garnet always claimed to have travelled for reasons of health – his own and perhaps Anne's too – and because he had been between houses. He had visited the shrine three years earlier, around the time that he had begun to lose control of his body. He had feared the palsy. He would rather 'shake at Tyburn than in his chamber'. He 'marvelled that he had lived so long'. His survival can be attributed, in part, to Anne and Eleanor, who 'have such care of him that he is able to endure such pains as his office requireth'. Those pains were increasingly mental as well as physical. Garnet suffered from depression and it was getting worse.[9]

At least he was eating well. He was 'full faced' and 'fat of body'. His hairline was receding as quickly as his waistline was expanding and his beard was 'grizzled'. He turned fifty in 1605 and looked older. 'He is always in hiding or in flight,' the Spanish envoy observed in March. But the music and the Masses continued and the feast days were celebrated with as much ceremony as was safe.[10]

On 22 April 1605, Garnet had received a visitor from Spain: Luisa de Carvajal, a fiery Spanish noblewoman on a self-appointed mission to save England's souls. She had arrived at Garnet's invitation and with his aid. 'Delicate, sick, physically weak' and unable to speak the language, she did not blend in well with Jacobean England and her letters were soon peppered with complaints. 'It is an unbearable country,' she would write in September 1606, 'and has certainly not fallen short of the expectation I had of suffering a great purgatory here.' She carped at the weather ('very damp and overcast'), the bread ('so heavy'), the vegetables ('almost tasteless'), the people ('no regard for propriety') and, above all, London, which was noisy, smelly, dirty, diseased and 'incredibly expensive'. 'This land,' she would conclude towards the end of 1607, 'is full to the brim with the bile of dragons.' She was an extraordinary witness to the time and place, but not the kind of person one would want around – far less invite to stay – if one was planning an act of terror.[11]

Although the evidence is not entirely conclusive, Luisa probably stayed with Garnet and the sisters for her first six weeks in England.[12] After a humiliating experience at Dover customs, when her 'instruments of penance' were laughed at and confiscated, she arrived at 'the desired location as to a pleasant paradise amid dense woods full of wild beasts'. She was bedridden for a fortnight, but nevertheless 'delighted' by the 'numerous' Masses, the 'beautifully decorated' chapel, the 'lovely garden' and, above all, the music: 'diverse, finely tuned voices and instruments' and after-dinner motets that were 'spiritual and moving'. (It was around the same time that a visiting Frenchman found Garnet 'in company with several Jesuits and gentlemen who were playing music, among them Mr William Byrd'.[13])

Luisa's paradise could not endure: 'Because of a warning that the house had been discovered, everyone scattered and fled, some across the fields, others by the river, and, dressing quickly, I had to rush away in the coach with the ladies to London.'[14] Garnet's account of their Corpus Christi celebrations points to the same episode: the feast day (30 May) was kept 'with great solemnity and music' and on the day of the octave (6 June) they 'made a solemn procession about a great garden, the house being watched, which we knew not till the next day when we departed twenty-five in the sight of all in several parties, leaving half a dozen servants behind'.[15]

If not the house from which they had fled, the manor in Erith on the Thames Estuary was also attracting attention. Local gossip that summer was of 'great resort' there,

by persons unknown as well as by five or six coaches upon a Sabbath day, coming in at a back gate newly made on the back side of the house,

as by sundry persons resorting thither by water who commonly returned
from thence daily in the afternoon or evening of the same day.

The neighbours knew that the house was 'well stored with wood,
seacoal and charcoals' and that it was 'usually' kept by 'a man and two
women with a maid'. Garnet and the sisters also still had White Webbs
in Enfield Chase – the Jesuits had a meeting there in November 1604
– but over the summer they feared it was 'discovered' and 'durst not
remain there past one night or two'. The house of a Mr Mainy at
Fremland in Essex was available to them until Michaelmas, 1605 (though
'pernicious' in late summer), and Anne also had a place in Wandsworth.
When visiting London, Garnet made use of a chamber in Thames
Street 'at the house of one Bennet, a costermonger hard by Queen-
hithe'.[16] Thames Street's location by the river, its length (almost wall
to wall), and its numerous taverns (because tide-dependent merchants
and travellers arrived and departed at strange times) made it a natural
choice for anyone wishing to preserve his anonymity. It was here, on
Sunday, 9 June 1605, two days after his flight to London, that Garnet
received a visit from Robert Catesby. The younger man posited a
hypothetical question, 'a case,' Garnet recalled, 'of killing innocents':

> Mr Catesby asked me whether, in case it were lawful to kill a person
> or persons, it were necessary to regard the innocents which were present
> lest they also should perish withal.

This, Garnet realised with hindsight, was 'the first breach afar off' of
the Gunpowder Plot. He replied:

> In all just wars it is practised and held lawful to beat down houses and
> walls and castles, notwithstanding innocents were in danger, so that
> such battery were necessary for the obtaining of the victory and that
> the multitude of innocents, or the harm which might ensue by their
> death, were not such that it did countervail the gain and commodity
> of the victory.

Catesby made a 'solemn protestation that he would never be known
to have asked [Garnet] any such question so long as he lived'. Only
then, Garnet later claimed, did he begin to worry. 'In truth, I never

imagined anything of the King's Majesty, nor of any particular, and thought it at the first but, as it were, an idle question.'[17]

Could Garnet really have been so naïve? In fairness, this was just the kind of issue in which a soldier on his way to Flanders – as Catesby claimed to be – might naturally engage a priest. Garnet's reply was grounded in a military context and upon the theology of Thomas Aquinas (which is still used to excuse collateral damage). He gave a logical answer to a question that he determinedly took to be hypothetical. But he knew Catesby very well. He knew that he was an angry, restless soul, who at least since the summer of 1604 had been agitating 'for the Catholic cause against the King and the State'. He knew that Catesby had found 'an invincible argument' in the papal breves on the succession, the breves that Garnet himself had shown him. Catesby had argued then that a mandate to keep the King out surely also applied to putting him out. Garnet had disagreed, had 'reproved' Catesby and reminded him of the Pope's ban on stirs; Catesby had 'promised to surcease'.[18]

That had been a year before their Thames Street conversation, but Catesby had not been quelled. According to the *Narrative* of his confessor, Tesimond, the next twelve months had seen a gradual build-up of tension between the priest and the gentleman, with Garnet urging peace and patience and Catesby asking 'if there was any authority on earth that could take away from them the right given by nature to defend their own lives from the violence of others'. Catesby had resented Garnet's 'lukewarmness' and accused him of preaching a draining doctrine that made England's Catholics 'flaccid and poor-spirited'. He began to avoid Garnet and his injunctions. The Jesuit superior wondered at Catesby's aloofness and soon learned that 'apart from the military preparations which he was making for his passage to Flanders, he was having frequent dealings, and that very secretly, with those special friends of his'. If Tesimond is to be credited – and his aim was to exculpate, not undermine, his superior – Garnet saw in Catesby all the signs of 'a man preoccupied with grandiose and far-reaching schemes'. He knew perfectly well that 'something was brewing' and, on 8 May 1605, had expressed his fear that 'a stage of desperation' had been reached.[19]

When Catesby came to Thames Street a month later with (Garnet later admitted) Tesimond in tow, it was surely obvious that it was not for some 'idle question'. Perhaps Catesby had had an attack of conscience, perhaps Tesimond had insisted he speak to Garnet, perhaps he just needed the Jesuit superior's name 'to persuade others'.[20] Whatever the case, Catesby left Garnet's chamber with a theoretical sanction for the killing of innocents, and Garnet, with his 'penetrating intellect', 'lofty but wide-awake' mind and 'deep and far-seeing' judgement, was left to stew.[21]

'For God's sake' talk to Robin, Anne Vaux implored Garnet around three months later on the pilgrimage to St Winifred's Well.[22] The Jesuit superior had tried, twice, to caution Catesby. 'Walking in the gallery' of the house in Essex a few weeks after the Thames Street meeting, he had told him 'that upon my speech he should not run headlong to so great a mischief' and that 'he must not have so little regard of innocents that he spare not friends and necessary persons for a commonwealth'. Garnet reiterated the papal command for quietness. 'Oh let me alone for that,' Catesby had replied, 'for do you not see how I seek to enter into new familiarity with this lord.'

The lord in question was Lord Monteagle, who had accompanied Catesby to Essex along with his brother-in-law (and Catesby's cousin), Francis Tresham. The four men had discussed 'how things stood with Catholics'. Garnet asked about their military capability – 'whether they were able to make their part good by arms against the King.'

'If ever they were, they are able now,' said Monteagle, 'the King is so odious to all sorts.'

Garnet pressed for a direct answer, for he would 'write to the Pope a certainty'. They answered in the negative.

'Why, then,' said Garnet, 'you see how some do wrong the Jesuits, saying that they hinder Catholics from helping themselves and how it importeth us all to be quiet, and so we must and will be.'

They talked some more: about the 1603 Bye Plot that Garnet had quashed and about the upcoming Parliament – Tresham wanted to see what laws would be made against them 'and then seek for help of foreign princes'.

'No, assure yourselves they will do nothing,' said Garnet.

'What?' queried Monteagle. 'Will not the Spaniards help us? It is a shame.'

Garnet concluded that he would assure Rome that 'neither by

strength nor stratagems we could be relieved, but with patience and intercession of princes'.[23]

This, in any case, was his testimony after the event. A few days later, he received a stern admonition from General Aquaviva against 'any violent attempt whatsoever'. It was the Pope's express command-ment that Garnet 'hinder by all possible means all conspiracies of Catholics'. Should anything happen, he read, 'nobody will be ready to believe that it was contrived without at least the consent' of the Jesuits.[24]

Not long afterwards, Catesby visited Garnet and the sisters again, 'as he was seldom long from us, for the great affection he bore the gentlewoman with whom I lived, and unto me'. They privately suspected that Catesby was also running from debtors in London, but it seemed that, having 'gotten leave', he wanted to tell the Jesuit superior about the plot. Both men were irritable and defiant. Garnet 'refused to know' any particulars and cited the papal prohibition. Catesby insisted that his plan was good for England, that the Pope would approve and that Garnet did not have the power to stop him. They finally agreed to send a messenger – Sir Edmund Baynham – to inform the Pope 'how things stood here' in general terms. Catesby promised to do nothing until Baynham's return. Garnet summoned and dispatched their emissary, but 'would not be the author of his going further than Flanders, for that the Pope would not take well that we should busy ourselves in sending messengers'.[25]

Thereafter, the Jesuit superior, who always seemed far more concerned about how the plot would play out in Rome than in West-minster, tried to bury his head in the sand. Within days, however, Tesimond had told him 'all the matter' of the powder plot. The burden of knowledge had been too great for Catesby's 'perplexed' confessor. He needed his superior's direction and so, by way of a walking confes-sion (it being 'too tedious to relate so long a discourse' kneeling), he had revealed everything he knew. 'I was amazed,' Garnet later declared, 'and said it was a most horrible thing.' He told Tesimond that it was 'unlawful' and must be hindered, 'for he knew well enough what strict prohibition we had'. According to Tesimond, Garnet wrote to Rome on 24 July: 'There is a risk that some private endeavour may commit treason or use force against the King, and in this way all the Catholics might be forced to take arms.'

He requested another prohibition. (It did not help that Pope Paul V had only held the keys for two months; Clement VIII had died on 5 March and his successor, Leo XI, had lasted seventeen days.) A few days later Garnet was still fretting about the reaction in Rome. 'Good Lord,' he exclaimed to Tesimond, 'if this matter go forward the Pope will send me to the galleys, for he will assuredly think I was privy to it.'[26]

If Garnet is to be believed – and it is by no means certain that the author of a treatise on equivocation should be – he had not known that John Grant was one of the plotters when he and his fellow pilgrims sojourned at Norbrook on their way to and from Wales in the early autumn; nor, indeed, Robert Wintour, with whom they stayed at Huddington Court, near Worcester. Nonetheless, Anne was highly suspicious.

They had set off from White Webbs on Friday, 30 August 1605: Garnet, Anne, Eleanor's son William and his wife Dorothy, 'Little John' Owen the carpenter, and several other servants. Mary, Lady Digby and John Percy, S.J., came from Gayhurst. Ambrose and Elizabeth Rookwood joined them further north. They numbered about thirty in all and for the final leg, from an inn to the well, 'the gentlewomen went barefoot' according to custom.[27]

Before the trip, Garnet had been 'in the greatest perplexity that ever I was in my life and could not sleep anights'. Anne would have noticed. 'I ceased not to commend the matter daily to God, so did I not omit to write continually to Rome.'[28] She would have noticed. During the pilgrimage,

> being at Wintour's and at Grant's and seeing their fine horses in the stable, she told Mr Garnet that she feared these wild heads had something in hand and prayed him for God's sake to talk with Mr Catesby and to hinder anything that possibly he might, for if they should attempt any foolish thing, it would redound to his discredit.[29]

Thomas Wintour might have wanted all the plotters to live the 'monastical' life, 'without women'. His disparaging remark in his 'jerkin' letter about Henry Morgan's 'she-mate' – quite possibly Morgan's wife, Mary, rather than a mistress[30] – suggests a streak of misogyny that might have been shared with other plotters: Percy was possibly a bigamist, Fawkes was a demobbed bachelor and Catesby, who made sure that Garnet was alone when he 'moved the matter' at Thames Street, was a widower.[31] But there were other plotters, including Robert Wintour, Robert Keys and the Wright brothers, who were married. Many also had sisters and female confidantes. It stretches credulity (just as, frankly, it often does today) to suggest that the women were completely excluded.

Anne Vaux was, in any case, deemed a superior type of woman, an honorary man, a virago, and like her sister-in-law Eliza, busy praying for Tottenham to turn French, she seems to have been privy to certain strategic conversations. She recalled, for example, Francis Tresham's visits, 'sometimes in the company of Mr Catesby', at which Garnet 'always gave him good counsel and persuaded him to rest contented'. She remembered Garnet's words: 'Good gentlemen, be quiet. God will do all for the best. We must get it by prayer at God's hands, in whose hands are the hearts of princes.'[32]

Anne may not have known the details of the Gunpowder Plot, but she knew enough by the autumn of 1605 to implore Garnet to talk to Catesby – not Grant, not Wintour, Catesby – and Garnet had agreed that he would. He 'assured' Anne afterwards that the horses were for the regiment Catesby was raising for Flanders. He had written to help advance him to 'a Colonel's place' and Catesby 'showed her his letter and said he would get a licence though it cost him £500'.[33]

Whether or not Anne believed them is another matter. 'In my cousin Catesby's promises there is so little assurance,' Francis Tresham had written to his father earlier in the year. 'You know his promises,' he added in another letter.[34] In all likelihood, Anne knew them too. She was certainly dismayed, after returning from Wales, to learn that Catesby had been having 'great meetings' at White Webbs. 'It would make the house more noticed,' she exclaimed to Garnet, 'and why did we absent ourselves but to have it out of suspicion?' Then some, or one, of the wives had asked her where she and Garnet planned to 'bestow themselves until the brunt was past in the beginning of the Parliament'. Clearly, they thought she knew what was going on. When she told Garnet about this, either at Harrowden Hall or at Gayhurst, she refused to name names; she had her own secrets and loyalties to uphold, but she knew then that 'some trouble or disorder' was coming, and Garnet could no longer pretend otherwise.[35]

Anne and Eleanor's return to Harrowden Hall in October 1605 must have been tense for other, more personal reasons. Here was the Vaux ancestral seat, the home of their dear, simple, late father and the place, for Anne at least, of first steps, words and memories. It was also the big house whither they had moved upon the death of their mother and the marriage of their father to Mary Tresham. It was the birth-place of their half-siblings and now the home of Eliza (technically their half-sister-in-law), her Jesuit chaplains and her children, including Edward, fourth Lord Vaux, who had just turned seventeen. Despite the 'moody atonement' that Sir Thomas Tresham had apparently discerned among the Vaux women in 1599, Anne and Eleanor 'had not been in that house for many years'. More than a decade had passed since Eleanor's rant there at Tresham, whom she had labelled (*in absentia*) a brass-faced, Machiavellian conman and 'a scandal to the Catholic religion and to all Catholics'.[36]

Now the old rogue was dead. He had passed away on 11 September 1605 after six weeks 'in such extremity, tossing and tumbling from one side and from one bed to another'. The pilgrims returning from the well had called in at Rushton Hall to pay their respects, for, whatever his personal flaws, Sir Thomas had not been a scandal to the Catholic faith. He had worked tirelessly for the right to worship his own faith in his own country in his own way. Had he retained his senses at the last, he would have died a disappointed man. His 'moth-eaten term of life' perhaps represented for the next generation the futility of 'Christian patience'.[37] His death marked the changing of the guard. Anne and Eleanor and Robert Catesby, who soon joined them at Harrowden Hall, could not but have been reminded of their own fathers' struggles; Tresham had been a brother-in-arms, if only figuratively, to Vaux and Catesby, as well as their brother-in-law.

About a month after Tresham's death, Catesby and Wintour tried to inveigle his son, Francis, into the Gunpowder Plot. If we are to believe Francis Tresham's account – and since most of the participants were lying or equivocating some of the time, any narrative of the Gunpowder Plot is necessarily based more on credibility than certainty – they had little success. Francis, whose recently inherited property was the attraction, subsequently told his servant that 'his soul and heart abhorred so foul an action', that he had refused to support it,

tried to stop it and had given the plotters money to escape abroad.*
He sold his father's chamber in the Inner Temple (where Garnet's
treatise on equivocation was subsequently found) and procured a
licence, dated 2 November, to travel 'beyond the seas' for two years.[38]

Whatever the truth of Francis's involvement, we may believe that
Catesby had an easier conversation with Sir Everard Digby, whom
he recruited as the two rode through Wellingborough after their
sojourn with the Vauxes at Harrowden Hall 'about St Luke's Day'
(18 October), 1605. Digby had sworn on a primer to keep the plot
secret and had subsequently received communion, though 'at whose
hands' he would never tell. He later claimed to have enlisted in the
'certain belief' that 'those which were best able to judge of the
lawfulness' of the plot had been 'acquainted with it and given way
unto it'. He had, he wrote, 'more reasons . . . to persuade me to
this belief than I dare utter', even secretly to his wife. Not one of
those reasons, however, was 'directly' of a priest and he had deemed
it 'best not to know any more'.[39]

Following Catesby's advice to take a 'convenient house in Warwickshire or Worcestershire' for the Midlands rebellion, Digby leased
Coughton Court from the recusant Throckmorton family.† Although
Garnet later admitted that he suspected Digby's recruitment, and
although he 'perceived also an intention in him to draw us to that
country for their own projects', he accepted Digby's offer to stay at
Coughton. Catesby and Digby promised to visit Garnet there on All

---

* 'I know,' Tresham reportedly told Catesby, 'that it is both damnable and that thereby
the Catholics will be utterly undone whether it be effected or no, for if it be effected
what can the Catholics do, what strength are they of, as of themselves, having no
foreign power to back them? For though at the first it might drive those of the
contrary religion into a maze and confusion, yet when they should find by whom
it was done, they would in their fury run upon the Catholics and kill them where-
soever they met them.'
  Tresham was extremely fearful of the Puritans and wondered 'what would they
not do to the utter subversion of the Catholics' if the plot was effected and 'there
was neither King nor nobility to bridle them'. (Wake, 'The Death of Francis Tresham',
p. 37)

† The sprawling Throckmorton kin network encompassed Catesbys, Treshams,
Wintours and Vauxes (Catherine Vaux, daughter of Nicholas, first Baron Vaux, was
the wife of Sir George Throckmorton, d. 1552). In 2009 the Throckmorton family
celebrated its 600th anniversary of residence at Coughton. The house is managed
by the National Trust and is open to visitors for ten months of the year.

Saints Day, 1 November. 'But they broke,' Garnet recalled, adding that had they kept their word, he would have 'entered into the matter with Mr Catesby and perhaps might have hindered all'. Instead, he preached his All Saints sermon, taking as his text two lines from the feast day hymn:

Gentem auferte perfidam
Credentium de finibus:
Take away the perfidious people
From the land of believers.[40]

22

Strange and Unlooked for Letters

Around seven in the morning on Tuesday, 5 November 1605, Henry Tattnall passed two agitated young men near the turnstile of Lincoln's Inn Fields. One was in 'a greyish cloak', the other 'a tawnyish cloak with broad buttons'. Suspecting them of 'some fray, or as cutpurses', he 'looked back towards them and they looked back also' before rushing round the back of Grey's Inn Fields towards Clerkenwell. 'God's Wounds,' he had heard one exclaim, 'we are wonderfully beset and all is marred.'[1]

Later in the day, at the Red Lion Inn on the fringe of Dunsmore Heath, Warwickshire, a servant tending to a large hunting party heard a man at an open window say, 'I doubt we are all betrayed.'[2]

The previous night, around midnight, 'a very tall and desperate fellow' had been found under the Parliament house with a watch, a match and thirty-six barrels of 'corn powder decayed'. He was fully dressed, booted and spurred. He said his name was John Johnson; he was, of course, Guy Fawkes.[3]

There had been an anonymous tip-off, a 'dark and doubtful letter' written in a disguised hand and foisted upon a servant of Lord Monteagle in a street by the house in Hoxton that he had received upon his marriage to Sir Thomas Tresham's daughter. 'As you tender your life,' it warned, 'devise some excuse to shift of your attendance at this Parliament, for God and man hath concurred to punish the wickedness of this time.' Chilling words, followed by a wink to the nature of the vengeance to be wrought: 'they shall receive a terrible blow this Parliament and yet they shall not see who hurts them.'[4] Ignoring the instruction to burn the letter, Monteagle took it to Salisbury, who took it to King James, who famously grasped its meaning, his own father having been the target of the Kirk o' Field explosion of 1567. 'Do I not ken the smell of pouther, think ye?' Sir Walter Scott would later have him ask.[5]

'The Monteagle Letter' survives, but its authorship remains a mystery. Francis Tresham, who had been 'exceeding earnest' to warn his brother-in-law Monteagle of the blast, and who 'had determined to frame a letter to Sir Thomas Lake' with the aim of pinning the plot on the Puritans, is a frontrunner. But so too is Monteagle himself, who received all the credit for uncovering the plot and none of the calumny for his involvement, at the very least, in the Spanish treason. On a *cui bono* basis, Monteagle triumphs, yet Catesby and Wintour instantly suspected Tresham and were not wholly convinced by his denials. Over the years, other candidates have been mooted, including Anne Vaux and nearly every other plotter and affiliate of plotter who could write.[6]

When the capital awoke to the news of 'this last treason, that treason of treasons, the unparalleled arch-treason of the world',[7] Catesby, Percy, Rookwood, Thomas Wintour and the Wright brothers were racing towards the Midlands and their rendezvous with Digby and his huntsmen. Percy and John Wright cast off their cloaks in their bid for speed. Ambrose Rookwood outstripped them all, riding thirty miles in two hours on one horse. Catesby's mount lost a shoe at Dunstable and while it was being shod, Henry Huddlestone, who was also on the road from London and had ridden with Catesby and John Wright for about seventeen miles, waited with him. Only when Percy arrived did Catesby tell Huddlestone to 'go home to his wife'. Dorothy Huddlestone was pregnant and staying at her cousin Vaux's house in Irthlingborough, a few miles from Harrowden Hall. Huddlestone supped at Harrowden with Eliza Vaux, two priests called Singleton and Strange, and John Gerard, the Jesuit who had converted him over a decade earlier and deemed him 'one of my most steadfast friends'.[8]

When the plotters arrived at the Red Lion Inn in Dunchurch, a dishevelled but determined Catesby urged the would-be rebels to join him. Most of them melted into the darkness. The following day his servant and co-conspirator, Thomas Bates, rode to Coughton with news of the plot's discovery and a letter from Digby begging Garnet's forgiveness and blessing. The Jesuit superior 'marvelled they would enter into so wicked actions and not be ruled by the advice of friends'. Digby seems to have been genuinely shocked by Garnet's censure. As

Garnet, Bates and Tesimond conferred, Lady Digby entered the room. 'What did she?' Garnet later recalled, 'Alas what but cry.' Actually, she did rather more than that, sending four 'great' horses, 'ready furnished for service' to the rebels at Huddington. When Bates left Coughton for Huddington, it was not with Garnet, but with Tesimond, the confessor of Catesby and Thomas Wintour.[9]

Moving from house to house, the rebels picked up supplies but haemorrhaged men. Sir Everard Digby peeled off with two servants at daybreak on Friday, 8 November, and was soon tracked to a dry ditch in a wood near Halesowen. With the sheriff's two-hundred-strong posse on their heels, the plotters made their final stand at Holbeach House in Staffordshire. An accidental explosion the previous night – a spark from a fire igniting the gunpowder that they had spread out to dry – had badly burnt some of the men and shredded their nerves. Still, it was a defiant Catesby, kissing his gold crucifix and brandishing his sword, who charged out of the house at about eleven o'clock on the morning of 8 November. It is said that he was killed by the same bullet that mortally wounded Thomas Percy. The Wright brothers also died at Holbeach. Ambrose Rookwood, Thomas Wintour and John Grant were injured and dragged away for questioning.

Francis Tresham, who had stayed in London throughout the Midlands rising, was arrested on 12 November and examined several times. His death of strangury on 23 December denied him a trial. His severed head was sent up to Northampton for display. His body, which 'smelt exceedingly' even before death, was 'tumbled into a hole without so much ceremony as the formality of a grave'.[10]

White Webbs was searched on 11 November 1605. Catesby's 'great meetings' there, 'grievous to the gentlewoman his cousin', had not gone unnoticed, but little remained in the house bar a skeleton staff, a case of pistols, two fowling pieces, 'popish books and relics' and a store of wine and sweetmeats. The house was a curiosity of 'many doors, trapdoors and passages out of all sides.' Three female servants and the caretaker, John Grissold, who gave his name as James Johnson (not to be confused with Fawkes's 'John Johnson'), were questioned about Garnet and recent visitors. Fourteen-year-old Jane Robinson confessed that a priest 'apparelled like a gentleman' had said Mass there about three months earlier.

Grissold was found to be 'very perverse and obstinate'. He said 'Mr Measy his master, a Berkshire man' (Garnet was from Derbyshire), had taken the house 'for his sister Mrs Perkins, widow' (Anne the spinster). He spoke of a Mr Perkins, Skinner the lawyer, Jennings (probably William Brooksby), who played the bass viole, and Turner the lutenist. He was committed to a dungeon in the Gatehouse and, according to Garnet, racked into admitting that Catesby had made 'merry' with some friends at White Webbs for several days before the feast of All Saints. As far as Anne was concerned, Grissold's most damaging statement was that she had directed him to 'entertain her friends that came thither'.[11]

Salisbury's surveyor, Thomas Wilson, who had conducted the search at White Webbs and later 'conveyed away' its contents, was determined to prevent it from becoming 'a nest for such bad birds as it was before'.[12] He had a fondness for animal analogies. On 20 November 1605, he briefed Salisbury on his enquiries into 'Mrs Perkins's abode'. There had been a sighting at Hartley Court in Berkshire in early November, but nothing since. It was frustrating, he complained, 'all of them use to change often one into another's place, especially at times when they suspect search', so that 'such a man by such a description' could never be found in the right place. 'Such cunning,' he concluded, 'have foxes in changing burrows when they smell the wind that will bring the hunt towards them.'[13]

The hunt was heading for Harrowden Hall. Eliza Vaux was in serious trouble. By the evening of 5 November, Salisbury was in possession of information from Lord Chief Justice Popham about 'an expectation that Mrs Vaux had of something to be done'. Popham claimed to know it 'by such a manner as I assure myself the matter is true'. Agnes Wenman's meddlesome mother-in-law, Lady Tasborough, had been talking again about *that* letter. 'Touching the contents of my cousin Vaux's letter to me,' Agnes would recall,

> it was chiefly concerning her son's marriage to my Lord of Suffolk's daughter, and some challenging of unkindness for my husband's not seeking her, he being so long in London, but she said the cause was for that those of her profession were now in disgrace. And she withal added: Notwithstanding pray, for Tottenham may turn French, or words to the like effect.[14]

Lady Tasborough, who wasted no time denouncing Eliza, remembered it slightly differently:

> The effect of that letter was that Mrs Vaux persuaded the Lady Wenman to be of good comfort and not to despair for that ere it were long she should see a remedy or toleration for religion or to such effect.[15]

The words that were passed on to Salisbury in November were different again:

> Contents of Mrs Vaux letter: fast and pray, that that may come to pass that we purpose, which if it do, we shall see Tottenham turned French.[16]

Three versions of the same letter offering subtly different interpretations.

According to Eliza, when Agnes's parents, Sir George and Lady Fermor, first told her that Lady Tasborough had said 'there was treason in the letter', she had merely 'smiled'. Agnes told Eliza in August that 'she kept the letter safely for both their discharges'.[17] Only in November did Eliza ask Agnes's mother, Lady Fermor, to retrieve it. 'My cousin [Eliza],' wrote Lady Fermor to her daughter,

> sendeth me word that your mother-in-law hath dealt very badly with her & yours, for she hath complained of a letter which my cousin Vaux writ something darkly to you about my Lord's marriage. My cousin most earnestly desireth that you will send her the letter, or the copy thereof, as soon as you can.[18]

If Eliza would have been content with a copy, perhaps she simply wanted to see what all the fuss was about. Or maybe she was feigning insouciance. Either way, Agnes replied that she had dealt with the letter 'as those did letters which were not regarded', that is, she 'either burnt it or lost it'.[19]

Eliza had to deal with other 'strange & unlooked for letters' that November, including one from her father, which she received at Harrowden on 9 November. The courier (appositely named Mr Race) was promised fourteen shillings for the round trip and waited for Eliza's reply. She told him it was a wasted journey: 'the letter needed not to have been sent to her for that she was very free from those matters whereof her father had written to her.' An hour and a half later she provided a more appropriate written response. She was clearly distressed, but if the few blots on the page are the result of her 'hot, indignant tears' as has been fancied, it is more than we can now tell. 'Sir,' she began,

> I cannot but marvel at your strange & unlooked for letters. I wish yourself & all others should know I am as innocent & free from the ever knowing of that plot as whosoever is most free & do as much abhor the intention; & for any letters of mine, I wish that may be showed & the uttermost made against me, so confident am I of ever writing anything, which it was impossible I should, never knowing nor imagining as God doth best know & as it is plain enough to friends here, how easy so ever yourself be to believe the worst upon I know not what report.

Eliza was expecting the Earl of Northampton to confirm the 'certainty' of Lord Vaux's hoped-for nuptials with Lady Elizabeth Howard. 'To that end,' she continued,

> my son had a purpose to have come up to London himself on Thursday or Friday last if by chance Sir George Fermor & his Lady had not come to supper to us on Wednesday night & told us the first news of this pitiful & tragical intendment & then I thought not best to send him.[20]

Eliza was lying to her father. Sir George Fermor had not gone to Harrowden 'by chance', nor had he provided her with 'the first news' of the plot. Readers will remember that (at the close of Part Three) he was *summoned* to Harrowden on the morning of Wednesday, 6 November, and that upon his arrival, Eliza had said that she had intended to ask him to accompany her son to London, but that because of 'some garboyl' there, she had changed her mind. She told Sir George that she had just heard the news – at that stage an unspecified rumour – from a servant of hers, who had heard it from 'Mr Markham's man'.[21]

This, too, was a lie, since Eliza had learned everything the previous evening when Henry Huddlestone, who had been riding with Catesby earlier in the day, came to Harrowden Hall for supper. Eliza and

Huddlestone would stick to their stories: they had not known about the plot until 6 November.[22] It took four months and, Anne Vaux would allege, the 'often racking and torturing' of Thomas Strange, a Jesuit who had been at the Harrowden supper, for the truth to come out. On 13 March 1606, Strange would confess that 'Henry Huddlestone brought the first news that ever I heard of the blowing up of the Parliament house to Harrowden'.[23]

John Gerard and another priest, Singleton, had also supped at Harrowden on 5 November and two days later, Strange, Singleton, Huddlestone, his servant William Thornbury, a Lancashire recusant called Matthew Batty and two other servants left Harrowden for Warwickshire. According to Gerard, both Strange and Singleton 'wanted to go and stay with Father Garnet'. Sir Richard Verney, the Sheriff of Warwickshire, who picked them up at Kenilworth, suspected them 'for the late conspiracy and insurrection'.[24]

In the small world of the shires, Verney happened to be an affiliate of Eliza Vaux. His nephew, Sir George Simeon, had recently married Eliza's daughter Mary. He was the kind of contact that Eliza used to good effect. Though a Protestant, he was no hard-liner, having once employed the Catholic musician John Bolt and recently, so Eliza heard, let one of Lady Digby's men go free. 'As you have often wished some fit occasion to show your good will unto me,' Eliza reminded Verney on 12 November, 'so now, if it please you, there is that to be done which may exceedingly pleasure me.'

Eliza was concerned about two gentlemen and a servant in Verney's custody. 'The younger gentleman,' she wrote of Father Strange, 'your niece Mary will rather give you her portion than have him come in question.' He was wealthy too, or at least his family was, 'and the very report that he were stayed in this fashion would kill his mother, whose only child he is'. This was a none-too-subtle bribe, but it also reminded Verney that his prisoner was valued as a person as well as a priest.* And there could be little doubt that the two 'gentlemen' *were* priests.

---

* Thomas Strange, S.J., was a convert of John Gerard. He was described by Henry Huddlestone as 'a gentleman-like man using the tennis court and sometime having music in his lodging'. The previous year he had written a book, 'a compendium of all the sciences', which he dedicated to Robert Catesby, his 'most distinguished and beloved' friend. (BL Royal MS 12 E. X; Fraser, *The Gunpowder Plot*, p. 93; Gerard, *Autobiography*, pp. 173, 248; PRO SP 14/16, f. 55v)

Eliza's pretence was flimsy. 'I will not now name them,' she wrote 'because _∧^{I hear} they go but as serving men & under that name you may please to let them have your pass home into Lancashire.' She dropped a few more bribes and a vow of requited kindness and then, just to make sure that Verney had the right men, she described them: 'The one which I chiefly respect' – Father Strange – was twenty-seven or twenty-eight. He had 'a clear complexion', brown hair 'and cut somewhat near, not much hair of his face'. The other – Father Singleton – was a redhead with 'a much redder beard' and 'much hair on both'. Their man – Matthew Batty – was about forty and 'very tall', with brown hair and beard. 'What names they give themselves I know not,' she continued, 'and therefore do not name them, but I assure myself this description is enough, & that you will deal worthily.'[25]

Whether it was panic, naïvety, or the confidence born of past favours, Eliza had totally misread the situation. 'A word to a true friend is enough,' she concluded, but it simply wasn't, not in the aftermath of the Gunpowder Plot. According to Gerard's harsh assessment, Verney behaved 'more like a Puritan as he is than a kinsman as he should be', but it was as Sheriff of Warwickshire that Verney hurriedly forwarded Eliza's letter to London at 9 p.m. on Wednesday, 13 November.* The Earl of Salisbury perused its contents and jotted down some thoughts:

L. Vaux at Mrs.
Grants
14 horses by ~~Singleton~~
Gerret
Ogle.[26]

Dorothy Grant (wife and sister of plotters) lived at Norbrook, Warwickshire, where the rebels had gone to collect arms on 6 November. The St Winifred pilgrims had stayed there on their way to and from the

---

* Gerard would, no doubt, have been delighted to learn that Verney did not receive his expected remuneration for the many arrests he made in November. Writing to Salisbury on 2 June 1606, he complained that his duty performed 'in the time of this late rebellion in Warwickshire' had been rewarded with 'hard measure and usage'. He reminded Salisbury of his 'extraordinary charge' and diligence in confiscating the goods of traitors, 'all being beforehand conveyed, either under water, or hid in the ground, or removed into far and remote places.' (CP, 116, f. 81)

well in September, but no one would testify that Eliza or her son, Lord
Vaux, were in the party. The note '14 horses' might suggest a suspected
contribution to the rebellion. 'Gerret' is surely John Gerard whose name
was often spelled that way. 'Ogle' is a mystery to me, not helped by
the fact that it was a name sometimes written as Oakley. Witness, in
1595: 'at Little Ogle, 8 miles distance from Rowell in Northamptonshire,
lieth Mr Bentley, who hath a priest in his house continually and
commonly a seminary priest, whom his wife calleth her chicken.'[27] The
Bentleys of Little Oakley were kinsmen of the Vauxes. In the November
round-up of Midlands rebels were the brothers Thomas and Edward
Okeley, both servants of the plotter Robert Wintour. The Earl of Northumberland, who was sent to the Tower for complicity in the plot, had
a man called Ogle.[28] These are just some possibilities.

It seems likely that the Vauxes of Harrowden were suspected of more
than foreknowledge of the Gunpowder Plot. Writing in December, the
Attorney General, Sir Edward Coke, thought it 'very probable' that
Huddlestone had been sent to Harrowden on 5 November 'to give
warning as well for conveying away of letters etc. and of Gerard the
priest'. Two days later, Huddlestone's departure for Warwickshire,
leaving his pregnant wife behind with Eliza, seemed to Coke to have
been 'by appointment into open rebellion'.

'Note the number of her horses,' Coke added, and 'Note Gerard
the priest ministered the sacrament to all the traitors etc., as well for
execution as for secrecy, and Gerard had continual access to Mrs
Vaux.'[29]

The revelation that Gerard had given communion to the original
five plotters straight after their private oath of secrecy in May 1604
had come from Guy Fawkes four days after his arrest. However, he
maintained, even under torture, that Gerard had not known about
the conspiracy. Still, the Jesuit was a wanted man and it was not
uncommon knowledge that Eliza's house was 'the chiefest place' of
his 'access'. Indeed, on 5 November Lord Chief Justice Popham had
informed Salisbury that it was also Garnet's 'and therefore like she
may know somewhat'.[30]

On 12 November 1605, the day that Eliza petitioned Verney for the
release of his prisoners, Lady Fermor of Easton Neston also wrote a
letter. It was to her daughter, Agnes, in Oxfordshire and in addition

to passing on Eliza's request for the swift return of her Tottenham missive, it related some news of the shire. Easton Neston, very near Towcester on Watling Street, was well placed to pick up news (perhaps one of the reasons why Eliza had chosen Sir George Fermor as her pretended channel of information). Lady Fermor's letter to her daughter conveys the anxious aftermath of the plot for those recusant women of the Midlands who knew so many of the men involved. Writing 'in haste' thus:

> I trust in God now Percy & Catesby are dead (who they say were the chief conspirators) we shall be more at quiet. Tom Hoult saw them both laid in one grave without any cloth about them. Many are still called in question. Sir Everard Digby is in Hereford jail; Mr Huddlestone in Warwick jail; Bates is in Warwick, but his wife & daughter & son are in Northampton jail. I trust in God they stand all sound at Harrowden: yet my cousin Tate is commanded to be in House with them till the Council's pleasure be farther known, as I hear . . . Our Lord bless us & send us peace in Christ our Lord . . . pray for your father & friends.[31]

Lady Fermor's source was reliable. As she bid her daughter good night, some twenty miles away at Harrowden a ring of torchlight encircled the home of Eliza Vaux.

23

In the Hole

'We had prepared,' John Gerard wrote simply.[1] It still must have been a shock for the seventeen-year-old Edward, Lord Vaux, to ride home around midday on Tuesday, 12 November, and find it surrounded by one hundred armed men. William Tate of Delapré had used 'all possible expedition' and 'as much secrecy as could be' to catch the inhabitants unawares. As he informed Salisbury the following day, 'we encountered the Lord Vaux returning out of the town, with whom we presently entered, making no stay in any place until we came unto his mother whom we found retired in her chamber through some indisposition of health.' (Eliza had been similarly 'indisposed' during the Irthlingborough raid of 1599.) Upon request, she immediately surrendered the keys of her closet, cabinet, trunks and coffers. Tate secured everything, rounded up the servants and, leaving some men 'to observe Mrs Vaux', commenced the search:

> As we passed through every room, we shut up the doors fast & kept the keys, which I yet retain, not admitting anyone to use them without some servant of mine own to accompany them. And after we had thus proceeded, having left no place unsought, outward or inward, we returned to Mrs Vaux her closet, where we applied ourselves with vigilant eyes to discover some matter of moment for the service. But having perused the rejected and treasured papers we found nothing that in any point did concern this late occasion. Then I ransacked the coffers of linen, trunks of apparel, the young Lord's lodging and his evidence house, to which he very honourably gave passage, and in all things disposed himself to expedite the service that he might stand justified from all imputation.

Tate questioned Lord Vaux informally, attempting 'by private discourse to evince something of circumstance' and 'by persuasion, nobly to discover what he knew in this late intended treason'. Vaux expressed his 'vehement detestation of the treason' and stiffly denied any knowledge of it, as did 'the mother', whom Tate worked on afterwards. As raids went, it had been 'very exact', but fairly civilised. 'There is neither armour nor stranger in the house,' Tate concluded, and 'I do keep a very sufficient watch about the house night & day so that no man can enter or issue forth without our knowledge.'[2]

On Day 2, Tate 'intermitted' the search and concentrated on questioning the servants and those caught in his cordon. Eliza's baker, Francis Swetnam, was interesting. He said that on the evening of 5 November he had gone to Wellingborough 'at the entreaty' of a man called Matthew, who bought twenty pounds of gunpowder from a local mercer. Swetnam did not know Matthew's surname, but he had claimed to be 'a Lancashire man' who 'served the Lord Monteagle'. Apart from that week, when he had stayed in town 'four or five nights' and resorted to Eliza 'divers times', Swetnam had not seen him. The man was Matthew Batty, one of the three men whom Eliza was so keen to have freed from Verney's custody. Like Huddlestone's servant, William Thornbury, who was arrested at the same time and had previously been implicated in the Babington Plot,[3] Batty seems to have been one of those stalwart recusant servants who could be very useful, but also quite damaging, to the English mission.

Although Batty had a story about sending the gunpowder up to Lancashire by a carrier in Kettering, he admitted to Swetnam (or so the baker claimed) that he intended to keep part of it 'for his own use' and part 'to bestow amongst his friends'.[4] The powder purchased late on 5 November would have been too late for Westminster, but not, perhaps, for the Midlands rebellion, or so the investigators might have wondered. Batty's version of events did not look good for Francis Swetnam:

Mathew Batty saith that he, serving the Lady Monteagle and living at Mrs Vaux's and Sir Francis Tresham's some few days before Allhallow-tide, did on Tuesday the vth of November buy a barrel of gunpowder, which he left with Francis, Mrs Vaux her man.[5]

Swetnam was taken to London for further questioning, 'but denieth that he was ever at any Mass, or that he knoweth any priest, and cannot deliver any other material thing to be set down'. He admitted that he was a recusant, 'but will now come to the Church, for that he had rather adventure his own soul, than loosen his five children'. (At least one son was safe in the Catholic fold: John Swetnam had been ordained abroad the previous year and would eventually return as a Jesuit missionary.)[6]

Tate's cordon, which extended three miles from Harrowden Hall, netted its first good catch on 13 November in the person of John Laithwood, a Lancashire man in his early twenties, who was approaching from the south. 'At his first examination,' Tate reported, 'he was insufferably insolent, but on the morrow he became of a better-tempered spirit.' He said he was returning home to Lancashire, via Kettering, and that he was a Catholic who had neither gone to Church nor travelled overseas. Tate was dubious: 'these priests & Jesuits masking under other habits, make me become jealous of any unknown to me professing themselves Catholics.'[7] He was right to be suspicious. Laithwood was a priest and had been staying at Harrowden Hall before the crisis. John Gerard tells his story:

> A few days before, when we first got word of the plot, he had left at my suggestion in order to see Father Garnet and ask him what we should do . . . On his way he was captured but managed to escape. Seized on the road and brought to an inn, he was to have been examined and committed to prison at once. But entering the inn, he took off his cloak and sword and walked out again to the stables as if he were going to attend to his horse and take him to drink. There was a stream near the inn and he asked the stable boy to lead his horse there at once. He went with him and when he reached the stream, he turned to the boy.
>
> 'Go and get the hay ready,' he said, 'and put down some straw for my horse to lie on. I'll be back myself when he has finished drinking.' The boy returned to the stable without further thought. Meanwhile, the Father mounted his horse, spurred him into the stream and swam him across to the other side. As his cloak and sword were lying in the inn, his stratagem was unsuspected until they realized he had been away a long time and the boy told them what had happened.

Immediately they set off in pursuit. But they were too late. The good Father knew the countryside well and reached a Catholic house before nightfall. There he hid for a few days, but when he found he could not get in touch with Father Garnet, he tried to return to me, thinking the danger had passed. He avoided Charybdis to fall into the clutches of Scylla.

Laithwood was sent to London for interrogation, 'but his priesthood could not be proved and his brother was allowed to pay a sum down for his release'.[8]

On Day 3 – Thursday, 14 November – William Tate, frustrated by his previous 'unprofitable endeavours', resumed the search of Harrowden Hall and concentrated on finding Gerard. He 'left no place unsought' where he thought 'any possibility might be of such secret retreat' and finally came to 'the place where this hidden serpent should seem to lurk'. There was nothing to give it away, even to the 'most exquisite inquisitor', but Tate 'insisted long upon that part of the house, upon some intimation given that there was a secret receptacle in the roof'. He used 'all sedulous industry to examine every corner' and threatened to break through the wall if the hide was not revealed. 'After some debate,' Eliza's butler relented, 'whereat I entered,' Tate reported,

and searched the same and found it the most secret place that ever I saw & so contrived that it was without all possibility to be discovered by any man that knew it not. And there I found many popish books & other things incident to their superstitious religion, but no man in it. And I am well assured that none could evade out thence after I entered the house, having guarded it day & night, round about & within, myself & my servants keeping the keys of all the doors from my first entrance.[9]

'I was in my hiding-place,' Gerard admitted in his *Autobiography* four years later.

I could sit down all right, but there was hardly room to stand. However, I did not go hungry, for every night food was brought to me secretly and at the end of four or five days, when the rigour of the search had relaxed slightly, my friends came at night and took me out and warmed me by a fire.[10]

These friends also furnished Gerard with the details that can now be read in his *Narrative of the Gunpowder Plot* – how 'the house was beset with at least a hundred men', how Eliza 'willed them to use their pleasure', how they probed the cellars and 'dark corners' with candles:

> They searched every cabinet and box in her own closet for letters, in hope to find some little scroll that might show Father Gerard had been an actor in this treason or that she or her son had received some knowledge of it. But they found not with all this diligence the least tittle of advantage in the matter, insomuch that the chief man in commission for this search (though an earnest puritan) yet sent a very full information unto the Council that he had found the house most clear, the young Lord and his mother very respective unto authority – admitting any kind of search or inquiry that he could desire – and yet very confident in their own innocency; and that he found not any preparation in the house for war or any show at all that they had the least knowledge of any such attempt intended.[11]

It is not known how Gerard came to read Tate's first report, but it seems that there were no hard feelings between searcher and searched: just over six years later William Tate would stand trustee for Lord Vaux in a deed of conveyance.[12] 'After nine days,' Gerard concluded in his *Autobiography*, 'the search party withdrew. They thought I could not possibly have been there all that time without being discovered.'[13]

Tate had to entrust the second half of the search to his deputies, for on 15 November he received orders to take Eliza to London. They were 'ill accommodated of coach and horses for so sudden a journey' and made 'slow, & troublesome' progress. They reached London on the night of 18 November and Eliza was immediately questioned.[14]

She was tired, but ready. She did not know Gerard the priest. Catesby and Digby had visited 'about 6 or 8 weeks last'. One 'Greene' came with Catesby 'and a day or two before there came in company with certain gentlewomen one called Darcy'. She first heard of 'the broils at London' from Sir George Fermor on Wednesday, 6 November, 'at night after the attempt should have been done'. He had come 'by accident' and 'the rumour at Towcester was that five Scots men should have done it'. She 'remembereth not the certain contents' of her Tottenham letter, but Agnes Wenman told her that she was keeping it safe 'for both their discharges'. She said that Henry Huddlestone had told her about his ride with Catesby on 5 November and had 'apprehended that all was not well', but had not pressed Catesby for the reason.[15]

Double double, toil and trouble. At least half of Eliza's testimony was a bubbling cauldron of lies and the Council suspected as much. Shakespeare's *Macbeth*, first performed in the months following the discovery of the plot, is a gunpowder play as well as 'the Scottish Play'. The porter's speech on the 'farmer' (an alias of Henry Garnet) is oft-quoted:

> Faith, here's an equivocator that could swear in both
> the scales against either scale, who committed treason
> enough for God's sake, yet could not equivocate to heaven.
>
> (Act 2, Scene 3)

But there are other equivocators in the play, including the duplicitous hostess, Lady Macbeth[16] and the witches with their strange, ambiguous prophecies:

> MACBETH: How now, you secret, black, and midnight hags,
> What is't you do?
> WITCHES: A deed without a name.
> MACBETH: I conjure you by that which you profess,
> Howe'er you come to know it, answer me.
>
> (Act 4, Scene 1)

We cannot know if Eliza Vaux informed Shakespeare's play in any meaningful way, but John Gerard's Gunpowder Plot *Narrative* is a different matter. He wrote it in English (unlike his Latin *Autobiography*) soon after the plot in order to clear himself, the Jesuits and their allies of the stain of complicity. His account of Eliza's examination must surely have come from the witness herself, for they were very soon reunited. It is authentic, therefore, if not necessarily the whole truth:

[She] was examined before the whole Council, where she did clear herself fully from all cause of suspicion in that treason and affirmed constantly that, although she were a firm Catholic and so would live and die by the grace of God, yet that fact [the plot] she did as much mislike and condemn as themselves; and that so she had been taught by those that had care of her soul.

They urged her that she knew Father Gerard and had received him many times into her house. She answered she hoped none could justly accuse her that she had received either him or any other priest and that she would not accuse herself, the same being a penal law. They insisted she was bound to tell of him, for that he was known to be a traitor and a chief plotter of this action. She answered with serious protestation that she had never the least cause to think so of him (if she did know him, as they presupposed) and said that she had heard so much good of the man (though she did not know him)* that she would pawn her whole estate, yea, and her life also, that he was not guilty of that plot, nor justly to be touched with it.

Then the Council produced a letter which she had written unto the Sheriff of Warwickshire, her cousin, for the delivery of two priests, who were taken passing through the country after the stirs were begun . . . She answered that she wrote for them indeed and that she desired much to set them free, but she knew them not to be priests but took them for Catholic gentlemen that came sometimes to her house, as others did, and looked nothing like priests.

Then finally some of the Council said that whereas she was now in the King's mercy to live or die, she should have her life and lose nothing of her estate if she would tell where Gerard the Jesuit was to be found. She answered she knew not, but if she did know, she would not tell it them to save her life and many lives.

'Why then,' said they, 'Lady, you must die.'

'Why then, I will die, my Lords,' said she, 'for I will never do the other.'[17]

Gerard included a few piquant details to this scene in his later *Auto-biography*. Instead of 'some of the Council' urging Eliza to save herself,

---

* The qualifying comments in parentheses are Gerard's, the tutor improving his student's work perhaps.

it was one formerly friendly lord of the Council,* who 'courteously accompanied her to the door' and said:

> 'Have a little pity on yourself and your children and tell them what they wish to know. If you don't, you will have to die.'
>
> In a loud voice she answered:
>
> 'Then I would rather die, my Lord.'
>
> As she spoke, the door was opened and her servants waiting outside heard her. They all burst into tears.[18]

It was all good dramatic stuff, but the mother of Lord Vaux was not going to die for harbouring the priest who couldn't be found or for writing the letter that couldn't be read, any more than she would for having friends round for supper or for lying about when and from whom she had heard about the news in London. The information against her, which emerged more fully over the coming weeks, was embarrassing, but hardly substantial. Besides, as she impishly informed Salisbury, not many people would 'put their lives & estates in the power & secrecy of a woman'. Even Lady Tasborough admitted that, while scenting treason in Eliza's letter, she had considered it, 'coming from a woman, to be of no great consequence'.[19]

Eliza Vaux joined Dorothy Wright, Martha Percy, Elizabeth Rookwood and others in a list of 'wives & kinswomen of the traitors who it was not thought fit to commit to prisons'.[20] They were dispatched to various aldermen of the city, the lot of Eliza Vaux falling on Sir John Swynnerton, who had the charge of the impost on wines. It was a wretched time for them all, even those wives allowed to stay in the country. Lady Digby's house was stripped 'to the very floor of the great parlour' and even her underwear was seized. 'Wholly destitute', she resorted to sending begging letters to Salisbury, as did Eliza's recent guest, Dorothy Huddlestone, 'great with child' and desperate for 'relief to sustain the present wants of myself and my poor comfortless infants'.[21]

---

* The formerly friendly councillor is traditionally thought to have been the Earl of Northampton, but was more probably the Earl of Salisbury, whom Eliza would entreat on 17 April 1606 to renew his 'honourable usage' towards her, 'as when I was last at the Council Table it pleased your Lordship in particular out of your noble disposition to show that care both of my health & estate as I could not think how to yield sufficient thanks'. (CP, 116, f. 22)

Eliza's butler, baker and other servants were committed to several prisons and examined 'with many menacings'.[22] Her younger sister Jane, Lady Lovell was questioned on 19 November. She admitted that in the months prior to the plot she had been visited by Digby ('my Lord Vaux with him' once), Catesby ('long of her acquaintance') and other suspect persons. Her servants were examined, her lodgings were ransacked and she was placed under house arrest. She, a widow, and her five- and eight-year-old daughters were put 'in much fear'; she was not used to such 'rude & unmannerly' treatment, she told Salisbury, and she begged 'the privilege of a poor gentlewoman' to be relieved of the searches of 'every base constable'.*[23]

The seventeen-year-old Lord Vaux was also questioned, though with more sensitivity than was shown to his outraged aunt. He was examined 'alone' by Salisbury and, according to Gerard, 'cleared himself so by his answer that he was no further restrained, but only commanded to stay in the city of London'. The news soon leaked and there were rumours that the young Lord Vaux was in the Tower. One contemporary diarist, the Puritan Member for Honiton, listed him as one of five noblemen who had, 'ut fama est', been privy to the plot.[24] It did not help that Fawkes and Vaux were so similar in pronunciation and, indeed, often in spelling – the form 'Guy Faux' was common; sometimes even 'Guy Vaux' was written. Reporting on 19 November 1605, Sir Edward Hoby wrote of John Johnson in the cellar: 'his name now is turned to Guy Vaux alias Faukes.'[25] No blood relationship has been discovered between Fawkes of York and Vaux of Harrowden.

Eliza's 'great and tried friend', Sir Everard Digby, tried to protect her and Gerard. In letters smuggled out of his Tower cell, he briefed his wife on his examinations. 'By that name, I did not know him,' he had

*Lady Lovell, her two girls and Eliza's daughter Joyce would leave England in June 1606. Lovell claimed to need treatment at the Spa in Belgium for breast cancer, but 'devotion of the soul' soon made her 'neglect the health of her body'. She changed her name to Mary, thought about joining various convents and eventually founded a house of English Carmelites at Antwerp. Joyce Vaux briefly joined her aunt's order before deciding upon Mary Ward's institute of unenclosed teaching nuns. She would, however, end her days quietly in Suffolk with her brother Henry. (CP, 119, ff. 30–3; BL Add. MS 11402, f. 112r; HMC Downshire, vol. 2, pp. 12, 71, 158; vol. 6, p. 71; C. M Seguin, 'Lovel, Mary', ODNB; Orchard, Till God Will, p. 92; Vaux Petitions, p. 19. Also Redworth, Letters of Luisa de Carvajal, II, p. 172 for many rich Catholics 'using poor health as a pretext' to escape England.)

replied when Salisbury had first challenged him about Gerard, 'nor at Mrs Vaux's, as he said I did, for I never saw a priest there.' When, later,

they told me that I was in the company of Father Walley [Garnet], Father Greenway [Tesimond], and Father Gerard at Mrs Vaux's, I told them that I had been in their companies, but not there or anywhere else with others but myself.[26]

Digby also managed to release verses to his 'dearest' wife and two sons:

> I grieve not to look back into my former state,
>   Though different that were from present case;
> I moan not future haps, though forced death with hate
>   Of all the world were blustered in my face
>   But Oh I grieve to think that ever I
>   Have been a means of others misery.
>
> When on my Little Babes I think, as I do oft,
>   I cannot choose but then let fall some tears:
> Me-thinks I hear the little Prattler, with words soft,
>   Ask, Where is Father that did promise Pears,
>   And other Knacks, which I did never see,
>   Nor Father neither, since he promised me.
>
> 'Tis true, my Babe, thou never saw'st thy Father since,
>   nor art thou ever like to see again:
> That stopping Father into mischief which will pinch
>   The tender Bud, and give thee cause to plain
>   His hard disaster; that must punish thee,
>   Who art from guilt as any Creature free.
>
> But Oh! when she that bare thee, Babe, comes to my mind,
>   Then do I stand as drunk with bitterest woe,
> To think that she, whose worth were such to all, should find
>   Such usage hard, and I to cause the blow,
>   Of her such sufferance, that doth pierce my heart,
>   And gives full grief to every other part.[27]

Eliza's butler, Richard Richardson, also managed to smuggle secret briefings out of his cell. As Anne, Lady Markham, informed Salisbury:

> I hear Ric. the butler is close in the Gatehouse, yet your lordship knows that prisons are places of such corruption as money will help letters to their friends to tell what they have been examined of, so they will guess shrewdly how to shift.

Lady Markham, a friend and neighbour of Eliza, was helping Salisbury with his enquiries. Her husband had been involved in the Bye Plot of 1603 and it was in the hope of terminating his banishment that she offered 'to deliver the person of Gerard . . . into the hands of the State'. She informed Salisbury in January that 'if the watch had continued but two days longer, Mr Gerard had been pined out at Harrowden'. But January was too late; Gerard was long gone. The 'wandering' Jesuit had been hard to track in Northamptonshire. As Lady Markham had protested:

> I fear this most vile and hateful plot hath taken deep and dangerous root, because I meet with many that will as easily be persuaded there was no gunpowder laid as that [that] holy good man was an actor in the plot; and surely the generality did ever so much admire him that they were happy or blessed in hearing him, and their roof sanctified by his appearance in their house.[28]

This was not the predominant view in the capital. 'Priests and Jesuits' lurked in the 'synagogue of satan', concocting theories of resistance against kings: they were the ones responsible for the Gunpowder Plot, thought Alderman Sir John Swynnerton:

> Yea, yea, it is a babe of their own begetting every inch of it: And though they search each corner of their wit to shift it off and father it upon others, yet shall it always be reputed theirs. They shall ever be enforced to keep it and bear it upon their backs as a notorious badge of their fornication and a durable monument of their shame.[29]

Swynnerton laid his prejudices – as well as his heart – bare in his *Christian Love-Letter* of 1606, a bizarre attempt to persuade a girl 'with mild and charitable phrase' to forsake her 'Romish religion' and marry him. The Earl of Salisbury, to whom it was dedicated, dismissed it as a 'toy'. One doubts that Mistress Katherine T. of Gloucestershire was won over by her suitor's assertion that her soul was benighted in 'Egyptian darkness', or the winsome: 'You lie slabbering in these corrupted puddles of man's erroneous inventions, yet never the more cleansed.'[30]

For Swynnerton, who also made a dig at 'your extraordinary unsanctified Saint Winifred's' Well, the Gunpowder Plot was reason enough for his darling to forsake the Church of Rome:

> I wonder what construction the favourers of your profession make of the accident. I know how they carry it outwardly, but what their inward man thinketh of it, in approbation or detestation of the plot, and touching the discovery, there's the point.[31]

It was, no doubt, a point that he put directly to Eliza, for Alderman Swynnerton was her London keeper. Five months before she came to reside with him at Aldermanbury, he had been involved in a mercantile dispute that saw his brother-in-law accuse him of 'many inhumane disgraces' and the Earl of Salisbury rate him for 'contempt and extreme proceedings'.[32] Eliza, however, was 'well respected' in Swynnerton's house, though 'not allowed any one servant of my son's to have access unto me to stead me in my needful occasions, all mine own men being committed to several prisons'. She entreated Salisbury for 'some enlargement'. On the subject of Gerard the priest:

> If your Lordship do hold me here out of an opinion to draw from me the discovery of that party which your Lordship is persuaded had so deep a finger in that most horrible treason, which none living hath a greater detestation of than myself, I do here protest unto your Lordship that it is not in the compass of my power to do it, but I pray heartily unto sweet Jesus that He in his Justice will deliver him into your Lordship's hands, if he be guilty, which I have very strong & forcible reasons to make doubt of, but that it becometh me not to contradict your Lordship's better judgement.[33]

Perfectly demure, perfectly deferential, perfectly uncooperative, Eliza
Vaux was released from Swynnerton's custody on the condition that
she remain in the city.[34] But London was expensive and unhealthy and
it was on both those grounds that she pressed Salisbury for leave to
return to the country. On 17 April 1606, she was still waiting and
wondering: 'I find both my suit & myself so wholly neglected that I
cannot but marvel what hath made so great a change in your Lordship
from whom I found such honourable usage before.'[35]

There was one reason why Salisbury might have been disobliged
to assist Eliza. Despite the 'great charges' of the capital, she was
finding the funds to help her priest. 'I was in London,' Gerard recalled,
having slipped past the shire watch, through the city gates and into a
safe townhouse:

> And as soon as she was released from custody, quite oblivious of herself,
> she wanted to look after me. Every day she sent me news by letter.
> She got all I needed for my house and when she heard that I wanted
> to go abroad for a time, she insisted that I should spare no expense
> that was necessary to ensure my safety. She would gladly pay for it
> even if it cost five thousand florins. And in fact she gave me a thousand
> florins for the journey.

On Saturday, 3 May 1606, John Gerard fled England in the retinue
of the Spanish envoy sent to congratulate James I on his deliverance
from the plot. As with all Gerard's adventures, it was a tense affair.
Having arranged to meet the fugitive at the port, the Spanish diplo-
mats 'took fright and said they could not stand by their promise'.
Time was running out, the ship was set to sail, the officials were
standing firm. 'Suddenly they changed their mind. The envoy came
personally to fetch me and helped me himself to dress in the livery
of his attendants so that I could pass for one of them.'[36] It was not a
time for working in England, Gerard concluded. There would be
several false sightings over the years, but he would never return to
his country, or the house that had kept him safe.

24

Two Ghosts

Miserable desolation! No king, no queen, no prince, no issue male, no councillors of state, no nobility, no bishops, no judges! O barbarous and more than Scythian or Thracian cruelty! No mantle of holiness can cover it, no pretence of religion can excuse it, no shadow of good intention can extenuate it. God and heaven condemn it, man and earth detest it, the offenders themselves were ashamed of it; wicked people exclaim against it, and the souls of all true Christian subjects abhor it.[1]

Sir Edward Coke had had almost three months to polish his speech. The King and Queen were apparently in private attendance. One MP complained in the Commons that his standing-room entry fee (10 shillings) was more than 'many of the baser sort' had paid. The trial of the eight surviving plotters at Westminster Hall on 27 January 1606 was a moment of national catharsis. Four days earlier, Sir Edward Montagu of Boughton (an old Vaux acquaintance) had been well supported in his motion to make 5 November a day of public thanksgiving.* When Sir Everard Digby, dressed in his 'tuff taffatie gown

---

* The thanksgiving prayer remained in the Church of England service book until 1859. From around the 1670s, it became popular to burn effigies of the Pope, sometimes with live cats trapped inside to mimic the wailing Whore of Babylon. William of Orange's landing at Torbay on 5 November 1688 reinforced the providential nature of the date. By the eighteenth century, effigies of Guy Fawkes had become common and today, with Bonfire Night continuing largely as a secular tradition, he has morphed into a more generic scarecrow-type figure. In Lewes, East Sussex, however, where the sectarian origins of 'the Fifth' are not ignored, images of any public figure, or thing, are considered fair kindling for the fire. In 2012 representations of Guy Fawkes and Pope Paul V were joined by those of Lance Armstrong, Angela Merkel, Mitt Romney, Geri Halliwell, the Olympics and the Queen.

and a suit of black satin', bowed out of the courtroom, he begged the lords for forgiveness. 'God forgive you' was the response, 'and we do.'[2] He was not, however, permitted to die by the axe. The eight men fell at the scaffold on the last two days of January.

But Robert Catesby could not be forgiven, or punished. Some satisfaction might have been derived from the exhumation of his corpse. People could go to Westminster and look at his impaled head, but they could not see him in the dock or witness his emasculation or smell his boiling flesh. While Guy Fawkes bore the brunt of popular odium (the fall guy), the mastermind had died on his own terms. Investigators had wondered, though, if Catesby's persuasive charm could really have worked without the endorsement of his religious and social superiors. They were sure that 'arch-traitors' were still at large. Even as the condemned plotters were led out of court, there was a sense of questions unanswered, secrets withheld and sins awaiting expiation.

In his speech Coke said of the Jesuits that they did not watch 'and pray', but watched 'to prey'. It was this eminent lawyer's sincere belief that the Gunpowder Plot was the spawn of the Society of Jesus. Henry Garnet, Oswald Tesimond, John Gerard 'and other Jesuits' had, according to Coke, provided the 'traitorous advice and counsel' upon which every detail of the plot – from the mine to the Midlands rising – was decided.[3]

Twelve days earlier, on 15 January 1606, a warrant had been issued in the King's name for the arrests of Gerard, Garnet and Tesimond – in that order. Detailed descriptions of the three were displayed, like wanted posters, throughout the parishes and markets of England. Their harbourers were to be dealt with severely, 'without hope of mercy or forgiveness', and were esteemed 'no less pernicious' to the King and commonwealth 'than those that have been actors and concealers of the main treason itself'. Tesimond – 'of mean stature, somewhat gross, his hair black, his beard bushy and brown' – was

---

The cellars at Westminster are ritually searched with lanterns before the Opening of Parliament. In 1812 the Yeomen of the Guard, coming to the vault of a wine-merchant, sensibly sampled the contents of the pipes 'to ascertain that they did not contain gunpowder'.
(Cressy, Champion and Jay, in *Gunpowder Plots: A Celebration of 400 Years of Bonfire Night* (2005); *thisissussex.co.uk*, 6 November 2012)

spotted in London. As soon as he and his captor shifted from busy street to quiet back-alley, he took to his heels and was gone before the hue and cry was raised. He eventually made it out of England with a boatload of dead pigs.[4]

Of the three accused Jesuits, he had probably been in the deepest. He was Catesby's and Wintour's confessor and had revealed the plot to Garnet. Catesby's man, Bates, had implicated him, telling his examiners that the Jesuit had urged secrecy 'because it was for a good cause'. Bates also confessed to the juncture of plotters and priests at Harrowden Hall in mid-October and to the messages exchanged between himself (on behalf of Catesby and Digby) and Garnet and Tesimond at Coughton on 6 November. He said that after delivering the news of the plot's discovery, he and Tesimond had left Coughton to see Catesby and the rebels at Huddington. Bates was subsequently 'heartily sorry' for his confession, but did not retract it.[5]

Against John Gerard, the most damning piece of evidence was Fawkes's testimony that he had given Communion to the first five plotters at their fateful May meeting in the Strand in 1604. None of the plotters suggested – and Gerard vehemently denied – that he had been admitted to the burning secret.

Henry Garnet appeared to have been everywhere and known everyone. That 'nest for such bad birds', White Webbs, had been his and Anne's before Catesby and his friends had come to roost. Investigators knew about the journey to St Winifred's Well and Garnet's prayers at Coughton. They knew about the earlier 'Spanish treason', and Garnet's 1602 letter recommending Wintour to the Madrid-based Jesuit, Joseph Creswell (the same Creswell who, in 1588, had served as chaplain to Parma's troops and penned the proclamation that would have been distributed in England in the event of a successful Armada[6]). They knew about Garnet's dispatching of Sir Edmund Baynham to Rome (Baynham, a notorious roisterer, who had briefly been imprisoned for 'some desperate speeches' against James and was now labelled by Coke 'a fit messenger for the devil'[7]). They knew about the papal breves on the succession, Robert Persons' pro-Spanish tract on the same subject and the latest Jesuit resistance theories that expounded the 'lawful and meritorious' case for the killing of 'heretic' rulers. They argued that the Gunpowder Plot had arisen 'out of the dead ashes of former treasons' and – a clinching observation here – Coke noted that 'gunpowder was the invention of a friar, one of the Romish rabble'.[8]

Thus: Tesimond had encouraged the plot, Gerard had sanctified it and Garnet had worked all the angles, domestic and foreign. If Bates had been the only plotter to make a direct accusation, if, indeed, the others had wilfully refused to acknowledge Jesuit involvement in the plot, 'what torture soever' was threatened, it was surely because they had been told it was a mortal sin to betray a priest. Rumour had it that Francis Tresham received a warning in his cell 'that if he accused this Garnet it was impossible for him to be saved'.[9] And so it was that this bloody band of elusive gentleman-priests, who wore hair shirts under their 'feathers and fashions',[10] who hunted in public and scourged themselves in private, who thirsted for murder and marched towards martyrdom, and taught Catholics how to lie – so it was that Anne and Eleanor and Eliza Vaux's friends and 'ghostly fathers' were depainted as the true villains of the piece.

Henry Garnet, meanwhile, who was terrified of torture, and Edward Oldcorne, who practised extreme self-mortification, were sitting in a hole knowing they could not hold out for much longer.[11] The Jesuit superior had been 'changing burrows'. On 4 December, he had joined Oldcorne at Hindlip, the grand mansion of the Worcestershire recusant, Thomas Habington. 'So large and fair a house that it might be seen over great part of the country', Hindlip's finest features were embedded in its masonry. It was a gamble to go there: a house in gunpowder country, known to officials, with a Jesuit-in-residence. But despite many searches, Hindlip had never given up her priests.[12] It may have felt sanctified, untouchable, at the very least it was familiar. Eleanor and the children seem to have gone elsewhere; their trail runs cold, though the presence of a French prayer book, inscribed 'Baronne Brooksby', in the library of neighbouring Harvington Hall (a place equipped with Owen-built hides), suggests that perhaps they did not stray far.[13]

Anne stayed with Garnet and the ever-faithful Owen. The carpenter, a Jesuit lay brother since around 1600, was about fifty now and lame (a 'resty' horse had fallen on him a few years earlier).[14] A month before their arrival, Hindlip had been turned upside down, not by pursuivants, but a baby – Mary Habington had given birth to a boy, William, a future poet, on 4 November 1605.

Garnet retired to a 'lower chamber descending from the dining room' and waited for 'the heat of this persecution' to pass.[15] He wrote to the Privy Council disavowing the plot and any Jesuit involvement. He stressed the importance of his order's fourth vow of 'holy obedience' to the Pope. There had been an 'express prohibition of all unquietness' and Garnet had 'inculcated' it, he wrote, 'upon every occasion of speech'. He had also sought a further ban 'under censures of all violence towards his Majesty'. 'I will infer,' he continued, 'that it is no way probable, in never so prejudicated a judgement, that the authors of this conspiracy durst acquaint me or any of mine with their purposes.'[16] *I will infer . . . no way probable* – neat words that prevented an outright lie. If the government's detraction of Garnet is a caricature, so is the saint of his apologists.

On the afternoon of Saturday, 18 January 1606, a recusant friend of the Habingtons tipped them off to an imminent raid. Only Mary Habington was home, her husband having ridden to Shropshire to execute a will. On Sunday the search was confirmed for 'one day in that week'.[17] At the break of the following day, Anne Vaux heard the dreaded noises. She knew the drill. Garnet and Oldcorne were helped into position. Owen, whose 'crooked' leg was an obvious tell, ducked into another hide with Oldcorne's servant, Ralph. Pictures, papers, books and vestments, rosaries, relics, chalices and other 'church stuff' were stashed 'in the most safe secret places they had'.

Sir Henry Bromley had the house surrounded with a 'seemly troop' of a hundred men. The Catholics played for time, 'sending to the gates, as the custom is, to know the cause of their coming and to keep them in talk with messages to and fro'. Bromley was wise to the tactic and 'caused the gates with great violence and force of men to be broken down'. He carried detailed instructions from London: 'You must take care to draw down the wainscot' in the east part of the parlour, where 'it is conceived there is some vault'. The lower floors 'must be tried with a broach' and the wainscoting pierced with a gimlet. 'For the upper rooms, you must observe whether they be more in breadth than the lower rooms and look in which places the rooms be enlarged.' Special attention was to be paid to chimneys and loft spaces, particularly any 'double loft' or seemingly inaccessible garret, 'for these be ordinary places of hovering'.

Armed with their tools, Bromely's men tried every room, but although they found a suspiciously large number of warm beds, 'parcels of apparel' and scholarly books, no 'hovering' was discerned. When Thomas Habington returned home that night, he vowed to 'die at his gate' if any priest could be found 'in his house or in that shire'. According to one manuscript account, 'this liberal or rather rash speech could not cause the search so slightly to be given over.'

Nicholas Owen and Ralph Ashley must already have been hungry; they had a single apple between them. The priests were better off. They had a store of marmalade and sweet meats and could receive warm broths and caudles (a medicinal mulled wine) through a reed in the masonry linked to Mary Habington's room. They had 'means to do *servitii piccoli* [urinate]', but they could not light a fire on these 'wet winter nights', since they were hiding in a chimney. Nor had there been time to take out incumbent books and altar furniture. It was a tight squeeze. 'We continually sat,' Garnet recalled, 'save that sometimes we could half stretch ourselves, the place being not high enough.' It was painful and 'both our legs, especially mine, were much swollen'. Despite this, 'we were very merry & content within' and heard each other's general confessions.

On Monday and Tuesday Hindlip retained its secrets. Thomas Habington continued to bluster. His wife refused to leave. Anne is not specifically mentioned, though if she behaved according to past and future form, she was probably more virago than virgo. 'I did never hear so impudent liars as I find here,' Bromely groused, 'all recusants and all resolved to confess nothing, what danger soever they incur.' He despaired of finding 'any man or any thing', but on the third day, Wednesday, his men started to pull up the floorboards and 'at last' he could return good news: 'popish trash hid under boards in three or four several places.'

Owen and Ashley, their solitary apple long gone, struggled through that cold January night. They were behind the wainscot panelling in the Gallery, a room 'foursquare going round about the house'. They could hear the patrol. The following morning, Thursday, when the footsteps were at their faintest, they slipped out 'so secretly and stilly, and shut the place again so finely that they were not one whit heard'. They made for the door, but it was shut, and the patrol returned, and they were taken. They refused to give up the hide and only after the wainscot was systematically stripped, and the walls smashed about a bit, were 'two cunning and very artificial conveyances' discovered in the wall, 'so ingeniously framed, and with such art, as it cost much labour ere they could be found'. Scant consolation for Nicholas Owen to witness admiration for his work.

Bromley redoubled the search. 'I have yet persuasion,' he informed Salisbury 'very late' that night, 'that there is one or two more in the house, wherefore I have resolved to continue the guard yet a day or two.' According to Luisa de Carvajal, who probably heard it from Anne, Bromley's men drilled 'lines of holes in the floors' and made such a mess of the walls that 'they feared that, despite the house being so sturdy and large, it might fall down about their ears'. More hides were uncovered, nearly all containing 'books, massing stuff and popish trumpery'. Habington continued to lie with impressive front, but he had no good answer when the deeds to his house were plucked out of a hide.

'Every day' the two priests heard men 'most curious over us'. Garnet believed that the search was 'not for me, but for Mr Hall' – Oldcorne's alias – and also for Gerard, but 'of me never no expectation'. There was evidently a lot of intelligence about. On Sunday, 26 January, a man who had sheltered Robert Wintour in Worcestershire* claimed from the county jail that Oldcorne was still at Hindlip. He also insinuated that the Jesuit had commended the plot. The search continued.

'After we had been in the hole 7 days & 7 nights & some odd hours, every man may well think we were well wearied & indeed,' Garnet recalled, 'so it was.' But the greatest nuisance was not fatigue, or cold, or even cramp, but the lack of a close stool. An eyewitness, possibly the pursuivant who discovered them on Monday morning, wrote that 'those customs of nature which of necessity must be done, and in so long a time of continuance was exceedingly offensive to the men themselves' did 'much annoy them that made entrance in upon them'. Garnet and Oldcorne 'confessed that they had not been able to hold out one whole day longer, but either they must have yielded or perished

---

* Wintour had fled Holbeach just before the siege that saw his younger brother taken and Catesby and others killed. He was a fugitive for two months, enduring 'hard bedding and diet' until his capture at Hagley on 9 January. Humphrey Littleton, the owner of Hagley, then turned informant. (BL Harl. MS 360, ff. 102–8; Fraser, *The Gunpowder Plot*, pp. 213, 216)

in the place'. In the end, wrote Luisa, 'they opened up the walls in such a way that it was impossible not to find the hiding place'.

'When we came forth,' Garnet later informed Anne,

> we appeared like 2 ghosts, yet I the strongest though my weakness lasted longest. The fellow that found us ran away for fear, thinking we would have shot a pistol at him, but there came needless company to assist him & we bade them be quiet & we would come forth. So they helped us out very charitably.

Their 'chimney conveyance' astonished the searchers, who had been expecting boarded-up corners. It was 'strangely formed' with an entrance 'curiously covered over with brick, mortared and made fast to planks of wood, and coloured black like the other parts'. Again, Owen's 'skill and industry' were admired. In all, eleven hides were found, the most recorded in any house.

Garnet and Oldcorne were seized on 27 January 1606. One hundred and twenty miles away, at the plotters' trial in Westminster Hall, lawyers fulminated against 'Jesuits not then taken'. It took a few days for Garnet's identity to be confirmed and the news to filter through, but finally the prosecution had its leading man. The last act of 'that heavy and woeful tragedy, which is commonly called the Powder-Treason', could begin.[18]

25

That Woman

Anne followed Garnet to London and spent her first night with Mary Habington in Fetter Lane. Thereafter she lived like a fugitive, staying no more than two or three nights in one place. Few were willing to put her up, 'even with money'. She was forty-three, her health was frail and it was February.[1]

On Valentine's Day, Garnet was transferred from the Gatehouse in Westminster to the altogether more foreboding Tower of London. By the bestowal of a gold coin, 'a cup of sack'[*] and some flattering words, he arranged for his new keeper to send messages to his nephew, Thomas, a priest in the Gatehouse. The first was written on a strip of paper enfolding a pair of glasses:

> I pray you let these spectacles be set in leather & with a leather case, or let the fold be fitter for the nose.
>   Yours for ever, H.G.

There was no other visible writing, but when held to a flame, new words, secretly etched in orange juice, appeared on the page. Garnet mentioned an earlier letter 'sent with biscuit bread', which he had been forced to burn without reading. 'I have acknowledged that I went from Sir Everard's to Coughton,' he wrote, and that when Bates had come from the rebel camp with news of the plot's discovery, Garnet had told him: 'I am sorry they have without advice of friends adventured in so wicked an action. Let them desist.'

---

[*] Sack (or sherry) was a sweet fortified wine famously appreciated by Falstaff: 'If I had a thousand sons, the first human principle I would teach them should be to forswear thin potations and to addict themselves to sack.' (2 *Henry IV*, Act 4, Scene 1)

I must needs acknowledge my being with the 2 sisters & that at White Webbs, as is true, for they are so jealous of White Webbs that I can no way else satisfy.

My names I all confess but that last.

Appoint some place near where this bearer may meet some trusty friend.

Where is Mrs Anne?[2]

On 23 February, hearing that Anne was in town, Garnet told Oldcorne in the adjacent cell that he had written 'a note that my keeper may repair to her near hand', so that she 'will let us hear from all our friends'.[3] Three days later, he sent an item to the Gatehouse 'to be new lined'. The covering note acknowledged receipt of 'the linen you sent' and requested socks and a black nightcap. 'The spectacles will not serve me,' he added, 'I only want spectacles to see afar off, for to read I need not.' (This provided the opportunity for more innocuous wrapping paper.) He would also need money, 'for we have not yet paid our fees'.

The invisible ink contained Latin instructions for the Jesuits, including the appointment of a provisional leader. Garnet continued in English with his own news:

They say I am obstinate & indeed they have nothing against me but presumptions.

I have indeed acknowledged Wintour's journey into Spain, but so that I cannot have hurt thereby. I acknowledged I was at White Webs, but one or 2 nights this twelve month.

The house is none of mine, though this day they will have me to be Mr Measy & brought James* to my face, who said nothing.

Neither have I confessed any particular but of Mrs Perkins [Anne] & the meeting of Catesby & Wintour in Q. Eliz.'s time. Yet they know all the persons & so I wish all be wary till their malice be wrought on me.

---

* 'James Johnson' *vere* John Grissold, Anne Vaux's servant and caretaker at White Webbs. Later that day he deposed that, 'having now seen Garnet the Jesuit', he had 'many times seen him with his mistress at her house at White Webbs and that he was called by the name of Mese when he came first and was said to be his mistress's kinsman.' (PRO SP 14/216/189)

The letter was meant for Anne. A superscription in juice to 'my very loving sister', urged caution:

> More hereafter: do not endanger yourself, but if you have any to bring
> you to me, by the Cradle [Tower] you may.[4]

It had been a month since Garnet was taken. Anne was desperate to receive his blessing and look for signs of his treatment. She was his conduit to the world, but 'your last letter,' he complained on 3 March, 'I could not read, your pen did not cast ink.' He had received the handkerchiefs, though, and the socks and the Bible. He hoped that Anne had paid his prison fees and could acquire beds 'for James, John, and Harry, who all have been often tortured'.[5]

The following day, he was more insistent: 'For God's sake provide bedding for these 3,' he wrote, 'your own necessities always regarded.'[6] If 'John' was Nicholas 'Little John' Owen, the request came too late. The carpenter had been found dead in his cell two days earlier, his bowels having 'gushed out'. His last examination had been just hours before his death and since the torture of 'the inferior sort' of prisoner had been authorised by special warrant, there is a strong suspicion that Owen, who may have had a hernia, was racked to death. The government was quick to put out its version: Owen 'killed himself in the Tower in the night, ripping up his own belly with a knife without a point.' Oswald Tesimond reacted incredulously: 'Does William Waad [the Lieutenant of the Tower] seriously expect us to believe that even after many days' torture, a man like Owen would abandon his hope of salvation by inflicting death on himself – and such a death?' The Venetian ambassador thought public opinion cleaved to the Catholic version. However he died, Owen took the secrets of his extraordinary priest-holes to the grave.[7]

If their friend's death made Anne even more afraid for Garnet, then his letter of 4 March, if safely received, must have come as sweet relief. Garnet had not yet been tortured. Indeed, considering the time and (alleged) crime, he was being treated rather well. This letter is much longer and more fluent than previous missives, which had not required context or elaboration. Headed 'for Mrs Anne or one of ours first', it aimed to put the record straight 'lest evil reports or untrue may do myself or others injury'.[8]

Garnet insisted that he had been 'exceedingly well used' by Sir Henry Bromley in Worcestershire. Before being taken to London, he had stayed at his captor's house, dined at his table and even celebrated Candlemas with the family. There had been 'a great dinner' and wine to toast the King. Garnet had 'pledged the health, yet with favour as they said, in a reasonable glass'. He had ridden to London on the best horse, at the King's charge, but had been 'much distempered' and could not eat anything on his first night at the Gatehouse. Thereafter, he had only managed 'bread, an apple & some wine according to my purse'. At the Tower:

> I have a very fine chamber, but was very sick the 2 first nights with ill lodging. I am allowed every meal a good draught of excellent claret wine & I am liberal with myself & neighbours for good respects, to allow also of my own purse some sack; & this is the greatest charge I shall be at hereafter, for now fire will shortly be unnecessary if I live so long, whereof I am very uncertain & as careless.

One 'evil report', apparently already doing the rounds, was that Garnet was a drunkard. To Oldcorne he confessed his fear that, in his weakened state, he might have hurt himself with 'too much abstinence and some excess of drink'. This does not sound like the admission of an inebriate, rather of someone who knew that he had drunk 'extra-ordinarily'. John Gerard's subsequent allegation that Garnet's food or drink had been spiked is not helpful in this context; nor is the decla-ration of a nineteenth-century Jesuit historian that 'the Son of God Himself was charged with being a drunkard'.[9]

However much Garnet appreciated his wine at this time – and it was just before Lent – he was sharp enough in examination to match some of the best minds in the country. To Salisbury, who treated him 'with all courtesy', Garnet defended the supremacy of the Pope 'plainly yet modestly & with great moderation'. To the question, 'May the Pope command anything unlawful for obedience?', Garnet had replied, 'No thing that is unlawful may be lawful for obedience.'

There had been odd moments of 'pleasant discourse'. Lord Chief Justice Popham had recognised the prisoner from the early 1570s when the then-teenaged Garnet had been a trainee publisher with thoughts of the law. The Attorney General, Sir Edward Coke, was 'very courteous'. William Waad, Lieutenant of the Tower, was 'very kind in usage & familiarity', but 'most violent' on the subject of religion. Once, when Garnet was asked about a christening he had performed at White Webbs – that of William and Dorothy Brooksby's daughter – Waad had insinuated that he was also 'there at the begetting'. Coke and Popham had agreed with Garnet that 'such calumniations were unfit'.

Garnet warned Anne that she was known to them. They had named Eleanor too 'and say they will have her.' There was 'a muttering' about a sermon. 'I fear mine at Coughton,' he wrote. He thought that 'Corpus Christi lodging' was still safe. 'They said they could believe me in nothing.'

'Why then, said I, you must bring witnesses.'

They had threatened torture and Garnet 'often' feared it, but 'in truth,' he informed Anne, 'I thank God I am & have been *intrepidus* & herein I marvel at myself, having had such great apprehensions before.'

When Garnet wrote this letter on Shrove Tuesday, he was unaware of Owen's death. He had no idea how Father Strange was faring either. The Tower was large enough to keep the prisoners segregated and Garnet's gaoler was not as helpful as he pretended, for while he soaked up Garnet's libations and compliments, he assiduously passed everything on – the letters, and the words, even those spoken in confession to Oldcorne in the adjacent cell.

The placement of the two Jesuits had been no happy accident. In the hope that they might incriminate themselves and others, they were put next to each other and shown 'a cranny in the top of a door' through which they could confer. They spoke in 'a low, whispering manner'. Cocks crowed, hens cackled and Oldcorne's husky, cancer-raddled voice was difficult to catch. Two hidden eavesdroppers craned their necks and noted everything down.[10]

The two priests were briefing each other, Garnet in particular telling Oldcorne what was, and was not, safe to mention. Thus, on 23 February: 'I think it not convenient to deny that we were at White Webbs; they do so much insist upon that place.' Two days later, Garnet said, 'I hope they have got no knowledge of the great . . .' The rest of the sentence was not heard. In the same session, he cited the prayers and Latin verses that he had 'indeed' used on All Saints Day at

Coughton.* The letters that he had sent into Spain 'were of no other matter, but to have pensions'. Garnet also said something 'of a gentle-woman, that if he were charged with her, he would excuse her conversing with him'. On 27 February, he said he had been questioned about a nobleman, 'but I answered it well enough I think'. He had been 'pressed again with Coughton, which I most feared'. And so it went on, Garnet 'well persuaded that I shall wind myself out of this matter', his examiners equally convinced that there was more to learn.[11]

In the many interviews that followed, Garnet might once have been tortured. In April he would refer to the threat of torture 'the second time'. There were rumours that he had been denied food and sleep. Anne said he was 'certainly' tortured; Salisbury insisted he was treated as tenderly 'as a nurse-child'. Luisa de Carvajal, who was no supporter of English officials, reported from London on 2 April that they had been 'soft' on Garnet. At the time she believed his trial statement that he had been treated 'with all courtesy'. In May, however, she was less sure, reporting that Garnet 'said that he had only been tortured for a brief while and that he had been well treated in the prison'. Later in the same letter, she wrote that 'they tried his patience in an extra-ordinary way, not by torturing his body, but by torturing his mind and understanding with false allegations, deliberate confusion and subtle fantasy'.[12] The Catholic poet and playwright Ben Jonson had a line in *Volpone* (1606) that has been seen as a waggish reference to the twin rumours of Garnet's torture and drunkenness: 'I have heard / The rack hath cured the gout' – neither apologists nor detractors would happily have granted both.[13]

Even when confronted with the minutes of the 'interlocutions', Garnet continued to evade his examiners. When challenged about 'the great . . .', he claimed he had meant 'the great house of Mr Mainy' in Essex, 'for Erith,' he admitted a month later, 'was not yet spoken of till Mrs Anne named it'. Garnet withheld information to protect people, places, his Society, his Church and himself. 'What should I have done?' he asked. 'Why should I not use all lawful liberty?'[14]

---

* This was Garnet's All Saints sermon on the text: 'Take away the perfidious people from the land of believers.' Garnet did not deny having given it, but he insisted that his prayers were 'against ill laws to be made' and not, as was alleged, to commend 'the business of the Parliament House'. (HMC Salisbury, 18, p. 109)

On 8 March, he finally admitted that he had had foreknowledge of the Gunpowder Plot. He had heard about it in general terms in June 1605, when Catesby had propounded the matter of the killing of innocents, and he had heard about it in particular when Tesimond had confessed the details in July. Garnet said he had tried to stop it by all lawful means. He had charged Tesimond to hinder the plot. He had urged Catesby to desist from any action. He had stressed the Pope's prohibition against stirs. He had begged Rome for a further ban that would threaten excommunication on all plotters (Paul V had not obliged, thinking the general ban would suffice). He had sent Sir Edmund Baynham to the Pope ('to inform generally') and he had secured a promise from Catesby that he would do nothing until his return. He had also prayed. 'Other means of hindrance I could not devise as I would have desired', because he had been bound to silence by the seal of the confessional. He said his penitent had only permitted him to divulge what he knew 'if ever I should come in question, the thing being laid to my charge'. So he had eventually confessed, believing Tesimond to be safely overseas. 'If I had not thought so,' he later wrote, 'I must have called my wits together to have made another formal tale, but the case standing as it did, it was necessary.'[15]

Questions remained. Had Garnet really not known about the messages that Catesby and others had handed Baynham before his departure for Rome? 'In all sincerity, I know not.' Why delate the plot of the appellant priest Watson in 1603, but not that of his friend Catesby in 1605? Fidelity to the seal of the confessional and, he would eventually admit, 'hope of prevention by the Pope and loathness to betray my friends'. But had Tesimond's revelation really been a confession? Garnet admitted that it had been given while walking, not kneeling, but that he had taken it as a proper confession. 'If it had been any less degree of secrecy,' he protested, 'I had written of it to Rome.'[16]

Rome, not Westminster. Garnet's allegiance to Rome is, I think, the most compelling argument for his relative innocence – and impotence – in the affair of the powder plot. His fear of disobeying not only his Jesuit superiors, but also the Pope to whom he had professed his solemn fourth vow of obedience, makes it unlikely that he would have gone rogue to support Catesby. He 'detested' the plot and condemned the 'devil's knights' who devised it.[17] He was only too happy to adhere to the papal prohibition against stirs. The seal of the confessional was a double-edged sword though. On the one hand, it gave Garnet deniability and excused him from betraying a friend to the enemy. On the other, it disabled him from giving Rome a full briefing and obtaining a specific directive in the case.

Garnet would apologise for not having disclosed his general knowledge of the plot, for not having done more to reveal what he had learned out of confession. He was probably guilty of wilful naïvety at Thames Street and a retreat into 'numb officialdom' thereafter.[18] He was certainly guilty, according to common law, of misprision of treason; that is, the knowledge, but non-disclosure, of a treasonable act. 'In respect of my superior's commandment,' he wrote, 'I kept myself aloof in all such matters.' He 'cut off all occasions' of discoursing with Catesby about the plot 'to save myself harmless both with the State here and with my superiors at Rome'.[19] Perhaps he should have assumed more responsibility and taken the blinkers off, as Anne seems to have urged on the pilgrimage – 'For God's sake talk to Mr Catesby!' He must dearly have wished that his General had accepted his resignation all those years earlier. 'I would to God I had never known of the Powder Treason,' he would exclaim at his trial.[20]

Henry Garnet lived and worked and died for the Church of Rome and it was to the Pope that he answered, not the King of England. He was always going to choose God, as he understood Him, over Caesar, and men like Coke, the Attorney General, were never going to understand that choice. At the last resort, Henry Garnet would have sat on his hands on 5 November 1605 and awaited instruction.

*

'I pray you, prove whether these spectacles do fit your sight.' Anne continued to write to Garnet after his confession. Here, in an undated orange-juice missive, the news lies amidst less momentous chatter about a lost letter:

> On Saturday at supper the attorney said that when you were in examining you feigned yourself sick to go to your chamber and coming thither you seem to take some marmalade, which even then was sent

you, and burned a letter which your keeper seeing did tell, and you being examined said that it was a letter that a friend had sent you and fearing that there might be anything of danger to the party, you burned it; and that you had acknowledged that you know of the powder action but not a practiser in it. The paper sent you with the box was concerning myself. If this come safe to you, I will write and so will more friends, who would be glad to have direction from you.

Who should supply you room for myself? I am forced to seek new friends, my old are most careless of me. I beseech you, for God sake, advise me what course to take. So long as I may hear from you [*illegible*] not out of London. My hope is that you will continue your care of me and commend to some that will for your sake help me. To live without you is not life but death. Now I see my loss. I am and ever will be yours and so I humbly beseech you to account me. O that I might see you.

Yours.[21]

This letter, which has been modernised for the sake of clarity, was poorly spelled and hardly punctuated. The original can be seen in Plate 36. Like the rest of their clandestine correspondence, it was intercepted, read, 'finely counterfeited' (since orange juice, once heated, is indelible) and filed. The copy was delivered to its recipient without suspicion.*[22]

'Concerning the disposing of yourself,' Garnet advised Anne, 'I give you leave to go over' to the nuns in Flanders. 'If you like to stay here, then I exempt you till a superior be appointed whom you may acquaint, but,' he added, 'tell him that you made your vow of yourself & then told me & that I limited certain conditions, as that you are not bound under sin except you be commanded in *virtute obedientiae*. We may accept no vows, but men may make them as they list & we after give directions accordingly.' Even now, with the prospect of a trial and horrible death before him, Garnet was worried about infringing Jesuit regulations. This

---

*The forger may have been one Arthur Gregory, who would petition Salisbury for work towards the end of the year. He reminded him of his past 'secret services' in 'discovering the secret writing being in blank, to abuse a most cunning villain in his own subtlety, leaving the same in blank again. Wherein, though there be difficulty, their answers show they have no suspicion.' Gregory was keen 'to write in another man's hand' again. (Hogge, *God's Secret Agents*, pp. 377–8)

letter is also undated, but it relates a dream that Oldcorne *alias* Hall seems to have had on 7 and 8 March, in which he and Garnet were given 'two fair tabernacles or seats' by the Jesuit General.[23]

'Mr Hall his dream had been a great comfort,' Anne replied, 'if at the foot of the throne there had been a place for me; God and you know my unworthiness.' Having been tied to Garnet for the past twenty years, Anne was now unmoored. Receiving his letter had been 'the greatest comfort that I have in this world', she wrote, but it was also the source of her 'greatest grief', since 'it seemeth you leave me'. Parts of this letter are illegible, but the writer's need for spiritual guidance is clear: 'How may I use my vow of poverty and what is your will absolutely for my going or staying?' Anne beseeched her 'good father' to help her with his prayers and, 'thus in most dutiful manner', she signed off:

> Yours and not my
>   own A.V.

She enclosed Garnet's doublet and hose. The keeper had demanded ten pounds. 'If you will,' she added, 'I will send.'[24] In practical matters, Anne was as competent as ever; spiritually, like her letter, she was in disarray.

Their correspondence revealed nothing substantial in relation to the plot, but Anne's devotion to Garnet was cruelly mocked. The prurient of Jacobean London worked the well-worn seam of hot holy ladies and randy priests. Even the Earl of Salisbury joined in. A letter from Anne apparently signed 'your loving sister A.G.' elicited the comment: 'What, you are married to Mrs Vaux: she calleth herself Garnet. What! *Senex fornicarius!* [dirty old man!]'

In all probability, the 'G' was a 'V'* and even if it wasn't, there was

---

* The letter in question has not survived, so one cannot be sure, but elsewhere Anne's capital V could easily have been mistaken for a G. For example, PRO SP 14/216/201 below:

Other contemporary hands also had strange Vs. In the examination of William Handy, for example, it looked like a 'b' (PRO SP 14/216/121). A portrait of William, third Lord Vaux (Plate 4), that was part of the contents of Grimshaw Hall sold by

nothing odd in Anne pretending to be Garnet's sister as she had done many times before. According to Garnet, Salisbury was embarrassed by the jibe and apologised at their next session, saying with a chummy arm on the priest's shoulders that he had spoken 'in jest'. The other examiners had apparently agreed that Garnet was 'held for exemplar in those matters'.[25]

The Jesuit superior had long been accused of 'face' for carrying a gentlewoman up and down the country, but to his last breath he protested that Anne was a true virgin. John Gerard railed against the *animalis* instincts of worldly men, who 'measure others by their own desires'. He placed Anne in the tradition of 'so many good Marys' who had followed Christ and his Apostles in the first days of the Church. Anne's devotion, he wrote, was as a mark of 'true charity' not 'fond affection', a thing of beauty not censure. He was of course partisan, but surely right in this instance. 'What greater comfort can there be in this world,' Garnet had written to his sister Margaret upon her entry to a convent in 1593, 'than wholly to be severed from the love of the world, and to love Him only who is better than the whole world.' To Margaret again, he had written in the summer of 1605: 'Love faithfully and constantly Him, which must be your perpetual lover.' Anne, admittedly, was not 'a religious', that is to say, she did not forsake the world to enter a convent, but she privately vowed chastity and her lifestyle was deemed so pure that the priest John Wilson would make her the dedicatee of *The Treasure of Vowed Chastity in Secular Persons*.[26]

Anne and Garnet's intimacy can be overstated. When, in 1594, the two Jesuits, Robert Southwell and Henry Walpole, were both incarcerated, Garnet found himself 'destitute of companions', explaining that 'although I have very many friends, I cannot confide in them with the same freedom as I can Ours'.[27] It was, however, the Jesuits who set up a discreet enquiry into all the gossip surrounding Garnet and the Gunpowder Plot. Griffith Floyd claimed to have been sent from the Jesuit College of Brunsberg 'to understand the truth whether Garnet were privy to that treason any other way than in confession' and 'to remove as far as he might any hard opinion which might be

Christie's in March 2000, was catalogued as 'Lo. Gauge' after a misread inscription (Sale 8689, Lot 286). Incidentally, Grimshaw Hall in Warwickshire is less than five miles from Baddesley Clinton.

held against some of the Jesuits for that action'. Among other things, Floyd was specifically charged by 'old Father Abercromby' to discover if there had been 'such familiarity' between Garnet and Anne as had been reported. 'Upon inquiry,' he said, 'he found too much.' Floyd was an unreliable witness – he was shunned by the Jesuits in London, imprisoned by the Jesuits on the Continent and offered his services to His Majesty's government – but even the act of his dispatch 'at the motion of [Robert] Persons, but by the commandment of Aquaviva the General', is telling.[28]

The relationship between the Jesuit superior and his spinster hostess might not have been entirely appropriate after all then, but not in the sense usually implied. According to the instructions with which Campion and Persons inaugurated the Jesuit mission in England in 1580, familiar conversation with women (and boys) was to be avoided. The Jesuit-authored *Exercise of a Christian Life* (1579) advised priests 'never to be in their company alone'. It was one of the best – and least extreme – remedies against lasciviousness.* Conversations were to take place in open spaces or in the presence of chaperones. Penitents were warned against becoming 'too indiscreetly addicted' to 'their chosen confessors'. *The Treasure of Vowed Chastity* gave the same advice with the unquestionable logic that 'if there were no conference in private, there would hardly any dishonesty be ever committed'.[29]

'Syneisactism' – the practice of men and women working together chastely for God – had been common among the primitive Christians, but was viewed with suspicion by their heirs.[30] Anne's active charity – and that of Eleanor, who was usually omitted from the gossip, but nearly always lived with her sister – enabled Garnet and his brethren

* Another was self-mortification: 'This remedy did Saint Benet use, feeling some fire in his flesh through the thinking of a woman; who, stripping off his clothes, rolled himself stark naked upon thorns and weltered so long there till his body became all of a goare [*sic*] blood, and so vanquished his temptation.'

   The *Exercise* also recommended thoughts of death and cited a priest who had opened the coffin of a woman he had fancied and, finding the corpse 'rotten and stinking very filthily', dipped his handkerchief in the 'carrionly filth'. Thereafter, 'when either this or any other woman came to his mind, he presently took this cloth, and all to be-smothered his face withal, saying "Glut thy self, thou luxurious wretch, glut thyself with this filthy saviour of stinking flesh", and by this means was rid of this temptation.' (Loarte, *Exercise*, sigs 108–9)

to survive in the mission field. One can easily imagine situations in twenty years of close cooperation in which they might have had private conversation. One can also extrapolate from Anne's letters that, as a penitent, she was 'too indiscreetly addicted' to her 'ghostly Father'. To Garnet's nervous superiors in Rome, for whom even the idea of unenclosed nuns was radical, this would have been 'too much' familiarity.

★

Sometime before 11 March 1606, Anne went to the Tower of London to glimpse Garnet at his cell window. It had been carefully arranged through the mother of Garnet's keeper. 'You may see me, but not talk,' Garnet had written on 3 March.[31] Anne kept the appointment, but something was wrong. She knew the signs. Men were waiting. She walked away. They followed. 'Perceiving herself to be dogged', she made for Newgate prison, which was full of Catholics. It was a sensible strategy that put no one in jeopardy. She passed St Paul's and entered Newgate, 'but when they saw she intended to go no further, they presently stayed her'. It was 'with some rough usage', Gerard wrote, that she was carried back to the Tower.[32]

According to Luisa de Carvajal, the Spanish lady whom Garnet had invited to England in April, Anne was 'alone' in the Tower 'without a servant' and not allowed to speak to anyone 'except the jailers and judge'.[33] She was questioned on 11 March. Asked first about White Webbs, she said she kept the house 'at her own charge' with help from 'such as did sojourn with her'. Catesby, Thomas Wintour, Tresham 'and others' had visited 'divers times', but she could not remember 'the particular times and the particular names of all that came'. Since leaving the house at Bartholomewtide, 'she hath passed the greatest part of her time with divers of her friends in the country'. After the search of 'Mrs Habington's house at Hindlip' – always good to keep the master of the house out of it – she had travelled to London with her hostess and stayed the night in Fetter Lane. She had not stayed more than two or three nights in one place, 'but where those places are she will make no other answer than that it is needless'.

Anne refused to disclose the whereabouts of her servants, nor would she name anyone on the pilgrimage beyond Lady Digby. 'She will not say that Walley was there,' her examiners noted. She would not say much at all, they realised. She 'knew nothing of any prayer that was said' at Coughton and 'she understood nothing from the women at St Winifred's Well what should be done in the beginning of the Parliament for the good of the Catholics'. She did, however, admit that the 'fine horses' at the stables of Wintour and Grant had made her fretful. She had implored Garnet to talk to Catesby and 'hinder anything that possibly he might'. She had reasoned that 'if they should attempt any foolish thing, it would redound to his discredit'. Anne told her examiners that Garnet had reassured her that the horses were for the war in Flanders and that Catesby had shown her his letter of recommendation.

The notes of this session are endorsed: 'The examination of Anne Vaux the maid.'[34] A few days earlier, Garnet had confessed that 'some wives' on the pilgrimage had asked Anne 'where we would be till the brunt were past, that is till the beginning of the Parliament'. It was this conversation, he claimed, that had made him realise that 'all was resolved'.[35] Now confronted with Anne's denial, he said that he must have been mistaken. 'I thought the gentlewomen past all examinations,' he lamented privately, and Anne 'so free from danger' that it would have been safe to name her. He had hoped that she 'would have kept herself out of their fingers'. He did not, however, think she was 'taken for me, but for White Webbs', and he was sure that 'all will turn to the best for she shall save all her goods'.[36]

Garnet's confidence in Anne was not misplaced. According to the *Narrative* of Tesimond, she bore her imprisonment with 'admirable steadfastness and a courage truly virile'.[37] Luisa de Carvajal thought that Anne had triumphed against her examiners. The Spaniard's letter to her friend in Brussels, Magdalena de San Jerónimo, is so engaging, and so rarely cited, that it deserves a lengthy quotation. It is, however, very much the pro-Jesuit account:

Mistress Anne Vaux was quite entertaining with them when they took her confession. (They have the habit of saying that all Catholic women are ladies of ill repute, so I have heard, because they have priests and Fathers living in their homes, because, aside from their malice and hate against the faith, they are ill able to judge others in this matter.) And they said that Mistress Anne has lived in sin with Master Farmer, who is Father Garnet, and they said as much to her and she, even though she was imprisoned there in the Tower, laughed loudly two or three times (for she is really quite funny and very lively) and she said,

'You come to me with this child's play and impertinence? A sign that you have nothing of importance with which to charge me.'

And she laughed bravely at them, making a great joke of their behaviour in that business.

They asked her whether she had known about the Gunpowder Plot. She said, of course she had known, for since she was a woman, how could anything possibly happen in England without her being told of it? They asked her if Master Farmer knew about it. She said that since he was the greatest traitor in the world [*mayor traidor del mundo*], he hadn't missed getting involved in that treason; and that she was in great debt to them because she hadn't been able to find a single place in all of London to stay, even with money, and they had given her room and board for nothing.

To more weighty questions, she responded very sensibly and she pays no attention whatsoever to them, and so she has them amazed and they are saying,

'We absolutely do not know what to do with that woman!'[38]

The day after her examination, Anne, perhaps mindful that sarcasm was not the wisest form of defence, made a statement:

I am most sore to hear that Father Garnet should be any ways privy to this most wicked action as himself ever called it, for that he made to me many great protestations to the contrary diverse times since.
Anne Vaux.[39]

Twelve days later, on 24 March, Anne was questioned again, almost entirely about Francis Tresham. On his deathbed in the Tower, Tresham had tried to exonerate Garnet from the 1602 'Spanish treason' by claiming that he had 'not seen him in sixteen years before'. His amanuensis, William Vavasour, wrote that Tresham had meant 'at that time', nor 'in fifteen or sixteen years before'.[40] Either way, Tresham had lied. He had seen Garnet at that time and the previous year, around the time of the Essex rebellion (February 1601). Garnet confessed as much in the Tower on 22 and 23 March, adding that

Tresham, Catesby and Wintour had 'dealt with me about the sending into Spain'.[41]

In her second examination, Anne divulged several other occasions when her 'cousin germane removed' had come to see her and Garnet. There had been the two or three visits by Tresham to White Webbs after the accession of the King, 'sometimes in the company of Mr Catesby'. There had been an afternoon chat with Garnet at a house in Wandsworth in the first year of James's reign. There had been a dinner at Erith 'between Easter and Whitsuntide last', when 'Catesby came hither likewise'. Tresham had also visited 'another house they had' in the summer and 'had some conference with Mr Garnet, where likewise he exhorted him to all patience'.

Anne must have wondered why her examiners were so particularly interested in her late cousin. She insisted that Garnet 'always' gave Tresham good advice 'and persuaded him to rest contented'. Her statement was shown to Garnet, who wrote on it: 'I do acknowledge these meetings & repair of Mr Tresham to be true.' Anne subsequently remembered paying her respects at Rushton Hall just after the death of Sir Thomas Tresham in September 1605. 'I also do well remember this above now, which I did not think of before,' wrote Garnet, who had claimed two days earlier that the last meeting with Tresham had been 'at Fremlands about July'.[42]

Anne had also given up Erith, the house that Garnet had lied to protect, but nothing else was revelatory. Garnet himself had already admitted that Catesby was 'seldom long from us, for the great affection he bore the gentlewoman with whom I lived'.[43] Anne's kinship ties were unspectacular. The whole point of her second examination, as Coke freely admitted to Salisbury, was 'the damnable execration of Tresham'.[44] At Garnet's trial four days later, Tresham's declaration that he had not seen Garnet 'in fifteen or sixteen years before' 1602 was twisted to appear to suggest that he had not seen Garnet in sixteen years before 1605. 'Yet Garnet,' Coke announced with a flourish,

and Mrs Anne Vaux (though otherwise a very obstinate woman) confessed that Tresham within these three years had been several times at their houses at White Webbs and Mrs Vaux confessed that he had been twice there this very last year, and had received very good counsel from him.

So 'what,' Coke asked, 'shall we think of this man?'[45]

Garnet floundered: 'It may be, my Lord, he meant to equivocate.' This spurred Coke in his denunciation of the Jesuits' deceitful doctrine, which was 'a kind of unchastity' as it perverted the marriage of heart and tongue. Tresham's death with a lie on his lips had proved that he and Garnet were 'stained with their own works and went a whoring with their own inventions'. Coke knew that Garnet had 'seen and allowed' the treatise of equivocation that he had discovered in December 'in a chamber in the Inner Temple wherein Sir Thomas Tresham used to lie'.[46] One wonders what the prosecutor would have made of the knowledge that Garnet had actually written it. Even so, he declared the Jesuit superior a 'doctor of dissimulation', as well as of 'deposing of princes, disposing of kingdoms, daunting and deterring of subjects, and destruction'. According to the indictment, Garnet was the author of a plot 'so inhuman, so barbarous, so damnable, so detestable as the like was never read nor heard of, or ever entered into the heart of the most wicked man to imagine'.

The plump clergyman with a bald patch and spectacles (if Anne ever found him a suitable pair) did not look much like an arch-villain (nor, for that matter, a Lothario), but, as Salisbury had briefed before the trial, it was 'the cause, not the person' that mattered. The 'poor seduced priest', who had surrendered his Englishman's heart and cleaved to 'an unnatural and unjust supremacy', symbolised the corruption of Rome. Indeed, he had become 'the little Pope of this kingdom'. His life had no intrinsic value,

> but seeing the law of nature and of nations teacheth all kings to prevent destruction practised under the mantle of religion, it is expedient to make it manifest to the world how far these men's doctrinal practice toucheth into the bowels of treason. Further and so forever after stop the mouths of their calumniation that preach and print our laws to be executed for difference in point of conscience.[47]

It was the point that Salisbury's father, Lord Burghley, had made in *The Execution of Justice* after the death of Edmund Campion.

The prosecution had Garnet conspiring against the State since his return to England in 1586, 'which very act was a treason'. Garnet had more than justified the need for the 1585 statute against seminary priests. The Gunpowder Plot was a manifestation of the evil that lurked under the cloak of religion, just as the Armada had been, and the Babington Plot, the Northern rising and the 1570 bull of excommunication against Queen Elizabeth (issued when Garnet was just fourteen). 'Before the bull of Impious Pius Quintus,' Coke announced, 'there were no recusants in England . . . but thereupon presently they refused to assemble in our churches.' Recusancy was grounded upon a 'disloyal cause'; it was 'a very dangerous and disloyal thing'. Garnet may have been the man at the bar, but his faith, his Society and his 'Jesuited Catholic' followers were all on trial.

Salisbury insisted that the court was impartial and that Garnet could draw on his own testimony and that of his friends for defence. 'This gentlewoman,' he added, 'that seems to speak for you in her confessions, I think would sacrifice herself for you to do you good, and you likewise for her.' Salisbury may have been right, but Anne's statement was only cited to expose Tresham's falsehood.

The trial at the Guildhall on Friday, 28 March 1606, lasted all day, from nine thirty in the morning to around six in the evening. The charge was that Garnet had conspired with Catesby and Tesimond on 9 June 1605 to kill the King and his heir, to stir sedition and slaughter throughout the kingdom, to subvert 'the true religion of God' and to overthrow the whole state of the commonwealth. It took the jury less than fifteen minutes to find him guilty. He was sentenced to be hanged, drawn and quartered.

26

Yours Forever

'I never allowed it,' Garnet protested to Anne a week after his trial, 'I sought to hinder it more than men can imagine, as the Pope will tell. It was not my part (as I thought) to disclose it.' Garnet had heard that five hundred Catholics had turned Protestant in the wake of the trial. Many were 'scandalized' by his acquaintance with the plot, 'but who,' he asked, 'can hinder but he must know things sometimes which he would not?' Other co-religionists deemed Garnet a coward for having given up too much information.[1] He begged them to consider what they would have done if they had been examined upwards of twenty-three times 'upon so many evidences'. He had hurt nobody, he informed his 'very loving & most dear sister' Anne, and 'howsoever I shall die a thief, yet you may assure yourself your innocency is such that I doubt not but if you die by reason of your imprisonment, you shall die a martyr'.

Garnet was concerned about Anne's health – her 'weakness' – and he hoped that if she did survive prison and escape abroad, she would not cloister herself in a convent. He also advised that St Omer was not as 'wholesome' as Brussels, but he thought it 'absolutely the best' if Anne could stay in England and 'enjoy the use of sacraments in such sort as heretofore'. He wished that she and Eleanor could live 'as before, in a house of common repair of the Society or where the superior of the mission shall ordinarily remain'. Again, he reminded Anne of the Rules: 'you must know that none of the Society can accept a vow of obedience of any, but any one may vow as he will & then one of the Society may direct accordingly.' She could 'do the like' with her vow of poverty, 'but this I would have you know, that all that which is out for annuities I always meant to be yours, hoping that after your death you will leave what you can well spare to the mission'.

Garnet entrusted Anne with his instructions for the Jesuits: Richard
Blount was to look after missionary business – the collections, distri-
butions and communications – while three priests were authorised to
take Jesuit confessions and the vow renewals 'until a superior be made'.
Garnet wanted his debts honoured, even the £4 2s that he owed,
'though not in rigour', to Thomas Wintour. This should be paid to
the late plotter's sister. 'As for the goods at your house', he was confident that anything on show would be left alone. 'I gave order that the
books should be taken away, neither was there any place fit to hide
them, but if they or anything else be found in holes, you must challenge them as yours as indeed they are. Otherwise let all things lie
that are hidden.'

Garnet wrote his final two sentences in Latin:

Tempus est ut incipiat judicium a domo Dei.
Vale mihi semper dilectissima in Xto et ora pro me.[2]

The first was a scriptural quotation:

The time is come that judgment should begin at the house of God.

(1 Peter 4:17)

The second was his farewell to Anne:

Goodbye my ever dearest in Christ and pray for me.

It was not, in fact, Garnet's last letter to Anne. Nor is it likely that
she read it. The Lieutenant of the Tower forwarded it to Salisbury
the following day recommending that it remain secret. He also
proposed that 'if good search be made at the house at Erith, his books
will be found there'.[3]

The last letter came on 21 April, Easter Monday (Plate 37). In the
interim, Garnet had been examined several more times and had been
told many things: that he might be spared death; that Tesimond had
been captured and had disclaimed their walking confession; that
Richard Fulwood and another servant had been taken with a letter
and a cipher; that Edward Oldcorne was dead. Only the last statement
was true. The Jesuit was executed on 7 April at Red Hill, near

Worcester, alongside his servant, Ralph, who had hidden in the hole at Hindlip with Nicholas Owen. 'It pleaseth God daily to multiply my crosses,' Garnet lamented to Anne, 'I beseech Him give me patience & perseverance *usque in finem.*' He catalogued his hellish year:

I was after a week's hiding taken in a friend's house. Here, our confessions & secret conferences were heard & my letters taken by some indiscretion abroad. Then the taking of yourself. After, my arraignment. Then the taking of Mr Greenwell [Tesimond]. Then the slander of us both abroad. Then the ransacking anew of Erith & the other house. Then the execution of Mr Hall [Oldcorne] & now, last of all, the apprehension of Richard & Robert with a cipher, I know not of whose, laid to my charge & that which was a singular oversight, a letter written in cipher together with the cipher, which letter may bring many into question. *Sufferentiam Job audistis et finem Domini vidistis, quoniam misericors Dominus est et miserator.*

Sit nomen Domini benedictum. 21 April.

Yours *in aeternum**

as I hope, H.G.[4]

There was almost half a page left, so Garnet, perhaps mindful that forged words could be added, filled it with an oversized Jesuit seal: the monogram IHS surmounted by a cross and encircled by the sun. Below, three nails pierce a heart with words from the psalm (72:26): '*Deus cordis mei: et pars mea Deus in aeternum* – God of my heart and God that is my portion forever.'

*

Henry Garnet was executed in St Paul's churchyard on Saturday, 3 May 1606. Easter week had been deemed too holy and May Day, the traditional day of misrule, too riotous. 'Will you make a May game of me?' he had asked. The 3rd of May – the feast of the Invention of the Holy Cross – seemed more apposite to him. It also suited John

---

* 'You have heard of the patience of Job, and you have seen the end of the Lord, that the Lord is merciful and compassionate (James 5:11).

Blessed be the name of the Lord.

Yours forever.'

Gerard, who quietly sailed away from England, assisted, he claimed, by Garnet's ascending spirit.[5]

'Dressed in a poor black habit and clothes reaching down to his feet', Garnet was taken from his cell and led through the courtyard towards the hurdle and horses that would take him along Cheapside to St Paul's. According to some Catholic reports, Anne rushed down from her cell to see him. Before either could speak, the Lieutenant of the Tower, who had only given permission for Anne to watch from her window, 'fell into a great rage, reviling the keeper with many oaths'. The man protested that he was only following orders, which sent the Lieutenant into a 'greater passion'. He demanded that Anne be taken away, 'which was suddenly done, the gentlewoman seeming much amazed at her so unexpected bringing down & so hasty returning'.[6]

At the scaffold, beyond the 'great fire prepared for the burning of his bowels', Garnet's supporters saw the face of a saint-in-the-making. According to a manuscript account that was preserved for years by friends of the Vauxes in Northamptonshire, he appeared 'very modest and grave, yet cheerful & somewhat smiling'. Luisa de Carvajal wrote of his 'peaceful and composed demeanour'.[7] Conversely, Garnet's critics saw a nervous, shifty man casting about for a last-minute reprieve.[8] Many dwelt on his association with equivocation. Although 'he will equivocate at the gallows', Dudley Carleton quipped, 'he will be hanged without equivocation'.[9]

When Garnet spoke, he repeated his defence, denounced the plot and defended Anne's honour:

> I understand since my arraignment that it is reported I am married. On my troth, as I hope to be saved, the honourable gentlewoman (so slandered) is as pure a virgin for any thing I know, as she was the first day of her birth & so I desire you all to think of her.[10]

John More, writing three days later, thought Garnet had 'served himself with his accustomed equivocations'. He did cede, however, that the Jesuit ended his life 'in a reasonable constant manner'.[11]

Stripped to his shirt (which he had sewn at the sides so 'the wind might not blow it up'), Garnet kissed the ladder and climbed. He begged that 'Catholics in general might not face the worst for his sake' and 'he admonished them all to keep their hands out of treason'. He said his prayers, crossed his arms to his breast, told the hangman he was ready 'and so was put off, commending his soul to God'.[12]

Accounts differ as to whether he 'had favour to hang till he was dead' or had his feet pulled by well-wishers.[13] Either way, he was spared the spectacle of his own evisceration.

*

Anne was kept alone in the Tower for three more months. 'She is in good health,' reported Luisa de Carvajal, 'and from what they tell me, happy.' On 7 June 1606, Eleanor's son, William, was buried at Great Ashby in Leicestershire. 'It was a shame,' wrote Luisa, 'for he was a very devout and honourable person.' The cause of death is unknown. 'His wife was very young and their children very small.'

Towards the end of August, Anne was released into plague-stricken London. Although 'on the customary bail', Luisa noted that she 'goes wherever she wants'.[14] She soon joined Luisa, John Gerard and others in the campaign to prove Garnet's martyrdom, saintliness and, thus, his innocence. There were stories about his crossed arms, locked in position even as he hung, and his parboiled head that 'never waxed black'.[15] But the tale that caught the imagination of London, and of Europe, was that of 'Garnet's Straw'.

A husk or ear of corn 'bedewed' with Garnet's blood had apparently jumped out of the straw-lined basket into which his severed limbs were thrown, and into the hands of a 'silkman' called John Wilkinson. (Some accounts, probably more truthfully, have Wilkinson plucking it from the basket.) He had been entreated by one Mrs Griffin of Drury Lane to obtain a memento of Garnet's 'passion'. The straw may not have seemed like much compared to the shirt bagged by 'a person of great account', or the 'modicum of the said Father's flesh' that Wilkinson 'fain would have snatched', but Mrs Griffin declared herself delighted with her 'jewel' and placed it in a crystal reliquary.[16]

Soon afterwards, the bloodstain reportedly transmogrified into 'a perfect face, as if it had been painted'. It even had a 'little reddish blemish' on the forehead, said to be the wound that Garnet received when he was thrown down from the gallows. The Griffins were discreet with their relic and only showed it to a few people, but as soon as Anne heard about it, she rushed to Drury Lane and instantly declared it a miracle. She begged to borrow it for a couple of days, took it to Clerkenwell and put it on display. Hugh Griffin was 'much troubled' before he could get it back. Soon England was 'belittered with the news'.

Anne's enthusiastic promotion of the straw was too much for the Italian Jesuit historian, Daniello Bartoli, who wrote later in the century that she was 'not infrequently excessive in her ardour'. He also noted her great devotion to Garnet. 'Spontaneous beatification by popular acclamation'[17] would not do in Rome, but it had been going on in England throughout the missionary period and Anne had learned from the master. Apparently she had only needed to look at the straw to recognise it as Garnet. Luisa had been less sure, but had shown great willing: 'At first glance it cannot be seen that well, but it can be seen clearly and distinctly after studying it and even better with a candle in my view.' The Earl of Suffolk thought it 'a marvel', but 'it did not look like the father'. Luisa reasoned that 'this is what he must have looked like after his death, because it is no doubt true what some say that if they are looking for whom it resembles, they will find no one in a thousand whom it looks like as much as the father.'

In public, the Spanish ambassador, Zúñiga, played the straw down, informing Salisbury that while he had seen it out of curiosity, 'I have never been such an enemy to my money as to give it for straws.' Privately, he kept it safe and smuggled a print out for his wife to circulate. One wonders if he also had a hand in the straw's journey towards Liège, where it was preserved by the English Jesuits there before disappearing around the time of the French Revolution.

However 'imposterous', 'feigned' or 'ridiculous' the straw appeared to the English ambassadors in Brussels and Madrid, it had to be confronted as reproductions were flooding the European markets. The Protestants put out their own versions, one with two faces as befitted the arch-equivocator. If it was true, John Gee later wrote, that the very sight of the straw had made five hundred converts, 'every thresher in England should become a Romanist because they deal with straws, which have as perfect an effigy of F. Garnet as any other straw without equivocation ever yet had'. Robert Pricket, who wrote a verse pamphlet lampooning 'the Jesuits' miracles', made the easy gag that 'such patched-up wonders' were 'not worth a straw'.

Arguably Anne and her friends had done their job. Whether the straw appalled, amused, edified, or even evangelised, it got people talking, just as the exorcisms of the mid-1580s had done. On the Continent, the *Spica Jesuitica* became a symbol of Counter-Reformation piety and English Catholic fortitude. The canonisation of Anne's confessor was not, however, forthcoming and the furore did not last. By the autumn of 1607, popular interest in the straw had waned along with that in another purported wonder, a little boy who healed people by making the sign of the cross. 'They never mention the child of the miracles now,' Luisa reported from London on 24 September 1607, 'nor is there any discussion of the straw. All the talk is of Spain breaking the peace and sending an armada against England.'[18] The plague was flaring up again too: 'One hundred and seventy-seven have died this week, which is fifty more than last week. It is a strange outbreak this one, which never seems to let up.'

Epilogue

A man walks into a bar.
> 'Are not you a Catholic?' asks a punter.
'Yes, marry am I,' he replies.
> 'Then y'are a knave.'
'I am no Catholic.'
> 'Why, then, y'are a scurvy, lying knave.'
> > The Jestbook of Sir Nicholas
> > le Strange (1603–1655)[1]

Anti-Catholicism remained, like the plague, a constant of English life, but the violent backlash that had been feared did not materialise and James I's preference for accommodation over persecution eventually prevailed. The recusancy laws, while still in place, were often relaxed depending on what else was going on within and without the realm. James's leniency was only relative, however. As the fourth Lord Vaux heard him explain to Parliament in 1624, the Catholic horse might sometimes have a slackened bridle, but the royal hands would never come off the reins.[2] Prominent recusants were not trusted, their reputations indelibly stained by the actions of those few 'wild heads' at the dawn of the seventeenth century. Those who refused to take a new oath of allegiance, which rejected the Pope's 'impious and heretical' power to depose kings, were deemed political malcontents and liable to loss of property and life imprisonment.

Anne Vaux continued to dedicate herself to the mission. After a period of readjustment – she was apparently 'much discontented' at not getting Richard Holtby as her new confessor – she soon resumed her work.[3] In the summer of 1607, at a house two miles from London, she took in a Jesuit who had recently come over from Austria. William

Wright *alias* Mr German had been abroad for so long that he no longer spoke good English. On the morning of Friday, 3 July, men began to circle the house. Wright fled to friends in the city. 'A little later, Mistress Anne arrived and, after her, the pursuivants.' Everyone was arrested, Wright was thrown into the Tower and Anne was freed on bail. Four days later, her house was 'minutely' searched. Wright was questioned by the Archbishop of Canterbury and denied, truthfully, that he was the new Jesuit superior. He was transferred to the plague-infested White Lion prison in Southwark. Two months later, he broke out, escaped to Leicestershire and, with the help of the Vaux sisters, sustained the Jesuit mission in the area for over thirty years.[4]

'Anna Vaux' and 'Helena Brooksby' kept house on the Brooksby estate at Shoby. They were sporadically cited for recusancy, but undeterred. Their priority was the young, 'the future tense of the Papists' as Parliament had put it. They founded a secret Catholic school. One pupil was Edward Thimelby, the sixth son of Eleanor's daughter Mary. He arrived as a baby in 1615 and left for the college of St Omer fourteen years later. He recalled his preparatory education under the tutelage of Father Wright and the continued care of his great aunt Anne after Eleanor's death around 1625.[5]

Not long afterwards, Anne transferred the school to Stanley Grange, 'a house standing alone in Appletree Hundred', near West Hallam in Derbyshire. It was searched in November 1625, when officials seemed more surprised by the amount of dormitories that Anne had crammed into 'that little house' than by the two interconnecting chapels prepared for Mass. Officials noted beds and furniture for 'forty or fifty persons at the least', but no action seems to have been taken and the school thrived for a decade until a former pupil gave it up. In 1635 a warrant was drawn up for the seizure of all the Jesuits, children, books, papers and 'massing stuff' at Stanley Grange. A tip-off ensured that no one and nothing was found. The school endured, but relocated. Anne, then in her seventies, seems to have stayed in the West Hallam area. In February 1637, she is mentioned in the local parish register as the mistress of a deceased servant, but there are no later references and her burial is not recorded.[6]

Anne's service to the English mission was acknowledged in two dedicatory epistles. In 1621 John Wilson, translator of *The Treasure of Vowed Chastity in Secular Persons*, praised her 'sincerity of heart and virtuous manner of life'. (He also recognised her 'two most worthy sisters' Eleanor and Eliza as exemplars of 'chaste widowhood'.) Six years earlier, Michael Walpole had presented his translation of the life of Ignatius Loyola to Anne, 'before all others', in recognition of her work with Loyola's children 'in our afflicted country'.[7] Perhaps the greatest tribute came during the reorganisation of the Jesuit mission in the 1620s. What had been known as the Leicester mission was turned into an official Jesuit 'Residence' covering Leicester, Derby, Rutland and parts of Nottingham. It was named the Residence of St Anne.[8]

Eliza Vaux continued to promote faith and family at Harrowden Hall. She was home again by September 1606 and soon struggling to stave off the fines and forfeitures associated with her recusancy. John Percy, S.J., took over from John Gerard, S.J. Catholics came for Mass and instruction as they had in the days before the plot.[9] Eliza's boys went abroad: Edward (who reached his majority in 1609) to travel in Italy, Henry to study at the English College in Rome and William first to St Omer, the Jesuit school that had been founded in 1593 and would relocate twice in the eighteenth century before finding a permanent home at Stonyhurst in Lancashire.[10] Of the girls, Mary had married Sir George Simeon in 1604, Katherine would stay at home until her marriage to Sir Henry Neville, later Lord Abergavenny, and Joyce would become a 'galloping girl' of Mary Ward's controversial new order of active, unenclosed nuns.

In the earliest hours of All Saints Day, 1611, upon a false report that John Gerard was back in the country, Harrowden Hall was attacked.[11] As its inhabitants slumbered, its walls were scaled and the locks were picked or otherwise smashed in. The chapel, which was prepared for the feast day, was desecrated. About one thousand pounds' worth of plate and jewels, including some diamonds, were seized. Eliza was stoic about the destruction of the walls, floors and ceilings. It was, she said, ever thus, but she was devastated by the loss of her garden. Her plants and fruit trees were uprooted and flung across the fields 'and they knocked down and flattened the charming shaded enclaves and summer houses which she had made there for her own enjoyment'. John Gerard had spent many happy hours in Eliza's garden.[12] Perhaps this was the pursuivants' revenge.

EPILOGUE 357

Although the man in charge, Gilbert Pickering of Titchmarsh (who also fancied himself as a witch-finder[13]), could not claim the wanted Jesuit, he bagged two others – John Percy and Nicholas Hart – as well as the mistress of the house herself. He entered London in triumph, his son John having been seriously injured by one of Eliza's servants. According to Luisa de Carvajal, Eliza had treated the wound herself 'with medicines that are often used in the houses here'. Gilbert Pickering was knighted on 10 November and wasted no time briefing the new Lady Pickering on the 'many hundreds' in London who had saluted him, and on the King's delight at his service in this 'religious and state cause of great consequence'.

Eliza, then about forty-six years old, was sent to the Fleet. She became quite ill and secured a transfer to a more salubrious house in Fleet Street. She had to pay prison fees for both places. The oath of allegiance was put to her, but she refused it, saying 'it was not something she understood'. Her perceived gender inferiority could not save her this time, nor her friends, not even a letter from Archduke Albert, the governor of the Spanish Netherlands, who was moved by Eliza's sister to beg King James 'to moderate the rigour of the laws' and have 'regard to her sex'. Eliza remained a prisoner. Edward, Lord Vaux, whose licence to travel had already expired, rushed back from Europe to see what he could do. He went straight to the Earl of Salisbury, who blamed Eliza for having chosen 'blood-soaked Jesuits' over a nice old Marian priest.

'Sir,' Edward replied, resisting the temptation to make the obvious point that Marian priests were practically extinct, 'my mother has been so great a Catholic for so long, and notoriously so throughout the whole kingdom, that I do not believe that you or anyone else in the land ever doubted that she would truly love and embrace all that is to be loved and esteemed in her religion.'

'You are very young,' Salisbury told the 23-year-old, 'look out for yourself.'

Soon afterwards Edward was presented with an ultimatum: take the oath or lose everything. In the five weeks that he was given to decide, he tied up his lands in a trust.[14] He refused the oath – or his offer to take a modified version was rejected – and he joined his mother in prison. Both were arraigned – Eliza on 19 February at the

Old Bailey,* Edward on 14 May at the King's Bench† – and sentenced to forfeiture of property and life imprisonment.

The case attracted a lot of interest at home and abroad. From the Low Countries, the latest Jesuit translation of Thomas a Kempis's *Imitation of Christ* was dedicated to Eliza in recognition of 'the public demonstration, which you have lately given of your true desire to follow the footsteps of our Lord'.[15] Edward received lectures and tracts. The King was reportedly 'in much anxiety on account of the Baron Vaux' and some peers felt that the social implications of his imprisonment ('a common insult to their grade') outweighed any potential political threat that he might have posed. Edward seemed rather to revel in his fate, writing that 'the consolation that I feel in my present state far exceeds anything that I have ever before experienced during the whole course of my life'. As Michael Questier has written, he even rivalled Viscount Montague in 'the suffering peer stakes', giving the Jesuits – Montague was the seculars' man – a 'quasi-martyr' of their own.[16]

The oath of allegiance divided the Catholic community rather as the issue of church conformity had done in Edward's grandfather's day.[17] Rome pronounced it unlawful, so for some, that was that. For others, including the imprisoned Archpriest Blackwell, the oath was acceptable, since it made no mention of royal supremacy. Blackwell was sacked, but some other priests and many of the laity took the oath and wondered why the hard-liners, and their tender consciences,

---

* Eliza argued that 'forasmuch as there was contained matter of learning, not yet discussed among the learned, about the Pope's power to depose princes, she being unlearned durst not with safe conscience take it. Yet if they pleased to take her oath of allegiance whereby she might free her integrity from disloyalty & secure, as she thought, the King from fear of her, she offered to swear fidelity to him notwithstanding any excommunication of the Pope granted against him. But when this would not suffice, she said if she had had money wherewith to have purchased her freedom, she should not have needed further to have been urged.' (AAW A XI, no. 34)

† 'The Lord Vaux made answer to the court that if any part of this oath did touch the conscience of his subjects, if it be the pleasure of the King to make a safe exposition of the oath, he would then take it accordingly.' Otherwise, 'he thought it better to swear from his heart his true allegiance to the King than to swear to a matter of the which he in his conscience hath some doubt, and that such an oath by him taken shall be for the greater safety of the King.' (Bulstrode, *Reports*, pp. 198–9)

had to make life quite so difficult for themselves. When, in June 1612, Eliza's keeper walked in on a Mass, he asked rather wearily: 'Has not your ladyship suffered enough already for this sort of thing?'[18]

The sentences were not perpetual. The Vauxes were allowed to keep their property, even the church plate that the Pickerings deigned to return. The enquiry into the family estate revealed an annual income of about £1,200, outgoings of £650 and more than £8,000 of debt.[19] The priests were exiled; both would return. Lord Vaux was transferred to the custody of the Dean of Westminster in October 1612 and slowly the controls on his movement (for example, he was only to meet with county gentry 'well affected in religion') were lightened. By the end of 1614 he was back at Harrowden on good-behaviour bonds. Eliza was released on 3 July 1613 'for eight months for recovery of her health' and thereafter sureties were entered for her too.

By 1616 she was living at Boughton, a manor on the Vaux estate (not to be confused with Boughton House, the Montagu seat near Kettering). There were tragedies (William's disgrace after a street killing in Madrid; Mary's death). There were triumphs (Edward's command of the English regiment serving under the Spanish banner in Flanders;* Joyce's appointment as mother superior of the 'English Ladies' in Perugia). And there were events that must have elicited mixed feelings. If Eliza allowed herself to feel the proud matriarch when Edward took his seat in the House of Lords on 19 February 1624, she was, presumably, the proud, bitter, recusant matriarch when, after just two more sittings, he had to withdraw for refusing the oath of allegiance. Edward did not attend James's Parliament again.[20]

The Vauxes also experienced the odd clash such as sometimes happened in counties like Northamptonshire where prominent recusants and Puritans lived side by side. On 31 October 1625, Richard Knightley of Fawsley, an outspoken Puritan, turned up at Boughton

---

*During the negotiations for a Spanish match for his son, James I permitted volunteer regiments to fight on both sides in the war between Catholic Spain and the Protestant United Provinces. On 8 April 1622, the Privy Council authorised Lord Vaux 'to pass the seas as Colonel to the voluntary soldiers licensed by His Majesty to go over to serve the King of Spain' (APC, 1621-3, p. 213). It did not end well. Vaux resigned his commission in July 1624 after his grant for reinforcements was revoked. By then, England and Spain were at war again.

with a posse of men and a mind to 'disarm' the house.[21] This was all above board, indeed 'according to his Majesty's pleasure'. Although recusants had to contribute to the local musters (the Vauxes always provided a fully armed and mounted soldier), they were not allowed to store weapons at home, a humiliation that was exacerbated by a 1619 directive that made them bear the cost of repairing weapons that had gone rusty in the hold of petty officialdom.[22]

Feelings ran high in 1625. Local Puritans resented Edward's martial swagger and he, having recently commanded thousands in Flanders field, baulked at the withdrawal of power and trust that came with the renewal of Anglo-Spanish hostilities. The real problems began when Knightley and his fellow deputy lieutenants, having found no 'martial munitions, arms and weapons' in the main house, moved on to the outhouses and farm. Edward's volatile younger brother, William (he of the Madrid murder), went with them. 'They could not be worse dealt withal,' he snarled, 'unless they should cut their throats', and 'with an oath' he wished 'it were come to that pass'. Knightley reproved William for his bad language and was repaid with further expletives.

Back at the house, Knightley effectively brought out the swearing box, citing the 1624 statute (21 Jac. I, c. 20), which prescribed a shilling an oath. The Vauxes refused to pay. Knightley ordered the constables to seize the equivalent value in goods. Edward warned him that 'if he found him in another place he would call him to a reckoning for this'.

'You know where I dwell,' said Knightley.

The officials made to leave. 'Now you have done your office you may be gone,' said Edward, shoving Knightley out of the hall. Knightley insisted he would only go when he was ready. Edward exploded, 'gave him a good blow on the face' and, in the ensuing fracas, struck down one of Knightley's servants with a cudgel. The sight of blood sent the officials packing, but they soon filed a report insisting that the Vauxes be held to account, lest 'dangerous encouragement' be given 'to such as we find are too daring and insolent already'.

The case went before the King (Charles I) in Council and not even Edward's 'prepared friends' could prevent an order to proceed to trial. As Edward left the room, he offloaded 'very intemperate words' on one of Knightley's witnesses and was promptly sent, with William, to the Fleet. The brothers endured the briefest, if frostiest, of prison spells and the following February, in order to gain the privilege of Parliament and have the case dropped, Edward swallowed the oath of allegiance. Knightley was made sheriff, which was not at all to his liking as it prevented him from promoting Puritan interests in the House of Commons. He returned to the county in a sulk and spent Boxing Day thinking up ways of flushing out every 'little papist' in the shire.

Eliza died not long afterwards. Her passing went unrecorded, her grave is unmarked. The last extant reference to her is a bequest from Lady Fermor, whose will was drawn up in August 1625, signed in April 1627 and proved two years later. She left Eliza a pair of narrow silver boxes engraved with elephant heads. One was for her treacle, the other for 'metridate' – both valued for their medicinal properties.* It conjures a rather touching last scene: Eliza, relaxed at home, comparing household remedies with her friend.[23]

Charles I might have wished that he had let the Catholics keep a few more weapons, for in the Civil War many would raise them under his standard. Edward, fourth Lord Vaux, was 'beyond sea' for much of the time and played no great part in those great events, though Charles would bowl on his green while a prisoner in Northamptonshire in 1647. The Parliamentarians registered Vaux a papist (though not a 'delinquent' Royalist) and sequestered his estate.[24] It was restored with the Stuart monarchy and Edward died the following year, on 8 September 1661, five years before the Great Fire of London, an accident that was, like 'every evil that occurs', blamed on the Catholics.[25]

Edward had only been seventeen at the time of the Gunpowder Plot, but it affected him deeply. He had been on the cusp of marrying the nineteen-year-old Elizabeth Howard, but her father, the Lord Chamberlain who investigated and tried the conspirators, took fright and married her off to a Puritan widower three times her age.[26] William

* 'Auicen sayeth: There be certain medicines . . . which will not suffer poison to approach near the heart, as treacle and metridate' (*Regimen Sanitatis Salerni*, 1541). 'Take a great onion, make a hole in the middle of him, then fill the place with mitridat or treacle, and some leaves of rue.' (*Defensative against Plague*, 1593 – *OED Online*)

Knollys, who later became Earl of Banbury, may have been more Malvolio than eminence those days (he was known as 'parti-beard' for his not entirely successful attempt to dye his beard[27]), but he was good to his young bride and tolerated both her Catholicism and her open affair with Edward Vaux.[28] He stood by 'my Bessy' when, on 10 April 1627, she gave birth to a boy, Edward, who was almost certainly named after his father.[29] Four years later, he visited his wife at Harrowden Hall after she was delivered of another baby, Nicholas, who had a Catholic baptism and was nursed for fifteen months at the Vaux seat. On 25 May 1632, at the age of eighty-seven, William Knollys, Earl of Banbury, died. Within six weeks, Edward and Elizabeth had legitimised their relationship.[30] It had taken them twenty-seven years.

The star-crossed lovers were admired for their recusancy, but the Catholic Church could hardly condone the fornication of the one and the adultery of the other. Even after their marriage, Edward was known in more hostile priestly circles as the man 'who kept another man's wife so publicly even to the scandal of our religion'.[31] Another painful consequence of the affair was the status of their surviving son, Nicholas. Elizabeth would argue just before her death in 1658 that 'my son [is] as worthy, though a mother see it, as any of his age to honour that title that descent has bequeathed him'.[32] But Nicholas's doubtful paternity meant that he was never regarded wholly as a Knollys or a Vaux. After the murder of his brother 'in a quarrel' on the road between Calais and Gravelines in 1645 (no details survive[33]), Nicholas was styled third Earl of Banbury and, in June 1660, sat in the House of Lords. His legitimacy was questioned, however, and he was not summoned back. Lord Vaux had not helped in this respect, having settled his estate in October 1646 on 'the Right Honourable Nicholas, now Earl of Banbury, son of the said Countess of Banbury, heretofore called Nicholas Vaux'.[34]

Nicholas made various efforts to regain his seat. In 1665, he accosted the Duke of York in his carriage and pulled his leg 'so hard that he had almost drawn off his shoe', but he was never readmitted to the Lords.[35] His son, Charles (1662–1740), who sold Harrowden Hall in 1694, was also disappointed and another attempt in the early nineteenth century led to a judgment that the heirs of Nicholas were 'not entitled' to the Earldom of Banbury. It was an important ruling and, for some, a 'gross and palpable injustice', since before Nicholas's exclusion, the law had presumed that the father of a child born in wedlock was the mother's husband, irrespective of adultery. Unless there was proof of divorce, impotence or absence from the realm at the time of conception, the law had hitherto cleaved to the proverb 'my cow, my calf'.[36]

Nicholas could not, of course, inherit the Vaux title either, though he received the bulk of the estate in 1646. In his will of 25 April 1661, Edward styled the son he could not claim 'the Earl of Banbury' and left him a token ten pounds to pay for mourning clothes.[37] Upon Edward's death on 8 September 1661, the title passed to his surviving brother, Henry, who lived a quiet single life in Suffolk and died with no heirs on 20 September 1663.[38] The barony fell into abeyance for 175 years.

During that period, 'test acts' were passed making the reception of Anglican communion and the abjuration of key Catholic tenets (including transubstantiation) a precondition of public employment. Catholics endured the Popish Plot of Titus Oates, the Exclusion Crisis and the 'Glorious' Revolution of 1688–9 when the Catholic King, James II, was overthrown by his Dutch Protestant son-in-law. They were made to pay double land tax and were barred from buying or inheriting property. They witnessed the raising of those august pillars of the British constitution: the Bill of Rights (1689) and the Act of Settlement (1701), both steeped in anti-popery. But they also sailed into the calmer waters of the 'long eighteenth century', where sensibilities shifted, priorities changed and, gradually, restrictions were lifted until, in 1829, they found a haven of sorts in the Catholic Relief Act. The issue of emancipation may have been forced upon a reluctant Parliament by the vigorous campaign of the Irish lawyer, Daniel O'Connell, but its acceptance was a sign of the times. When, in 1834, the Palace of Westminster was destroyed by accidental fire, Catholics were not automatically blamed as they had been in 1666.

By 12 March 1838, when the Vaux barony was revived in favour of the descendants of Eliza's eldest daughter, Mary, Catholics could lawfully hear Mass and receive priests. They were entitled to join the army, work for the government, serve the court, practise law, teach, acquire land, sit in Parliament and vote. They were no longer fined for not going to church. They were no longer recusants, even if they were still frequently denounced as papists, or worse, and even if a Catholic could not (and still cannot) inherit the throne.

When, in 1962, Peter Hubert Gordon (Fr Gabriel) Gilbey, ninth Baron Vaux of Harrowden, became the first Benedictine monk since 1559 to address the House of Lords, references to the past were light and congratulations hearty. 'I think historically,' the Bishop of London said in response to Vaux's maiden speech,

> it may be of some comfort to him to know that my predecessors in office were never able to exercise any authority over his predecessors in the Community of which he is now a member . . . We welcome in this House a voice, which, in a sense, has been silent for 400 years, and we hope that we shall hear more of that voice.[39]

There was, however, one discordant note: a letter, marked 'confidential', handed to Lord Vaux by an attendant. Scribbled in black ink on lined paper, the words have no greeting or signature:

> I am surprised you are thinking
> becoming a monk
> The RCs are practically heathen
> company
> The pope is only a figurehead in
> fact a very old man and a nonentity
> The previous pope died an agonizing
> death knowing the scheming that went
> on to start the last war
> Fancy a Gilbey becoming a monk
> My advice is please reconsider.[40]

Almost fifty years later, the first state visit of a Pope to the United Kingdom – that of Benedict XVI in September 2010 – was a happy and fruitful occasion. On 13 March 2013, his successor, Pope Francis, became the first Jesuit Bishop of Rome, something unthinkable in the early modern period when the controversial new order was tarred by 'black legend' propaganda. In 1679, Thomas Barlow, Bishop of Lincoln, described the Gunpowder Plot as

> a villainy so black and horrid (I do not say unchristian only, but) so inhumane and barbarous, as has no parallel in any age or nation (Jewish,

Pagan or Turkish), nor indeed could have before the invention of gunpowder and the unhappy institution of the Jesuitical Society by (a fanatical lame soldier) Ignatius Loyola. For before that time, the world had no instrument or means so pernicious as gunpowder and congruous for effecting such a mischief, nor any order of men so impious as to approve, design, and endeavour to execute a villainy so manifestly repugnant to the law of nature and scripture.[41]

One might wish for gunpowder to be the threat it once was. Torture, persecution, fundamentalism, fanaticism, martyrdom, the tangle of religion and politics: many issues are as live today as they were then. Combatants and weapons may change, but in its ambition for mass destruction, the powder conspiracy was a precursor for the callous and calculated plots of our own time. In the aftermath of its discovery, Robert Wintour told Guy Fawkes about a strange dream that haunted him: of a scarred city with steeples blown 'awry' and charred, disfigured faces.[42] Such images are now all too real.

Abbreviations

AAW	Westminster Diocesan Archives
APC	*Acts of the Privy Council of England*, ed. J. R. Dasent et al., 46 vols (1890–1964)
ABSI	Archivum Britannicum Societatis Iesu
ARSI	Archivum Romanum Societatis Iesu
BL	British Library
Bod	Bodleian Library
CP	Cecil Papers
CRS	Catholic Record Society
CSP	*Calendar of State Papers*
DEP	*A Declaration of Egregious Popish Impostures* by S. Harsnett (1603), in F. W. Brownlow, *Shakespeare, Harsnett, and the Devils of Denham* (1993)
ERL	English Recusant Literature 1558–1640, 394 vols selected and edited by D. M. Rogers (1968–79)
HMC	Historical Manuscripts Commission
LJ	*Journals of the House of Lords*
LRO	Leicestershire Record Office
NRO	Northamptonshire Record Office
NRS	Northamptonshire Record Society
ODNB	*Oxford Dictionary of National Biography*, ed. H. C. G. Matthew and B. Harrison, 60 vols (Oxford, 2004)
PRO	Public Record Office: the National Archives, Kew
RH	*Recusant History*
TP	'The Tresham Papers belonging to T. B. Clarke-Thornhill. Esq., of Rushton Hall, Northants', HMC 55: *Report on Manuscripts in Various Collections*, vol. III (1904)
Vaux Petitions	*A Collection of documents, printed and manuscript, relating to the petitions of G. Mostyn and E. B. Hartopp, claiming to be coheirs of the Barony of Vaux of Harrowden* (1836–8)

Notes

Introduction

1   The following account is taken from the two examinations of Anne Vaux, reported on 11 March and 24 March, and her 'declaration' of 12 March 1606 (PRO SP 14/216, nos 200, 201, 212). The official 'interrogatories' are not extant, but one can glean them from Anne's answers and from the letter of Luisa de Carvajal to Magdalena de San Jerónimo, 12 April 1606 (NS), in Rhodes, *This Tight Embrace*, pp. 237–9. I have also drawn on Garnet's several examinations and statements, the Proclamation of 15 January 1606, the orange-juice letters exchanged between Garnet and Anne, and various examinations of conspirators, suspects and servants taken in the aftermath of the discovery of the Gunpowder Plot. Full details and context can be found in Part Four. Quotations given here can be found at: CP, 110, f. 33v; 115, f. 15v; 193, no. 57; Larkin and Hughes, *Stuart Royal Proclamations*, p. 132.

2   BL Add. MS 39829, f. 10r. For Campion's praise of Eleanor, see Anstruther, *Vaux*, p. 101.

3   *A Tract on the Succession to the Crown* (1602), cited by Kilroy, *Edmund Campion*, p. 114.

4   Geoffrey Nuttall ('The English Martyrs') counted 189 English Catholic 'martyrs', but acknowledged the difficulty in defining martyrdom. Patrick McGrath (*Papists and Puritans*, pp. 177n, 255–6), Penry Williams (*Later Tudors*, p. 475) and Diarmaid MacCulloch (*Reformation*, p. 392) give the figure of 191 executions: 131 priests and 60 laypersons.

5   Margaret Ward, cited by Crawford, *Women and Religion*, p. 63.

6   Bod MS Eng. Th. B. 1, p. 3.

7   Bossy (*English Catholic Community*, ch. 8) defines a Catholic as one who habitually, though not necessarily regularly, used the services of a priest. The diocesan returns of 1603 recorded 8,590 recusants, though local influence, poor enforcement, 'riding up and down the country', etc.

meant that many escaped presentation for recusancy. Also see Miola, *Early Modern Catholicism*, pp. 26–9.

Prelude: *The Calm before Campion*

1   Simpson, *Campion*, p. 248.
2   BL Harl MS 859, f. 44r.
3   Edmund Campion to Henry Vaux, 28 July 1570, trans. Anstruther, in *Vaux*, pp. 100–2.
4   PRO C 81/863, no. 4673.
5   *Letters and Papers, Henry VIII*, I, i, 257(32), 357(45).
6   PRO E 36/215, f. 65r.
7   *Letters and Papers, Henry VIII*, IV, ii, 4040.
8   *Vaux Petitions*, p. 4. Dugdale, *Baronage* (1676), pp. 304–5. It is unlikely that he was the Thomas Vaulx who wrote to the Duke of Norfolk from Ampthill in April 1533 about the resistance of Catherine of Aragon and her household to her new status as Princess Dowager (BL Cotton MS Otho CX, f. 177). Unfortunately, the letter is not signed, but other references to this man never refer to 'Lord Vaux', only 'Thomas Vaux'. Anstruther (p. 41) suggests that this man was a member of the Vauxes of Odiham, Hampshire. See too: BL Cotton MS Otho CX, fols. 199r–205v; *State Papers, Henry VIII*, I, ii (1831), p. 394; *Letters and Papers, Henry VIII*, II, ii, p. 1548.
9   *LJ*, I, pp. 65–82 (esp. at pp. 75, 77, 81–2). S. E. Lehmberg, *The Reformation Parliament* (Cambridge, 1970), p. 199.
10 *Vaux Petitions*, p. 4; BL Harl MS 158, f. 143v; *LJ*, I, p. 297.
11 PRO SP 1/100, f. 92.
12 Rollins, *Tottel's Miscellany*, I, no. 212; II, pp. 283–6. Puttenham, *The Arte of English Poesie*, pp. 60, 62, 239–40. Puttenham confuses Thomas with his father, Nicholas.
13 Rollins, *The Paradise of Dainty Devices*, no. 89, lines 1–4.
14 Bowler, *Recusant Roll No. 2*, note 160 on p. xliv.
15 PRO SP 1/98, ff. 74–82.
16 Loarte, *The Exercise of a Christian Life*, p. 55.
17 Bod MS Eng. Th. B. 2, p. 159; Vaux, *Catechisme*, pp. 108–9.
18 T. More, *Treatise on the Passion*, Yale, *Complete Works*, vol. 13, p. 143.
19 In 1535 the chaplain was 'Mr Moote' (PRO SP 1/98, f. 75r).
20 Garnet, *The Societie of the Rosary*, pp. 149–50; Loarte, *The Exercise of a Christian Life*, pp. 90–1.
21 Vaux, *Catechisme*, p. 76.
22 PRO PROB 11/21/178.

23   Williams, 'Forbidden Sacred Spaces', pp. 111–12.
24   The authority on the subject is Eamon Duffy's *The Stripping of the Altars*, esp. ch. 13.
25   Fincham and Tyacke, 'Religious Change and the Laity in England', p. 43.
26   Anstruther, *Vaux*, pp. 60–1 and App. D.
27   Ingram, *Church Courts, Sex and Marriage*, ch. 3, esp. pp. 116 (for quotation) and p. 123 for the 'unspectacular orthodoxy' of the majority. See too Marsh, *Popular Religion*, ch. 2.
28   Duffy, *Fires of Faith*, *passim*; MacCulloch, *Reformation*, pp. 282–4.
29   Foxe, *Acts and Monuments* (1563 edn), bk 5, p. 1131.
30   Duffy, *Fires of Faith*, p. 87.
31   Foxe, *Acts and Monuments* (1570 edn), bk. 11, p. 1703.
32   Ibid. (1563 edn), bk 5, p. 1699. Subsequent editions depict a woodcut of the burning.
33   NRO WR 337; Anstruther, *Vaux*, p. 101.
34   NRO Parish Register, Irthlingborough, 1562.
35   BL Lans. MS 33, f. 64r. John Murray (*English Dramatic Companies*, vol. 2, 1910, pp. 97, 209, 291, 308) gives instances of the bears on tour in the reign of Elizabeth, and of Lord Vaux's players at the beginning of the seventeenth century. The *Letter-Book of Gabriel Harvey* (1884, p. 67) shows that the players were also active in the 1570s.
36   BL Add. MS 39828, f. 270v.
37   BL Lans. MS 991, f. 164r.
38   Strype, *Annals*, I, pt II, pp. 390–1; D'Ewes, *Journals*, p. 8.
39   Jones, *Faith by Statute*, p. 100.
40   For the Elizabethan Settlement as a 'frozen tableau of her brother's Church', see MacCulloch, 'Latitude', pp. 45–52.
41   Parker, 'Messianic Vision', pp. 181–2, 191.
42   Alford, *Burghley*, pp. 124–5.
43   Ibid., p. 155.
44   *CSP Rome, 1558–1571*, p. 266.
45   NRO WR 337; BL Lans. MS 15, ff. 181r, 186r.
46   Simpson, *Campion*, p. 226.
47   Kilroy, *Edmund Campion*, Transcription I (quotations at pp. 177, 193). Kilroy (p. 4 and Ch. 2) argues that 'the epic reveals Campion's secret intellectual journey to the Roman church'.
48   Vossen, *Two Bokes*, pp. 1–13 (quotations at pp. 3, 6, 13). See too McCoog, *The Reckoned Expense*, pp. xiv–xxii.
49   Vossen, *Two Bokes*, p. 8n.
50   Haynes, *State Papers*, pp. 579–88 (quotation at p. 579).
51   Longley, *Margaret Clitherow*, p. 35.

52 Rex, *Elizabeth*, pp. 9–10.

53 PRO SP 12/59, no. 22; Trimble, *Catholic Laity*, pp. 52–5; NRO Parish Register, Irthlingborough, 26 January 1569/70.

54 Miola, *Early Modern Catholicism*, pp. 486–8.

55 Alford, *Burghley*, p. 161.

56 Bod MS Eng. Th. B. 1, p. 477; *CSP Spanish* II, p. 254.

57 Taylor, *Tracts*, 15, pp. 18–19.

58 13 Eliz. c. 1–3.

59 Neale, *Elizabeth I and Her Parliaments*, pp. 213–14.

60 Ibid., p. 215.

61 Ibid., p. 216; La Mothe Fénélon, *Correspondance Diplomatique*, 1571–2 (1840), p. 106.

62 *LJ*, I, pp. 681–8.

63 Neale, *Elizabeth I and Her Parliaments*, p. 216.

64 Plowden, *Danger to Elizabeth*, p. 95.

65 NRO WR 337.

66 *CSP Rome, 1558–1571*, pp. 393–400. See too *Letters of Mary Stuart*, ed. W. Turnbull (1845), p. 206n; Williams, *Fourth Duke of Norfolk*, pp. 199–201.

67 Parker, 'Messianic Vision', p. 197n.

68 Cecil, *Salutem in Christo*, sig. A6v.

69 Parker, 'Messianic Vision', quotations at pp. 195, 197.

70 Ibid., pp. 215–16; Alford, *Burghley*, p. 168.

71 Guy, *My Heart is My Own*, pp. 467–8.

72 Frieda, *Catherine de Medici*, p. 271.

73 Plowden, *Danger to Elizabeth*, p. 106.

74 Parker, 'Messianic Vision', *passim*, but especially pp. 177, 185, 206–9. For the commemorative medal, also see Parker, *Grand Strategy*, p. 4 and Plates 2 and 3 on p. 5.

75 *CSP Rome, 1558–1571*, pp. 393, 394, 396, 400.

76 BL Lans. MS 15, ff. 181r, 186r.

77 *LJ*, I, p. 728. For Vaux's involvement in the county, see J. J. LaRocca, 'Vaux, William, third Baron Vaux', *ODNB*; *CSP Dom 1547–80*, pp. 343, 375; PRO SP 12/86, f. 135r; PRO KB 9/653, pt. II, ff. 106–7.

78 Neale, *Elizabeth I and Her Parliaments*, p. 347.

79 Wiburn, *A checke or reproofe of M. Howlets untimely shreeching in her Maiesties eares* (1581), f. 15v; Collinson, *The Elizabethan Puritan Movement*, p. 27. For the Puritan movement in Northamptonshire, see Sheils.

80 BL Add. MS 39828, f. 59r; *APC*, XI, pp. 179–80, 207; PRO SP 12/86, f. 135r; HMC Buccleuch, 3, p. 18.

81 Folger MS Bd.w. STC 22957. f. 86.

82 PRO STAC 7/4/26; Anstruther, *Vaux*, pp. 87–90.

83 *APC*, XXII, p. 546.

84   S. Lipscomb, *1536: The Year That Changed Henry VIII* (Oxford, 2009), pp. 62–3; K. Thomas, 'Age and Authority in Early Modern England', *Proceedings of the British Academy*, 62 (1976), pp. 207–8.

85   Marsh, *Popular Religion*, p. 35.

86   Loarte, *The Exercise of a Christian Life*, p. 34.

87   BL Add. MS 39828, f. 169r.

PART ONE: WILLIAM AND HENRY

1 *The Enterprise is Begun*

1   Simpson, *Campion*, p. 228.

2   Cross, 'Letters of Sir Francis Hastings', Introduction and pp. 3, 19, 23.

3   Caraman, *Garnet*, p. 200.

4   Cross, 'Letters of Sir Francis Hastings', pp. 6–7, 19.

5   Caraman, *Garnet*, p. 201; PRO SP 14/19, f. 136.

6   Anstruther, *Vaux*, p. 101.

7   Ibid., p. 100; Folger MS Bd.w. STC 22957, ff. 78v–79v, 83v–86r.

8   Gerard, *Autobiography*, p. 195.

9   Alexandra Walsham's *Church Papists* (1993) is the authority on this subject and any material not referenced below can be found there, especially at pp. 73–96. For Throckmorton's complaint, see Wake, *Brudenells*, p. 117n. For Sheldon's chapel: Williams, 'Forbidden Sacred Spaces', p. 98. For Mallory: PRO SP 12/190, f. 130v. For the articles against the parishioners of Preston: Peel, *Seconde Parte of a Register*, I, p. 295. For links between the Flamsteads and the Vauxes and Treshams: TP, p. 47; NRO V 385: Harpole deeds; PRO C2/Eliz./U2/12; PRO WARD 3/17part1. For William Flamstead and John Shakespeare: Hodgetts, 'Certificate', II, pp. 13–14. For John Finche's attempted suicide: *CSP Dom 1581–90*, p. 131.

10   *Recusancy and Conformity*, ed. Crosignani et al., p. 23. Also, pp. 262–84 for the views of Henry Garnet, S.J., who would later advise the Vauxes. This is an invaluable collection of documents with an excellent introduction.

11   Haigh, *Plain Man's Pathways*, p. 197.

12   Miola, *Early Modern Catholicism*, p. 488.

13   Cross, 'Letters of Sir Francis Hastings', p. 23.

14   NRO WR 337.

15   Devlin, *Southwell*, pp. 18–21; *A discoverie of the treasons*, sig. Aiiir.

16   Loarte, trans. Sancer [Brinkley], *The Exercise of a Christian Life*, sigs **iir, v

17   Southwell, *Short Rule*, sig. a7v.

18   Brown, 'Robert Southwell', p. 193.

19   Persons, 'Memoirs', pp. 200–1; Persons, 'Life and Martyrdom', 12, pp. 28–9; Foley, *Records*, III, pp. 626–8; Simpson, *Campion*, pp. 141–2, 222–3, 292–3, 296–9.

20   Gerard, *Autobiography*, p. xxiv.

21   Ditchfield, 'The Jesuits', pp. 54–6.

22   McCoog, *The Society of Jesus*, p. 141.

23   Simpson, *Campion*, pp. 141–2; McCoog, 'French Match', p. 200n.

24   See McCoog, 'French Match', and Lake and Questier, 'Campion in Context'.

25   McCoog, 'Playing the Champion', p. 125; Simpson, *Campion*, pp. 139–40.

26   Reynolds, *Campion and Parsons*, p. 177.

27   Ibid., p. 127; Simpson, *Campion*, p. 175.

28   Simpson, *Campion*, pp. 174–5.

29   Ibid., p. 247.

30   Reynolds, *Campion and Parsons*, pp. 73–4.

31   For the way in which Persons and Campion used recusancy as 'a wedge issue' to prise apart the government's rendition of the religion/politics divide, see Lake and Questier, 'Puritans, Papists, and the "Public Sphere" in Early Modern England: The Edmund Campion Affair in Context', pp. 608–12. I am indebted to the insights in this article.

32   Ibid., p. 602.

33   Simpson, *Campion*, p. 226.

34   McCoog, 'Playing the Champion', p. 128n.

35   Simpson, *Campion*, p. 228.

36   Lake and Questier, 'Campion in Context', p. 604; McCoog, 'Playing the Champion', p. 129.

37   Simpson, *Campion*, p. 245.

38   Ibid., pp. 242–3.

39   BL Lans. MS 30, f. 201r; Anstruther, *Vaux*, p. 100.

40   Simpson, *Campion*, pp. 247–8.

41   BL Harl MS 859, f. 44r.

42   BL Harl. MS 360, f. 3v. Persons seems to have been mistaken when he later named Lord Vaux as one of those arrested. Vaux was not on Burghley's list and the following month he signed a musters certificate in Northamptonshire.

43   Reynolds, *Campion and Parsons*, p. 155.

44   Simpson, *Campion*, p. 249.

45   Questier, *Catholicism and Community*, p. 191; Larocca, 'Popery and Pounds', pp. 249–63.

46   Simpson, *Campion*, pp. 226–8.

47   PRO SP 12/142, f. 78r.

2 *To be a Perfect Catholic*

1   *LJ*, II, pp. 23–53.

2   Hartley, *Proceedings*, pp. 502–5.

3   23 Eliz. c. 1. For commentary, see Bowler, *Recusant Roll No. 2*, pp. xii–xxi; Larocca, 'Popery and Pounds', pp. 260–3.

4   Bowler, *Recusant Roll No. 2*, pp. xliv–v, citing Thomas Wilson's 1601 survey.

5   Simpson, *Campion*, p. 244.

6   Anstruther, *Vaux*, p. 113, citing f. 20 of the Visitation Book of 1581–3 in the NRO. Unfortunately the mansuscript is so fragile that it cannot currently be viewed.

7   Persons, 'Memoirs', 2, p. 200; McCoog, 'Slightest Suspicion of Avarice', pp. 103–4; Simpson, *Campion*, pp. 222, 292–3, 296–9.

8   Devlin, *Southwell*, p. 53. The paintings commissioned by Gilbert and undertaken by Niccolò Circignani no longer survive, but engravings were made and bound in a book, published as *Ecclesiae Anglicanae Trophae* (Rome, 1584).

9   Hicks, *Letters and Memorials*, pp. 331–40. See too Questier, 'Like Locusts', pp. 272–3.

10   Persons, 'Life and Martyrdom', 12, p. 30; McCoog, *The Society of Jesus*, p. 152.

11   Lake and Questier, 'Campion in Context', pp. 604–5.

12   Persons, 'Memoirs', 2, pp. 29, 182; Simpson, *Campion*, pp. 260–2, 287, 296, 526 (n. 190). See too Brown, 'Robert Southwell', pp. 193–6; Waugh, *Edmund Campion*, pp. 146–7.

13   Lake and Questier, 'Campion in Context', p. 605.

14   Simpson, *Campion*, pp. 303–4; Campion, *Ten Reasons*, p. 142.

15   Campion, *Ten Reasons*, p. 90.

16   Simpson, *Campion*, p. 266.

17   Four debates were held within the precincts of the Tower of London on 31 August and 18, 23, and 27 September. A fifth conference, scheduled for 13 October, was cancelled. See McCoog, 'Playing the Champion', pp. 135–8.

18   Reynolds, *Campion and Parsons*, p. 200.

19   Ibid., pp. 161–2.

20   Alford, *Burghley*, p. 250. For further analysis and text, see Kingdon's double edition.

21 Simpson, *Campion*, p. 155; Reynolds, *Campion and Parsons*, p. 172.

22 Lake and Questier, 'Campion in Context'.

23 Fitzherbert, *A Defence of the Catholyke Cause* (Antwerp, 1602), sig. G2r.

24 Reynolds, *Campion and Parsons*, pp. 150, 154–6, 202–4.

25 Simpson, *Campion*, pp. 455, 466–8; *DEP*, pp. 266–7, 295–6; Bod MS Eng. Th. B. 1, p. 490.

26 For an absorbing analysis of Persons' subsequent state of mind, see Bossy, 'The Heart of Robert Persons'.

27 *APC*, XII, pp. 271, 294–5; XIII, p. 144.

28 Gerard, *Autobiography*, p. 116n.

29 Reynolds, *Campion and Parsons*, pp. 133–4.

30 Graves, *Thomas Norton*, pp. 275–7; Alford, *Burghley*, p. 241.

31 Reynolds, *Campion and Parsons*, pp. 179–80; BL Harl MS 859, f. 44r.

32 'Loves Exchange', cited by Stubbs, *Donne*, p. 93.

33 Reynolds, *Campion and Parsons*, p. 138.

34 *APC*, XIII, p. 164; Cross, 'Letters of Sir Francis Hastings', pp. 18–19.

35 *APC*, XIII, pp. 155–6.

3 *Lying Lips*

1 Folger MS Bd.w. STC 22957. f. 77v.

2 BL Add. MS 39828, f. 59r; Kingdon, *The Execution of Justice*, p. 12; Alford, *Burghley*, pp. 249–50.

3 BL Add. MS 39828, f. 59r.

4 PRO KB 9/653, pt. II, ff. 106–7.

5 Bod MS Eng. Th. B. 2, p. 822.

6 Ibid., B. 1, p. 4.

7 Anstruther, p. 278. PRO SP 12/233, f. 21.

8 Bod MS Eng. Th. B. 2, p. 822.

9 *APC*, XI, pp. 179–80, 207.

10 BL Add. MS 39828, ff. 59r–60r.

11 Bod MS Eng. Th. B. 2, p. 822.

12 *APC*, XIII, p. 176.

13 Ackroyd, *London: The Biography* (2000), pp. 556–7; R. L. Brown, *A History of the Fleet Prison, London* (1996), p. 3; Foxe, *Acts and Monuments* (1583 edn), bk II, p. 1530; BL Harl MS 78, fo. 24.

14 BL Add. MS 39828, ff. 43r, 59r.

15 BL Add. MS 39828, f. 77r; Bod MS Eng. Th. B. 2, pp. 823–36; Persons, 'Memoirs', 2, p. 29.

16 BL Add. MS 39828, ff. 59r–60r.

17 Ibid., ff. 60r–61v.

18   PRO SP 12/233, f. 21.
19   Ibid., f. 22; BL Add. MS 39828, f. 262r.
20   For the trial, I have relied upon the eyewitness account in the British Library: BL Harl MS 859, ff. 44–50. There are also two printed versions: Bruce, 'Observations', and Simpson, 'A Morning at the Star-Chamber'. For Mildmay's speech, see BL Harl MS 6265, ff. 86v–87v (also printed in Bruce, 'Observations', pp. 101–4n).
21   TP, pp. 17–19; BL Add. MS 39830, f. 46v.
22   Kaushik, 'Resistance, Loyalty and Recusant Politics', p. 52.
23   Reynolds, *Campion and Parsons*, p. 201.

4 Worldly Woes

1   BL Add. MS 39828, f. 72v.
2   Questier, *Catholicism and Community*, pp. 188–90; Challoner, *Memoirs*, p. 113.
3   PRO SP 12/152, fo. 97r; Pollen, *Unpublished Documents*, p. 27. Lady Vaux was indicted several times during her Southwark residence 'for not resorting to the church according to the statutes' (Hyland, *A Century of Persecution*, pp. 379, 381, 384–7, 401).
4   BL Add. MS 39828, f. 74r.
5   *CSP Spanish* III, pp. 236, 364.
6   Pollen, 'Official Lists', pp. 223, 229; Pollen, *Unpublished Documents*, pp. 27–8; Persons, 'Memoirs', 4, p. 47; Anstruther, *Seminary Priests*, pp. 261–2. For the alleged threat of torture, see Allen's *True, Sincere, and Modest Defense*, in Kingdon, *The Execution of Justice*, pp. 75–6.
7   *APC*, XIII, pp. 353, 360.
8   Gerard, *Autobiography*, p. 270.
9   Pollen, *Unpublished Documents*, p. 28; Bowler and McCann, *Recusants in the Exchequer Pipe Rolls*, p. 180.
10   Pollen, 'Official Lists', pp. 223, 228–9; PRO SP 12/168, f. 86r. For the dating, see D. Flynn, '"Out of Step": Six Supplementary Notes on Jasper Heywood', in McCoog, *The Reckoned Expense*, p. 185n.
11   BL Add. MS 39828, f. 269v.
12   Ibid. For her jointure, Eleanor received a manor house and tenements in Ashby Magna, Leicestershire (PRO SP 12/183, f. 76r).
13   Persons, 'Memoirs', 4, p. 49; BL Add. MS 39828, f. 278r.
14   BL Add. MS 39828, ff. 59v, 72r.
15   'Isham Correspondence', p. 29. See too Finch, *Wealth*, p. 179.
16   NRO YZ 5622, 8235–40.
17   PRO SP 78/7, f. 35v.

18   Knox, *Douay Diaries*, pp. 174–5. See too Anstruther, *Seminary Priests*, p. 252.

19   Knox, *Douay Diaries*, p. lxxxii.

20   Ibid., pp. lxxi–lxxvi.

21   Ibid., pp. 186–7.

22   BL Add. MS 39828, f. 74r.

23   Bossy, 'The Heart of Robert Persons', pp. 144–5; Philip Benedict, *Rouen during the Wars of Religion* (Cambridge, 1981), pp. 170–1, 178, 184, 195, 202; Hicks, *Letters and Memorials*, pp. 107–8.

24   PRO SP 78/7, f. 93v. Cobham reported on 10 April (Old Style), which would be two days after 18 April (New Style).

25   Cf. Duffy, 'Allen, William', *ODNB*; Mattingly, 'William Allen and Catholic Propaganda in England', pp. 335–9; Kingdon, *The Execution of Justice*, pp. xxxiii–xxxvii.

26   Christie, *Letters of Sir Thomas Copley*, pp. xxxv–xxxvii, 136; Michael A. R. Graves, 'Copley, Thomas', *ODNB*.

27   Christie, *Letters of Sir Thomas Copley*, p. xxxvi. For Polidore Morgan, see Anstruther, *Seminary Priests*, pp. 234–5; Pollen, 'Official Lists', pp. 219, 225, 230. For Nicholas Morgan: Poulton, *John Dowland*, pp. 419–20; W. H. Grattan Flood, 'Nicholas Morgan of the Chapel Royal', *The Musical Antiquary* 4 (1912), pp. 59–60; W. Barclay Squire, 'John Dowland', *The Musical Times* 37 (1896), pp. 793–4, and 38 (1897), pp. 92–3. For Roland Morgan: Anstruther, *Seminary Priests*, pp. 235–6. For Thomas Morgan: A. Plowden, 'Morgan, Thomas', *ODNB*; Bossy, *Under the Molehill, passim*; *A discoverie of the treasons*, sig. Bi^v. Cobham's reference to surnames only might perhaps argue that he meant the most obvious Morgan, i.e. Thomas.

28   Plowden, *Danger to Elizabeth*, p. 201. For Walsingham's intelligence operation, see Bossy, *Under the Molehill*.

29   Foley, *Records*, VI, p. 726; PRO SP 15/27A, f. 199r.

30   PRO SP 78/8, f. 166r.

31   Knox, *Douay Diaries*, pp. 192, 194.

32   BL Add. MS 39828, ff. 83r, 187v, 209r; 39829, f. 13r; PRO C2/Eliz./U2/12.

5 *Refuse of the World*

1   Tierney, *Dodd's Church History*, III, p. 157.

2   BL Lans. MS 103, ff. 25–8; Alford, *Burghley*, pp. 245–6. BL Add. MS 39828, f. 78r.

3   BL Add. MS 39828, f. 187v.

4   Ibid., f. 84r.

5   Jeaffreson, *Middlesex County Records*, I, pp. 143–4, 150, 158, 163, 167, 173; KB 9/666, pt I, no. 51; Bowler and McCann, *Recusants in the Exchequer Pipe Rolls*, p. 180. Lord Vaux and his household were sometimes referred to as 'of Tottenham', but usually as 'of Hackney'.

6   Foley, *Records*, V, p. 470; VI, p. 717.

7   BL Harl. MS 286, ff. 52–3, 267r.

8   PRO C 54/1162/29; BL Add. MS 39828, f. 86v. See too NRO YZ 8235. For Holborn as a rendezvous for the Catholic community, see McClain, *Lest We be Damned*, p. 147.

9   *CSP Spanish* III, p. 236; Mattingly, 'William Allen and Catholic Propaganda in England', pp. 336–7.

10   Caraman, *The Other Face*, p. 109.

11   Caraman, *Garnet*, pp. 59, 180; Gerard, *Autobiography*, pp. 98–9; BL Harl. MS 6998, ff. 65r, 71v. Also, McGrath, 'The Bloody Questions Reconsidered'.

12   Talbot, *Recusant Records*, p. 206; Anstruther, *Seminary Priests*, pp. 226–7; *A discoverie of the treasons*, sig. Bii.

13   PRO SP 12/173, ff. 100–1. For Browne, see Knox, *Douay Diaries*, p. 199. Also pp. 204, 217.

14   Simpson, *Campion*, pp. 242–3.

15   Weston, *Autobiography*, p. 39n.

16   Foley, *Records*, VI, pp. 17, 727; Anstruther, *Seminary Priests*, p. 135; J. G. Elzinga, 'Howard, Philip, thirteenth earl of Arundel', *ODNB*.

17   Wilson, *Walsingham*, p. 180.

18   PRO SP 12/163, f. 140v.

19   27 Eliz. c. 1; Guy, *My Heart is My Own*, pp. 474–6; Rex, *Elizabeth*, pp. 187–9.

20   TP, pp. 37–43.

21   Alford, *Burghley*, p. 199. See too Kaushik, 'Resistance, Loyalty and Recusant Politics', pp. 57–9.

22   *Markham Memorials*, I, pp. 103–4.

23   Hicks, *Letters and Memorials*, pp. 334–7.

24   PRO SP 12/183, f. 218v.

25   PRO SP 12/178, ff. 88–90, 170r.

26   Persons, 'Life and Martyrdom', 12, pp. 29–30.

6 Flibbertigibbets

1   *The History of King Lear* (The Quarto Text, 1608), Scene 15.

2   *DEP*, pp. 211–12, 295–6.

3   *Vaux Petitions*, Minutes, p. 203; BL Add. MS 39829, f. 12v.

4   *DEP*, pp. 400, 408.
5   Bod MS Eng. Th. B. 1, Lib. 25: 'Of Exorcisms', pp. 485–91. The 'true witness' of Sara's exorcism may have been the priest and future government informant, Anthony Tyrrell (*DEP*, p. 394).
     The 'Brudenell manuscript' is discussed by Kilroy in *Edmund Campion, passim*, but esp. at pp. 5, 13–15. Kilroy suggests that that author, 'Thomas Jollet', was Sir Thomas Tresham, but it may not be a pseudonym: a certain Thomas Jollett/Jellett/Jallet of Edmonton and Shoreditch was cited for recusancy several times in the reign of James I (Jeaffreson, *Middlesex County Records*, II, pp. 115, 131, 134, 144, 211–12).
6   Weston, *Autobiography*, p. 24.
7   Walsham, 'Miracles', p. 801.
8   *DEP*, pp. 350, 375.
9   Ibid., p. 390; Weston, *Autobiography*, p. 25. Also, Holmes, 'Witchcraft and Possession', pp. 71–3.
10   The book was dedicated to 'the seduced Catholics of England'. Quotations are from the edition by Brownlow [*DEP*].
11   *DEP*, p. 318. Holmes, 'Witchcraft and Possession'.
12   Brownlow, *Shakespeare, Harsnett, and the Devils of Denham,* pp. 76–83.
13   Holmes, 'Witchcraft and Possession', p. 70.
14   *DEP*, p. 350.
15   Ibid., pp. 297, 266, 312–13, 350.
16   Crawford, 'Attitudes to Menstruation', p. 49.
17   *DEP*, pp. 224–5, 352.
18   Ibid., p. 357.
19   Brownlow, *Shakespeare, Harsnett, and the Devils of Denham*, pp. 23, 88.
20   Weston, *Autobiography*, pp. 26–7; also p. 30n.
21   Bod MS Eng. Th. B. 1, p. 491.
22   *DEP*, pp. 357–9.
23   Bod MS Eng. Th. B. 1, p. 485; BL Add. MS 39828, ff. 203r, 239r; PRO PROB 11/88/344 & 11/92/52; NRO YZ 8240. John Cheney was also Sir Thomas Tresham's solicitor (BL Add. MS 39829, f. 21r). Pollen, 'Official Lists', p. 269; Bowler and McCann, *Recusants in the Exchequer Pipe Rolls*, p. 36; Bridges, *History and Antiquities*, II, p. 152; Jeaffreson, *Middlesex County Records*, I, p. 163.
24   *DEP*, pp. 311, 357.
25   Ibid., pp. 208, 211, 391, 405.
26   Jeaffreson, *Middlesex County Records*, I, p. 160. The other surety was 'Henry Marshe of London, letherseller', who appears to have been a moneylender operating by St Paul's Cathedral (ibid., p. 267).
27   PRO SP 12/179, f. 1r.

28 Weston, *Autobiography*, p. 99.

29 PRO SP 53/19, no. 28.

7 *Atheistical Anthony Babington's Complotment*

1 *DEP*, p. 208.

2 Pollen, *Babington Plot*, pp. 18–22, 52–3. This is an invaluable resource. Two excellent recent accounts of the plot are by John Guy (*My Heart is My Own*, ch. 29) and Stephen Alford (*The Watchers*, chs 13–15). Also very useful are: Fraser, *Mary Queen of Scots*, ch. 24; Bossy, *Under the Molehill*, pp. 140–1; and the *ODNB* entries for Anthony Babington (by Penry Williams), Gilbert Gifford (by Alison Plowden) and Thomas Phelippes (by William Richardson).

3 Weston, *Autobiography*, p. 101.

4 Pollen, *Babington Plot*, pp. 38–46.

5 PRO SP 53/20, no. 26.

6 Camden, *Annales,* p. 142; Read, *Bardon Papers*, pp. 45, 47.

7 Weston, *Autobiography*, p. 87n.

8 BL Harl MS 360, f. 8; PRO SP 12/203, f. 100r; SP 53/19, no. 28.

9 PRO SP 12/179, f. 3r; Pollen, *Babington Plot*, pp. 58, 92, 108; Pollen, 'Official Lists', p. 269; BL Add. MS 39828, f. 170v.

10 PRO E 133/10/1656. Almost a decade later, Sir Thomas Tresham recalled that 'one Babington which was executed, or some other to his use, bought lands of the said Lord Harrowden & his sons, as he taketh it, which lands lie in Lincolnshire or Nottinghamshire as he remembreth' (PRO WARD 3/17 part 2).

11 BL Harl MS 360, ff. 8r, 12r; PRO SP 53/19, no. 28.

12 PRO SP 12/193 f. 119r. Five years later, one Robert Weston, the son of 'a notable recusant dwelling in Clerkenwell', was apprehended with letters on his person from his father to John Palmer and 'Francis Babington, brother to Anthony Babington the traitor' (PRO SP 12/238, f. 185r).

13 Howell, *State Trials*, I, cols 1135, 1150; BL Harl. MS 286, f. 52v; PRO SP 12/178, f. 170r.

14 *DEP*, p. 391; P. Holmes, 'Tyrrell, Anthony', *ODNB*.

15 *DEP*, p. 362 and Brownlow's commentary in this edition, pp. 30–4.

16 Weston, *Autobiography*, p. 88.

17 *DEP*, p. 350; Pollen, 'Official Lists', pp. 258, 280.

18 PRO SP 12/191, f.101r.

19 *CSP Spanish* III, p. 605.

20 Pollen, *Babington Plot*, p. 108.

21   BL Add. MS 39829, f. 105r.

22   *CSP Spanish* III, p. 607.

23   Miola, *Early Modern Catholicism*, pp. 180–1.

8   *Lambs to the Slaughter*

1   Devlin, *Southwell*, p. 107. See too Caraman, *Garnet*, ch. 3.

2   Caraman, *Garnet*, p. 244; ABSI Collectanea P II, f. 551.

3   Bod MS Eng. Th. B. 1, p. 758; N. P. Brown, 'Southwell, Robert', *ODNB*.

4   T. M. McCoog, 'Garnett, Henry', *ODNB*.

5   Caraman, *Garnet*, p. 20.

6   Devlin, *Southwell*, p. 99.

7   Ibid., pp. 107–8; Caraman, *Garnet*, p. 28.

8   PRO SP 12/178, f. 88r.

9   Weston, *Autobiography*, pp, 69, 75n.

10   Devlin, *Southwell*, p. 109.

11   Ibid., p. 116; More, *Historia*, p. 235; Bartoli, *Dell' Istoria*, p. 374.

12   Devlin, *Southwell*, p. 109.

13   Southwell, *Humble Supplication*, p. 22.

14   Weston, *Autobiography*, p. 31.

15   Pollen, *Unpublished Documents*, pp. 308, 309, 313, 314; Devlin, *Southwell*, pp. 117, 122.

16   Morris, *Troubles*, II, pp. 428–9. There is no record of a priest called (or having the alias) Sale. It has plausibly been suggested that it was a mishearing of the elided form of Southwell (pronounced Suthall). See Devlin, *Southwell*, p. 123; N. P. Brown, 'Southwell, Robert', *ODNB*.

17   Pollen, *Unpublished Documents*, p. 313.

18   PRO SP 53/20, no. 26; SP 12/192, f. 92r. For Henry Davies, see: PRO SP 12/194, f. 95r; SP 12/202, f. 2r.

19   Morris, *Troubles*, II, pp. 428–9.

20   PRO SP 53/20, no. 26.

21   *APC*, XV, p. 89.

22   LRO Parish Register, Ashby Magna, 19 November 1587.

23   Persons, 'Life and Martyrdom', 12, p. 30; Gerard, *Autobiography*, p. 195; Caraman, *Garnet*, pp. 44, 209.

24   Anstruther, *Vaux*, p. 100; BL Add. MS 39829, f. 12v; Caraman, *Garnet*, p. 209; Persons, 'Life and Martyrdom', 12, pp. 29–30. Catilyn's report can be found at PRO SP 53/20, no. 26. Elsewhere, he describes Clerkenwell as 'a very college of wicked papists' (PRO SP 12/194, f. 95r).

25   Gerard, *Autobiography*, p. 195; BL Add. MS 39828, f. 275r. Henry's verses are bound up with Robert Southwell's in a seventeenth-century manuscript

volume in the Folger Shakespeare Library, Washington, DC: MS Bd.w. STC 22957, ff. 69r–88v (quotation at f. 88r). They are also accessible online courtesy of Timothy Hacksley's MA thesis, 'A Critical Edition of the Poems of Henry Vaux'. Full details in the bibliography. I am most grateful to Timothy Hacksley for kindly permitting me to cite his thesis.

26   Anstruther, *Vaux*, pp. 100–1.

27   Caraman, *Garnet*, p. 128.

28   Pollen, *Unpublished Documents*, p. 317.

29   Parker, *Grand Strategy*, p. 189.

PART TWO: ELEANOR AND ANNE

1   Miola, *Early Modern Catholicism*, p. 193.

9 *The Widow and the Virgin*

1   Anstruther, *Vaux*, p. 101; Persons, 'Life and Martyrdom', 12, p. 30.

2   LRO Parish Register, Ashby Magna, 19 November 1587.

3   Lessius and Androtius, *The Treasure of Vowed Chastity*, sig. *5 & p. 310.

4   Anstruther, *Vaux*, p. 188.

5   ABSI Anglia A I, 73, f 138v; Cross, 'Letters of Sir Francis Hastings', p. 19; *DEP*, p. 400.

6   Anstruther, *Vaux*, p. 189; BL Add. MS 39828, f. 271v; Rhodes, *This Tight Embrace*, p. 237.

7   BL Add. MS 39828, f. 277r; 39829, f. 13r.

8   Lessius and Androtius, *The Treasure of Vowed Chastity*, sig. *6r.

9   Pollen, *Unpublished Documents*, p. 320.

10   ABSI Anglia A I, 73, f 138v; HMC Salisbury, 18, p. 109; Foley, *Records*, IV, p. 141; Anstruther, *Vaux*, p. 276; Caraman, *Garnet*, pp. 63–4, 187, 258, 296; PRO SP 12/287, f. 72r.

11   PRO SP 14/20, f. 29r.

12   PRO SP 14/216/121, f. 23r.

13   Inner Temple, Petyt MS 538.38, f. 415r. Francis Taylor was Catholic, but supported the faction of secular priests who opposed the Jesuits. He accused the Society of luring away his wife, keeping her from him for almost two years, slandering him as an excommunicated 'lewd fellow' and seeking his death at the gallows.

14   PRO SP 14/20, ff. 29r, 30v for the quotations. For the controversy, see ch. 25 below.

15   Devlin, *Southwell*, p. 140.

16   BL Add. MS 39828, f. 60r.
17   Foley, *Records*, VII, p. 1352.
18   Colleton, *A Just Defence*, p. 248.
19   Caraman, *Garnet*, p. 250.
20   Palmes, *Dorothy Lawson*, pp. 18–19, 40. Also, Lux-Sterritt, *Redefining Female Religious Life*, pp. 121–2 and *passim*.
21   Stubbs, *Donne*, p. 15.
22   Colleton, *A Just Defence*, p. 248. At the time, Colleton and Garnet were on opposing sides of the intra-clerical dispute known as the Archpriest Controversy. See ch. 14 below.
23   Gardiner, 'Two Declarations', p. 515; CP, 110, no. 16.
24   *DEP*, p. 296; Caraman, *Garnet*, p. 198; PRO SP 14/19, f. 136.
25   Rowlands, 'Recusant Women', p. 163.
26   Sheldon, *Survey*, p. 135.
27   Anstruther, *Vaux*, p. 189.
28   Weber, 'Little Women', p. 144.
29   Palmes, *Dorothy Lawson*, p. 13.
30   Hamilton, *Chronicle*, II, p. 166.
31   Anstruther, *Vaux*, p. 188.
32   BL Harl. MS 6998, f. 199r.
33   Rowlands, 'Recusant Women', pp. 152–5, 176n.
34   BL Add. MS 39828, f. 275r.
35   PRO SP 14/216/193.
36   PRO SP 14/20, f. 29v. See McCoog, 'Slightest Suspicion of Avarice', p. 114.
37   Hodgetts, 'Certificate', II, p. 12.
38   PRO SP 12/208, ff. 75r, 91r, 93r.
39   Lake and Questier, *The Trials of Margaret Clitherow*, pp. 106–8, 198. This is the best and most recent account.
40   Foley, *Records*, VII, p. 1039; Bod MS Eng. Th. B. 2, p. 118.
41   Caraman, *Garnet*, pp. 200–2; J. H. Baker, 'Beaumont, Francis', *ODNB*.
42   NRO FH 124, f. 83 (The Privy Council to Lord Chancellor Hatton, Lieutenant General of Northants., 4 January 1588).
43   Mattingly, *The Defeat of the Spanish Armada*, pp. 190–1.

10 *Fright and Rumour*

1   Mattingly, *The Defeat of the Spanish Armada*, p. 160.
2   Parker, *Grand Strategy*, pp. 188, 203; Hogge, *God's Secret Agents*, p. 5.
3   Alford, *Burghley*, p. 306.
4   Younger, 'If the Armada Had Landed'.

5   John Ponet, *A Shorte Treatise of Politike Power* (1556), sig. LIVr.

6   Aubrey, *Brief Lives*, pp. 147, 156.

7   NRO FH 124, f. 83; HMC Rutland, 1, p. 232.

8   HMC Bath, 5, p. 92.

9   BL Add. MS 39828, f. 140r; Bod MS Tanner 118, no. 14.

10   Pollen, *Unpublished Documents*, pp. 325–7.

11   *LJ*, II, p. 151. Also pp. 153–65.

12   PRO SP 12/233, f. 21; Bowler and McCann, *Recusants in the Exchequer Pipe Rolls*, pp. 180–1. Also Bowler, *Recusant Roll No. 2*, p. xxxi.

13   BL Add. MS 39828, f. 207r; PRO C 89/7/22: Private Act, 35 Eliz I, no. 16 (*SR* IV, p. 841).

14   BL Add. MS 39828, ff. 178r, 187v, 190r.

15   NRO WR 337.

16   PRO SP 12/183, f. 218v; 12/187, f. 78r.

17   Goring and Wake, 'Northamptonshire Lieutenancy Papers', p. 64; Bowler and McCann, *Recusants in the Exchequer Pipe Rolls*, p. 34. For the Earl of Arundel, see: Brigden, *New Worlds, Lost Worlds*, p. 294.

18   Heale, 'Contesting Terms', pp. 197–8; Laughton, *State Papers*, p. 30.

19   Allen, *Admonition to the Nobility*, sig. D3.

20   PRO SP 12/239, f. 36r.

21   *CSP Rome, 1558–1571*, p. 400; PRO SP 12/191, f.101r.

22   *CSP Spanish* IV, pp. 184–6.

23   BL Add. MS 39828, f. 140v.

24   Parker, *Grand Strategy*, p. 214.

25   Alford, *Burghley*, p. 307.

26   Dekker, *The Wonderful Year*, p. 167.

27   BL Add. MS 39828, f. 139v.

28   Clark, *England's Remembrancer*, opening passage.

29   BL Add. MS 39828, f. 142v. For 'Ely, my familiar prison', see Ibid, f. 227r.

30   Southwell, *Humble Supplication*, ed. Bald, App. I.

31   BL Add. MS 39828, f. 230r.

32   Ibid., ff. 139v, 142r.

33   Caraman, *Garnet*, pp. 71–2, 79–81; Devlin, *Southwell*, p. 167.

34   PRO SP 12/208, ff. 91–3.

11 *Mrs Brooksby's Household*

1   Caraman, *Garnet*, pp. 152–3.

2   PRO SP 12/229, f. 137r; Gerard, *Narrative*, p. 282; Gerard, *Autobiography*, pp. 41–3.

3   For Baddesley Clinton, see Squiers, *Secret Hiding-Places*, pp. 28–34;

Gerard, *Autobiography*, App. B. It may be significant that Thomas
Tomlinson and Nathaniel Birkhead, who were involved in the release
of the moiety of Baddesley Clinton on 13 July 1601, were witnesses
(along with Ambrose Vaux) to the lease of the manor of Isham (formerly
part of the Vaux patrimony) on 27 March 1599 and a related deed a
fortnight later (Shakespeare Centre, DR 3/349; NRO YZ 8241–2). On 27
March 1599 Nathaniel Birkhead and Ambrose Vaux also witnessed the
lease of Kirby Hall, 'a princely mansion' in Northamptonshire, which
Eliza Vaux hoped to set up as a Jesuit stronghold (NRO FH 3013; Gerard,
Autobiography, p. 149).

On 19 February 1596 Baddesley Clinton was conveyed to George
Shirley of Staunton Harold, Leicestershire, who had very close links to
the Vauxes: Shakespeare Centre, DR 3/338; NRO WR 337; PRO SP
12/183, f. 76r; PRO SP 12/238, f. 188r; SP 38/9; PRO E 178/3628; E 377/32
& 33; *Stemmata Shirleiana*, pp. 39, 63, 69, 83–8. For Henry Garnet's letter
to George Shirley's sister Elizabeth in 1605, see Caraman, *Garnet*, p. 320.

For Rowington Hall, see Brown, 'Paperchase', pp. 134–7; Woodall,
'Recusant Rowington', pp. 6–11. For John Grissold of Rowington *alias*
James Johnson, see Hodgetts, 'Certificate', I, p. 28; II, p. 12; PRO SP
14/216, nos. 70, 188.

The close proximity of Baddesley Clinton to Rowington Hall means
that evidence pointing to one tends also to support the other. Anne
Vaux's servant, John Grissold, may have come from Rowington, for
example, but so did several servants of Henry Ferrers of Baddesley
Clinton (cf. Laurence Cowper and William Shipton in BL Add. MS 4102,
f. 13r and Hodgetts, 'Certificate', I, p. 28; II, p. 20). Thurstian Tubs of
Rowington, examined in 1584, said that he heard of a priest at William
Skinner's house who 'read upon a Latin portesse in his orchard or
garden'. Three years earlier, at Skinner's brother-in-law's house 'of
Bushwood', Tubs had met a priest 'with his chalice and a book in his
hand going toward Baddesley, but whether the same were the man
which was said to be harboured at Mr Skinner's or no, he knoweth not'
(PRO SP 12/167, f. 61r). Incidentally, Bushwood (*alias* Lapworth) Hall
was the birthplace of Anne and Eleanor's cousin, Robert Catesby, the
architect of the Gunpowder Plot (Hodgetts, 'Certificate', I, 28).

For the Catholicism of the Arden area more generally, see Brown,
'Recusant Community', pp. 297–9.

4   PRO SP 12/229, f. 137r; Tesimond, *Narrative*, p. 185; ABSI Anglia A I, 73,
    f. 140r.

5   Lessius and Androtius, *The Treasure of Vowed Chastity*, sigs *2, *5.

6   Ibid., sigs *4v, *5r; pp. 3, 86–8, 93–100, 110–117; 151, 159, 176–7, 193, 196,
    237.

7   Southwell, *Short Rule*, sig. a5v.

8   Ibid., pp. 48–59.

9   Ibid., pp. 128–31.

10   Ibid., pp. 30, 47; Rowlands, 'Recusant Women', pp. 163–4.

11   Southwell, *Short Rule*, pp. 103–4, 135.

12   PRO SP 14/19, f. 136.

13   Finucane, *Miracles and Pilgrims*, p. 26. For the following discussion, I am particularly indebted to Alexandra Walsham's article, 'Miracles and the Counter-Reformation Mission to England'.

14   Walsham, 'Domme Preachers?', esp. pp. 80–1, 93–123.

15   Gerard, *Autobiography*, p. 49; Pollen, *Unpublished Documents*, p. 291.

16   *DEP*, p. 296; Walsham, *Providence*, pp. 238–40.

17   McClain, *Lest We be Damned*, p. 154.

18   Redworth, *Letters of Luisa de Carvajal*, II, pp. 291–4.

19   Holmes, *Elizabethan Casuistry*, pp. 82–3.

20   Ibid., p. 87; Gerard, *Autobiography*, pp. 183–4; Holroyd, 'Rich Embrodered Churchstuffe', pp. 75–8.

21   Lux-Sterritt, *Redefining Female Religious Life*, p. 97; Lessius and Androtius, *The Treasure of Vowed Chastity*, p. 172; *The Egerton Papers*, ed. J. Payne Collier (1840), p. 164.

22   Gerard, *Autobiography*, p. 40.

23   Holmes, *Elizabethan Casuistry*, pp. 24, 86. The spy Thomas Dodwell, who had informed on the Vauxes at Hackney, reported on the use of a tin chalice by priests in prison (Gerard, *Autobiography*, p. 216n).

24   Holmes, *Elizabethan Casuistry*, pp. 39–40, 60, 104–6, 109 and Introduction.

25   Ibid., pp. 4, 23, 81–3; Williams, 'Forbidden Sacred Spaces', pp. 97–103.

26   Cox, *Derbyshire Annals*, I, p. 284.

27   Gerard, *Autobiography*, p. 130.

28   HMC Downshire, 3, p. 180.

29   Rex, 'Thomas Vavasour', p. 442.

30   Ibid.; Hodgetts, *Secret Hiding-Places*, pp. 9–12, 117; Hodgetts, '*Loca Secretiora*'.

31   Hodgetts, *Secret Hiding-Places*, passim; Hogge, *God's Secret Agents*, pp. 118–19.

32   *Hierarchomachia*, cited by Shell, *Oral Culture*, p. 145.

33   Caraman, *Garnet*, p. 125.

34   Foley, *Records*, V, p. 470.

35   Caraman, *Garnet*, p. 168; Hodgetts, '*Loca Secretiora*', pp. 390–1.

36   Caraman, *Garnet*, p. 55; Holmes, *Elizabethan Casuistry*, p. 77.

37   Sheldon, *Survey*, pp. 29–31. 'The perjury of Thomas Cornford' is also cited in John Gee's *The Foot out of the Snare* (1624).

38   Bod MS Laud Misc. 655, f. 2; Sheldon, *Survey*, p. 31.

39 Holmes, *Elizabethan Casuistry*, pp. 103, 123; Caraman, *Garnet*, p. 113.

40 PRO E 377/32.

41 Presumably this is why the third Lord Vaux bequeathed Frances £100 in his will, but 'to the rest of her brothers and sisters one hundred pounds to be equally divided amongst them' (PRO PROB 11/88/344). Hamilton, *Chronicle*, II, pp. 164–8.

42 Williams, 'Forbidden Sacred Spaces', p. 113; Holmes, *Elizabethan Casuistry*, p. 23.

43 Caraman, *Garnet*, p. 104n.

44 Colleton, *A Just Defence*, p. 248; Shell, 'Furor juvenilis', p. 191. Caraman, *Garnet*, p. 218.

45 Hamilton, *Chronicle*, II, p. 165.

46 Foley, *Records*, V, pp. 598–600.

47 Dillon, 'Praying by Number'; Dekker, *The Wonderful Year*, p. 167. For other imaginative forms of Catholic renewal in England, see Walsham, 'Translating Trent?'

48 Hodgetts, 'Certificate', I, pp. 19, 28.

49 ABSI Collectanea P II, f. 551.

50 Caraman, *Garnet*, p. 215.

51 Morris, *Troubles*, I, p. 177; Bod MS Eng. Th. B. 1, pp. 488, 490; Southwell, *Short Rule*, p. 69.

52 Gerard, *Autobiography*, pp. 10, 17, 44–5.

53 Bod MS Eng. Th. B. 1, p. 486; *DEP*, p. 216; Gerard, *Autobiography*, p. 239n.

54 Southwell, 'Two Letters', p. 5.

55 Hodgetts, 'Certificate', II, p. 7; McGrath and Rowe, 'The Marian Priests'.

56 ARSI Anglia 37, f. 259r (from discs held at ABSI); Foley, *Records*, VII, pp. 1347–55.

57 ABSI Collectanea P II, f. 552.

58 PRO SP 14/16, f. 55v. Strange stayed 'for nearly two years' (Gerard, *Autobiography*, p. 173, p. 248n).

59 Gerard, *Autobiography*, p. 40; Caraman, *Garnet*, pp. 92, 204–5, 222–3, 233–4, 296.

60 Caraman, *Garnet*, pp. 222, 276, 327; Gerard, *Autobiography*, pp. 45–8, 205.

61 They had been captured at sea on their way to Goa in 1602 and taken to England, where they promptly escaped. Caraman, *Garnet*, pp. 297–8, 301.

62 ABSI Collectanea P II, f. 551; Persons, 'Memoirs', 2, pp. 18, 36–7.

63 Caraman, *Garnet*, pp. 122, 213, 217, 233.

64 ARSI Anglia 37, f. 265v: 'Fr Cowling's Relation of our Fathers in England' (from discs held at ABSI).

65 HMC Salisbury, 17, p. 611; Bod MS Eng. Th. B. 2, p. 136; ABSI Collectanea P II, f. 580v.

66   Gerard, *Autobiography*, pp. 40–1, p. 225*n*.
67   Caraman, *Garnet*, p. 128.
68   Gerard, *Autobiography*, p. 41.

12 *Virgo Becomes Virago*

1   ABSI Anglia A I, 73. Garnet's account is in Latin. Morris (*Troubles*, I, pp. 149–51), Caraman (*Garnet*, pp. 128–35) and Anstruther (*Vaux*, pp. 186–91) all give lengthy translated extracts. The account above is taken largely from Anstruther with the kind permission of the Trustees of the English Province of the Order of Preachers. There is, sadly, no account of the raid in the State Papers.

13 *Hurly Burly*

1   Gerard, *Autobiography*, p. 42.
2   Southwell, *Humble Supplication*, ed. Bald, App. I. The proclamation is dated 18 October 1591, but seems to have been issued towards the end of the following month.
3   PRO SP 12/229, f. 137r.
4   Caraman, *Garnet*, pp. 140–1.
5   Southwell, *Humble Supplication*, pp. 2, 17, 34.
6   Caraman, *Garnet*, p. 136; Devlin, *Southwell*, pp. 255–6; Petti, *Letters and Despatches*, pp. 39, 42.
7   *The Rambler*, new series, 7 (1857), pp. 112–15.
8   See the entries for Topcliffe by S. T. Bindoff in *The History of Parliament: HoC 1558–1603*, ed. Hasler, and by W. Richardson, in *ODNB*. For specific quotations, see: Gerard, *Autobiography*, pp. 68–70; Caraman, *Garnet*, p. 107; Hogge, *God's Secret Agents*, p. 123.
9   Bod MS Eng. Th. B. 1, p. 758.
10   BL Harl. MS 6998, f. 185v.
11   HMC Middleton, pp. 530–1; Jeaffreson, *Middlesex County Records*, I, p. 73; Gerard, *Autobiography*, p. 68.
12   BL Harl. MS 6998, f. 250v; Jeaffreson, *Middlesex County Records*, I, p. 73.
13   Petti, *Letters and Despatches*, pp. 97–8: original MS and copy by Grene.
14   Southwell, 'Two Letters', p. 78.
15   Ibid., p. 82; Petti, *Letters and Despatches*, pp. 67–8.
16   BL Lans. MS 72, f. 113.
17   Southwell, 'Two Letters', pp. 77–8, 121*n*.
18   Gerard, *Autobiography*, p. 26.

19 Caraman, *Garnet*, pp. 197–8.

20 Southwell, 'Two Letters', ed. Brown, pp. xvi, xxxix–xl.

21 Petti, *Letters and Despatches*, p. 68.

22 Ibid.; Caraman, *Garnet*, pp. 162, 195, 198.

23 Caraman, *Garnet*, p. 196; Southwell, 'Two Letters', pp. xlii–xliii.

24 Devlin, *Southwell*, pp. 88, 235.

25 Ibid., p. 314; Southwell, 'Two Letters', p. 7; Petti, *Letters and Despatches*, p. 79.

26 Southwell, 'Two Letters', pp. 81, 83.

27 Caraman, *Garnet*, p. 162; Gerard, *Autobiography*, p. 26.

28 Devlin, *Southwell*, p. 179.

29 Caraman, *Garnet*, p. 168. Also Caraman, *The Other Face*, p. 129.

30 Caraman, *Garnet*, pp. 152–3, 163, 177.

31 Pollen, *Unpublished Documents*, pp. 237, 257, 259; Bod MS Eng. Th. B. 1, p. 758; Caraman, *Garnet*, pp. 190–1.

32 Morris, *Troubles*, I, p. 177; Anstruther, *Vaux*, pp. 193–4.

33 Caraman, *Garnet*, p. 152.

34 ABSI Collectanea P II, f. 550; Caraman, *Garnet*, p. 185.

35 Alford, *The Watchers*, pp. 300–8. For Walpole's alleged involvement with the Irish assassins, see Hogge, *God's Secret Agents*, p. 240.

36 ABSI Collectanea P II, f. 550; Caraman, *Garnet*, pp. 185–7; Gerard, *Autobiography*, p. 54.

37 Gerard, *Autobiography*, p. 59.

38 Ibid., p. 65.

39 Caraman, *Garnet*, pp. 188–9.

40 Gerard, *Autobiography*, pp. 68, 77; ABSI Collectanea P II, f. 550.

14 Hot Holy Ladies

1 Lessius and Androtius, *The Treasure of Vowed Chastity*, sigs *2r–*6v; Walpole, *The Life of B. Father Ignatius*, sig. A2.

2 Watson, *Decacordon*, pp. 17, 37, 39, 40.

3 Christopher Bagshaw, *A Sparing Discoverie of Our English Jesuits* (1601), in Donnelly, *Jesuit Writings*, pp. 252, 254.

4 Watson, 'Preface' to John Mush's *A Dialogue betwixt a Secular Priest and a Lay Gentleman*, in Donnelly, *Jesuit Writings*, p. 256.

5 McCoog, 'Construing Martyrdom', pp. 106–20; Watson, 'Preface', in Donnelly, *Jesuit Writings*, p. 255.

6 Watson, *Decacordon*, p. 109; Persons, 'Memoirs', 2, pp. 37, 41; Caraman, *The Other Face*, p. 131.

7 Caraman, *Garnet*, p. 207.

8   Watson, *Decacordon*, pp. 37, 40, 44. Bagshaw, *Sparing Discoverie*, p. 252.
9   Bruce, 'Observations', p. 74.
10   BL Add. MS 39828, f. 260r; 39829, f. 11r.
11   Finch, *Wealth*, App. VIII, lists nineteen principal lawsuits. It excludes
     subsidiary cases and, as the Tresham Papers reveal, is by no means
     exhaustive. See, for example, Tresham's letter to his sister, Lady Vaux,
     of 22 February 1593 (BL Add. MS 39828, ff. 191–2), in which he complains
     of 'restless vexation in the law'.
12   BL Add. MS 39829, f. 11r.
13   BL Add. MS 39828, ff. 269r–270r.
14   Ibid., f. 269r.
15   BL Add. MS 39829, f. 11v. Also: 39828, f. 278r. For the proclamation of
     10 January 1581, see Strype, *Annals*, III, pt I, pp. 58–9.
16   BL Add. MS 39829, f. 13.
17   BL Add. MS 39828, f. 277r.
18   Ibid., ff. 271–2.
19   Brigden, *New Worlds, Lost Worlds*, p. 300.
20   McGrath, *Papists and Puritans*, pp. 177n, 255–6.
21   Lord Burghley, quoted by Alford, *Burghley*, p. 323.
22   See, for example, Marsh, *Popular Religion*, p. 23.
23   BL Add. MS 39828, f. 277r; PRO SP 12/287, f. 72r; Foley, *Records*, III, p.
     502; Fitzalan-Howard, *Lives*, pp. 225–6.
24   Morris, *Troubles*, I, pp. 177–8.
25   ABSI Collectanea P II, f. 551.
26   Gerard, *Autobiography*, pp. 156–7; Morris, *Troubles*, I, p. 178–80. For the
     possibility that Garnet kept a printing press at the house in Spitalfields,
     see Brown, 'Paperchase', pp. 132–40.
27   ABSI Collectanea P II, f. 551.
28   PRO SP 14/216/188–9.
29   Caraman, *Garnet*, pp. 245–6.
30   ABSI Collectanea P II, ff. 553v, 554v.

PART THREE: ELIZA

15 *Brazen-faced Bravados*

1   Carvajal, *Epistolario*, no. 135. I am grateful to George McPherson for his
     translation from the Spanish.
2   Gerard, *Autobiography*, pp. 148–9. According to a document in the Court
     of Wards (PRO WARD 3/18 part 2), Eliza was thirty-three in 1598.
3   BL Add. MS 39829, f. 12v.

4 BL Add. MS 39828, f. 169r.

5 Ibid., ff. 187v, 270v; Gerard, *Autobiography*, p. 148.

6 BL Add. MS 39828, ff. 169r, 270v; PRO C2/Eliz./U2/12 (Ambrose Vaux *contra* George Vaux, 6 November 1590); *Vaux Petitions*, Minutes, p. 203.

7 BL Add. MS 39828, ff. 169r, 187v, 191r, 209r.

8 PRO SP 12/233, f. 13.

9 Vallance, 'The Ropers and Their Monuments', pp. 148, 151–6; J. G. Nicholas, 'Sepulchral Memorials of the English Formerly at Bruges', *The Topographer and Genealogist*, II (1853), p. 469.

10 HMC Downshire, 6, no. 167, p. 71; CP, 114, ff. 84–5 (quotations at f. 84r).

11 PRO SP 14/70, f. 54v.

12 Poulton, *John Dowland*, pp. 433–4.

13 BL Add. MS 39828, ff. 169, 176r; 39829, f. 10v.

14 BL Add. MS 39828, f. 170r.

15 PRO SP 12/233, ff. 13, 22.

16 BL Add. MS 39828, f. 270v.

17 BL Add. MS 39829, ff. 11v, 35v; PRO SP 12/233, f. 21.

18 BL Add. MS 39829, f. 14r.

19 Kaushik, 'Resistance, Loyalty and Recusant Politics', p. 49.

20 BL Add. MS 39828, ff. 169r, 187v. Also Add. MS 39829, f. 203r (for another instance of Vaux borrowing on Tresham's credit). For Tresham's finances, see Finch, *Wealth*, ch. 4, and App. VI.

21 BL Add. MS 39828, ff. 192r, 217r; 39829, f. 12r.

22 BL Add. MS 39828, f. 131v (Lady Tresham's expenditure), 39829, f. 31r (mysticism), 39830, *passim* for the library, f. 211 (books in closet); TP, pp. 43 (cards), 72 (Easter), 92 (servants reading).

23 Finch, *Wealth*, pp. 76, 77, 80, 82, 91; TP, pp. 59–60 (supporting his servant Vavasour); BL Add. MS 39831, f. 72v (pears).

24 BL Add. MS 39828, f. 8r. All eleven volumes of the Tresham Papers can be found in the Additional Manuscripts collection at the British Library: BL Add. MSS 39828–39838.

25 BL Add. MS 39829, f. 192r.

26 Ibid., f. 10v.

27 PRO SP 12/192, f. 92r; 12/194, f. 95r; Kaushik, 'Resistance, Loyalty and Recusant Politics'.

28 PRO SP 14/14, ff. 93–4, 106, 108; TP, pp. 128–32; Kaushik, 'Resistance, Loyalty and Recusant Politics', pp. 61–2.

29 N. R. Ker, 'Oxford College Libraries in the Sixteenth Century', *The Bodleian Library Record*, 6/3 (1959), pp. 511–15; Kilroy, *Edmund Campion*, pp 136–45; TP, pp. xix–xxi; xxiii–lvi; Kaushik, 'Resistance, Loyalty and Recusant Politics', pp. 47–8; Gotch's *Complete Account* provides wonderfully detailed drawings of the buildings.

30   BL Add. MS 39828, ff. 115r; 191–2, 271r; 39829, f. 105r.

31   BL Add. MS 39829, ff. 10v, 14r.

32   College of Arms Vinc. MS 7, ff. 230–2; NRO Clayton 95: Copy of Final Concord between Antony Naylhart and Ambrose Vaux, Trinity 31 Eliz.; Anstruther, *Vaux*, pp. 207–8; BL Add. MS 39828, ff. 169, 170r, 187v, 209r.

33   PRO SP 12/233, ff. 21–2.

34   BL Add. MS 39828, ff. 178v, 187v, 190r.

35   Ibid., ff. 207r, 270v; 39829, f. 13r.

36   *APC*, XXIII, pp. 192–3 (14 September, 1592); Trimble, *Catholic Laity*, p. 213. Lord Vaux appeared in all the Recusant Rolls from this year till his death: CRS 18, pp. 1, 148, 234–5; CRS 57, pp. 1, 9, 88, 113; CRS 61, pp. 1, 8, 44, 64–5, 129, 134, 178, 196–7.

37   BL Add. MS 39828, f. 262r; Donne, Satyre II, line 10; *Vaux Petitions*, Minutes, p. 39; NRO Parish Register, Irthlingborough, 21 August 1595.

38   *Vaux Petitions*, Minutes, pp. 39–41; BL Lans. MS 991, f. 164r; Anstruther, *Vaux*, p. 232.

39   Gerard, *Autobiography*, p. 144; BL Add. MS 39828, f. 262r.

40   BL Add. MS 39828, f. 270.

41   BL Add. MS 39828, ff. 191r, 197v; 39829, f. 13r. Also NB: 39828, f. 180r: Tresham to George, 15 January 1593: 'The time was when I had that interest in you, I boldly might counsel you, in a sort command you . . . I sithence have been estranged from you.'

42   BL Add. MS 39828, f. 269.

43   BL Add. MS 39829, ff. 11v–12r; PRO WARD 3/17 parts 1 & 2. For Lord Vaux's codicil, see PRO PROB 11/88/344.

44   BL Add. MS 39828, f. 176r.

45   BL Add. MS 39828, f. 189v; 39829, ff. 9v, 13v–14r, 19r.

46   BL Add. MS 39828, f. 141r, 39829, f. 19r; TP, p. 104.

47   BL Add. MS 39829, f. 12v.

48   PRO STAC 5/T2/39, 1598; BL Add. MS 39828, f. 187v; 39829, ff. 9v–10v; Anstruther, *Vaux*, pp. 227–31.

49   BL Add. MS 39829, ff. 10v, 11r.

16 *Assy Reprobateness*

1   BL Add. MS 39829, f. 11r.

2   Ibid., f. 14v. Also 39828, f. 269.

3   TP, p. 74; BL Add. MS 39828, f. 271r.

4   BL Add. MS 39828, f. 230r.

5   Holmes, *Elizabethan Casuistry*, p. 107.

6   Knox, *Douay Diaries*, pp. 186–7, 207, 211–12; Anstruther, *Vaux*, p. 60.

7 *APC*, XX, p. 303; XXII, p. 546.

8 BL Add. MS 39828, f. 197.

9 PRO C 54/1459; Anstruther, *Vaux*, p. 215.

10 PRO C 54/1335; *APC*, XXVII, pp. 83, 334; PRO STAC 5/T2/39.

11 NRO YZ 8241; NRO FH 3013; BL Add. MS 39829, f. 31.

12 PRO SP 77/7, ff. 329v, 331v.

13 M. A. R. Graves, 'Copley, Anthony', *ODNB*; Hamilton, *Chronicle*, I, pp. 89–91, 261–2.

14 HMC Downshire, 2, p. 405.

15 PRO C 24/468, pt 2: *Wyseman v Smyth*, 1621.

16 PRO STAC 8/289/3; SP 14/175, f. 30. The antagonism between the rival entourages of the second Viscount Montague and the fourth Lord Vaux may also have influenced the dispute (Questier, *Catholicism and Community*, pp. 369–70).

17 PRO STAC 8/88/9; SP 77/7, f. 329r. See too Ostovich and Sauer, *Reading Early Modern Women*, pp. 35–9.

18 BL Add. MS 39828, f. 209v.

19 Bod MS Ashmole 38, f. 75.

20 BL Add. MS 39828, ff. 187v, 197v; 39829, f. 10.

21 PRO STAC 8/289/3.

17 *Long John with the Little Beard*

1 Caraman, *Garnet*, p. 204; Gerard, *Autobiography*, pp. 78–9.

2 The Privy Council authorised the use of 'the manacles and such other torture as is used in that place' on 13 April 1597 (*APC*, XXVII, p. 38). See Hogge, *God's Secret Agents*, pp. 242–5.

3 Gerard, *Autobiography*, pp. 107–9. Unless otherwise stated, hereafter the source for Gerard's time in the Tower is his *Autobiography*, chs 15–17.

4 ABSI Collectanea P II, f. 550.

5 HMC Salisbury, 7, p. 260.

6 NRO FH 124, f. 32. Ardens are mentioned in the will of Nicholas, first Lord Vaux (PRO PROB 11/21/178).

7 Gerard, *Autobiography*, p. 72. Gerard, describing here the manacling of Fulwood and Owen, was writing from experience.

8 Weston, *Autobiography*, Foreword by Evelyn Waugh, p. viii; Gerard, *Autobiography*, Longman's jacket blurb and pp. xvii, xxiv.

9 Gerard, *Autobiography*, pp. 5–6, 33, 39, 76, 167.

10 Ibid., pp. 78, 90; *CSP Dom 1595–7*, p. 389.

11 Gerard, *Autobiography*, pp. 15, 68, 70, 170.

12 Ibid., pp. 33, 122–3, 166.

13   Ibid., pp. 94, 100, 102–3.

14   Ibid., App. J.

15   HMC Salisbury, 11, p. 365; 15, p. 25; Gerard, *Autobiography*, pp. 17–18, 165.

16   Caraman, *Garnet*, pp. 84–6, 190; Gerard, *Autobiography*, pp. 17, 135, 201.

17   Gerard, *Autobiography*, pp. 91, 122; PRO SP 14/19, f. 136.

18   Watson, *Decacordon*, p. 14.

18   *St Peter's Net*

1   Gerard, *Autobiography*, p. 144. If not detailed below, the source for Gerard in this chapter is his *Autobiography*, chs. 18–22.

2   ABSI Collectanea P II, f. 551.

3   Gerard, *Autobiography*, pp. 144–5, 148.

4   CP, Petitions 701; Anstruther, *Vaux*, pp. 231–2. Also PRO C 3/274/14.

5   Gerard, *Autobiography*, pp. 25, 145–6, 148, 174.

6   BL Add. MS 39829, f. 12v. Tresham wrote this letter a year after Gerard had taken up residence with Eliza.

7   Gerard, *Autobiography*, pp. 147–8.

8   *APC*, XXII, p. 546; PRO STAC 5/T2/39.

9   Gerard, *Autobiography*, p. 150.

10   Ibid., pp. 153–4; Caraman, *Garnet*, pp. 261–2.

11   Gerard, *Autobiography*, p. 148.

12   NRO FH MSS 3013, 3015; Also PRO C 3/274/14.

13   Gerard, *Autobiography*, pp. 158–60.

14   Ibid, p. 195. See too PRO E 178/3628: schedule of Vaux goods and chattels, 1 March 1612.

15   Tesimond, *Narrative*, p. 157.

16   See, for example, CP, III, f. 31.

17   CP, 76, f. 58.

18   PRO 16/9, f. 26v; BL Harl. MS 1580, f. 342r.

19   Carvajal, *Epistolario*, no. 135. I am grateful to George McPherson for his translation from the Spanish.

20   Gerard, *Autobiography*, pp. 195–6.

21   Ibid., p. 174; Anstruther, *Seminary Priests*, p. 169; Anstruther, *Vaux*, p. 244; CP, 115, ff. 22, 34; vol. 119, f. 154.

22   Anstruther, *Vaux*, pp. 244, 436–7.

23   Gerard, *Autobiography*, pp. 151, 166, 194. Lisa McClain (*Lest We be Damned*, p. 39) is not alone in questioning 'Gerard's depiction of his success rate in converting Catholics'.

24   Gerard, *Autobiography*, pp. 168–9.

25   ARSI, Anglia 36II, ff. 277, 325 (from discs held at ABSI); McCoog, 'The Society of Jesus in England', pp. 193–5. I am extremely grateful to Fr

McCoog for permitting me to cite his thesis and also for his help at the Jesuit archives in London.

26 Walsham, 'Translating Trent?', p. 299.

27 Gerard, *Autobiography*, pp. 189–92.

28 Gee, *New Shreds*, sig. BIV and p. 17.

29 Ibid., pp. 1–9.

30 Gee, *The Foot out of the Snare*, p. 156.

31 See Harmsen's comments: ibid., pp. 60–9, 197–8 and his entry on John Gee in the *ODNB*. Also Walsham, 'Miracles', pp. 807, 813–14.

32 PRO SP 89/3, f. 152v.

33 HMC Downshire, 4, p. 167.

34 Carvajal, *Epistolario*, no. 171. I am grateful to George McPherson for his translation from the Spanish. A published translation is also now available: Redworth, *Letters of Luisa de Carvajal*, II, pp. 325–6.

35 Gerard, *Narrative*, p. 137; CP, III, f. 31; W. B. Devereux, *Lives and Letters of the Devereux, Earls of Essex* (1853), II, p. 223; P. Croft, 'Howard, Thomas, first earl of Suffolk', *ODNB*.

36 Gerard, *Autobiography*, p. 169. Hopes would be realised on 30 July 1628, when Sir Richard was created first Viscount Wenman.

37 PRO SP 14/216, nos. 141, 229.

38 PRO SP 1/105, f. 245v.

39 *The Proverbs, Epigrams, and Miscellanies of John Heywood*, ed. J. S. Farmer (1906), pp. 17, 450.

40 CP, III, f. 31r; PRO SO 3/3 (July 1605).

41 PRO SP 14/216/226.

42 Ibid., nos 98, 150.

PART FOUR: POWDER TREASON

19 *This Stinking King*

1 Loomie, *Spanish Elizabethans*, p. 82.

2 Wake, 'The Death of Francis Tresham', p. 36; Fraser, *The Gunpowder Plot*, pp. 91–2; PRO SP 14/16, f. 55v.

3 Gardiner, 'Two Declarations', p. 512 (CP, 110, f. 31v).

4 Caraman, *Garnet*, p. 242; CP, 112, f. 137; Sir Thomas Tresham also seems to have been involved in the Erith lease (cf. BL Add. MS 39828, f. 287; 39829, f. 155).

5 Tesimond, *Narrative*, p. 61; Fraser, *The Gunpowder Plot*, pp. 91–2, 98, 155, 205.

6   Gerard, *Narrative*, p. 55; Tesimond, *Narrative,* pp. 61, 80.

7   PRO SP 14/14, f. 106v.

8   BL Add. MS 39828, f. 169r.

9   Ibid., 150r; TP, pp. 60–1; *APC*, XXI, pp. 360, 368–9, 384, 386, 422, 467, 470.

10 Wake, 'The Death of Francis Tresham', p. 39.

11 M. Nicholls, 'Catesby, Robert', *ODNB*; *The Parish Register of Rushton*, ed. P. A. F. Stephenson (Leeds, 1930), I, pp. 18, 40. Baby Thomas Tresham, who only lived for eight months, was buried on 31 March 1599. His twin sister, Lucy, survived and, in accordance with her father's dying wish, became a nun (Wake, 'The Death of Francis Tresham', p. 39).

12 Quinn, *Voyages*, pp. 71–5, and associated documents; Merriman, 'Some Notes', pp. 492–500.

13 Quinn, *Voyages*, doc. 87.

14 Hughes, *History of the Society of Jesus in North America*, p. 5.

15 Quinn, *Voyages*, doc. 90.

16 Hughes, *History of the Society of Jesus in North America*, p. 4.

17 Sorlien, *Diary of John Manningham*, p. 208; McClure, *Letters of John Chamberlain*, p. 188.

18 Harington, *Nugae Antiquae*, II, pp. 134, 264; Alford, *Burghley*, pp. 188–9; Razzell, *Two Travellers*, p. 70.

19 Caraman, *Garnet*, p. 305.

20 Doleman [pseud.], *A conference about the next succession to the crown of Ingland* [1594]; Nicholls, *Investigating Gunpowder Plot*, p. 69.

21 McClure, *Letters of John Chamberlain*, p. 190; M. Nicholls, 'Catesby, Robert', *ODNB*.

22 Stubbs, *Donne*, p. 179.

23 Croft, 'The Gunpowder Plot Fails', in Buchanan et al., *Gunpowder Plots*, pp. 9–14 (quotation at p. 13).

24 BL Add. MS 39829 ff. 95–101 (quotations at 99v, 100r); Kaushik, 'Resistance, Loyalty and Recusant Politics', pp. 60–1, p. 71n.

25 Vallance, 'The Ropers and Their Monuments', p. 150; Gerard, *Narrative*, pp. ccxlvi, 27.

26 Wormald, 'Gunpowder, Treason, and Scots', p. 148.

27 Gerard, *Narrative*, p. 21; TP, p. xxv; Caraman, *Garnet*, p. 305.

28 Nicholls, *Investigating Gunpowder Plot*, p. 69.

29 Wormald, 'Gunpowder, Treason, and Scots', p. 149.

30 Nicholls, *Investigating Gunpowder Plot*, p. 132.

31 Jones, 'Journal of Levinus Munck', p. 247; *Markham Memorials*, I, pp. 96–101; HMC Salisbury, 12, p. 229; M. Nicholls, 'Watson, William', *ODNB*; Fraser, *The Gunpowder Plot*, pp. 63–5; Hogge, *God's Secret Agents*, pp. 309–314.

32 BL Add. MS 39829, f. 103r; Harington, *Nugae Antiquae*, II, p. 117.

33 Caraman, *Garnet*, pp. 310, 313, 315.
34 Croft, 'The Gunpowder Plot Fails', in Buchanan et al., *Gunpowder Plots*, p. 16; Fraser, *The Gunpowder Plot*, pp. 84–5, 88–90; Hodgetts, 'Certificate', I, p. 19; Gerard, *Narrative*, p. 181; Camm, *Forgotten Shrines*, pp. 320–2.
35 Wormald, 'Gunpowder, Treason, and Scots', pp. 150–1.
36 Gerard, *Narrative*, p. 25.

20 *Desperate Attempts*

1 J. Wormald, 'James VI and I', *ODNB*; ibid., 'Gunpowder, Treason, and Scots', p. 149.
2 HMC Salisbury, 17, p. 513; Nicholls, *Investigating Gunpowder Plot*, pp. 37–9, 57, 69. For a detailed examination of the various strands of the 'Spanish treason', and the identification of Anthony Dutton as one of the petitioners, see Loomie, 'Guy Fawkes in Spain'.
3 'His Majesty's Speech . . .', p. 248.
4 Tesimond, *Narrative*, p. 88.
5 Nicholls, 'Strategy and Motivation', p. 790; PRO SP 77/7, ff. 329v, 331v; PRO SP 12/271, f. 56r.
6 Gardiner, 'Two Declarations', p. 514; 'His Majesty's Speech . . .', p. 248. For what follows, I have also drawn on the scholarship of Fraser and Nicholls.
7 Barlow, *The Gunpowder-Treason*, p. 250; Nicholls, 'Strategy and Motivation', pp. 794–6, 803.
8 Fraser, *The Gunpowder Plot*, pp. 102, 110, 132–3.
9 Wake, 'The Death of Francis Tresham', p. 37.
10 Travers, *Gunpowder*, p. 41.
11 Gerard, *Narrative*, pp. 50, 56; Loomie, *English Polemics*, p. 80.
12 Travers, *Gunpowder*, p. 115.
13 Tesimond, *Narrative*, p. 105.
14 PRO SP 14/19, f. 19r; SP 14/18, f. 182v; SP 14/216, nos 70, 188, 214, 240.

21 *Quips and Quiddities*

1 McClure, *Letters of John Chamberlain*, p. 205.
2 *King Lear*, Act 1, Scene 2.
3 Caraman, *Garnet*, p. 327.
4 PRO E 101/433/3, f. 26r; SP 14/17, f. 83r; SP 14/216, nos 182, 240, f. 196r.
5 PRO SP 14/216, nos 103, 105, 141, 147, 156, 229, 230; CP, 113, ff. 70, 148.
6 Travers, *Gunpowder*, p. 42.
7 Tesimond, *Narrative*, pp. 80, 100.

8   Gee, *The Foot out of the Snare*, pp. 121–2; Gerard, *Autobiography*, pp. 46–8;
      Gerard, *Narrative*, pp. 275, 284–5; Garnet, *A Summe of Christian Doctrine*,
      pp. 625–6. Garnet added three supplements to his translation of Peter
      Canisius's catechism, which was printed at his secret press in London
      c.1592–6: on the veneration of images, on indulgences and on pilgrim-
      ages. For more on the well, see Walsham, 'Holywell'.

9   ARSI Anglia 37, f. 265v (from discs held at ABSI); Caraman, *Garnet*,
      pp. 298–9.

10   Larkin and Hughes, *Stuart Royal Proclamations*, p. 133; Hogge, *God's Secret
      Agents*, p. 335.

11   Redworth, *Letters of Luisa de Carvajal*, I, pp. 115, 196, 282; II, pp. 39, 195.
      Also, Redworth, *The She-Apostle*, pp. 106–9, 114, 128–9.

12   Owen Rees ('Music in an English Catholic House', pp. 272–3) has recently
      argued that Garnet's order to Luisa's escort to take her directly to 'su
      casa' could refer to the escort's house just as well as Garnet's. The
      latter, however, still seems more likely in light of the similarity of Luisa
      and Garnet's accounts of the house's discovery and their subsequent
      flight 'in several parties'. If Luisa did stay at one of Garnet's houses, it
      would have to have been no more than two days away from London,
      since Garnet departed on 7 June (the day after the octave of Corpus
      Christi) and met Catesby in London on the 9th. Perhaps Erith is the
      most likely site (Luisa's reference to 'a pleasant paradise amid dense
      woods full of wild beasts' is surely a simile), though Garnet and the
      sisters had probably only had the house since about November 1603
      (CP, 112, f. 137), which is a shorter duration than the 'more than three
      years' specified by Luisa. Garnet's later reference to 'Corpus Christi
      lodging' (PRO SP 14/19, f. 19v) might have been to Erith, or somewhere
      else, but was not to White Webbs.

13   HMC Salisbury, 17, p. 611. Also Harley, *William Byrd*, pp. 142–4.

14   Rees, 'Music in an English Catholic House', p. 273.

15   Foley, *Records*, IV, p. 141.

16   PRO SP 14/19, f. 87r; SP 14/216/212; Gardiner, 'Two Declarations',
      p. 515; HMC Salisbury, 18, pp. 109–110, 138.

17   Gardiner, 'Two Declarations', pp. 510–11, 517; HMC Salisbury, 18, pp. 96,
      107.

18   Hogge, *God's Secret Agents*, pp. 333–4.

19   Tesimond, *Narrative*, pp. 81–2, 87, 90.

20   HMC Salisbury, 18, p. 108.

21   Tesimond, *Narrative*, p. 82.

22   PRO SP 14/216/200.

23   Gardiner, 'Two Declarations', pp. 511–12. It seems unlikely that Garnet
      would have fabricated this conversation as it reveals him discussing

matters of state. That Tresham advocated waiting to see what laws would be made in Parliament is corroborated by his servant Vavasour's later account (Wake, 'The Death of Francis Tresham', p. 37). However, one cannot rule out an element of revenge in the treacherous words that Garnet attributes to Lord Monteagle, the man who would betray the plot to the authorities. See Nicholls, *Investigating Gunpowder Plot*, p. 77.

24   Gardiner, 'Two Declarations', p. 512; Caraman, *Garnet*, pp. 321–2.

25   Gardiner, 'Two Declarations', pp. 512–13, 515.

26   Ibid., pp. 513–15, 517; Tesimond, *Narrative*, p. 91; Loomie, *English Polemics*, p. 80.

27   PRO SP 14/216, nos. 121, 153, 240; Walsham, 'Holywell', pp. 229–30.

28   Gardiner, 'Two Declarations', p. 515.

29   PRO SP 14/216/200.

30   Mary Morgan deposed that 'her husband & she serveth at Grant's' (PRO SP14/216/105, f. 158v).

31   Ibid.; Travers, *Gunpowder*, pp. 41–2, 43; M. Nicholls, 'Percy, Thomas', *ODNB*.

32   PRO SP 14/216/212.

33   PRO SP 14/216/200.

34   BL Add. MS 39829, ff. 176r, 180r.

35   PRO SP 14/19, f. 88r; Gardiner, 'Two Declarations', pp. 515–16; HMC Salisbury, 18, p. 109.

36   Tesimond, *Narrative*, p. 155; BL Add. MS 39828, f. 277r; 39829, f. 11r.

37   Bod MS Eng. Th. B. 1, p. 572; B. 2, p. 823; Wake, 'The Death of Francis Tresham', p. 39; PRO SP 14/216/212; BL Add. MS 39828, f. 141r; Pollen, *Babington Plot*, p. 58.

38   Wake, 'The Death of Francis Tresham', pp. 37–8; HMC Salisbury, 17, p. 528; Bod MS Laud Misc. 655, first leaf; PRO SO 3/3 (November 1605). Antonia Fraser (*The Gunpowder Plot*, pp. 145–6) is sceptical of Tresham's 'exculpatory confession'; Mark Nicholls (*Investigating Gunpowder Plot*, p. 50) is inclined to give it more credit.

39   PRO SP 14/16, ff. 170–4; SP 14/216/135; PRO 31/6/1, f. 32r; Gerard, *Narrative*, p. 136; Barlow, *The Gunpowder-Treason*, pp. 241–2.

40   Gardiner, 'Two Declarations', p. 516; HMC Salisbury, 18, p. 109; PRO SP 14/16, f. 170r.

22 *Strange and Unlooked for Letters*

1   PRO SP 14/216/11.

2   Nicholls, *Investigating Gunpowder Plot*, p. 43.

3   Ibid., pp. 8–9; Nicholls, 'The Gunpowder Plot', *ODNB*; 'His Majesty's Speech . . .', pp. 244–5.

4   PRO SP 14/216/2; Fraser, *The Gunpowder Plot*, p. 150.

5   Scott, *The Fortunes of Nigel* (Edinburgh, 1822) III, pp. 96–7; Wormald, 'Gunpowder, Treason, and Scots', p. 144.

6   Fraser, *The Gunpowder Plot*, pp. 150–8, 307n; M. Nicholls, 'Tresham, Francis', *ODNB*; Wake, 'The Death of Francis Tresham', p. 38. For Anne Vaux's proposed candidacy, see D. Jardine, *A Narrative of the Gunpowder Plot* (1857), pp. 84–6.

7   Swynnerton, *A Christian Love-Letter*, sig. L2r.

8   PRO SP 14/16, f. 55; SP 14/17, ff. 19–20; Gerard, *Autobiography*, p. 33; T. F. Teversham, *A History of the Village of Sawston*, vol. 2 (Sawston, 1947), pp. 99–101.

9   PRO SP 14/216/240, 241; M. Nicholls, 'Digby, Sir Everard', *ODNB*; Barlow, *The Gunpowder-Treason*, pp. 242–3, 250–1; Tesimond, *Narrative*, p. 156.

10   Wake, 'The Death of Francis Tresham', pp. 39–40; PRO SP 14/17, ff. 75r, 85r.

11   Gardiner, 'Two Declarations', pp. 516; PRO SP 14/216, nos. 70, 188; PRO 31/6/1, f. 34r. Fr Garnet heard that Grissold was 'upon the rack for three hours': Foley, *Records*, IV, p. 151.

12   CP, 193, no. 57.

13   CP, 113, ff. 20–1.

14   PRO SP 14/216/229.

15   PRO SP 14/216/105.

16   PRO SP 14/16, f. 131r.

17   PRO SP 14/216/103.

18   Bod MS Tanner 75, f. 214v.

19   PRO SP 14/216/229.

20   PRO SP 14/216, nos 83, 226. Anstruther, *Vaux*, p. 295.

21   PRO SP 14/216, nos 98, 150.

22   For Eliza, see PRO SP 14/216, nos 103–4; CP, 113, ff. 148–9. For Huddlestone: PRO SP 14/16, f. 55; SP 14/17, ff. 19–20.

23   PRO SP 14/19, f. 93r. Strange confused his dates, but was referring to the supper at Harrowden on 5 November. For his alleged torture, see Gerard, *Autobiography*, p. 173, and ABSI Anglia A III, 64.

24   Gerard, *Autobiography*, p. 199; PRO 14/216/134.

25   PRO SP 14/216/227.

26   CP, 112, f. 173; Gerard, *Narrative*, p. 140.

27   Foley, *Records*, V, p. 470.

28   PRO 14/16, f. 175r; SP 14/216/123; HMC Salisbury, 18, pp. 426–7, 453.

29   CP, 113, ff. 148–9.

30   PRO SP 14/216/10. For Fawkes's confession, see Fraser, *The Gunpowder Plot*, p. 189.

31   Bod MS Tanner 75, f. 214v.

23 *In the Hole*

1   Gerard, *Autobiography*, p. 197.

2   PRO SP 14/216/92.

3   BL Harl. MS 360, f. 8r; Harl. MS 6998, f. 71r.

4   PRO SP 14/216/93.

5   PRO SP 14/216/240.

6   PRO 31/6/1, f. 25r; T. M. McCoog, 'Sweetnam [Swetnam], John (1579–1622), *ODNB*.

7   CP, 191, f. 71; PRO SP 12/118, ff. 59–60.

8   Gerard, *Autobiography*, pp. 198–9.

9   CP, 191, f. 71.

10 Gerard, *Autobiography*, pp. 197–8.

11 Gerard, *Narrative*, pp. 138–9.

12 PRO E 178/3628.

13 Gerard, *Autobiography*, pp. 197–8.

14 CP, 191, ff. 71, 75.

15 PRO 14/216/103–4. See too CP, 113, ff. 148–9.

16 For an interesting recent take on this, see Baynham, 'Twice done and then done double'.

17 Gerard, *Narrative*, pp. 140–1.

18 Gerard, *Autobiography*, p. 208.

19 CP, 113, f. 65; PRO 14/216/105.

20 BL Add. MS 11402, f. 108r.

21 Anstruther, *Vaux*, pp. 324–6; Fraser, *The Gunpowder Plot*, pp. 199–200.

22 Gerard, *Narrative*, p. 141.

23 PRO SP 14/16, f. 168; CP, 113, no. 19; vol. 114, ff. 84–5; vol. 119, f. 31.

24 Gerard, *Narrative*, p. 140; Roberts, *Diary of Walter Yonge*, pp. 1–2.

25 BL Stowe MS 168, f. 235r.

26 Barlow, *The Gunpowder-Treason*, pp. 241, 245; Gerard, *Narrative*, p. 137.

27 Barlow, *The Gunpowder-Treason*, pp. 261–2.

28 Anstruther, *Vaux*, pp. 328–30.

29 Swynnerton, *A Christian Love-Letter*, sig. K.

30 Ibid., sigs Ar, B–B3r; CP, 119, f. 110.

31 Swynnerton, *A Christian Love-Letter*, sig. K4v.

32 CP, 110, f. 121; CP, Petitions 1375.

33 Gerard, *Narrative*, p. 141; CP, 113, f. 65.

34 BL Add. MS 11402, f. 108r; Gerard, *Autobiography*, p. 208.

35 CP, 116, f. 22.

36 Gerard, *Autobiography*, pp. 208–9.

24 Two Ghosts

1 Howell, *State Trials*, II, col. 176.

2 Ibid., col. 194; Hawarde, *Les Reportes*, pp. 256–7; Willson, *Diary of Robert Bowyer*, pp. 4–8, 10.

3 Howell, *State Trials*, II, cols 162, 182.

4 Larkin and Hughes, *Stuart Royal Proclamations*, pp. 131–3; Tesimond, *Narrative*, pp. 162–3.

5 Nicholls, *Investigating Gunpowder Plot*, p. 50; Gerard, *Narrative*, p. 211.

6 A. J. Loomie, 'Creswell, Joseph', *ODNB*.

7 Hasler, *The History of Parliament: HoC 1558–1603*: Baynham, Edmund; Nicholls, *Investigating Gunpowder Plot*, pp. 67–8.

8 Howell, *State Trials*, II, cols 165, 168, 183.

9 Nicholls, *Investigating Gunpowder Plot*, p. 49; Roberts, *Diary of Walter Yonge*, p. 5.

10 Coke at the trial in June 1606 of Lords Mordaunt and Stourton: Nicholls, *Investigating Gunpowder Plot*, p. 75.

11 PRO SP 14/19, f. 20r. Caraman, *Garnet*, pp. 152–3; Gerard, *Autobiography*, p. 45.

12 Gerard, *Autobiography*, pp. 44–5; *Narrative*, pp. 149–50.

13 Hodgetts, *Life at Harvington*, p. 28. The Harvington library is now at Oscott College, near Birmingham.

14 PRO SP 14/216/121; Gerard, *Narrative*, p. 185.

15 PRO SP 14/216/194; Gerard, *Narrative*, p. 149.

16 ABSI Anglia A III, 58.

17 Gilbert, 'Thomas Habington's Account', p. 417. For the following narrative, I have also drawn on Bromley's and Garnet's own relations of the search: PRO SP 14/18, ff. 48, 65 ('wet winter nights'), 68, 86; SP 14/19, ff. 17–18r; HMC Salisbury, 18, p. 109 (general confessions). Also: Bromley's instructions from London (PRO SP 14/18, f. 35); an official manuscript account on 'the service performed at Hinlip', which was intended for publication (BL Harl. MS 360, ff. 93–101), and Gerard's *Narrative*, pp. 151–6. Although they differ in some details, the accounts tend to agree substantively. Much information is printed in Foley, *Records*, IV, pp. 69–81, 154, 223–5, 269. Glyn Redworth's excellent English-language edition of *The Letters of Luisa de Carvajal* provides fresh details (I, p. 122).

18 Howell, *State Trials*, II, cols 165, 219.

25 *That Woman*

1   PRO 14/216/200; Luisa de Carvajal to Magdalena de San Jerónimo, 12 April 1606 (NS), in Rhodes, *This Tight Embrace*, p. 239.

2   PRO SP 14/216/241.

3   Foley, *Records*, IV, p. 148.

4   CP, 110, no. 16.

5   PRO SP 14/216/242.

6   PRO SP 14/19, f. 20v.

7   BL Add. MS 11402, ff. 190v–110r; BL Stowe MS 168, f. 364r; CP, 227, p. 209; Hogge, *God's Secret Agents*, pp. 363–5; M. Hodgetts, 'Owen, Nicholas', *ODNB*.

8   PRO SP 14/19, ff. 17–20.

9   HMC Salisbury, 18, pp. 108–9; Gerard, *Narrative*, pp. 173–4; Foley, *Records*, IV, p. 153.

10 Foley, *Records*, IV, p. 153n.

11 Ibid., pp. 148–53.

12 HMC Salisbury, 18, p. 108; ABSI Anglia A III, 64; Howell, *State Trials*, II, col. 243; Rhodes, *This Tight Embrace*, p. 237; Redworth, *Letters of Luisa de Carvajal*, I, pp. 156, 158.

13 Travers, *Gunpowder*, p. 155.

14 Foley, *Records*, IV, p. 155; HMC Salisbury, 18, pp. 109–110.

15 Gardiner, 'Two Declarations', p. 516; HMC Salisbury, 18, pp. 107, 109.

16 Gardiner, 'Two Declarations', p. 518; HMC Salisbury, 18, pp. 96, 107, 111.

17 Bod MS Eng. Th. B. 2, p. 134; Foley, *Records*, IV, p. 157.

18 Alice Hogge's words (*God's Secret Agents*, p. 344).

19 HMC Salisbury, 18, p. 108; Gardiner, 'Two Declarations', p. 517.

20 Howell, *State Trials*, II, col. 256.

21 PRO SP 14/216/244.

22 Gerard, *Narrative*, p. 168.

23 PRO SP 14/216/245. Gerard, *Narrative*, p. 306.

24 PRO SP 14/216/246.

25 HMC Salisbury, 18, p. 111 (CP, 115, f. 16r).

26 Lessius and Androtius, *The Treasure of Vowed Chastity*, dedication; Inner Temple, Petyt MS 538.38, f. 415r; Gerard, *Narrative*, p. 172; Caraman, *Garnet*, pp. 175, 321; Fraser, *The Gunpowder Plot*, pp. 237–9.

27 Caraman, *Garnet*, p. 193.

28 PRO SP 14/81, ff. 122–3.

29 McCoog, *The Society of Jesus*, p. 138; Loarte, *The Exercise of a Christian Life*, pp. 80, 105; Lessius and Androtius, *The Treasure of Vowed Chastity*, p. 199.

30   McNamara, *Sisters in Arms*, esp. chs 1 and 16; Lessius and Androtius, *The Treasure of Vowed Chastity*, ch. 2.

31   PRO SP 14/216/242.

32   Gerard, *Narrative*, pp. 171–2.

33   Luisa de Carvajal to Magdalena de San Jerónimo, 12 April 1606 (NS), in Rhodes, *This Tight Embrace*, p. 239.

34   PRO SP 14/216/200.

35   Gardiner, 'Two Declarations', p. 515 (CP, 110, f. 33v).

36   HMC Salisbury, 18, pp. 109–10 (CP, 115, f. 15).

37   Tesimond, *Narrative*, p. 190.

38   Rhodes, *This Tight Embrace*, pp. 236–9.

39   PRO 14/216/201. The words that I have transcribed as 'any ways' are problematic. In the original, they are 'ane yease' and have been interpreted variously. Anne sometimes wrote 'y' for 'w' (e.g. SP 14/216/244, lines 2 & 9).

40   PRO 14/216/211; Wake, 'The Death of Francis Tresham', p. 40.

41   PRO SP 14/216/205–6.

42   PRO SP 14/216, nos. 205, 212.

43   HMC Salisbury, 18, p. 109 (CP, 115, f. 14v); Gardiner, 'Two Declarations', p. 512.

44   PRO SP 14/216/215.

45   For the trial, see Howell, *State Trials*, II, cols 217–355; Gerard, *Narrative*, pp. 224–64; Foley, *Records*, IV, pp. 164–90; Rhodes, *This Tight Embrace*, pp. 235–7.

46   Bod MS Laud Misc. 655, first leaf.

47   HMC Salisbury, 17, p. 595; PRO SP 14/19, f. 40r.

26 *Yours Forever*

1   Redworth, *Letters of Luisa de Carvajal*, I, p. 156; Gerard, *Narrative*, p. 175.

2   PRO SP 14/20, ff. 29–30.

3   HMC Salisbury, 18, p. 97.

4   PRO SP 14/20, f. 91.

5   PRO SP 14/21, f. 2r; Foley, *Records*, III, p. 513; Gerard, *Narrative*, p. 288; Gerard, *Autobiography*, p. 209.

6   Bod MS Eng. Th. B. 2, p. 133. Also Anstruther, *Vaux*, p. 368.

7   Bod MS Eng. Th. B. 2, p. 133; Redworth, *Letters of Luisa de Carvajal*, I, p. 158. See too Gerard, *Narrative*, pp. 289–97.

8   Howell, *State Trials*, II, cols 355, 357.

9   PRO SP 14/21, f. 2r.

10   Bod MS Eng. Th. B. 2, p. 134.

11 HMC Buccleuch, 1, p. 64.

12 Gerard, *Narrative*, p. 294; BL Add. MS 34218, f. 82v; Bod MS Eng. Th. B. 2, p. 135.

13 BL Add. MS 34218, f. 82v; Howell, *State Trials*, II, col. 358; Gerard, *Narrative*, pp. 295–6; Redworth, *Letters of Luisa de Carvajal*, I, p. 158.

14 Redworth, *Letters of Luisa de Carvajal*, I, pp. 165, 174, 196; ABSI Anglia A III, 64; LRO Parish Register, Ashby Magna, 7 June 1606.

15 Bod MS Eng. Th. B. 2, p. 134; BL Add. MS 21203, f. 22r.

16 For what follows, see Bod MS Eng. Th. B. 2, pp. 135–6; AAW A VIII, nos. 13–18; Redworth, *Letters of Luisa de Carvajal*, I, pp. 201–3, 292–3; Bartoli, *Dell' Istoria*, pp. 582–5; Foley, *Records*, IV, pp. 121–33, 195–210; Gerard, *Narrative*, pp. 297–305; Gerard, *Autobiography*, pp. 201–2, 274–6. HMC Salisbury, 18, p. 357; HMC Downshire, 2, p. 454; BL Stowe MS 169, f. 27r; Gee, *The Foot out of the Snare*, p. 137; Sheldon, *Survey*, pp. 94–5; P[ricket], *The Jesuits Miracles*, *passim* (quotation at sig. B3r). Also Caraman, *Garnet*, App. D; Walsham, *Providence*, pp. 242–3, and, for a fascinating discussion of the straw as a rebus, Shell, *Oral Culture*, pp. 134–5.

17 The phrase is Alexandra Walsham's ('Miracles', p. 791).

18 Redworth, *Letters of Luisa de Carvajal*, I, p. 279.

Epilogue

1 Lippincott, *Merry Passages and Jeasts*, no. 361.

2 *LJ*, III, pp. 209–10.

3 ABSI Anglia A III, 64.

4 Redworth, *Letters of Luisa de Carvajal*, I, pp. 256–7, 278; T. M. McCoog, 'Wright, William', *ODNB*; Foley, *Records*, II, pp. 275–86.

5 BL Add. MS 34765, f. 27r; PRO SP 38/9; PRO E 377, nos. 31, 33; Fraser, *The Gunpowder Plot*, p. 236; Foley, *Records*, V, pp. 598–600.

6 Anstruther, *Vaux*, pp. 460–2; McCoog, 'The Society of Jesus in England', pp. 293–5; Beales, *Education Under Penalty*, pp. 209–11.

7 Lessius and Androtius, *The Treasure of Vowed Chastity*, sigs *2r–*6v; Walpole, *The Life of B. Father Ignatius*, sig. A2.

8 McCoog, 'The Society of Jesus in England', pp. 290–3. The full title was: the Residence of St Anne with the Leicester mission. In 1633 it became the College of the Immaculate Conception with the mission of Nottingham and Derby.

9 Redworth, *Letters of Luisa de Carvajal*, I, p. 196; Anstruther, *Vaux*, pp. 381–2. See McCoog, 'The Society of Jesus in England', pp. 193–5 for the 'church' of AP (Percy) in 1609.

10 Anstruther, *Vaux*, pp. 377–8; H. Chadwick, *St Omers to Stonyhurst: A History of Two Centuries* (1962).

11 Carvajal, *Epistolario*, no. 135. I am grateful to George McPherson for his translation from the Spanish. The letter can now also be read in translation in Redworth, *Letters of Luisa de Carvajal*, II, pp. 188–90. Several *Newsletters from the Archpresbyterate of George Birkhead* (nos 19, 20, 22, 23, 25, 26, 28, 29, 31, 32, 36, 41) are instructive on the raid and its aftermath, as is the editor Michael Questier's excellent commentary. Gilbert Pickering's gloating letter can be read in BL Add. MS 15625, f. 3r (endorsed on f. 4v). Otherwise see the detailed account provided by Anstruther, *Vaux*, pp. 392–407, 414–21, 426–9.

12 Gerard, *Autobiography*, p. 181n.

13 Gilbert Pickering, whose sister was Elizabeth Throckmorton (BL Add. MS 15625, f. 3r), was involved in the witches of Warboys story. See D. P. Walker, *Unclean Spirits: Possession and Exorcism in France and England in the Late Sixteenth and Early Seventeenth Centuries* (1981), pp. 49–52; Philip C. Almond, *The Witches of Warboys: An Extraordinary Story of Sorcery, Sadism and Satanic Possession* (2008), *passim*, but esp. pp. 31–2.

14 PRO E 178/3628. The eleven-year trust was ostensibly to secure a dowry for Lord Vaux's sister, Katherine. The four trustees were Sir George Shirley, Sir George Fermor, Sir Richard Wenman and Sir William Tate. The first two were conforming Catholics. Wenman was the Protestant husband of Eliza's friend, Agnes, and apparently disapproving of Eliza. Tate was the courteous official in charge of the search of Harrowden Hall in November 1605.

15 *The Following of Christ*, trans. 'B.F.' (Anthony Hoskins, S.J.), sig. *2. The dedication is dated 1 November 1612 NS. Hoskins had previously written *A Briefe and Cleare Declaration of Sundry Pointes* (St Omer, 1611).

16 Foley, *Records*, VII, pp. 1039–40; Questier, *Catholicism and Community*, p. 369.

17 The Jacobean oath still provokes lively debate. Cf., for example, Sommerville, 'Papalist Political Thought', and Questier, 'Catholic Loyalism in Early Stuart England'. For one way of dealing with the oath, see Redworth, *Letters of Luisa de Carvajal*, I, pp. 285–6.

18 ABSI Anglia A III, 111.

19 BL Lans. MS 153, ff. 89–90. Also ff. 44–7 for the £2,000 offered by the Vaux tenants in composition for Lord Vaux and his mother. For the Vaux estate, see also PRO E 178/3628. For Lord Vaux's pardon and the restitution of his lands, see PRO SO 3/5 (October 1612 and April 1613).

20 *LJ*, III, pp. 209, 211, 216; Questier, *Catholicism and Community*, pp. 409–10.

21 PRO 16/9, f. 26; BL Harl. MS 1580, ff. 201r, 342–3; HMC Buccleuch, 1, pp. 261–2; vol. 3, pp. 254, 258, 267; HMC Cowper, 1, p. 235; *APC*, 1625–6, pp. 228–9, 231, 234, 237–8, 248, 249; Pollen, 'Notebook of John Southcote',

p. 101; *LJ*, III, p. 496. See too PRO SO 3/8 (June 1626); SP 14/155, ff. 31v–32r; SP 16/12, f. 106; Questier, *Stuart Dynastic Policy and Religious Politics*, pp. 27–8; 124–7; R. Cust, 'Knightley, Richard', *ODNB*; Seaver, 'Puritan Preachers and Their Patrons', pp. 141–2.

22 Wake, *The Montagu Musters Book*, p. 224 and note on p. xlv. For the Vaux contribution to the musters, see ibid., pp. 6, 18, 21, 45, 51, 61, 76, 92, 100, 117, 145, 163, 189, 205.

23 PRO PROB 11/155/169.

24 Foley, *Records*, II, p. 561; PRO C 203/4, no. 46; BL Add. MS 61681, f. 95r; Cal. Committee for Compounding, p. 88; *LJ*, IX, pp. 67–8 (18 June 1660).

25 Champion, 'Popes and Guys and Anti-Catholicism', in Buchanan et al., *Gunpowder Plots*, pp. 104–5; M. Murphy, *St. Gregory's College, Seville*, CRS 73 (1992), p. 174. For Edward's death, see *The Case of William Earl of Banbury*, Minutes, pp. 14–15.

26 William Knollys was born on 20 March 1545. See Varlow, 'Sir Francis Knollys's Latin Dictionary', App.

27 L. Hotson, *The First Night of Twelfth Night* (1954), pp. 97–119; Lady Newdigate-Newdegate, *Gossip from a Muniment Room* (1897), *passim*.

28 The main sources here are *The Case of William Earl of Banbury*, which includes minutes of the evidence given before the Committee of Privileges, and Nicolas, *A Treatise on the Law of Adulterine Bastardy*.

29 Nicolas, *Adulterine Bastardy*, pp. 302, 311–16, 319. Knollys did not mention the boy in his will of 19 May 1630.

30 *The Case of William Earl of Banbury*, Minutes, pp. 57–9, 254.

31 Questier, *Newsletters from the Caroline Court*, p. 122. John Southcot, who wrote those words, was, admittedly, incensed that Edward had assented to the 'Protestatio Declaratoria' against the jurisdiction of Richard Smith, Bishop of Chalcedon, in England, although secular disapproval of Edward and Elizabeth's relationship seems to have pre-dated the petition. See ibid., pp. 78–81.

32 HMC Salisbury, 22, p. 433.

33 BL Harl MS 5808, f. 9r.

34 *The Case of William Earl of Banbury*, Minutes, pp. 219–30.

35 V. Stater, 'Knollys, William', *ODNB*.

36 Nicolas, *Adulterine Bastardy*, *passim*, but esp. pp. 65–6, 72, 529–31.

37 PRO PROB 11/305/356.

38 *Vaux Petitions*, p. 5.

39 Hansard, 21 Feb. 1962, 4.44 pm (cols 758–9).

40 NRO V 375. The anonymous author seems confused; Lord Vaux was already a monk.

41 Barlow, *The Gunpowder-Treason*, pp. 1–2.

42 PRO SP 14/216/180; Howell, *State Trials*, II, cols 186–7.

Select Bibliography

MANUSCRIPTS

Archivum Britannicum Societatis Iesu, London
Collectanea Manuscripts
Anglia Manuscripts

Bodleian Library, Oxford
Ashmole Manuscripts
Laudian Collection
MSS Eng.
Rawlinson Manuscripts
Tanner Manuscripts

British Library, London
Additional Manuscripts
Cotton Manuscripts
Harley Manuscripts
Lansdowne Manuscripts
Royal Manuscripts
Stowe Manuscripts
Microfilms of the Cecil Papers at Hatfield House, Hertfordshire

College of Arms, London
Vincent Collection

Folger Shakespeare Library, Washington, D.C.
Henry Vaux Poems (Bd.w. STC 22957)

Inner Temple Library, London
Petyt Manuscripts

Leicestershire Record Office
Parish Registers, Ashby Magna

National Archives, Kew
Records of: Chancery (C), the Exchequer (E), the Court of King's Bench (KB), the Prerogative Court of Canterbury (PROB), the Court of Wards and Liveries (WARD), the Signet Office (SO), the Court of Star Chamber (STAC)
State Papers (SP): Domestic, Scotland (53), Flanders (77), France (78) and Portugal (89)
Transcripts (PRO 31)

Northamptonshire Record Office
Clayton Collection
Family and Estate Collections: Brudenell (BRU), Finch Hatton (FH), Vaux (V), Watson (WR)
Parish Registers, Irthlingborough
YZ series

The Shakespeare Centre, Stratford-upon-Avon
Baddesley Clinton Deeds (DR 3)

Westminster Diocesan Archives, London
A Series

PRIMARY SOURCES

Unless otherwise stated, the place of publication is London.

A discoverie of the treasons practised and attempted against the Queenes Maiestie and the Realme, by Francis Throckmorton (1584)
The Case of William Earl of Banbury, on his petition to the King, to be summoned to Parliament for the Banbury Earldom (1809)
Allen, W., *An Admonition to the Nobility and People of England and Ireland* ([Antwerp?], 1588)
Bowler, H. (ed.), *Recusant Roll No. 2 (1593–1594)*, CRS 57 (1965)
—, *Recusant Roll No. 3 (1594–1595) and Recusant Roll No. 4 (1595–1596)*, CRS 61 (1970)
—, and McCann, T. J. (eds), *Recusants in the Exchequer Pipe Rolls 1581–1592*, CRS 71 (1986)
Bruce, J., 'Observations upon certain Proceedings in the Star-Chamber against Lord Vaux, Sir Thomas Tresham, Sir William Catesby, and others, for

refusing to swear that they had not harboured Campion the Jesuit', *Archaeologia*, 30 (1844)

The Reports of Edward Bulstrode of the Inner Temple, pt 1 (1657)

Calendar of the Proceedings of the Committee for Compounding, 1643–1660, ed. M. A. E. Green (1889)

Calendar of Letters and State Papers relating to English Affairs, preserved principally in the Archives of Simancas: Elizabeth, ed. M. A. S. Hume (1892–9)

Calendar of State Papers, Domestic, ed. R. Lemon, M. A. E. Green (1856–72)

Calendar of State Papers relating to English Affairs, preserved principally at Rome: Elizabeth, ed. J. M. Rigg (1916–26)

Camden, W., *Annales* (1625 edn)

Campion, E., *Ten Reasons proposed to his adversaries for disputation in the name of the faith and presented to the illustrious members of our univesities* (1914)

Caraman, P. (ed.), *The Other Face: Catholic Life under Elizabeth I* (1960)

Carvajal y Mendoza, L. de., *Epistolario y Poesías*, ed. C. M. Abad, Biblioteca de Autores Españoles, 179 (Madrid, 1965)

Cecil, W., *Salutem in Christo* (1571)

Christie, R. C. (ed.), *Letters of Sir Thomas Copley* (1897)

Clark, S., *England's Remembrancer: containing a true and full narrative of that never-to-be-forgotten deliverance, the Spanish Invasion in 1588* (1657; repr. 1819)

Colleton, J., *A Just Defence of the Slandered Priestes* (1602)

Cox, J. C. (ed.), *Three Centuries of Derbyshire Annals*, 2 vols (1890)

Cross, C. (ed.), 'The Letters of Sir Francis Hastings, 1574–1609', *Somerset Record Society* 69 (1969)

Dekker, T., *The Wonderful Year 1603*, in *Three Elizabethan Pamphlets*, ed. G. R. Hibbard (1951)

D'Ewes, S., *The Journals of all the Parliaments during the Reign of Queen Elizabeth* (1682)

Donnelly, J. P. (ed. and trans.), *Jesuit Writings of the Early Modern Period, 1540–1640* (Indianapolis, Ind., 2006)

Fitzalan-Howard, H. G. (ed.), *The Lives of Philip Howard, Earl of Arundel, and of Anne Dacres, his wife* (1857)

Foley, H. (ed.), *Records of the English Province of the Society of Jesus*, 7 vols in 8 (1875–83)

Foxe, J., *The Unabridged Acts and Monuments Online* (HRI Online Publications, Sheffield, 2011). Available from: http://wwwjohnfoxe.org

Gardiner, S. R. (ed.), 'Two Declarations of Garnet Relating to the Gunpowder Plot', *English Historical Review*, 3/11 (1888)

Garnet, H., *A Summe of Christian Doctrine: Composed in Latin by the R. Father P. Canisius of the Society of Jesus* [n.d. *c*.1592–6], ERL, 35 (1971)

—, *The Societie of the Rosary* (1st edn, *c*.1593; 2nd edn, *c*.1596)

G[arter], B., *A Newyeares Gifte dedicated to the Popes Holinesse, and all Catholikes addicted to the Sea of Rome* (1579)

Gee, J., *The Foot out of the Snare* (1624), ed. T. H. B. M. Harmsen (Nijmegen, 1992)

—, *New Shreds of the Old Snare* (1624)

Gerard, J., *The Condition of Catholics under James I: Father Gerard's Narrative of the Gunpowder Plot*, ed. J. Morris (1871)

—, *The Autobiography of an Elizabethan*, trans. P. Caraman (1951)

Gilbert, C. D., 'Thomas Habington's Account of the 1606 Search at Hindlip', *RH*, 25/3 (2001)

Godeau, A., *The Life of the Apostle St Paul, written in French by the famous Bishop of Grasse, and now Englished by a person of honour* (1653)

Goring, J. and Wake, J. (eds), *Northamptonshire Lieutenancy Papers and Other Documents, 1580–1614*, NRS, 27 (1975)

Hamilton, A. (ed.), *The Chronicle of the English Augustinian Canonesses Regular of the Lateran, at St Monica's in Louvain*, 2 vols (1904–6)

Harington, J., *Nugae Antiquae*, 3 vols (1779)

Hartley, T. E. (ed.), *Proceedings in the Parliaments of Elizabeth I*, vol. 1 (Leicester, 1981)

Hawarde, J., *Les Reportes del Cases in Camera Stellata, 1593 to 1609* (1894)

Haynes, S. (ed.), *A Collection of State Papers . . . at Hatfield House* (1740)

Henson, E. (ed.), *Registers of the English College at Valladolid, 1589–1862*, CRS 30 (1930)

'His Majesty's Speech in this last Session of Parliament, concerning the Gunpowder-Plot . . . Together with a Discourse of the Manner of the Discovery of this late intended Treason, joined with the Examination of some of the Prisoners, 1605', *Harleian Miscellany* 4 (1745)

Hodgetts, M. A., 'A Certificate of Warwickshire Recusants, 1592', *Worcestershire Recusant* 5, 6 (1965)

Howell, T. B. et al., *A Complete Collection of State Trials*, 34 vols (1809–28)

Hughes, T., *History of the Society of Jesus in North America: Documents*, vol. I, pt I (1908)

Hyland, S. K., *A Century of Persecution under Tudor and Stuart Sovereigns from Contemporary Records* (1920)

'Isham Correspondence', *Northamptonshire Past and Present* 1/1 (1948)

Jeaffreson, J. C. (ed.), *Middlesex County Records*, 4 vols (1886–92)

Jones, H. V. (ed.), 'The Journal of Levinus Munck', *English Historical Review*, 68/267 (1953)

Kempis, Thomas a, *The Following of Christ, 1613*, ERL, 369 (1977)

Kingdon, R. M. (ed.), *The Execution of Justice in England by William Cecil and A True, Sincere, and Modest Defense of English Catholics by William Allen* (Ithaca, NY, 1965)

Knox, T. F. (ed.), *The First and Second Diaries of the English College, Douay* (1878)

—, *The Letters and Memorials of William Cardinal Allen* (1882)

Larkin, J. F. and Hughes, P. L. (eds), *Stuart Royal Proclamations*, vol. I (Oxford, 1973)

Laughton, J. K. (ed.), *State Papers Relating to the Defeat of the Spanish Armada*, vol. 2 (Havant, 1981).

Lessius, L. and Androtius, F., *The Treasure of Vowed Chastity in Secular Persons. Also the Widdowes Glasse, trans. I.W.P., 1621*, ERL, 214 (1974)

Letters and Papers, Foreign and Domestic, of the Reign of Henry VIII, ed. J. S. Brewer, J. Gairdner and R. H. Brodie, 21 vols and addenda (1862–1932)

Lippincott, H. F. (ed.), '"Merry Passages and Jeasts": A Manuscript Jestbook of Sir Nicholas le Strange (1603–1655)', *Elizabethan & Renaissance Studies*, 29 (1974)

Loarte, G., *The Exercise of a Christian Life, [1579]*, ERL, 44 (1970)

Markham, C., *Markham Memorials*, 2 vols (1913)

McClure, N. E. (ed.), *The Letters of John Chamberlain*, vol. I (Philadelphia, 1939)

Miola, R. S., *Early Modern Catholicism: An Anthology of Primary Sources* (Oxford, 2007)

More, H., *Historia Missionis Anglicanae Societatis Jesu* (St Omer, 1660), ed. and trans. F. Edwards, in *The Elizabethan Jesuits* (1981)

Morris, J. (ed.), *The Troubles of our Catholic Forefathers related by themselves*, 3 vols (1872–7)

Orchard, M. E. (ed.), *Till God Will: Mary Ward through Her Writings* (1985)

Palmes, W., *Life of Mrs Dorothy Lawson of St Anthony's near Newcastle-upon-Tyne in Northumberland*, ed. G. B. Richardson (1851)

Peel, A. (ed.), *The Seconde Parte of a Register: Being a Calendar of Manuscripts under that title intended for publication by the Puritans about 1593, and now in Dr Williams's Library, London*, 2 vols (Cambridge, 1915)

Persons, R., 'Of the Life and Martyrdom of Father Edmond Campian', *Letters and Notices* 11 & 12 (1877–8)

—, 'The Memoirs of Father Robert Persons', ed. J. H. Pollen, CRS 2 & 4 (1906–7)

Petti, A. G. (ed.), *The Letters and Despatches of Richard Verstegan*, CRS 52 (1959)

Pollen, J. H. (ed.), 'The Notebook of John Southcote, 1628–36', CRS 1 (1905)

—, 'The Official Lists of Catholic Prisoners during the Reign of Queen Elizabeth, pt 2: 1581–1602', CRS 2 (1906)

—, *Unpublished Documents Relating to the English Martyrs, I: 1584–1603*, CRS 5 (1908)

P[ricket], R., *The Jesuits Miracles, or new Popish Wonders* (1607)

Puttenham, G., *The Arte of English Poesie*, ed. G. D. Willcock and A. Walker (Cambridge, 1936)

Questier, M. C. (ed.), *Newsletters from the Archpresbyterate of George Birkhead*, Camden Fifth Series, 12 (1998)

—, *Newsletters from the Caroline Court, 1631–1638: Catholicism and the Politics of the Personal Rule*, Camden Fifth Series, 26 (2005)

Razzell, P. (ed.), *The Journals of Two Travellers in Elizabethan and Early Stuart England: Thomas Platter and Horatio Busino* (1995)

Read, C. (ed.), *The Bardon Papers: Documents Relating to the Imprisonment & Trial of Mary Queen of Scots*, Camden Society, Third Series, 17 (1909)

Recusancy and Conformity in Early Modern England: Manuscript and Printed Sources in Translation, ed. G. Crosignani, T. M. McCoog, and M. Questier with the assistance of P. Holmes, Pontifical Institute of Mediaeval Studies, Studies and Texts 170 (Toronto, 2010)

Redworth, G. (ed.), *The Letters of Luisa de Carvajal y Mendoza*, 2 vols (2012)

Roberts, G. (ed.), *Diary of Walter Yonge, Esq., Justice of the Peace, and M.P. for Honiton . . . 1604 to 1628*, Camden Society, 41 (1848)

Rollins, H. E. (ed.), *The Paradise of Dainty Devices (1576–1606)* (Cambridge, Mass., 1927)

—, *Tottel's Miscellany (1557–1587)*, 2 vols (Cambridge, Mass., 1928–9)

Shakespeare, W., *The Complete Works*, ed. S. Wells, G. Taylor et al. (Oxford, 1986)

Sheldon, R., *A Survey of the Miracles of the Church of Rome, proving them to be Antichristian* (1616)

Simpson, R., 'A Morning at the Star-Chamber', *The Rambler,* new series, 7 (1857)

Sorlien, R. P. (ed.), *The Diary of John Manningham of the Middle Temple 1602–1603* (Hanover, NH, 1976)

Southwell, R., *An Humble Supplication to her Maiestie*, ed. R. C. Bald (Cambridge, 1953)

—, *A Short Rule of Good Life*, ERL, 78 (1971)

—, 'Two Letters and Short Rules of a Good Life', ed. N. P. Brown, *Folger Documents of Tudor and Stuart Civilization*, 21 (Charlottesville, Va, 1973)

Strype, J., *Annals of the Reformation*, 4 vols (Oxford, 1824)

Swynnerton, J., *A Christian Love-Letter Sent particularly to K.T. a Gentlewoman mis-styled A CATHOLICKE, but generallie intended to all of the Romish Religion, to labour their conversion to the true faith of Christ Iesvs* (1606)

Talbot, C. (ed.), *Recusant Records*, CRS 53 (1961)

Taylor, J. (ed.), *Tracts relating to Northamptonshire*, second series (Northampton, 1881)

Tesimond, O., *The Gunpowder Plot: The Narrative of Oswald Tesimond alias Greenway*, trans. and ed. F. Edwards (1973)

Tierney, M. A., *Dodd's Church History of England*, 5 vols (1839–43)

Varlow, S., 'Sir Francis Knollys's Latin Dictionary: New Evidence for Katherine Carey', *Historical Research* 80/209 (2007)

Vaux, L., *A Catechisme, or a Christian Doctrine, necessary for Children & ignorant people* (Antwerp, 1574 edn)

Vossen, A. F. (ed.), *Two Bokes of The Histories of Ireland compiled by Edmunde Campion* (Assen, 1963)

Wake, J. (ed.), *The Montagu Musters Book, A.D. 1602–1623*, NRS, 7 (1935)

Walpole, M. (trans.), *The Life of B. Father Ignatius of Loyola, Authour, and Founder of the Society of Jesus. Translated out of Spanish into English, by W. M. of the same Society* (1616)

Watson, W., *A Decacordon of Ten Quodlibeticall Questions Concerning Religion and State* (1602)

Weston, W., *The Autobiography of an Elizabethan*, trans. P. Caraman (1955)

Willson, D. H. (ed.), *The Parliamentary Diary of Robert Bowyer, 1606–1607* (Minneapolis, Minn., 1931)

SECONDARY WORKS

Alford, S., *Burghley: William Cecil and the Court of Elizabeth I* (2008)

—, *The Watchers: A Secret History of the Reign of Elizabeth I* (2012)

Allison, A. F. and Rogers, D. M., *The Contemporary Printed Literature of the English Counter-Reformation between 1558 and 1640*, 2 vols (Aldershot, 1989–94)

Anstruther, G., *Vaux of Harrowden: A Recusant Family* (Newport, Monmouthshire, 1953)

—, *The Seminary Priests: A Dictionary of the Secular Clergy of England and Wales*, vol. I: *Elizabethan 1558–1603* (Ware, Durham, 1968)

Barlow, T. (ed.), *The Gunpowder-Treason, with a Discourse of the Manner of its Discovery* (1679)

Bartoli, D., *Dell' Istoria della Compagnia di Giesu l'Inghilterra* (Rome, 1667)

Baynham, M., '"Twice done and then done double": Equivocation and the Catholic Recusant Hostess in Shakespeare's *Macbeth*', in *The Accession of James I*, ed. G. Burgess, R. Wymer and J. Lawrence (Basingstoke, 2006)

Beales, A. C. F., *Education Under Penalty: English Catholic Education from the Reformation to the Fall of James II, 1547–1689* (1963)

Bossy, J., *The English Catholic Community: 1570–1850* (1975)

—, 'The Heart of Robert Persons', in McCoog, *The Reckoned Expense* (1996)

—, *Under the Molehill: An Elizabethan Spy Story* (2001)

Bridges, J., *The History and Antiquities of Northamptonshire*, 2 vols (Oxford, 1791)

Brigden, S., *New Worlds, Lost Worlds: The Rule of the Tudors, 1485–1603* (2000)

Brown, C. C., 'Recusant Community and Jesuit Mission in Parliament Days: Bodleian MS Eng. poet. b.5', *The Yearbook of English Studies* 33 (2003)

Brown, N. P., 'Paperchase: The Dissemination of Catholic Texts in Elizabethan England', *English Manuscript Studies 1100–1700* I (Oxford, 1989)

Brown, N. P., 'Robert Southwell: The Mission of the Written Word', in McCoog, *The Reckoned Expense* (1996)

Brownlow, F. W., *Shakespeare, Harsnett, and the Devils of Denham* (1993)

Buchanan, B., Cannadine, D., Champion, J., Cressy, D., Croft, P., Fraser, A. and Jay, M., *Gunpowder Plots: A Celebration of 400 Years of Bonfire Night* (2005)

Camm, B., *Forgotten Shrines: An Account of Some Old Catholic Halls and Families in England and of Relics and Memorials of the English Martyrs* (1910)

Caraman, P., *Henry Garnet 1555–1606 and the Gunpowder Plot* (1964)

Challoner, R., *Memoirs of Missionary Priests*, ed. J. H. Pollen (1924)

Collinson, P., *The Elizabethan Puritan Movement* (1967)

Colthorpe, M., 'Edmund Campion's Alleged Interview with Queen Elizabeth in 1581', *RH*, 17/3 (1985)

Cooper, J., *The Queen's Agent: Francis Walsingham at the Court of Elizabeth I* (2011)

Corthell, R., Dolan, F. E., Highley, C. and Marotti, A. F. (eds), *Catholic Culture in Early Modern England* (Notre Dame, Ind., 2007)

Crawford, P., 'Attitudes to Menstruation in Seventeenth-Century England', *Past and Present* 91 (1981)

—, *Women and Religion in England 1500–1720* (1993)

Cressy, D., *Birth, Marriage, and Death: Ritual, Religion, and the Life-Cycle in Tudor and Stuart England* (Oxford, 1997)

De Lisle, L., *After Elizabeth: How James, King of Scots Won the Crown of England in 1603* (2004)

—, and Stanford, P., *The Catholics and Their Houses* (1995)

Devlin, C., *The Life of Robert Southwell, Poet and Martyr* (1956)

Dillon, A., 'Praying by Number: The Confraternity of the Rosary and the English Catholic Community, *c*.1580–1700', *History* 88/291 (2003)

Ditchfield, S., 'The Jesuits: In the Making of a World Religion', *History Today*, 57/7 (2007)

Dolan, F. E., 'Reading, Work, and Catholic Women's Biographies', *English Literary Renaissance* 33/3 (2003)

Duffy, E., *The Stripping of the Altars: Traditional Religion in England c.1400–c.1580* (1992)

—, *Fires of Faith: Catholic England under Mary Tudor* (2009)

Edwards, F., *Robert Persons: The Biography of an Elizabethan Jesuit 1546–1610* (St Louis, Mo., 1995)

Finch, M. E., *The Wealth of Five Northamptonshire Families 1540–1640*, NRS, 19 (1956)

Fincham, K. and Lake, P. (eds), *Religious Politics in Post-Reformation England: Essays in Honour of Nicholas Tyacke* (Woodbridge, 2006)

Fincham K. and Tyacke, N., 'Religious Change and the Laity in England', *History Today*, 58/6 (2008)

Finucane, R. C., *Miracles and Pilgrims: Popular Beliefs in Medieval England* (1995 edn)

Fraser, A., *Mary Queen of Scots* (1969)

—, *The Gunpowder Plot: Terror & Faith in 1605* (1997 edn)

Frieda, L., *Catherine de Medici* (2003)

Gotch, J. A., *A Complete Account, illustrated by measured drawings, of The Buildings Erected in Northamptonshire by Sir Thomas Tresham* (1883)

—, *The Old Halls & Manor-Houses of Northamptonshire* (1936)

Graves, M. A. R., *Thomas Norton: The Parliament Man* (Oxford and Cambridge, Mass., 1994)

Greenblatt, S., 'Shakespeare and the Exorcists', in *Shakespearean Negotiations: The Circulation of Social Energy in Renaissance England* (Berkeley and Los Angeles, 1988)

Guy, J., *'My Heart is My Own': The Life of Mary Queen of Scots* (2004)

Hacksley, T. C., 'A Critical Edition of the Poems of Henry Vaux (*c*.1559–1587) in MS. Folger Bd with STC 22957' (MA thesis, Rhodes University, 2008)

Haigh, C., *The Plain Man's Pathways to Heaven: Kinds of Christianity in Post-Reformation England, 1570–1640* (Oxford, 2007)

Harley, J., *William Byrd: Gentleman of the Chapel Royal* (Aldershot, 1999)

'Harrowden Hall', *Country Life*, 24/625 (1908)

Heale, E., 'Contesting Terms: Loyal Catholicism and Lord Montague's Entertainment at Cowdray, 1591', in *The Progresses, Pageants, and Entertainments of Queen Elizabeth*, ed. J. E. Archer, E. Goldring and S. Knight (Oxford, 2007)

Hicks, L (ed.), *Letters and Memorials of Father Robert Persons, S.J., I: 1578–1588*, CRS 39 (1942)

Hodgetts, M., *Secret Hiding-Places* (Dublin, 1989)

—, 'Loca Secretiora in 1581', *RH*, 19/4 (1989)

—, *Life at Harvington 1250–2000* (Birmingham, 2002)

Hogge, A., *God's Secret Agents: Queen Elizabeth's Forbidden Priests and the Hatching of the Gunpowder Plot* (2005)

Holmes, C., 'Witchcraft and Possession at the Accession of James I: The Publication of Samuel Harsnett's *A Declaration of Egregious Popish Impostures*', in *Witchcraft and the Act of 1604*, ed. J. Newton and J. Bath (Leiden and Boston, 2008)

Holmes, P. J., *Elizabethan Casuistry*, CRS 67 (1981)

—, *Resistance and Compromise: The Political Thought of the Elizabethan Catholics* (Cambridge, 1982)

Holroyd, S., '"Rich Embrodered Churchstuffe": The Vestments of Helena Wintour', in Corthell et al., *Catholic Culture in Early Modern England* (2007)

Ingram, M., *Church Courts, Sex and Marriage in England, 1570–1640* (Cambridge, 1987)

Jones, N. L., *Faith by Statute: Parliament and the Settlement of Religion 1559* (1982)

Kaushik, S., 'Resistance, Loyalty and Recusant Politics: Sir Thomas Tresham and the Elizabethan State', *Midlands History* 21 (1996)

Kilroy, G., *Edmund Campion: Memory and Transcription* (Aldershot, 2005)

Lake, P., 'Anti-popery: the Structure of a Prejudice', in *Conflict in Early Stuart England*, ed. R. Cust and A. Hughes (1989)

—, and Questier, M. (eds), *Conformity and Orthodoxy in the English Church, c.1560–1660* (Woodbridge, 2000)

—, and Questier, M., 'Puritans, Papists, and the "Public Sphere" in Early Modern England: The Edmund Campion Affair in Context', *The Journal of Modern History* 72/3 (2000)

—, and Questier, M., *The Trials of Margaret Clitherow: Persecution, Martyrdom and the Politics of Sanctity in Elizabethan England* (2011)

LaRocca, J. J., 'Time, Death, and the Next Generation: The Early Elizabethan Recusancy Policy, 1558–1574', *Albion* 14/2 (1982)

—, 'Popery and Pounds: The Effect of the Jesuit Mission on Penal Legislation', in McCoog, *The Reckoned Expense* (1996)

Loades, D., 'Foxe's Book of Martyrs and the Face of England', *History Today*, 55/12 (2005)

Longley, K. M., *Saint Margaret Clitherow* (Wheathampstead, 1986)

Loomie, A. J., *The Spanish Elizabethans: The English Exiles at the Court of Philip II* (1963)

—, 'Guy Fawkes in Spain: The "Spanish Treason" in Spanish Documents', *Bulletin of the Institute of Historical Research*, special supplement, 9 (1971)

—, *English Polemics at the Spanish Court: Joseph Creswell's Letter to the Ambassador from England, the English and Spanish Texts of 1606* (New York, 1993)

Lux-Sterritt, L., *Redefining Female Religious Life: French Ursulines and English Ladies in Seventeenth-Century Catholicism* (Aldershot, 2005)

MacCulloch, D., *Reformation: Europe's House Divided 1490–1700* (2003)

—, 'The Latitude of the Church of England', in Fincham and Lake, *Religious Politics in Post-Reformation England* (2006)

MacDonald, M., *Witchcraft and Hysteria in Elizabethan London: Edward Jorden and the Mary Glover Case* (1991)

Marsh, C., *Popular Religion in Sixteenth-Century England* (Basingstoke, 1998)

Mattingly, G., 'William Allen and Catholic Propaganda in England', *Aspects de la Propagande Religieuse*, ed. E. Droz (Geneva, 1957)

—, *The Defeat of the Spanish Armada* (1959)

McClain, L., *Lest We be Damned: Practical Innovation and Lived Experience among Catholics in Protestant England, 1559–1642* (2004)

McCoog, T. M., 'The Society of Jesus in England, 1623–1688: An Institutional Study' (Ph.D. thesis, Warwick, 1984)

—, 'The Creation of the First Jesuit Communities in England', *The Heythrop Journal* 28/1 (1987)

— '"The Slightest Suspicion of Avarice": The Finances of the English Jesuit Mission', *RH*, 19/2 (1988)

—, *English and Welsh Jesuits, 1555–1650*, 2 vols, CRS 74 and 75 (1994–5)

—, '"Playing the Champion": The Role of Disputation in the Jesuit Mission', in McCoog, *The Reckoned Expense* (1996)

— (ed.), *The Reckoned Expense: Edmund Campion and the Early English Jesuits* (Woodbridge, 1996)

—, *The Society of Jesus in Ireland, Scotland, and England 1541–1588: 'Our Way of Proceeding?'* (Leiden, New York, Köln, 1996)

—, 'The English Jesuit Mission and the French Match, 1579–1581', *The Catholic Historical Review* 87/2 (2001)

—, 'Construing Martyrdom in the English Catholic Community, 1582–1602', in Shagan, *Catholics and the 'Protestant nation'* (2005)

McGrath, P., *Papists and Puritans under Elizabeth I* (1967)

—, 'The Bloody Questions Reconsidered', *RH*, 20/3 (1991)

— and Rowe, J., 'The Marian Priests under Elizabeth', *RH*, 17/2 (1984)

— and Rowe, J., 'The Elizabethan Priests: Their Harbourers and Helpers', *RH*, 19/3 (1989)

McNamara, J. A. K., *Sisters in Arms: Catholic Nuns through Two Millennia* (1996)

Merriman, R. B., 'Some Notes on the Treatment of the English Catholics in the Reign of Elizabeth', *The American Historical Review*, 13 (1908)

Murphy, J. L., *Darkness and Devils: Exorcism and King Lear* (Athens, Ohio, 1984)

Neale, J. E., *Elizabeth I and Her Parliaments: 1559–1581* (1953)

Nicholls, M., *Investigating Gunpowder Plot* (Manchester, 1991)

—, 'Strategy and Motivation in the Gunpowder Plot', *The Historical Journal*, 50/4 (2007)

Nicolas, H., *A Treatise on the Law of Adulterine Bastardy, with a report of the Banbury case, and of all other cases bearing upon the subject* (1836)

Nuttall, G. F., 'The English Martyrs 1535–1680: A Statistical Review', *Journal of Ecclesiastical History*, 22/3 (1971)

O'Malley, J. W. (ed.), *Catholicism in Early Modern History* (St Louis, Mo., 1988)

Parker, G., *The Grand Strategy of Philip II* (1998)

—, 'The Place of Tudor England in the Messianic Vision of Philip II of Spain', *Transactions of the Royal Historical Society*, sixth series, 12 (2002)

Peck, L. L., *Northampton: Patronage and Policy at the Court of James I* (1982)

Plowden, A., *Danger to Elizabeth: The Catholics under Elizabeth I* (1973)

Pollen, J. H. (ed.), *Mary Queen of Scots and the Babington Plot: Edited from the Original Documents*, Scottish History Society, third series, 3 (Edinburgh, 1922)

Poulton, D., *John Dowland* (rev. edn, 1982)

Questier, M., '"Like Locusts over all the World": Conversion, Indoctrination and the Society of Jesus in late Elizabethan and Jacobean England', in McCoog, *The Reckoned Expense* (1996)

—, 'Elizabeth and the Catholics', in Shagan, *Catholics and the 'Protestant nation'* (2005)

—, *Catholicism and Community in Early Modern England: Politics, Aristocratic Patronage and Religion, c.1550–1640* (Cambridge, 2006)

—, 'Catholic Loyalism in Early Stuart England', *English Historical Review*, 123/504 (2008)

— (ed.), *Stuart Dynastic Policy and Religious Politics 1621–1625*, Camden Fifth Series, 34 (2009)

—, see also entries under Lake

Quinn, D. B., *The Voyages and Colonising Enterprises of Sir Humphrey Gilbert*, 2 vols (The Hakluyt Society, 1940)

Redworth, G., *The She-Apostle: The Extraordinary Life and Death of Luisa de Carvajal* (Oxford, 2008)

Rees, M. A., *The Writings of Doña Luisa de Carvajal y Mendoza, Catholic Missionary to James I's London* (Lewiston, Queenston, Lampeter, 2002)

Rees, O., 'Luisa de Carvajal y Mendoza and Music in an English Catholic House in 1605', in E. Hornby and D. Maw (eds), *Essays on the History of English Music in Honour of John Caldwell* (Woodbridge, 2010)

Rex, R., 'Thomas Vavasour M.D.', *RH*, 20/4 (1991)

—, *Elizabeth: Fortune's Bastard?* (Stroud, 2007 edn)

Reynolds, E. E., *Campion and Parsons* (1980)

Rhodes, E., *This Tight Embrace: Luisa de Carvajal y Mendoza (1566–1614)* (Milwaukee, Wis., 2000)

Rowlands, M. B., 'Recusant Women 1560–1640' in *Women in English Society 1500–1800*, ed. M. Prior (1985)

— (ed.), *English Catholics of Parish and Town 1558–1778*, CRS mon. 5 (1999)

Salgādo, G., *The Elizabethan Underworld* (Stroud, 2005 edn)

Schroder, T. (ed.), *Treasures of the English Church: A Thousand Years of Sacred Gold & Silver* (2008)

Seaver, P., 'Puritan Preachers and Their Patrons', in Fincham and Lake, *Religious Politics in Post-Reformation England* (2006)

Shagan, E. (ed.), *Catholics and the 'Protestant nation': Religious Politics and Identity in Early Modern England* (Manchester and New York, 2005)

Sheils, W. J., *The Puritans in the Diocese of Peterborough, 1558–1610*, NRS, 30 (1979)

Shell, A., '"Furor juvenilis": Post-Reformation English Catholicism and Exemplary Youthful Behaviour', in Shagan, *Catholics and the 'Protestant nation'* (2005)

—, *Oral Culture and Catholicism in Early Modern England* (Cambridge, 2007)

Shirley, E. P., *Stemmata Shirleiana: or the Annals of the Shirley Family* (1873)

Simpson, R., *Edmund Campion: A Biography* (2nd edn, 1896)

Sommerville, J. P., 'Papalist Political Thought and the Controversy over the

Jacobean Oath of Allegiance', in Shagan, *Catholics and the 'Protestant nation'* (2005)

Squiers, G., *Secret Hiding-Places: The Origins, Histories and Descriptions of English Secret Hiding-Places Used by Priests, Cavaliers, Jacobites & Smugglers* (1933)

Stubbs, J., *Donne: The Reformed Soul* (2006)

Thomas, K., 'Art and Iconoclasm in Early Modern England', in Fincham and Lake, *Religious Politics in Post-Reformation England* (2006)

Travers, J., *Gunpowder: The Players behind the Plot* (Kew, 2005)

Trimble, W. R., *The Catholic Laity in Elizabethan England, 1558–1603* (Cambridge, Mass., 1964)

Vallance, A., 'The Ropers and Their Monuments in Lynsted Church', *Archaeologia Cantiana*, 44 (1932)

Wake, J., *The Brudenells of Deene* (1954)

—, 'The Death of Francis Tresham', *Northamptonshire Past and Present* 2 (1954–9)

Walsham, A., *Church Papists: Catholicism, Conformity and Confessional Polemic in Early Modern England* (Woodbridge, 1993)

—, *Providence in Early Modern England* (Oxford, 1999)

—, '"Domme Preachers?" Post-Reformation English Catholicism and the Culture of Print', *Past & Present* 168 (2000)

—, 'Miracles and the Counter-Reformation Mission to England', *Historical Journal*, 46/4 (2003)

—, 'Holywell: Contesting Sacred Space in post-Reformation Wales', in *Sacred Space in Early Modern Europe*, ed. W. Coster and A. Spicer (Cambridge, 2005)

—, 'Translating Trent? English Catholicism and the Counter-Reformation', *Historical Research* 78/201 (2005)

Weber, A., 'Little Women: Counter-Reformation Misogyny', in *The Counter-Reformation*, ed. D. M. Luebke (Oxford, 1999)

Williams, N., *Thomas Howard Fourth Duke of Norfolk* (1964)

Williams, P., *The Later Tudors: England 1547–1603* (Oxford, 1995)

Williams, R., 'Forbidden Sacred Spaces in Reformation England', in *Defining the Holy: Sacred Space in Medieval and Early Modern Europe*, ed. A. Spicer and S. Hamilton (Aldershot, 2005)

Waugh, E., *Edmund Campion* (1935)

Wilson, D., *Sir Francis Walsingham: A Courtier in an Age of Terror* (2007)

Woodall, J., 'Recusant Rowington', *Worcestershire Recusant* 31 (1978)

Wormald, J., 'Gunpowder, Treason, and Scots', *Journal of British Studies*, 24/2 (1985)

Younger, N., 'If the Armada Had Landed: A Reappraisal of England's Defences in 1588', *History*, 93/311 (2008)

List of Illustrations

Main Text

Plate Section 1

alumni to Christ', from *Ecclesia Anglicanae Trophaea* (Rome, 1584), P.2.33(2) plate 31. Reproduced by kind permission of the Syndics of Cambridge University Library

10. Edmund Campion, S.J. Engraving from *A Particular Declaration or Testimony of the Undutifull and Traiterous Affection Borne Against her Maiestie by Edmond Campion Jesuite, and Other Condemned Priestes* (London, 1582) © Jesuit Institute

11. Campion on the rack. Engraving after a lost fresco by Niccoló Circignani commissioned by George Gilbert for the English College in Rome, from *Ecclesia Anglicanae Trophaea* (Rome, 1584), P.2.33(2) plate 36. Reproduced by kind permission of the Syndics of Cambridge University Library

12. Campion's Rope © Jesuit Institute

13. The pressing to death of Margaret Clitherow, 25 March 1586, from Richard Verstegan, *Theatrum Crudelitatum Haereticorum Nostri Temporis* (Antwerp 1587) © The British Library Board. G.11732

14. Mary Queen of Scots' cipher endorsed by Anthony Babington © The National Archives, ref. SP 12/193/54

15. Sir Thomas Tresham (1543–1605), artist unknown. Reproduced by kind permission of the Duke of Buccleuch and Queensberry

16. Aerial view of The Triangular Lodge at Rushton, Northamptonshire © www.skyscan.co.uk

17. Aerial view of Lyveden New Bield, Northamptonshire © National Trust Images/Paul Wakefield

18. *Popish Plots and Treasons from the Beginning of the Reign of Queen Elizabeth, Illustrated with Emblems and Explained in Verse*, engraved by Cornelis Danckerts (*c*.1603–56) (engraving) (b&w photo), English School, (17th century) / Private Collection / The Bridgeman Art Library

Plate Section 2

19. Elizabeth I, Armanda Portrait, 1588, attr. to George Gower. Bedfordshire, Woburn Abbey © akg-images

20. Philip II of Spain, artist unknown © National Portrait Gallery, London

21. Portrait of William Cecil, 1st Baron Burghley (1520–98) Lord High Treasurer (oil on panel), by or after Arnold von Brounckhorst (*c*.1560–70) / National Portrait Gallery, London, UK / The Bridgeman Art Library

Acknowledgements

I owe a great deal to the many works of the many scholars listed, with gratitude, in the Notes and Bibliography. I would particularly like to salute the Dominican friar, Godfrey Anstruther, who first wrote about the Vaux family in 1953, as well as the more recent scholarship of Alexandra Walsham, Peter Lake, Michael Questier and Thomas McCoog. I have benefited enormously from, and thoroughly enjoyed, numerous conversations with Antonia Fraser on 'the recs', for which my heartfelt thanks. Support and advice have also come from Saul David, William Dalrymple, Simon Sebag Montefiore, Adrian Tinniswood and Richard Foreman. John Holland helped with the Latin, George McPherson with the Spanish and Nicola Newson and Giovanni Gabassi with the Italian.

I am most grateful to the Trustees of the English Province of the Order of Preachers for allowing me to use Father Anstruther's translation for chapter 12. Timothy Hacksley kindly permitted me to cite his thesis on the poems of Henry Vaux; the Revd Thomas McCoog, S.J., graciously did the same with his doctoral thesis on the Society of Jesus. I am also indebted to Father McCoog and his colleague at Farm Street, Anna Edwards, for their warm welcome to the British Jesuit archives and their determined help sourcing manuscripts for me there.

Thanks, too, to the talented and friendly librarians and archivists who have lent assistance at the Bodleian Library, the British Library, the National Archives, the College of Arms, the Inner Temple Library, the London Library, Northamptonshire Record Office, Leicestershire Record Office, the Shakespeare Centre, Westminster Diocesan Archives and the Folger Shakespeare Library, Washington, D.C.

I am immensely grateful to Jan Graffius for showing me the remarkable collections at Stonyhurst; to David Waite, Managing Director of Wellingborough Golf Club, for heroically shifting the office furniture so I could peer at the Harrowden Hall priest-hole; and to the staff at Rushton Hall Hotel, who kindly showed me the Tresham oratory and priest-hole. I should also like to take this opportunity to thank the owners and custodians of the various historic houses whose priest-holes are on public view. Mentioned in this book, but by no means the only ones, are Baddesley Clinton and Coughton Court in Warwickshire and Harvington Hall in Worcestershire. Every school trip should include one of these places.

Anthony Gilbey, the current Lord Vaux, was kind enough to encourage my pursuit of his ancestors and answer all my queries. Tom Baring of Baring Fine Art went out of his way to hunt the provenance of the third Lord and Lady Vaux's portraits. Jo Baring and Sarah Keller read the typescript with eagle eyes and generous hearts.

It has been an enormous privilege, as well as a great pleasure, to work with Andrew Lownie, Will Sulkin, Stuart Williams and Georgina Capel. I am immensely grateful. Thanks, too, to everyone at Bodley Head and Vintage who made an improving mark on the book, namely: Julia Connolly for the jacket, Darren Bennett for the map and family tree, Mark Handsley for the copy-edit, Jane Howard for the proofread, Ben Murphy for the index; Kay Peddle, Katherine Ailes, Eoin Dunne, Emmie Francis and Áine Mulkeen, and last, but certainly not least, Ruth Waldram. You have all been wonderful.

My daughters, Isabella and Lara, made a considerable contribution to the delay in delivering this book, but also gave me the wonderful perspective of motherhood. I would like to thank them both, along with my nieces Matilda and Poppy, for our experiments in orange-juice writing; if only historical research and childcare were always so compatible. Fletch, you got me through it and I thank you for more than I can possibly put down here.

Extraordinary women lie at the heart of this book, so it is fitting that it should be dedicated, with love and thanks, to my mother, Jane Childs, and my sister, Anna Richards.

Index

Entries in *italics* indicate illustrations.